CW00828547

Dedication

To Win & Cyril Smith
and
Cathy & Edward Black

The spirit of Corby

Yae cannae shove your Grannie aff a bus!

ALIVE IN THE DEAD OF NIGHT

A town in search of soul

by

Clive Smith and David Black

CHROME MOLLY
publications

MMX

Published by Chrome Molly Publications Ltd

Copyright © Clive Smith and David Black 2010

Designed, printed and bound by D. Black Printers

ISBN 978 0 9565882 0 3

All rights reserved. No part of this publication may be reproduced, stored in a retrieval system, or transmitted, in any form or by any means, electronic, mechanical, photocopying, recording or otherwise, without prior permission of Chrome Molly Publications Ltd.

Any copy of this book issued by the publishers as clothbound or paperback is sold subject to the conditions that it shall not by way of trade or otherwise be lent, re-sold, hired out or otherwise circulated without the publisher's prior consent, in any form of binding or cover other than that in which it is published, and without a similar condition including this condition being imposed on any subsequent publisher.

CONTENTS

Acknowledgements

Our thanks go to everyone who gave up their time and provided us with information, advice, photographs and the odd pint of Red Barrel.

John Black
Ray Brett
Alistair Brodie
Andy Brown
Pete Buckby
Bob Crawford
Stuart Davidson
Dick Dighton
Ricky Dodd
Ian Eccles
Ricky Geoghegan
Mick Harper
John Kenrick
Billy Mathieson
Barry Noble
Dennis Priddy
Jack Stewart
Dewi Toleman
Bip Wetherell
Trevor Wright
Brian 'Barney' Keenan (our man in Plymouth)
Bob & Judy Knight
Steve Hadjuk
Dennis Taylor
Pete 'Plop' Robb
Paula Boulton
Dave Martin
Maxi McCafferty
John Grimley
Bob Grimley
Kenny Payne
Pat Lavin
Johnny Heron
Pat Ravey

Tony Haseslip
Jim 'The Big Clunk' Smith
John Proctor
Derek Cowie
Mick Ferguson
Mr. & Mrs. Noel Rayson
Peter Dorrington
Malcolm Wright
Ted Foster
Johnny Morrison
Margaret McDowell
Adrian Holland
Ian Murray
Andy Fraser
Bill Wyman
Ian McLagen
Jim Dale
Pete Dyne
Carol Anne Kane
Margaret Leaker
Frank Mullen
Corrie Grey
Franny Lagan
Bernie Crawford
Roger Johnson
Howie Casey
Anne Marie McGeachy
Ian McGeachy
Dougie Wilson
Alex Henderson
Graham Henderson
Stuart Allen
John 'Wilf' Smith

Foreword

I was always surrounded by music. I suppose you could say that the whole of my childhood and teenage years in Corby were just one big musical learning curve. The same applies to my late brother Bob and sister Lilian - their lives were also steeped in music. First and foremost there was the unmistakable influence of our parents, Babs and Charlie Grimley, who were excellent singers and were always in demand at the local clubs (a sort of Mickey and Griff of their day if you like.) As youngsters we three kids would relish the times when Mum and Dad allowed us to accompany them to the Welfare (S&L Club) for a glass of Vimto and a packet of crisps, and I recall that it was on one of those occasions (a warm summer's evening when we were sitting outside on one of the green park benches overlooking the bowling green) that we discovered, by peering through the windows of the Smoke Room, that it was not only our parents who possessed talent in abundance, but that there were also many other gifted amateur entertainers in the town. These were people who could sing well and could play their chosen instruments with accomplishment. One such person was my cousin Murray. It was Murray Glen who encouraged me during my early endeavours to master the guitar. Whilst I looked to my parents for guidance as a vocalist, it was Murray who became my mentor as far as the guitar was concerned.

Musically speaking, things changed for me at around the age of thirteen - when Jimi Hendrix appeared on *Top of the Pops*. Jimi's rendition of *Hey Joe* made a big impression on both me and on the Corby music scene as a whole, and consequently, as the 1960s rolled into the 1970s several up-and-coming local bands began to reveal a much harder edge to their acts. In contrast, playing alongside them were other bands like Corby's St. Cecilia - who made it to number 12 in the charts with *Leap Up And Down (Wave Your Knickers In The Air)*. Unfortunately, the BBC refused to play the record and as a result denied some of our own their moment of *TOTP* fame. It's ironic when you think about it, because just a few years later there came the much more aggressive, more offensive culture of punk rock. Throughout the early 1970s (and particularly during the Arts Festival weeks) the Festival Hall in Corby's Civic complex played host to a number of famous names. These included Amen Corner, the Tremeloes, the Equals, Zoot Money and the Nice - all of whom used local bands as support. At the end of the Nice concert I remember leaving the Civic and going on to a midnight matinee at the Odeon cinema. That was a first for me.

Also of significance to music lovers in the town was the way in which during the 1970s Corby's bowling alley was transformed into a dynamic and forward-looking venue. (In 1972 the then unknown Irish band Thin Lizzy put in an appearance there). In the first stage of its makeover the lounge bar of the Corby Bowl became the Exclusive Club. However, because of its strict shirt and tie policy, it proved to be a little 'too' exclusive to the average club-goer in the town, and so the name was relatively short-lived. Its next reincarnation as Shafts' saw the venue adopt a more casual and relaxed atmosphere. The newly named club engaged the services of many talented local bands and (to the delight of musicians and punters alike) there was a very late bar!

Another successful live music venue of that era was the Nags Head in Corby. When Bip Wetherell took it over he promoted both local and out-of-town bands and was instrumental in organising the first proper jam sessions in the town. Elsewhere, local entrepreneur Franny Lagan was promoting cutting-edge bands - whenever and wherever he could. Who from that generation will forget the afternoon at Corby Rugby Club's marquee where the line-up included Harry Garter's Elastic Band, Stutz, Suparlik and Knobbs (all for an admission price of 30p!)

If you were out and about in Corby during the 1970s, I'm sure this book will bring back many fond and humorous memories. *Alive In The Dead Of Night* captures the heart and soul of a rough, tough, steel town - at a time when it was struggling against economic adversity and was facing an uncertain future. From a purely personal perspective, it reminds me of everything that I loved about being a Corby musician.

John Grimley

Introduction

A Scottish Roman Catholic priest once described Corby as being 'a town of broken bottles and ragged weans.' Fortunately, those days are long since gone. What it should more rightly be remembered for, is for being at the most advanced point of this country's progress towards greater social integration. Prior to 1932 Corby was a greystone Northamptonshire village with thatched roofs, a church (part of which dates back to the thirteenth century) and a population of less than two thousand inhabitants. In stark contrast, by 1970 there were more than forty-nine thousand people living in what was now Corby New Town, and, astonishingly, the local dialect had been overtaken to a large extent by a distinct Scottish lilt (there was even a bus stand marked 'Glasgow'.) In fact the town was made up of no fewer than twenty different nationalities, it had virtually no middle class and the birth rate eclipsed that of nearly every other community in Britain.

The single most important reason for such huge change was the existence, within the immediate vicinity of Corby, of the great Northampton Sand Ironstone bed (one of the largest stratified ironstone beds in the world - and at that time the most important deposit of iron ore in Britain.)

In 1932, at the lowest point of the industrial depression, the Scottish tube-making firm of Stewarts & Lloyds made the courageous decision to open up an iron, steel and tube works in Corby. It was to be situated on the site of a small ironworks which had been operating there since 1910.

The years spanning the 1930s were a time of heavy unemployment - bringing fear to men who had already felt its brutal impact in the past. When S&L came down to Corby from Scotland, many of the company's key workers also relocated here. These were joined soon afterwards by friends and relatives, and then by families from some of the most depressed areas in Wales.

S&L was both a benevolent and forward-thinking company. So much so that between the years of 1932 to 1938 (in addition to the firm's massive iron, steel and tube works) it oversaw the construction in the town of 2,200 houses for its workers, a large recreation club and a football ground.

By the end of the 1960s Corby was experiencing a steady increase in light industry. With the majority of the town's men-folk working for one dominant industry, it was imperative that gainful employment be available to their wives and partners - hence (in addition to the corset factory, shoe factory and crisp factory which were already up and running) several others were in various stages of development. Everything that could be done to create a blueprint for the success of the town was being done, however, there were limits to what this could achieve for the community. For instance, although the factories were being built in anticipation of a fast-increasing population, commercial enterprises such as cinema chains etc. were more economical with their predictions and were reluctant to move to the town. The Odeon had been Corby's only picture house since the 1930s and, with the exception of the Stewarts & Lloyds Recreation Club, the lack of public evening entertainment was viewed by many as a serious hindrance to the development of the community - especially if it meant that people were obliged to look to neighbouring towns in order to fill the void. Of course many of the factors to which Corby owed its unique cultural status were still in evidence back in 1970. The town's population was still predominantly of Scottish descent (indeed most of the children who were born here spoke with Scottish accents - even if they had never been north of the border in their lives!) In addition, the Scottish *Sunday Mail* and *Sunday Post*, together with the *Irish Sunday Press*, were still amongst the most popular newspapers in 'Little Scotland'.

As for culinary tastes, it was incredible for a town set in the heart of England that Aberdeen buttery rolls and 'Scotch' bread took pride of place in the local bakers' shops.

Interestingly, despite the presence of Poles, Ukrainians, Yugoslavs and people of other nationalities, the Scottish influence tended to have an isolating effect on the character of Corby as a whole. To outsiders the town was slightly alien - a strange growth in the middle of Northamptonshire. However, there were two other main features which set the tone of Corby - they were the handsome wages and the ever-prevailing social influence of the steel works where they were earned.

Evidence of the growing prosperity of the community was demonstrated by the fact that taxis, on the look-out for fares, could be seen cruising up and down the green, tree-lined avenues of the housing estates - a sight largely unknown in surrounding towns.

As for culture? There were Burns clubs, highland dancing, musical societies, a Latvian choir and an Amateur Dramatic Society (generally thought to be highbrow) amongst many other pursuits.

Corby was a town where three-phase shift work meant that one third of the population was always asleep whilst the other two thirds were awake. It was a town where the streets were never silent in the dead of night.

Besides being the source of its daily bread, Corby New Town was indebted to Stewarts & Lloyds for many other things. The recreation club wasn't just an additional amenity but a vital factor in the social integration of the community. The firm also made a contribution towards the invaluable Diagnostic Centre (set up on Cottingham Road by the Nuffield Institute.) Moreover, as the town entered the 1970s it was generally accepted that Stewarts & Lloyds would always play an essential part in Corby's future. After all, the two were mutually synonymous.

Although Corby was a town in which many individual emotional and psychological adjustments had still to be made, there was an air about the place which suggested that, in spite of its solid foundations and relatively high levels of prosperity, the town was not entirely sure of itself.

Whether it was the fisherman from Peterhead who having lost his means of making a living in Scotland decided to head south, or the miner from the Rhondda Valley who wanted to give his family a better chance than they would have at home, many saw a great opportunity here. Be that as it may, a local doctor once diagnosed: "Corby is a harsh place. It's not mellow as a town should be - it has no soul." But that would come presumably? Surely, out of all the things that such a benevolent employer could bestow upon a town - a soul, one hoped, would be one of them?

Chapter One 1970
Down The Dustpipe?

On December 31, 1969, the Diddymen were gathered in the bar of the Raven Hotel in Corby. Champions-elect of the Kettering and District Licensed Victuallers Darts League, they had come together on New Year's Eve to celebrate what had been a spectacularly fast and unconventional rise to prominence within Northamptonshire darts circles. With only a few minutes of the old decade remaining, Johnny Morrison (accompanied by Rod Bailey on plastic guitar) led the team in a rousing rendition of *We Are The Diddymen*.

As midnight approached, the team drained their two-pint mugs, returned the cracked brass handbell to its place of honour behind the bar, pocketed their kazoos and then, with their ritual at an end, set off en route to various hogmanay parties - with the intention of 'seeing-out-the-auld' year and 'bringing-in-the-new'.

On January 2nd the *Evening Telegraph* reported:

> *'A bleary-eyed Corby awakened to face a new year, not with the sound of bells, but with the fizzing of a veritable sea of bubbling hangover preparations. The most obliterated of revellers were still navigating a somewhat precarious path homeward as dawn was breaking. As some lights were being switched out to herald the sweet oblivion at the end of an all night house party, others were winking on as somewhat befuddled workers struggled with the intricacies of boiling a breakfast egg - to be washed down with sweet black coffee. Yes, 1970 was well and truly welcomed in by Corby in a manner befitting its strong Scottish connections.'*

The new decade was ushered in by Thunderclap Newman's one-hit-wonder *Something In The Air*. It turned out to be prophetic - as Hong Kong Flu swept the country and claimed nearly 4,000 lives.

Along with the flu epidemic, January saw the introduction of the first Pan Am jumbo jet airliner. With three hundred and sixty-two passengers on board (double that carried by a Boeing 707 jet) it was scheduled to fly from New York to Heathrow, and then on to Frankfurt. *Leaving On A Jet Plane* (Peter, Paul and Mary's mantra to the jet age) could have been Pan American Airline's theme for the day - but would have been inappropriate as bad weather caused the Frankfurt leg of the trip to be abandoned! An hour long return trip via the Bristol Channel was arranged instead. Invited on board the jumbo was a Kettering journalist by the name of Murray Bailey, who was covering the flight for *Airways* magazine. Murray was highly impressed and extolled: "It was extremely smooth, rather like an ocean liner on a calm sea". It was the kind of passage that the astronauts of Apollo 13 might have been wishing for that April when their spacecraft limped back to earth after suffering an explosion in the service module. Crewed by James Lovell, Fred Haise and Jack Swigert, the third moon mission

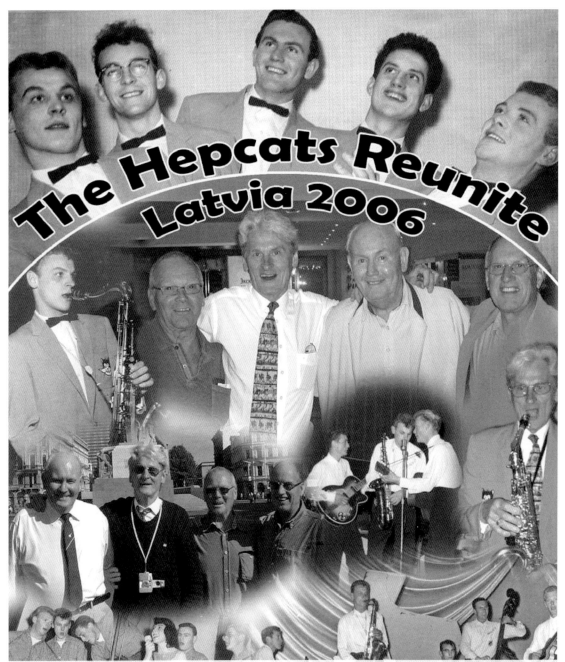

Reunited! In September 2004 the publication of the first volume of this book ('It's Steel Rock 'n' Roll To Me') led to a long overdue reunion involving four former members of the Hepcats. In 2006 Brian Jones, Alan Doy and Mal Prodger travelled to Latvia in order to meet up with Kru Zakss whom they had not seen since the band broke up in 1960. The group of old friends spent an eventful weekend catching up on the past, meeting the press and being interviewed on Latvian television about the country's earliest links with Rock 'n' Roll. Pictured here with Kru in his home town of Riga are L-R: Brian Jones, Alan Doy and Mal Prodger.

was aborted and 'as the world held its breath' the astronauts (who were squeezed into the lunar module and had just the bare minimum of supplies and oxygen) coaxed the craft home.

Some social historians claim that 1970 was not an 'altogether dynamic year'. If that is the case, then the deaths within weeks of each other, of Jimi Hendrix and Janis Joplin, proved to be two career moves that certainly bucked the trend. Sadly, their posthumous elevation to iconic status didn't make the loss of two such exceptional talents any less regrettable.

Regrettable too was the stepping down of Nellie and Bernard Connaughty as caretakers of the Our Lady of Walsingham School in Corby. The departure of Mr. and Mrs. Connaughty also signalled the end for 'Nellie's Bin' (a thrice-weekly dance in the school hall) which for nearly two decades had provided the teenagers of Corby with both a sanctuary and a focal point.

In addition to this, the Size Seven (one of the Bin's earliest groups) disbanded, crushing speculation that they would continue into a third decade. Singer Brian Dowell said: "It was time for us all to move on." Dowell, along with guitarist Billy Geary, continued to feature in cabaret-style bands for a number of years to come. Brian: "I was considerably happier and more comfortable when singing Sinatra and Dean Martin material."

The Formula, who had been rivals of the Size Seven since the heady days of the sixties, also split up in 1970. Kru Zakss (their leader and the band's original saxophonist) resurfaced in Henley-on-Thames - where he went on to become an influential local politician. Latvian-born Kru then moved to Riga and no doubt regaled friends and business acquaintants with tales of the time when he was, in all likelihood, Latvia's first rock 'n' roll star. Sadly in 2008 Kru died after suffering a brain tumour. As for the rest of the group? After leaving the Formula vocalist Mick Harper fronted several of the most popular outfits of the 1970s, Drummer Tommy Guthrie spent some time in Canada before re-crossing the Atlantic to work in the London music business - eventually returning home to Corby to become a taxi driver; the group's bass player, Bruce Carey, settled in South-East London and guitarist Martin Fallon ended up in Spain. It was Ricky Dodd who had arguably the most success - by progressing to playing professionally with the Roy Young and Kevin Coyne bands. He later became a sought-after session musician.

Disintegrating in acrimony, the Beatles bowed out in May with their final album release - *Let It Be*. It was to be the end of a musical phenomenon that had been the catalyst for a social and cultural revolution. Simon and Garfunkel also called it a day (having released their classic *Bridge Over Troubled Water* album) but theirs was an even less harmonious exit. In the meantime, the 'Stones continued to roll - catching a second wind and embarking on a trek that would eventually take them well beyond their sell-by date. As for Bob Dylan? Bob was engaged in a brief flirtation with the country and western genre - resulting, unfortunately, in the largely disappointing *Self Portrait* album (a follow-up to 1969's *Nashville Skyline*).

During this time the career of Kettering's Barry Noble appeared to be going well - he had released a new single, entitled *Take Your Time*, which had been penned by Roger Greenaway and Roger Cook. The flip side *Life Is For Living* (written by Barry and Fingers 'n' Fumbs star Steve Fearn) reflected Noble's approach to life in general, however, Elvis, his big rival, outgunned him that year with three top-selling records - the biggest and most enduring being *The Wonder Of You*.

On the recording front, Noble was working in the famous Abbey Road No. 2 Studio with arrangers Ron Richards (of Hollies fame) and George Martin (who made his name producing Jim Dale, the Goons and - more notably - the Beatles.) Barry wrote his next release himself. It was called *Mary Put The Lights Out*, and although it was recorded at Derek Tompkins' Beck Studios in Wellingborough, production was later relocated to Chappell Studios in London's Bond Street, so that strings could be added (courtesy of several 'moonlighting' BBC Light Orchestra violinists).

Unfortunately for Barry, his contract with EMI Records expired that same year and was not renewed.

His final British television appearance also took place in 1970, when he was on *The Golden Shot* (ITV's Sunday afternoon show) to promote what would be his penultimate single for the record company - a number entitled *Give Me Your Word*.

The start of a revolution in air travel - the first 'Jumbo' jet airliner (a Pan American Boeing 747) arrived on 12 January 1970 at London's Heathrow Airport.

Corby's reputation as a breeding-ground for musical talent remained intact. This was despite many of the town's most popular rock musicians taking the arrival of the new decade as a point of departure - leaving behind both the sixties and performing live on stage. However, some veterans continued under various guises and played country and western or folk music on the lucrative cabaret circuit or in working men's clubs. Crusaders Jack Stewart, Alistair Sinclair and Tommy Smith teamed up with Bob McAuslin to become the Tartan Combo and having done so played as regularly as in their Crusader days. The Kirbys (John Dolby, vocalist Cathy Maguire, ex-Blueprint Paul Smith and ex-Pacific Jimmy Cave) won a talent contest at Burton Latimer's Britannia Club and scooped a prize of £25 for their performance of the Everly Brothers' classic *All I Have To Do Is Dream* - the three lads promising Cathy that they would spend the money on new clothes!

The Carnations blossomed - Corby's contribution to the flower power craze of the late 1960s ended up working the Carribean cruise ships with a new line-up. Ex-Blueswailer Frank Devine (fresh from a season at Pontins Holiday Camp in Selsey) replaced Ted Ward to team up with John Hill, Dick Ashworth and June McLaughlin. Frank: "I saw an advert in the paper inviting people to audition. When I did so, I got the job and embarked on an adventure on the cruise ships that lasted for almost two years. We worked on the Cunard Line as a fifteen minute cabaret spot between orchestras - it was great. We played all of the Seekers and Woody Guthrie folk stuff, including *This Land is Your Land* and *The Carnival Is Over*. The money wasn't great, however, everything was free. The passengers were always buying us drink as well. Now and again we'd go down into the bowels of the ship to entertain the crew and the booze would really flow! This was where singer June McLaughlin met her husband Fred - a Geordie. He was an engineer and a really nice guy. When we returned to Britain, June decided to leave the group. I believe she settled in the North East with Fred. As we needed a replacement, we poached Cathy Maguire from John Dolby's band, the Kirbys. After spending a considerable amount of time getting Cathy into the swing of things, we discovered that she was too young to get a visa for the States - which was a problem. We ended up having to forgo the cruise ships and worked up north a lot, at clubs in Rotherham and the like. Dick Ashworth was 'the main man'. He was like a model - a good-looking guy who always had a smile on his face and who had the patter. The women seemed to love him!"

When the Carnations disbanded, Frank and his wife Katherine left Corby to open a café in Walsall. They stayed there for ten years before taking up residence in Tenerife for two years. On their return to the UK in 1996, they moved to Troon in Ayrshire.

The Carnations enjoy the party atmosphere during a working cruise aboard the Carmania. L-R: Frank Devine, Cathy Maguire, Dick Ashworth, and John Hill.

The seeds of St Cecilia were sewn when the jazz-oriented Unadopted Society split - following the departure of their saxophonist, Bob Clark, who had left in order to sample the bright lights of Soho. When Dave Johnson also quit, the remaining members teamed up with Ricky Moss and John Proctor to become the first line-up of the hit-making band. John Proctor: "It was a seven-piece with Norrie McMullen on baritone sax, Steve Holmes from Kettering on drums and Keith Hancock on bass. After several weeks of rehearsal, we had our first outing at Stamford YMCA for which we were paid the princely sum of £15. Ken Cox became our manager and soon had us working three or four nights a week. Our fee went up to £25 at Cambridge, and £35 later on at Sheffield. As we were playing more and more events up and down the country, it soon began to take its toll. Norrie and Rab McLintock weren't long in deciding that they'd had enough, and then Steve Holmes reached the conclusion that he too would prefer 'an ordinary life' and left to go and work in a factory. When Graham Smith (the drummer with Natural Gas) came in, we finally had the line-up that would bring us chart success - and notoriety!"

Before a change of 'underwear' some said they were pants - but in reality the first line-up of St. Cecilia was a highly rated harmony group. L-R: Ricky Moss, Les Smith, Steve Holmes, Norrie MacMullen, Keith Hancock, John Proctor, Rab McLintock .

Despite merchants of doom constantly predicting its inevitable demise, Corby was still dependent on the steelworks as its one main source of employment. However, any doubts about its long-term future were surely dispelled when British Steel published the details of a massive investment programme for the former Stewarts and Lloyd's complex. £4 million was to be spent on improvements to the Iron Ore Preparation and Sinter Plants, and the announcement prompted BISAKTA union official George McCart to eulogise: "This is a terrific boost for the steelside, killing fears that the town's future in the production of steel could be limited." His brother members were delighted. The news would ensure a continuation of social activities such as perusing the *Seventh Pan Book of Horror Stories* or a Mickey Spillane novel on night shift, honing *Daily Sketch* cryptic crossword skills on day shift - or practicing new moves on the domino board during the back shift. Card schools were another favoured pastime. "Who's in for a quick haund?" was a familiar shout whenever a mill went down. Duncan Robertson, a former steelworker and Alistair McLean fan, confirmed as much from the cab of his Corby taxi when, speaking on the eve of the millennium, he remarked: "Leisure activities were essential - as conditions in the Works were abominable!"

The record-breaking output in 1969, of 70,000 tons of steel tubes from the tubeworks, probably influenced British Steel's decision to invest. It was the icing on the cake when they announced that a further cash injection of £2.6 million was to be spent on a new power plant. This would mean that the Blast Furnaces would be able to operate at a higher level than ever before. McCart was exultant: "This is a massive vote of confidence for the giant complex and should allay fears that the works are finished!"

The 'works. Build it, and they will come - and they did.

Demonstrating an in-depth grasp of commercial affairs,Kelvin Glendenning, Chairman of Corby Urban District Council, was buoyant. "It's great news. We are here to stay as a steel-making town!" he exclaimed. To the sceptics who doubted that the Works had a future, he proffered the following advice: "The dismal Johnnies should either understand economics or just say nothing at all. With the Tubes Division of the British Steel Corporation coming to Corby, it is obvious that we must make steel for the tubes here - and this is a sign that British Steel realise it." Considering what lay ahead, Glendenning must have wished that he had kept his mouth shut. Even the humblest production worker, with a less than elementary grasp of economics, understood that the BSC gravy train of profligate waste, over-manning and outdated working practices could not be sustained indefinitely. The news of British Steel's intended expansion plans had come hot on the heels of the previous November's announcement that Corby was to become one of the country's 'big four' steel centres, but it was tempered slightly when the local MP, Sir Geoffrey De Freitas, cautioned all interested parties 'not to get carried away'. During an appearance on Anglia Television's *Probe* programme, Sir Geoffrey warned of the possibility - indeed likelihood - of what would happen should the Tories regain power at the next general election. He said "Corby Works would be shut down!" The Labour man's frank appraisal sent a chill down the back of the vast majority of the town's 14,000 steelworkers, however, there were some employees who were guilty of 'just killing time' in the tubeworks, men who appeared to be indifferent to the speculation surrounding the plant's future. One such worker was Johnny Bradshaw of Franklin Fields - who was a building worker in summer. He was also a keen pub sportsman and had little intention of allowing shift work to interfere with his hobbies. Clocking in one Monday afternoon, for his first 'three to eleven' back shift, didn't sit too well with young Bradshaw, and come seven o'clock he was making tracks for the changing rooms of the CW Detail Department. His foreman, Dan Whittle, who was a six-foot-something brummie and had a fearsome reputation, stared in disbelief as Johnny collected his donkey jacket and made ready to leave. "Where do you think you're going?" he bellowed.
"The Raven." Johnny replied nonchalantly.
A bewildered Dan roared: "You're back shift and you don't finish till eleven!" To which Johnny responded: "You might be back shift pal. I've got a darts match in the Welfare Club!"

When British Steel employees handed in their notice, they were often treated with disdain by junior management. It seems that many of the foremen (the majority of whom were in contention for a Trebex gold watch - awarded in recognition of thirty years' service) begrudged any attempt by 'malingerers' to escape the dreary clutches of the tubeworks.
Things were no different for Clive 'Big C' Smith and 'Big Ted' Foster when in 1970 the two aspiring young upstarts decided that they'd had enough of working in the C W Mills. (Nearly everyone in Corby was known as Big or Wee something - e.g. Big Alex, Wee Jammy, Big Yin). On learning of the pairs intention to quit, 'Wee' Andy Sneddon (foreman and gold watch recipient circa '69) delivered the patronising and mocking riposte: "You'll be back."
Standing by the Cooling Rack on Number 3 Mill and bemoaning their lot, during a stiflingly hot Friday back shift, the lads had been yearning for something better out of life when, suddenly, they stared open-mouthed as a prospective gold watch 'awardee' in the next bay dropped down dead in front of them!
"That's what happens if you stay too long in this hole," Big Ted reflected.
Barely out of their teens, Clive and Ted decided that the time had come to move on - they wouldn't be 'going for gold'.
Within weeks they were job hunting.
"How do you fancy a building site?" asked Big C. (Wimpey's had recently started construction work on the Celebration Arts factory on the town's Earlstrees Industrial Estate).
"Any jobs goin' pal?" Foster asked of a squat Irishman who was emptying the contents of a rusty old teapot outside his hut.
"When can ye start?" he responded in a thick Belfast brogue.

Dispute hits oil supplies

'Corby doomed unless it gets new industry'

CORBY WILL DIE if the town does not attract basic new industries within the next five years. This warning came from Mr. Jack Stevens after a stormy debate at last night's meeting of Corby Urban Council.

Earlier both he and Mr. Kelvin Glendenning had been ruled out of order by council chairman Mr. Tom Bayliffe, when trying to force home their controversial points during a debate on a traffic study.

"We must not bury our heads in the sand. Unless we get basic new industries in the next five years, this town will die," said Mr. Stevens.

"We have come to the cross-roads and we must examine the situation," he said. "I think the numbers of people employed in the steel works is going to go down and new industry will not have come."

The council were debating the recent announcement of the reduction in the labour force at the cashire and Strip Mills.

Mr. Stevens was not getting for the more publicity.

DISTU
"This metho ceeded. It w not say it no about it nov ever night... concern... sta... something... Earlier Mr described th...

disturbing news and called for an immediate meeting with Corby Development Corporation and trades unions about the future position of industry in Corby.

Mr. William Stewart feared that the future of the steel industry lay in deep water ports, pointing to develop- ments at Middlesborough of deep water facilities.

He warned Stewarts and Lloyds...

'Town is losing many potential customers

CORBY DEVELOPMENT Corporation were accused of turning away potential customers because of the high prices of land, shops and factories, by Mr. Kelvin Glendenning, at last night's meeting.

"I believe many dealers should not would have come to Corby," he said. "With the prices of land, shops and factories as they are, we have given firms empty. I am sure we could attract more people if they were relieved."

Mr. Glendenning had...

away that to make a point in the meeting was getting a debate on a traffic survey when he was ruled out of order and then the situation of industry the town was discussed.

"This town is still a minority town. I believe it is by time that Corby is where it was years ago. Are going to stay with Scottish Steel Corporation for the we come to realise before other town?

"Let's get moving and something have said...

'No threat' to shoe trade from abroad

BRITISH shoe industry nothing to fear from for- competition in a world is moving into an era of ly international trade.

is was Mr. Stewart Ken- 's message of encourage- t to 1,300 footwear dele- s when he officially opened British Boot and Shoe In- ation's exhibition and con- nce at Harrogate last t.

r. Kennedy, president of British Footwear Manufac- ers' Federation, and manag- director of Church and Co., thampton, said: "This is international affair with a

very large contingent of visi- tors from overseas.

"And this is a jolly good thing for they can see for themselves just how up to date and progressive we are."

He told delegates that he was most impressed by the variety of machinery and materials on display.

"When one hears so much these days about foreign com- petition and the threat from

foreign manufac... future and sta... British shoe tra... it is very hear products such a... here which in... second to none...

"Obviously th... created these f... of vision and in... and determined to succeed a... are not afraid of competition from whatever source it may come," he said.

A SON FOR CHRISTMAS

Mrs Janice Modesitt, aged 23, of 41 Kensington Walk, Corby, with son Stephen Joseph, born late on Christmas Day.

Joseph Modesitt Christmas Day his parents he all be

Stephen, who weighed in at 8 pounds 3½ ounces, is the son of Joe and Janice Mode- sitt of 41 Kensington Walk, Corby.

Sitting up in bed with Stephen on Boxing Day, 23-year-old Mrs. Modesitt said: "It was a wonderful way to spend Christmas."

"My husband is delighted, this is the best Christmas present we have ever had.

Karen Abraham of Roth well is another of our Christmas Day babies Kar- en who was born at Corby Maternity Unit shouldn't really have been a Christ mas baby at all she wa due almost two weeks ago.

"My husband Roge wasn't very pleased at bein woken so early. We wer hoping the baby would wai until after Christmas, said Mrs. Abraham, of 2 Coronation Avenue, Roth well, with a smile.

Karen, Mrs. Abraham's first child, was born just before nine o'clock on Christmas Day...

Despite concerns that Great Britain PLC wasn't adequately prepared to deal with the various challenges posed by a fast-growing global economy, back in 1970 some sectors of UK industry insisted on adopting a 'head in the sand' approach to matters (e.g. Northamptonshire shoe manufacturers.) Exacerbating the problem, industrial disputes continued to dog the nation. Shown here gathering for a strike meeting are Corby binmen Gilbert Riley, John Black, Cyril O'Neil, Tommy McFadden and Hughie Mellors. Although local headlines that December may have indicated that the great days of Corby steel-making were coming to an end, hope for the future was symbolised by the photo of Mrs. Janice Modesitt of Corby proudly presenting to the camera her 'Christmas Day baby' Steven Joseph Modesitt.

"Next week" said Big Ted.
Bursting with anticipation, the two pals reported for work the following Monday - only to be greeted with a brusque "Yes?" from an oblivious Irish ganger.
"We're starting work today."
Shuffling his feet, 'Belfast' scratched his unshaven chin.
"We came here last week. Remember?" Big C prompted.
Struggling to recall events, the Irishman paused before replying.
"Ah yes, I remember now," he said. Then, with a dismissive wave of his hand, he declared "Ach! Those jobs have gone!"
For Smith and Foster it was a rude awakening to the ways of the construction world, and with the words of Andy Sneddon ringing in their ears, the 'Big' guys sloped off, forlornly.
While they were coming to terms with their predicament, the lads found that they weren't the only ones to endure such feelings of despair. Employees of York Trailers (a Canadian-owned firm which had been doing business in Corby since the 1950s) received news that the company was contemplating a move out of the town, in order to set up a base at Northallerton in Yorkshire. Jim Smith, the production manager of the plant in St James Road, revealed that the problem lay in the fact that the existing site was adjacent to a pair of disused, water-filled excavation pits (known locally as 'the Clayholes') that were on land belonging to British Steel. Thus with there being no possibility for expansion, relocation seemed inevitable.

'Disenchanted' would have been the best way to sum up Anthony Roye's feelings in January. The manager of the New Midland

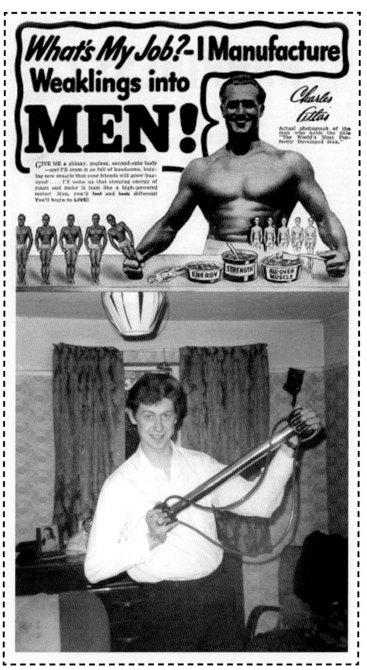

British Steel employee 'Big' Ted Foster training with his bullworker for a job in the outside world. Four years earlier Ted had spurned an opportunity to join the Corby Barbell Club - citing irreconcilable differences with the Charles Atlas 'Dynamic Tension' method of body-building. "It's a load of bull!" claimed Foster.

Theatre Company (which was based in Corby) was threatening to sue the Post Office for £200 because they had taken more than twelve days to deliver a parcel from Loughborough. The package, containing urgent billposters for his next production in Peterborough, eventually turned up at Kettering sidings in a railway wagon marked 'Empty'.

Roye fumed: "I ordered a reprint and collected them from Loughborough myself. I am convinced that because the posters were late arriving, bookings were down by £200." Letters of complaint were written and despatched to relevant Members of Parliament and one was even sent to the Prime Minister.

Above: The two water-filled claypits which put paid to expansion plans for York Trailers Ltd. Over three decades, illegal swimming by trespassers led to several drowning incidents. Despite authorising regular patrols of the area, BSC were unable to discourage this dangerous activity, and as a last resort sited lifebelts around the perimeter.

Anthony also fired this broadside at the Corby public: "Unless the number of people attending the plays put on by the New Midland Theatre Company at the Civic Centre improves, the town will find itself without a professional company. The business is going backwards daily, nightly and weekly. The sort of audience we get is very disheartening for the standard of production we provide. The threat is absolutely serious. Unless business improves during the next play, T.S. Eliot's *The Confidential Clerk*, scheduled for March, I will close the company down!"

Corby Theatre Group faced similar problems when their third production, *Paint Your Wagon*, was abandoned. A spokesman complained of apathy within the group and that members were somewhat lackadaisical when it came to attending rehearsals. "We originally had difficulty in attracting people to cast. When we did succeed, we then found it hard to get the 'Wandrin' Stars' to turn up for rehearsals," complained a dejected Stan Stewart (CTG's business manager). "It was the straw that broke the camel's back for producer Derek Prax - he resigned."

Another victim of the postal service was Father Dan Cronin of St Brendan's Church in Beanfield Avenue, Corby. When his supply of shamrocks failed to show up on the morning of St Patrick's Day, it appeared that the luck of the Irish had deserted him. He complained: "It was the same last year. I blame the postal service because we ordered the shamrocks three weeks ago."

Keeping things confidential was the dying wish of Earle Stanley Gardner - the eighty-year-old crime novelist and creator of Californian TV lawyer Perry Mason. Relatives and staff were left under strict instruction not to discuss details of his death other than to reveal that the popular writer had suffered a fatal 'mystery illness'. For those people over here in Britain who were addicted to television crime drama,

Displaying his long-awaited parcel Anthony Roye, manager of the New Midland Theatre Company, deems it a very poor performance from the Post Office - a feeling shared in March by Father Dan Cronin of St Brendan's Church, Corby when his St Patrick's Day shamrock failed to materialise.

Perry Mason had become essential viewing. On a weekly basis they had marvelled at the lawyer's ability to establish the innocence of his client, even when faced with overwhelming and incriminating evidence of first degree murder. Gardner's six secretaries acted as one in maintaining the secrecy surrounding the demise of their employer - to the extent that the exact cause of death remains a mystery to this day. Speculating on the matter, a sixty-two-year-old Corby fan, Bella Brodie of Pen Green Lane, had this to say: "It's obvious that somebody's murdered the poor guy for his money!" Betty McClements from the house next door agreed: "Aye, he must have been loaded - especially when ye consider that his output kept six secretaries on the go. It's too bad Perry isnae around tae unravel the mystery!"

In spring Shanks & McEwan Ltd. (one of the main subcontractors to the British Steel Corporation) began the task of dismantling several cable-car pylons which had been redundant since 1966. The overhead ropeway had been constructed in 1960 at a cost of £172,000. It ran from quarries near Rothwell - via Oakley - to the Blast Furnaces and Sinter Plant.
"A plum job!" enthused Smith. "Fresh air, the sun beating down on your back, working in the countryside - and in the pub by six! What could be better?" declared Foster.
So it was that, on the following Monday, a second attempt to obtain employment in the 'outside world' began. In company with ten other recruits, they lined up to receive the standard kit issue of donkey jacket, Totector boots, shovel and safety helmet, from a diminutive Irishman who was masquerading as a supervisor (and who, incidentally, had hands like shovels and feet to match!)
The new squad boarded Shanks' van and were driven off in the direction of the main gate, assuming that they were about to be whisked away to Rothwell. The vehicle accelerated around the side of the Coke Ovens and travelled on towards the beckoning main gate, but then suddenly, with a screech of brakes and an abrupt left-hand-down, the 'sunseekers' found themselves heading up the long Mill Road.

"Where we goin'?"

"The BOS Plant."

"So much for the sun!" groaned Terry Cotton.

Alighting from the bus (and still smarting at the thought of remaining on the inside) the gang were met by a scrawny Irish ganger called Pat, who bade them a sarcastic "Welcome to sunny Costa del BOS," Pat was no doubt a comedian - because as fate would have it, he would be smirking on the other side of his face come the end of the shift.

Pictured above: Crossing the A6 Rothwell to Desborough Road, the British Steel Corporation's aerial ropeway spanned the five-mile distance from Rothwell Hill Quarry to Great Oakley. In a journey which took precisely fifty-three minutes (with a hod arriving every twenty-six seconds at the destination point) it was able to transport seventeen cwt. of ore in each of its one-hundred-and-twenty-four hods. On arrival at Great Oakley, the cargo was then taken by rail to the Ore Reception Sidings at Corby steelworks. As the A6 was only one of several roads to be crossed en route by the ropeway, extensive precautions were taken to prevent accidental spillage. In addition, should anyone venture onto one of the bridges, a tripwire would immediately stop the mechanism.

The workers task for the day was to tarmac a square which was about the size of a football penalty area. It was located beneath a nest of hissing, odorous pipes that lay alongside a tall chimney which was belching out acrid, yellow smoke. Big C immediately christened the worksite 'the Cauldron'.

As they knuckled down to the job, throughout the morning lorry loads of 'the black stuff' arrived and were dumped, steaming, on the ground. A small hand-controlled road roller was then pressed into action.

"This is looking interesting," said a beaming Terry. The rest of the gang, licking their lips in anticipation, nodded in agreement. Unfortunately, their hopes were dashed when Pat, gesturing for the gang to stand well back, solemnly announced "I'll do this, lads." Terry stood his ground and pointed questioningly at his chest - still hopeful of a chance to drive the roller.

"Sorry laddie," Pat commiserated, "this is a job for an experienced operative."

Infuriatingly, the machine refused to start - despite its operator having tried his best to coax it into life. "Come on bejesus!" he cursed, - as the workforce stifled an attack of the giggles.

After several failed attempts, Pat reluctantly gave up on his roller and called for a lunch break. He then sent the gang off to the nearby Open Hearth canteen, so he could work on Plan B for the afternoon session - a line of attack which would prove to be equally diverting for the lads!

Strolling back to the Cauldron after lunch, they were greeted by the spectacle of 'Irish' seated atop a gigantic road roller. "Welcome back boys," he called, grinning from ear-to-ear, a sure indication that in his mind, Christmas had come early!

An incredulous Terry Cotton inquired: "You're not going to drive that thing over the tarmac, are you Pat?"

"To be sure I am laddie," the genial Irishman assured him.

Running parallel to the Mill Road, a pug makes its way past the abandoned Bessemer Plant towards the Blooming (Rolling) Mills and Soaking Pits - a sight familiar to workers taking the scenic route to the 'Costa Del BOS'.

Audience duly assembled, the roller was cranked into gear and sent on its way. Pat was a joy to behold as he steered the huge front roll onto the tarmac. Back and forth it rolled as it tamped down the tar - its driver guiding the '*Leviathan*' with consummate skill, whilst playing to a spellbound gallery. So immense was his pleasure at being the centre of attention that Pat momentarily took his mind off the job and failed to register that the three ton road roller was sinking into the soft, wet tar. The '*Leviathan*' had become the *Titanic*!

"That really didn't go down too well," Cotton observed dryly. "Launch the lifeboat!" he added sarcastically.

Another hour was squandered in trying to steer the *Titanic* out of its black and very gluey predicament. Finally, abandoning his vessel, a frustrated 'captain' declared: "Well lads, I reckon that's it. I'll have to phone for a crane to drag the thing out." As he waded off in the direction of the

BOS plant office, he left his bemused audience with the instruction: "You lot may as well get yourselves a cup of tea while I sort this mess out."

"Chancer!" Cotton muttered under his breath as he turned and headed once more for the Open Hearth canteen.

The next three days were spent on increasingly futile enterprises. On the fourth day came further glad tidings when Pat informed his men: "I've got good news for you. Next week we'll be working twelve-hour nights - knocking bricks out of the Blast Furnace." Distinctly underwhelmed at the prospect, Clive Smith announced: "I'm off!" He and Ted Foster then filed requests for immediate transfers - which were summarily dismissed by the labour officer for Shank's, Crawford Jamieson. Barely able to conceal his disappointment, Crawford cautioned them not to be too hasty, saying: "Pat can ill afford to lose two good men and true. I'm sure you'll feel differently once the job inside the furnace is finished."

Foster's reply was direct and to the point. "Listen pal - there's no chance of us working in that shite furnace! You can keep yer job!" Big C was in complete agreement with him, and so off they went in search of pastures new.

Those seeking a distraction from the weekly woes of Anthony Aloysius Hancock, of Railway Cuttings in East Cheam (a Thursday night *Hancock's Half-Hour* repeat on BBC 1) would be sure to find it in the form of the Kettering and District LV Darts League, in which competing pubs and clubs from across the north of the county sent their finest darts players to take part in a series of nine-leg matches. Those Thursday nights throughout the winter months were always accompanied by ear-shattering noise in the bars from supporters who were fervently cheering on their team. Amongst the most vociferous were the followers of the side from the Raven Hotel in Corby - who accompanied their team to away games in a convoy of cars and minibuses. With winning displays from the oche, the Diddymen inspired their fans to indulge in madcap antics and singing and chanting - which invariably left the opposition shell-shocked and marmalised!

Such raucous behaviour often provoked objections from other teams in the league (the majority of which came from pubs in Kettering and the surrounding villages.) Their complaints, although occasionally bordering on the hysterical, were partly justified as - it must be said - the vocal support for the team from the Raven Hotel was indeed unrivalled!

The Diddymen went on to become part of Corby's folklore during their four-year existence. On their travels they met with criticism and praise, anger and resentment, laughter and controversy. In the same way that the world-famous jam butty mines in Knotty Ash had boasted the highest sunshine rate in the world, on many a dreary Thursday night the Diddymen from the Raven would scatter sunbeams around the local darts league. In full ceremonial costume of Diddyhats, Diddycloaks and the occasional kilt, and bearing two-pint beer mugs, kazoos (and last but not least) a set of Jim Pike darts, the Diddymen ventured forth to take on the best that 'Kettering and District' had to throw at them.

Their supporters were dressed in similar attire and always carried with them an appropriately cracked brass handbell, and sang songs that were bawdy enough to make the Hon. Nigel Ponsonby-Smallpiece flee to the safety of his caviar allotment!

The two-pint mugs owed their existence to the fact that Peter Kane, bar-manager of the Raven Hotel, had mentioned to Rod Bailey that Ansells Brewery were selling them for a bargain price of 3s. 6d, and when Rod promptly ordered one for each of the team, dozens of Diddymen supporters followed suit.

Led by their chief bell-ringer Vince Farag, and with Rod Bailey on plastic guitar, they would storm into out-of-town pubs, deposit dozens of two-pint mugs on the bar and collectively order "Two pints please, m'duck" (guaranteed to create bedlam behind any bar!)

Captain of the Diddymen, Alec 'Fudge' Redmond said: "Kettering's pubs in particular didn't take kindly to it. A horde of us - and some nights there'd be a bus-load - all dressed in peculiar-looking hats and singing away as we walked single-file into the bar, had many of the locals frightened to death! It was all a good laugh and meant to be fun, however, some people were put off by the noise

Above: Members of the Raven Hotel's Diddymen (accompanied by one of their female supporters) gather in 'The Pit' bar. Formerly the 'Tartan Room', by the time of this photograph the bar had been revamped in typical 1970s style - e.g. Day-Glo skeletons, fluorescent lighting and psychedelic wallpaper. Standing. L-R: Colin Took, Johnny Morrison and Frank McMahon. Sitting. L-R: Walter McDonald, Alan 'Toots' McKenzie, Mary McMahon, Rod Bailey, Billy Mitchell and Charlie Black.

and the antics. It was probably part of the reason why we romped away with the Kettering and District L.V. Darts League during the two consecutive years in which we participated. I remember one night when we played the Cardigan Arms in Stanion and decided to tone things down a bit. We left the hats in the bus and forgot about the singing, but when we walked in everybody was disappointed. 'Where's the gear?' they asked. 'What's happened to your songs?' That was weird. We went back out to put on our hats and then we made our normal entrance. There was uproar. The Stanion punters loved it!"

Geoffrey De Frietas's fears for the steel industry intensified when the Prime Minister of the day, Harold Wilson, called a general election for June - the first in which eighteen-year-olds would be entitled to vote. Although Wilson believed he would be returned to Downing Street, the inflationary effects of big pay rises (especially those awarded during the six months prior to the election) had alienated many of his supporters within the Labour Party. In addition, close ties to the increasingly unpopular trade unions were gradually eroding the party's support throughout the country.

An issue central to the opposition party's campaign was the high cost of living under the Labour government and during a walkabout in Holborn Wilson was manhandled and heckled mercilessly by a baying crowd of Young Conservatives. In the middle of the undignified scramble, an egg was hurled and hit him on the forehead. Though boiling with rage, the P.M. somehow managed to maintain his composure, cracking: "The cost of living can't be that high if the Tories can afford to throw eggs at me!"

Pre-election polls had indicated that the Tories' chances of winning were looking slim. It was therefore against all the odds when Edward Heath, a keen yachtsman, swept to power. On the eve of victory he had described Labour as "men of straw trampled over by greedy, strike-prone unions responsible for rising prices."

With unemployment figures soaring to their highest level for thirty years, Ted was soon to discover that life at Number Ten was far from plain sailing. The Industrial Relations Bill was introduced in an effort to limit the power of the trade unions, but when the Prices and Incomes Board recommended a 25 per cent pay rise for the armed forces (triggering demands from the teachers for a 20 per cent increase and from the dockers for a basic weekly wage of £20) Heath's response was to put troops on standby to keep Britain's ports open.

Corby steelworkers joined in the fray - with 2,000 engineers, electricians and foundryworkers going on strike when their demands for pay rises (of up to £2.10s. per week and equal pay for all craftsmen) were rebuffed. Production from the tubeworks had already been reduced to half capacity (affecting 4,850 workers) when the painters and decorators working for contractors H. B. Pearce also joined the strike. A troubled British Steel spokesman warned of 'a grave situation facing Corby'. The industrial action lasted a month. Perversely, a mass meeting during the strike, held at Corby Town F.C.'s Occupation Road ground, gave the Steelmen their biggest attendance for years. An increase of between 15s. and £3.0s.3d per week was eventually agreed upon and it was a relieved Tom Bayliffe, Chairman of Corby Urban District Council, who said: "It's the best news that Corby's had on its breakfast tables for weeks."

Tom's gastronomic glee was short-lived, however, as in August a sting in the tail was delivered - the Lancashire & Corby cold strip rolling mill was to shut. The closure (part of Lord Melchett's rationalisation plan) would begin with the transfer of some of the workers to other tubeworks plants. This would be followed by redundancy packages in February 1971.

Elsewhere, strike-fever was also hitting Corby Town Centre. Ninety-two construction workers from the Queen's Square development site had walked out in protest when twelve subcontractors refused to join the Transport and General Workers Union. A spokesman for the ninety-two explained: "It goes against an agreement between management and union that there would be 100 per cent union membership on this site."

Apart from the General Election and a vow from Robin Kimmerling (Corby's new Publicity Officer) to rid 'Little Scotland' of its unwarranted reputation, the summer of 1970 was best remembered for the World Cup Finals in Mexico. The tournament was televised live for the first time in 'magnificent technicolor' (or not so magnificent in some cases!) Alan Smith, landlord of the Open Hearth in Studfall Avenue, was the lucky owner of a colour television set which he'd had installed in his living quarters above the pub. Extending his most generous hospitality, Alan invited a few of his regulars to join him in following the progress of a brilliant Brazilian team (showcasing the talents of Pelé Rivelino and Jairzinho) as it weaved its way to winning the coveted Jules Rimet Trophy. The critics hailed the players as being the greatest footballing side ever. Pity the TV picture wasn't as great!

Despite the absence of striker Alex Dawson (the Steelmens' ex-Manchester United centre forward and leading goalscorer) a strike meeting held by BSC employees on June 23rd, 1970 attracted a record crowd to Corby Town's Occupation Road ground!

The F.A. Cup that year produced one of the most exciting and brutal finals in British football history. Chelsea and Leeds United battled for the trophy over two tremendous games - with the Pensioners eventually claiming a 2 – 1 victory in a replay at Old Trafford. Stuart 'Chelsea' Allen remembers the night vividly. He says: "I was watching the game at home on a British Relay black and white telly. Some of my mates had been playing 'slam' around the garages that were behind our house - but I'd sneaked away through a hedge and disappeared home to watch the game. Mum treated me to a bag of out-of-date cheese and onion crisps (times were hard) which I washed down with a glass of water. As soon as the game finished, I was sent to bed and the telly was switched off to save putting another 5d. in the 'lecky' meter. Next day at school I felt like the king of the castle!"
It was around that time that Robin Kimmerling was given an early insight into the task ahead of him, when an irate Alfred Dennis Turner (the general manager of Restrail Haulage in Little Addington) described two of his former drivers as being 'typical of Scotsmen in Corby - absolutely useless and they want their money for nothing!' A response to this insult came from a fifty-five year old Scottish driver named Sam Hart. "The man's an eejit!" remonstrated Sam. The other driver, Derek Harms elaborated, saying: "I'm not surprised Mr. Turner can't get drivers. The hours are long and the money is terrible. He's only got himself to blame."

Characteristically, news of a proposed boating lake for Corby - described at the time as being a gift from the Development Corporation - was greeted with sarcasm. "So the plans have not been sunk after all," commented one old salt. After years of discussion between the Development Corporation and Corby Urban District Council, the £60,000 scheme had finally been approved. "It's very likely that we'll all be messing about in boats next spring," ventured Captain W. Ross of Nelson Road.

Thanks in part to Anthony Roye's outburst, *The Confidential Clerk* turned out to be a relative success at Corby Civic Theatre, and provided the inspiration for 'A Gala Performance' of William Douglas Home's *A Friend Indeed*. The public were promised that the event, which was to take place in April, would be a 'splendid occasion graced by the Duchess of Gloucester.' The other main guest was to be the Lord Lieutenant of Northamptonshire.

If Anthony felt that he was winning the war on apathy, he was brought crashing back down to earth by the outspoken comments of councillor Jack Stevens, who said: "It's an evening for snobs. For a start off, the ticket price is too much at £2.3s. for most and £1.1s. for the gallery. Regarding 'formal dress will be obligatory for the evening', I would say this is the classical snob appeal technique - as 95 per cent of Corby people would have to hire a dinner jacket if they wanted to go." Councillor Stevens revealed that he had met the duchess and Lt. Col. Chandos-Pole and that they were charming people who would be the last to want to impose conditions of this sort.

Anthony Roye was enraged. He

Sam Hart (one half of the Addington Two) complained that he and fellow Scot Derek Harms were being maligned by former employer, Alfred Dennis Turner, 'purely on the basis of where we were born and now live.' Sam remonstrated: "People like Turner can damage the reputation of a great town like Corby!"

countered: "It's childish to call the Gala a penguin parade and it's also a wildly inaccurate statement to say that 95 per cent of Corby people don't have evening dress. In February 1968, when it was suggested that the world première of William Douglas Home's *Ambassador Extraordinaire* be an evening dress occasion, over 80 per cent of the audience dressed accordingly. People in Corby like to dress up."

Support for Roye came from Councillor Mr. E. Wright - who disagreed entirely with Jack Stevens. Cllr Wright: "Any event that adds to the tone of Corby as a town should be supported. This town has been dubbed artisan. I think it would be a retrograde step to do anything to hinder a show like this. It can only heighten the tone of the town." This was a view which was shared by joint-organiser Mrs. Margaret Axe. She said: "Prices don't seem to be putting people off. We have taken a number of block bookings. Several people have said they want to attend in formal dress as they are looking forward to a sense of occasion." She also pointed out that the price of the ticket would include a sherry reception and that free cigarettes would be handed out by girls from W. D. and H. O. Wills.

Thrilling the audience on March 7th at the Civic, were Cleo Laine and the Johnny Dankworth Quartet. "A bewitching performance from Cleo and some sparkling improvisational jazz by Johnny's quartet, had an audience 700 strong baying for more, with thunderous applause," trilled Corby music journalist Billy Piper. Bill, who later became the night editor of the *Scottish Daily Mail* (following a round robin tour of English newspapers - including the *Corby Leader*, *Manchester Evening News* and *Accrington Chronicle*) was a self-confessed 'free spirit' in the early 1970s. He had recently returned from a trek 'up the hippie trail'. This involved hitchhiking around the Mediterranean countries and Morocco - whilst soaking up sun, peace and love. A jazz aficionado, his return to home port was perfectly timed as it coincided with the concert by Cleo & Johnny. Breaking into journalistic mode, Billy espoused: "The music was the sort to please young and old - both those familiar with jazz and those who had popped in to see what all the fuss was about."

For rock and pop enthusiasts, the Open Hearth was packing them in on Tuesday, Saturday and Sunday nights. Bip Wetherell's discothèque (with Dennis Taylor at the turntables) commandeered the lounge at the rear of the pub, while next door an equally jam-packed Smoke Room catered for the other pub-goers, by providing them with a jukebox on which to play their own records e.g. classics such as *Beatnik Fly* by Johnny and the Hurricanes.

In conjunction with running his disco, Bip was working full time as an accounts clerk for Golden Wonder in Market Harborough. He recalled: "It was during the time when I was playing keyboards with the Rhubarb Tree that I began to see the way ahead. We were on at the Flamingo Club in London, where instead of the usual two bands alternating throughout the night, there was just us and a newfangled thing called a discotheque - or as they pronounced it a 'discotay'. The idea, which had originated in France, consisted of just one guy spinning discs and talking into a mic. I said to myself 'I could do that' - and that's how I came to do my first disco. It was on November 30, 1969 and was at the White Hart. (It was actually my brother Alan's 21st birthday party). The room was packed and things went down so well that shortly afterwards two of my mates, Tony Smith and Nick Adams booked me for their joint 21st birthday bash. This time it was for a Tuesday night and at the Open Hearth. Though I say it myself, that night went even better - so well in fact that the landlord, Alan Smith, decided to hold a disco there every Tuesday. I was off and running!

Towards the end of the night, across a roomful of people, Tony signalled to my brother Alan (who was sharing the stage with me) to ask what our fee would be. I told Alan to say a fiver, so he held up his right hand to indicate £5. However, because Alan has half a finger missing on that hand, Tony only paid us £4.50p!"

For those willing to travel, the pubs and clubs of Kettering remained an attractive alternative. Despite having endured decades of their rowdy behaviour, Kettering still had to put up with the nocturnal visits from 'the wild men from up the A43'. On most evenings they spilled out of the green-liveried double-decker buses which bore the routes Nos. 254 and 256. They were merely intent on enjoying a concentration of nightlife that was unheard of in their home town of Corby, as they invaded the numerous drinking establishments that were dotted along the narrow backstreets of the town. Sadly, in spite of their well-meaning (albeit rather clumsy) attempts to develop a camaraderie with their southern neighbours, they failed miserably to do so.

With two distinctly different youth cultures clashing by night in Kettering's watering holes, it was inevitable that trouble would never be far away. A typical confrontation occurred at the North Park Club when an axe-wielding skinhead, John McCann, threatened a bouncer with an impromptu makeover. "I'll make your face like your arse!" he snarled. McCann's pals chuckled at what they considered might be an improvement for Terry Page (the resident doorman who had just turfed them out for threatening behaviour and foul and abusive language.)

Having survived in one piece the Corby to Kettering leg of its journey, a Northampton-bound United Counties Number 256 climbs the A43 towards Broughton - leaving behind its steel town cargo of well-paid but culturally-starved pleasure-seekers to enjoy the much sought-after amenities that neighbouring Kettering had to offer - e.g. the Granada, USF Club and Drill Hall. There was also the Odeon cinema, which from the 1950s through to the early 1970s showed newly-released films up to six weeks prior to their appearance at the corresponding venue in Corby.

Skinheads were the latest branch of ne'er-do-wells to irritate the Establishment - following hot on the heels of the Teddy boys of the 1950s, and the Mods and Rockers of the sixties. Fortunately Page and his cohorts were used to threats of this nature from their Corby patrons - and especially from Corby's skinheads. The 1970s were with us and nothing had changed. *Plus ça change, plus c'est la meme chose!*

Stephen Milne, who once was one of those adventurers on United Counties route 256, but who later boarded a 747 and emigrated to Seattle in the U.S.A., remembers the North Park Club as being one of the last outposts of Northern Soul - hosting stars like Ben E. King, the Showstoppers and Jimmy Ruffin. He said: "I used to go to the North Park when Motown was all over the charts. It was around the time of the skinheads but I wasn't one of them - I still had my long hair. Come to think of it, I don't know how I managed to go the clubs without being murdered!"

Among the assorted tribes to frequent the Hearth Disco of a Tuesday night, was a group of lads consisting of Pat Ravey and Ginger McCleland plus their pals from the Strathclyde Hotel. The youths would often add a touch of menace to proceedings at the pub, before heading off to the more up-market surroundings of the Hunting Lodge in nearby Cottingham - where they would 'socialise' until the early hours of the morning.

Ginger: "The Lodge was a great place to take a woman, or to chat one up. You could have a late drink and then bop the night away to the likes of Creedence Clearwater Revival's *Up Around the Bend* and Frigid Pink's *House Of The Rising Sun*. Unfortunately, our trips down there often ended in carnage!" (The Corby contingents - who were mostly tanked up, womanless and belligerent - were apt to do battle with the doormen on duty at the Hunting Lodge. They in turn were big bruisers who were more than willing to oblige). Ginger: "I can testify to that because one of them once whacked me across the back with a cricket bat and almost broke my shoulder!"

It was only a matter of time before *Evening Telegraph* headlines were screaming:

'MIDNIGHT MOB TERRIFY VILLAGE'.

The newspaper reported:

> *'Yelling, fighting and drunken discotheque teenagers, hell-bent on destruction, are turning life in the peaceful village of Cottingham into a nightmare. Some villagers are afraid to go out and others patrol their gardens to ward off violent gangs who storm into the street after the Hunting Lodge closes at two in the morning. Residents claim that at night "it's worse than Soho!" They use the gardens as toilets, break down walls to throw stones at each other, battle with chairs, bottles, car aerials - and the language is awful!"*

Though a spokesman for the Hunting Lodge blamed Corby skinheads for the disturbances, reveller John Friel gives another insight. Describing what happened when Sandy McWilliams (one of his friends) accused the bar staff of supplying short measures, John said: "Sandy complained about the lack of alcohol in the vodka and orange that he'd just bought for his girlfriend Joyce, and although they tried to fob him off, it was blatantly obvious that they'd merely rubbed their finger around the edge of the glass - the oldest scam in the book! When Sandy informed the bar manager that he was going to report them to the Weights and Measures Department, it must have done the trick - because for the rest of the evening they gave us free drinks!"

After 'the worst night ever' that September (an altercation resulting in the village being turned into a battleground) the Lodge had no choice but to close its doors to the disco-goers. The new manager, Mr. Paul Naffine, warned that he would not tolerate any hooliganism and stipulated: "The Lodge will revert to its original use as a restaurant." The news was met with sighs of great relief by villagers. Mick York, one of the residents and a former chairman of Corby Historical Society, congratulated the owners for taking the decision to close the disco. He added: "I hope our problems are now consigned to the history books and we can get back to normality." Naffine straight away set about the task of

WHATS GOING ON...

GRANADA KETTERING 323

open 1.10   today and all next week   last show 7

James Bond 007 is back!

HARRY SALTZMAN and ALBERT R. BROCCOLI
present IAN FLEMING'S
"ON HER MAJESTY'S SECRET SERVICE" A
"PANAVISION" · TECHNICOLOR
United Artists

RUTLAND CORBY 2276
THEATRE · BINGO CLUB

BINGO: Tonight 8.0 : Members Only

LATE FILMS TONIGHT OPEN 10. 3

HOW I LIVED AS EVE x
Colour. 11.50. And TABU x 10.40

FILM. Saturday Afternoon. Open 1.30.
OH! WHAT A LOVELY WAR a 1.40

Inner Wheel Club of Rushden
JUMBLE SALE
St. Peter's Church Hall,
Station Road,
SATURDAY, 25th APRIL
Doors open 2 p.m.
Admission 3d.

NAGS HEAD
WOLLASTON
Two Live Progressive Bands
1—AXE
2—JONS FARMYARD
3—JORK   only 4/-

Saturda
THE BIG-B
8 start   (BA

Sunday
with BIG
LITTL
8 start

TUESDAY,

SALON BALLROOM
FRANKLINS GARDENS
NORTHAMPTON

SEAHORS
CLUB DEENE
DISCOTHEQUE

EVERY
WEDNESDAY
FRIDAY
SATURDAY

from 8.30 p.m.

BUS EACH NIGHT
Corporation Street
8.45 p.m. There 'r
back

R GIRLS ONLY
—Suits, Collars, Tie
please
CENSED BAR

CORBY CIVIC THEATRE
Telephone GORBY 3482
SPECTACULAR MUSICAL SHOW
NEW MOON
27th APRIL — 2nd MAY, 7.39 p.m.
Best seat in the house and dinner after the show at
the Strathclyde Hotel : 24/- all in

NAGS HEAD
WOLLASTON
LIVE TONIGHT
JOHN PEEL
and FRENDS
lus SWEGAS and JO
oors open 7.30 : Ba

EVERY SAT. SUN.
BIG-BOB
DISCO
TWO NIGHTS OUT
Start 8 (3 BARS)
plus Rick plus Alf

CIVIC CENTRE
CIVIC THEATRE
THE URBAN DISTRICT COUNCIL OF CORBY
presents
WEDNESDAY, 6th
at 7.30 p.m.
BALLET FOR A
WITH DANCERS OF THE R
in
THE WORL
Tickets 8/-

NORTH PARK CLUB
KETTERING
FRIDAY— ROCK AND ROLL LIVE Swinging to
BOBBY LEROY and the fabulous NORTHMEN
ADMISSION 1
N
SATURDAY— DANCE and C
featuring the Girl with th
ANN WA
Dancing to RAY KELLE
TOMBOLA
P
GRAND DANC
SUNDAY THE DEB
TOMBOLA

CORBY SOCIAL AND EX-SERVICE CLUB
LLOYDS ROAD
Tonight at 8.15 p.m.
ROY BISHOP SOUN

reinventing the Hunting Lodge - starting by hiring a talented duo (keyboard player Neil Campbell and drummer Bob Gowen) to provide background music for the diners. Bob: "It worked out quite well. We played soft jazz - with me using the sticks rather than the brushes - and the numbers coming to the restaurant gradually began to increase. We only got paid about a fiver - not to mention the odd sausage roll thrown in! Paul was a shrewd businessman.

With his dark good-looks and pinstriped suits, he resembled a Mafioso straight out of a Hollywood gangster movie. I remember one time when we all went down to London and Paul introduced us to a PR girl who worked for Island Records. When she told him that Stevie Winwood was looking for a drummer, Paul put my name forward for an audition. I was up for it at the start - I'd had a drink and was game for it. However, when I thought about it in the clear light of day, I changed my mind. I knew my limitations. Winwood was one of the major players in rock music at that time, having just worked with former Cream drummer Ginger Baker. With hindsight I wish I had gone through with the audition - if only for the experience."

In an effort to placate the locals and win back their support, Paul Naffine revealed that a new specialty dish named 'Suprême de Volaille Cottingham' was to be served up for the very first time in the Hunting Lodge's new restaurant. He explained: "It will probably be a surprise to most of the villagers. I hope the gesture - after all that the village has had to put up with during the warring disco days - will prove to be a very popular item."

Meanwhile, in Kettering, a somewhat overblown press release announced the re-opening of the Windmill Club after a £50,000 facelift. First opened in 1926, it was now claiming to be the biggest ground floor club in the town.

> 'Far from the misty streets of Kettering, downtown Paris may offer a galaxy of nightlife where a businessman, with a fortune in his pocket, can secure a good night's entertainment. Its centre is Montmarte. Without stretching their resources to this extent, the Windmill Club in Kettering does its best to transport you from a world of boots and shoes. But the Windmill is not a poor man's substitute. Its atmosphere is relaxing, plush and classless. Its attractions include good professional cabarets, first class wrestling bouts, discotheques and a wealth of routine club activities.'

Spinning the discs at their Big Wheel Disco, the resident DJs at the Windmill were three young, dynamic Corby lads - Dougie Wilson, Rob Filik and Ian Eccles (former frontman of 60's groups the Sensitive Set and Quick Reaction.) Dougie, who was soon to adopt the stage name 'Martell', was also a member of the fledgling Corby Pioneers Rugby League Club. Unfortunately, thoughts of a career in Rugby League soon evaporated when he broke a leg, after just eight minutes of play, whilst representing Southern England in a testimonial game for Wakefield Trinity stalwart, Neil Fox. Dougie said: "We were still only novices at the game, and when I was lying in hospital I thought 'I can do without this!' That's when I decided to take up an offer to become a Redcoat at Butlins Holiday Camp in Skegness."

The Big Wheel Discotheque gathered momentum with Ian and Rob at the helm, and was in demand throughout the country - laying the foundations of a long and prosperous career in the music business for Ian. He not only ran his own booking agency in Milton Keynes (under the name of Robbie Stewart) but also managed a nightclub for many years.

Amid controversy, the Fourth Corby Arts Festival Week was opened on July 11th by Lady Hesketh, Chairwoman of the South Northants Conservation Association and a member of the Northampton Repertory Theatre Board. Corby Sea Cadets, who had been engaged to act as a guard of honour for her ladyship, claimed that the organising committee had snubbed them by failing to forward any instructions about or to notify them of any proposed arrangements regarding the visit. Lt. Commander

R. Nithine revealed that twenty-five of his boys had been training for two weeks. He said: "We waited but heard nothing. The lads are very disappointed." Further to that, their disillusioned Commanding Officer, Lt. R.N.W. Howe, commented: "We're all at sea over this matter!" Mr. Harry Maddams, Chairman of Corby Urban District Council, apologised to them because they had missed the launch, putting it down to 'an unfortunate misunderstanding.'

As an alternative to Highland dancing (a tradition much loved by Scottish inhabitants of the town) a group of morris dancers kicked off the week with an exhilarating display outside the Civic Centre. The sight of grown men skipping and bouncing around in fancy dress, with dangling ribbons and bells, brought a mixed response from passers-by. Roger Johnson was delighted. "We should have more of this kind of event in rural England - not beer-swilling clansmen prancing about in skirts!" he ventured.

James 'Hamish' Cox, a first generation 'Corbyite' and understandably proud of his Scottish heritage, took the opposite view. "I find it all rather twee - men wearing Totector boots, brandishing oversized baby-rattles and stamping their feet in the Civic car park. It's not at all what we are used to in Corby," he countered.

Paul Naffine of the Hunting Lodge in Cottingham may have looked like a Sicilian mobster, however this didn't prevent him fearing reprisals from both residents and members of Pat Ravey's gang. By way of a peace-offering (and to avoid having to sleep with the fishes!) the Lodge's manager offered residents a culinary apology - a dish named 'Suprême de Volaille Cottingham'. Having retired to the 'Strath' by this time, Ravey and his boys were distinctly unimpressed - preferring a pint of Tartan bitter and a Forfar bridie!

Described as being 'one of Liverpool's finest', the Spinners were the first headline act of the week to appear at the Festival Hall. Their folk-music and sea shanties, *Liverpool Judies* and *The Manchester Rambler*, had the audience singing along with gusto. A blues pianist, Champion Jack Dupree (another act promoted by Trevor Wright of Arts and Leisure) claimed the Thursday night spot at the Willow Room and treated the audience to some of his best-known numbers - such as *Chain Gang Blues* and *Down In The Valley*. Dupree was nicknamed 'The Champ' on account of being an ex-boxer with over one hundred bouts to his name. That night at the Civic, his barrelhouse blues packed a punch which knocked out the punters of Corby in minutes!

The other highlight of what turned out to be a fairly low-key Arts Festival, came when the New Midland Theatre Company managed to overcome postal problems and get on the road with their production of the bawdy musical *Lock Up Your Daughters*.

Also in July of that year, those who owned taxis in Corby were up in arms over a council plan to introduce London-style black cabs on the streets of the town. Corby Urban District Council declared that all taxi firms would have to switch over to the London cabs by 1972. Mrs. E. E. Stewart, Vice-Chairman of the Urban District Council Streets and Buildings Committee (the department responsible for the decision) defended the proposal by saying: "They are purpose-built to do the job - for instance, they can turn in their own length."

A spokesman for Tommy's Taxis complained: "They are trying to introduce old-fashioned cabs into a New Town. Elected councillors should not be dictating to those who are trying to run a business."

Mr. Joe Nelson, the owner of Nelson's Cabs, also vehemently opposed the idea. He protested: "Ordinary people don't want the black cabs - and the drivers don't want them. We are bound to lose all the seaside runs - as I doubt that anyone will relish the prospect of a trip to Skeggy in a London-style cab."

In August, following routine maintenance checks at the Civic complex, structural faults were discovered in the concrete floors of the four-year-old building. On learning how much the repairs would cost (estimated to be £22,000) John McGuiness, the head barman, quipped: "It was those heavy-footed morris dancers who caused the damage!" A spokesman for Corby Council was quick to assure the public that the Annual Police Ball, scheduled for October, would not pose a further threat to the building. An unconvinced McGuiness responded: "Hundreds of flat-footed coppers stomping about the place? Where's the exit?"

Arguments over the running of the Civic Centre continued to arise, and Arthur Pitcher, the manager of the Rutland Cinema, certainly had his tanner's worth.

A concerned James 'Hamish' Cox put his foot down over the weighty issue of men in Totectors dancing in car parks.

"What is the percentage of Corby people attending these events?" he asked. "Very few!" he answered. "Regarding the design of the complex, I think one word sums it up. Hopeless! Why build a dance floor above a theatre? Who put the toilets so far away from the patrons? Pop music would also be more suited to the Willow Room than the Festival Hall where, if you only get a couple of hundred turn up, they are lost in the vastness of the room. Why not have Sunday night discos? Midweek ballroom dances were started, ran at a loss and were then dropped. Would they have been ditched if they were deemed to be 'cultural entertainment'? The Civic is under-used as well as misused and the blame has to be attached to the Civic Amenities Committee."

Caught on camera was this dastardly (but unsuccessful) attempt by morris dancers to destabilise the foundations of the Festival Hall. Thirty-nine foot-stomping years later both the hall and the town's swimming pool (pictured in the background) would be gone - demolished under the Corby Regeneration programme.

More concerns were aired - this time by women dissatisfied with having to shell out for a new pair of tights every time they went to a show. Helen Aitchinson stated her grievance: "The chairs are snagging and laddering our tights. They must have got them from a factory canteen or something." Her best friend, Marion McKinney, backed her up: "We were there for Champion's concert and I had just taken my seat when the damn thing snagged my leg. The resulting tear soon developed into a big hole and I had to walk around for the rest of the night looking like a right tramp."
Helen added: "I know women normally carry spare pairs of tights in their bag - but how many? It's time the management replaced these second-rate chairs with some decent seating!"
While Corby's so-called premier entertainment venue continued to be dogged by complaints, the Crows Nest Coffee Bar and Youth Club, also to be found in George Street, closed its doors for the

very last time. Alderwoman Mrs. Dora Oxenham (a committee chairwoman who had been awarded a CBE in the New year's honours list of 1970) broke the news: "I think the club has now served its purpose and is no longer a viable proposition - especially with the change in taste of the rising generation and development of the Corby Youth Centre in Cottingham Road." Opened a decade earlier by Youth Ventures Ltd. of Reading, the Crows Nest was originally intended to help get youngsters off the streets and develop their social skills. No one in authority lost any sleep as yet another gathering-place and refuge for teenagers vanished from the town. A Chinese restaurant took over occupancy of the building and remains there to this day.

'Your story sounds touching but it sounds like a lie'

COMPLIMENTS *From*

Mr. & Mrs.

Champion Jack Dupree

BLUES PIANIST

of NEW ORLEANS L.A. U.S.A.

173 OVENDEN WAY OVENDEN HALIFAX

YORKSHIRE
0422
Tel. Hx. 65389

The two sides of Champion Jack Dupree. The Champ's business card offered little in the way of consolation to friends Helen Aitchinson and Marion McKinney - who regularly complained to management that the spiralling cost of hosiery was making the Festival Hall an expensive night out.

It wasn't all bad news though - Les Tolhurst, landlord of the Lilacs pub in Isham, was planning a jazz club. "This will be a place where jazz-lovers can come together to hear and discuss their common interest." The announcement was welcomed by John Sandy from Corby. He responded: "At last! Jazz has been poorly served around here since the days of Studio 49 and of the Halfway Jazz Clubs of the 1950s and '60s. I've missed the sheer, ethereal pleasure of listening to Mingus and Monk - whilst nursing a *Ritz Fizz*, fortified by a liberal dash of *Crème de Cassis*. This is indeed excellent news!"

Pat Ravey and his boys were involved in another fracas during a Friday midnight movie at the Rutland Cinema on Rockingham Road. The only difference was that this time they came off second-best. Pat sustained both a black eye and a cut to his face, when Eddie Panter (one of the ushers) was forced to eject twenty youths from the cinema for making a nuisance of themselves. Ravey: "Nobody went to the midnight movie with serious intentions of watching the film! Snog a bird, sleep, conduct belching or farting contests, or throw things at the screen - they were all part of the fun! The films were often rubbish anyway!"

Mick Dickson: "We were always steaming when we went to the pictures. I remember one night when four of us came out of the Rutland, got a cab to Kettering and then a train to London - to go to the free Blind Faith concert in Hyde Park. When we got there, we tried to get some sleep in St James's Park, however, the police kept moving us on. As soon as the pubs re-opened, we were back in for another session - before making our way to the performance. There were thousands of people in Hyde Park, and you couldn't see the stage because it was miles away. Not that it mattered - as soon as we hit the grass, we all fell asleep and missed the show!"

A much better time was had at one of their get-togethers which took place at Billing in Northamptonshire. John Kenrick: "Joe Cocker and the Grease Band were headlining at the show, which was due to take place inside a big marquee. The good news was that it was very easy to gatecrash - we just crawled under the side of it! Another stupid thing was that the bouncers were giving pass-outs to everyone who left the marquee - so we collected ours and then sold them outside for half the entrance fee. We did that quite a few times. To cap things off, the beer and spirits were kept in another big marquee that was just next door to the show tent. Suffice to say - a good time was had by all!"

Although photographed near the police station - it's an urban myth that Pat Ravey and friends had just been released from custody that day (for a start the polis wouldn't have allowed them to keep that 'dug' with them overnight!)

'Teddy the booze loving badger is a regular at the Bluebell Inn, Gretton' so said the *Evening Telegraph* in March 1970. It appears that the amiable pet not only enjoyed the friendly banter at his local pub but had also developed a penchant for the occasional drop of beer. Mr. and Mrs. Tony Weber (who ran the pub at the time) said that Teddy would soon have to go on the wagon because they and their daughter Lesley were leaving the district and would be unable to take with them the twelve-month-old orphaned badger whom they had rescued from the Pytchley badger hunt. The Weber family were hoping that despite Teddy's unusual tastes (which included sausages with bread and treacle - washed down with a saucer of beer) someone in the village would take him in and cater to his needs. "But not too much beer - it's not good for him," said Lesley. Mrs. Weber added: "He's affectionate, house-trained and really quite domesticated. I'm sure that he'll make someone a lovely pet."

The Rutland was the scene of absolute farce when police, following a tip-off about alleged illegal gambling, interrupted a bingo session. Arriving in police vans and panda cars, thirty 'boys in blue' sealed off the area and surrounded the building - thus bringing an unscheduled halt to proceedings. The Chief Constable took the stage and announced to a startled audience: "This is a raid. Will everyone please leave the premises quietly and in an orderly fashion." Seven hundred bingo players then exited the building - grumbling about the 'cairry on'. "That clown has just cost me the jackpot," complained Dougie Spiers. "I was waiting for two fat ladies to come out of the bag," he mused. Manager Arthur Pitcher appeased disconsolate punters by reassuring them that the £300 kitty would carry forward to the following month's jackpot session.

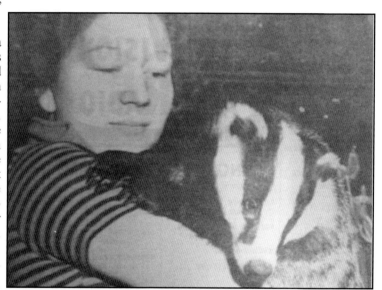

Another incident involving a disgruntled Corby punter was that featuring a chap named John McGhee, who ended up in front of the town's magistrates - pleading a 'misunderstanding'. After placing a £1 bet on a horse in Martin's (the bookies on Occupation Road) McGhee claimed to have heard the result of the race over the loudspeakers, as he was about to leave. He returned to the counter and asked for a refund - which was politely refused. Dissatisfied, he leaned over and took his money out of the till, then left the shop. "Cowboys!" he was heard to exclaim. The magistrate ordered McGee to pay a £1 fine and a further £3 in costs.

Lesley Weber explains the dangers of under-age drinking to one-year-old Teddy the badger. Unfortunately for this thirsty pet it was chucking-out time as his owners were about to leave the district.

Corby's crime figures continued to soar as a wave of burglaries swept through the town. They included the theft of a vacuum cleaner from a flat in Argyll Street, and in another case a clock and a biscuit barrel were taken from a house in Maxwell Walk. Among those residents battening down the hatches was Mrs. McClatchey at Number 14, who fumed: "Ah'm scunnered. I'd only just filled the barrel with digestives as well! I hope the glaikit wee toley chokes on them!"

The most exciting and original musical group on the local circuit was Principal Edwards Magic Theatre - a travelling rock/theatre group who were based in Kettering. With up to fourteen members - including eight Exeter University students - the line-up also included four girls who danced and sang. When John Peel from Radio One saw the band he took a shine to them and signed them to his Dandelion record label (which was managed by Clive Selwood.) The group also featured on his *Top Gear* programme. Appearances at major festivals and bookings on the university and college circuit followed, with the group sharing the bill with Roxy Music, Hawkwind and the Faces. During his contribution to John's obituary in 2004, Selwood recalled the signing of the Kettering outfit and the unnerving effect their presence had on him: "John had a penchant for signing unusual artists so we signed this 'acid rock' folk band called Principal Edwards Magic Theatre. There were up to thirteen members - but it was a bit of a moveable feast. John put the band up and, if he ever had any food in, they'd just eat it. He'd get up and the fridge would be empty. I thought they'd put black magic on me.

They would occasionally come into the office and, after they'd gone, I found I just couldn't do anything. We didn't argue or have fights but somehow I lost my reason. It was strange. I'd just have to call it a day and go home. I felt some kind of grey magic was involved."

Principle Edwards concert at Kettering's Central Hall provided a rare opportunity for local followers of the group to see them play live. Billy Piper, who was both a fan and a music hack, reported: 'The Principals have undoubtedly brought culture and art into modern music. They have the most weird and wonderful costumes. Their dressing room was littered with yards of net and silks, strands of tinsel and coloured foil paper. Christopher Runciman, in charge of the lighting and effects, told me: "We try to do something original." Percussionist Lyn Edwards explained the unusual name: "It came about when I once mentioned that my Uncle Edward was principal of some college in Wales. It became a private joke and then we thought it would be a good name for a group."

Corby postal worker Brian Coyle (who was a Marine Engineer in the Royal Navy back in 1970) remembers coming across Principal Edwards on several occasions when returning to Chatham to join his ship *HMS Jaguar*. Brian: "At the end of a weekend pass I used to travel back to London on the milk train - which left Kettering at around 2 o'clock in the morning. The first time I saw them was when the door of the luggage car opened and all these long-haired, dishevelled, hippie types fell out - carrying drum cases, guitars and all sorts of equipment. I was amazed at the amount of gear they had. Sitting on the platform, shivering, I felt like asking one of them if I could borrow a kaftan coat. Someone told me that they had taken over a farmhouse in the Kettering area because they wanted to get away from it all. As I was a music fan and they intrigued me, I followed their progress and even bought an album of theirs called *Soundtrack*."

The rapacious Principal Edwards Magic Theatre was famous for eating John Peel out of house and home. They also preyed on the mind of Peel's manager Clive Selwood, who felt that 'grey magic' was at work.

In February 1970, Margaret Barker served her last cup of tea from behind the counter of the snack bar at Kettering's Granada Cinema. Margaret, who was aged sixty-six, had worked at the cinema for two decades and retained many fond memories of the various pop stars and entertainers who had appeared there. Frank Mullen, who lived in Corby as a young lad, remembers Margaret assisting him in his quest to return a photograph to Cliff Richard when the star visited the Granada. The photo had been given to Frank by a brother of his who had once worked in a Glasgow hotel where Cliff had been staying, and who had been unable to resist the urge to purloin it from the pop star's room. The snapshot in question was of a young Harry Webb. It portrayed him standing in his parents' back garden - at a time when he was just on the threshold of stardom.

Frank: "I was a regular customer at the tea-stand during the intervals, and I had gotten to know Margaret well enough to ask her if she would return the photo, on my behalf, to its rightful owner. Although she promised me that she would do her utmost to ensure that Cliff got it back, as it turned out, he left by the back door immediately after coming off stage - so the opportunity never arose. We were both disappointed, however, hopefully I will get the chance to hand it back to him one day."

Frank returned to Scotland when he reached adulthood and (inspired by Cliff Richard and the Shadows) started his own rock 'n' roll group called Airport. He returned to Corby, on a permanent basis, a decade later. The photograph of Cliff remains in his album - a reminder of the days he spent as a starstruck youngster!

That summer Corby police were to be found hobnobbing with the Finedon Constabulary. It was rumoured that their remit was to establish whether or not the theft of an eight ton lorry-load of biscuits from the premises of the United Biscuit Company (with an estimated market value of £1000), could in any way be linked to the recent disappearance of Mrs. McClatchey's biscuit barrel.

"It's driving the Finedon police crackers!" said aspiring comedian PC Roger Wells of Corby.

Margaret Barker 'Tea Lady To The Stars' recalls the days when artists like Cliff Richard enjoyed a cuppa at the Granada snack bar - a bargain at tuppence ha'penny (the tea that is!)

Despite assisting a neighbouring division with their enquiries, officers from Corby were coming under mounting pressure from the local media. The criticism heaped upon them by the press was predominantly due to a mini-crimewave which had swept through the town during that year. Apart from the on-going mystery of the missing biscuits, the Corby constabulary was also in the process of investigating a case of burglary at a house in Burghley Drive - the victims of which were a family who had awoken to discover that their living room carpet and vacuum cleaner had been stolen. A similar crime involving the theft of a vacuum cleaner had also reportedly taken place at a house in Halifax Square. A bemused PC Wells joked: "Hoovered thought it?"

It would seem that the laughing policeman soon grew weary of searching for crumbs of evidence - not long after that he left the force to become landlord of the Coach and Horses pub in Lubenham.

During mid-winter the *Evening Telegraph* ran this headline: 'USELESS SCOTS CAN SHIFT SNOW FAST'. T. Walton (a Kettering resident with business interests in Corby) had advised members of Kettering Borough Council 'to employ some of those useless Scots to clear the snow from the town centre and main bus routes' if they should be unfortunate enough to encounter weather conditions as severe as those recently endured by their neighbouring town of Corby. "Maybe they don't make it as long distance lorry drivers," he said, "but when it comes to clearing snow - they sure make everyone else look slow!"

The local tabloid also reported that Corby was in line to get a second mural - this one to be created by Grammar School teacher Anthony Parsons, who said: "I am hoping that the Council will be able to find a suitable site for it." Councillor Jack Stevens, a proponent of the idea, added: "I hope that, if the town accepts the mural, we won't cover the thing up like we did the last one!"

In inflation-hit Papua New Guinea (part of the Australian Trust Territory) the rising cost of brides was causing some concern to local government officials. Although the President of the New Guinea Local Council, Mr. Toua Kapena, announced his intention to bring in new regulations that would set a cap on prices, matters were not made any easier by the fact that shell armbands - the traditional currency - still constituted part of the bridal negotiations. Despite having no means of converting such goods into the currency of dollars and cents, Kapena

Above: Frank Mullen's guilty secret. A baby-faced Cliff Richard (1958) enjoys a few moments of relative anonymity - relaxing in his parents' garden prior to embarking on the 'Summer Holiday' of a lifetime!

disclosed that he had devised a scheme whereby all interested parties would have to declare in writing the value of the bride-to-be, which was expected to lie within a range of 1000 - 2000 Australian dollars (the sterling equivalent being £466 & £933.) Recorded in 1968 - the highest amount paid out stood at 3000 dollars (£1400).

Billy Paton, enjoying a pint of NBC in the Welfare Club Smoke Room, expressed his views on the price of a bride, saying: "If I'd known then what I know now aboot my Gracie, I widnae have given tuppence for her - never mind a shell airmband!" (Billy's wife Gracie had recently run off with a local barman!)

Reaching for the stars (in his case Cliff and the Shadows) Frank Mullen left his former group Airport back home in Drumchapel, Glasgow and flew south to Corby. The young guitarist was hoping that the town's proximity to London (hub of the British music industry) would assist him in his efforts to emulate his idols. Frank Mullen is pictured third from left with fellow Airport members John, Chic, Owen & Alex.

In 1969 Kip Trevor (former guitarist with the Invaders) joined Pesky Gee - a rock group from Leicester. Their first album, which was recorded at Derek Tompkins' Beck Studios in Wellingborough, and released later that year on the Pye Records label, sadly didn't strike a cord with the music press - who described it somewhat unflatteringly as 'an album of mediocre blues rock'. In light of that, changes were made to personnel which saw them adopt a harder-edged style under the new and more sinister name of Black Widow. The new formation played what was likened to 'a wild, orgiastic, black mass oriented rock, a sound similar to the jazz/rock fusion of John Hiseman's Coliseum'.

It was while they were performing in Ryde, on the Isle of Wight, that the band came into contact with Wilf Pine - who had once managed the chart-topping group, the Move, and who by this time was in charge of security at all of the nightclubs and ballrooms on the island.

Kip Trevor: "I remember Wilf very well. He was a formidable character who often said, 'If you wanna be successful in da bizniz Kip, be a bit 'umble'. That's one thing that you definitely had to be around him!" (An uncompromising figure, Pine went on to work for Don Arden - another hard-nosed individual in the music business. Arden's clients included, amongst others, the Small Faces and Amen Corner, and it was after working with Don that Wilf decided to try his hand at managing again - this time an up-and-coming band called Black Sabbath. Arden was convinced that Sabbath was destined to become one of the biggest bands in rock history. It came as no surprise therefore, that when Pine poached them from right under his nose, in an act of perceived betrayal, the diminutive, self-appointed 'Godfather of British Pop' never forgave the 'Uriah Heep' of heavy metal!)

Elizabeth Street, December 1972: Showing their patronising southern neighbours just how it's done - 'lazy' Scots workers from Corby clear snow in double quick time.

Released on the CBS label, Black Widow's debut album *Sacrifice* was described in the music press as 'progressive rock with lots of flute, sax and organ - bringing to the forefront the dark elements, with mystical and demonic lyrics set to a contemporary rock backdrop.' *Come To the Sabbath* (a track from *Sacrifice*) was a minor hit for Widow and became the band's signature tune. Their stage act (which came to a climax with the title track of the album) was soon courting controversy because it included the 'ritual sacrifice' of a naked girl called Joyce - who was also from Leicester. Alex Sanders (a prominent male witch who had been to one of the group's performances) issued a warning that they should stop. He said: "Black Widow's stage act is dangerously near to the doors of hell. Their naked sacrificing and other such black deeds are too near the real thing. They are in danger of conjuring up a she-devil, which sounds fun but on the other hand could be a bit nasty." The band played on regardless - relishing publicity such as that provided by music journalist Carol Boucher of *Disc*, who wrote:

'Black Widow hit on the idea of using black magic as a musical act, and now, swept along by a barrage of outcries and sensationalism, there is no stopping them. Not that they want to stop. At the moment they're hot property - in constant demand all over the country with a possible tour of America lined up. They've sparked off controversies on TV and in the Sunday newspapers, and been taken under the wing of head witch, Alex Sanders.
The question most people want to know is just how safe and genuine are they? Is this six-piece group in danger of conjuring up something evil or being possessed? Kip

Trevor, vocalist, reckons they're quite safe. And yet after the outcry they caused at London's Lyceum recently, when the girl in their act stripped off against the management's orders and whipped Kip until, his back bleeding, she passed out and Sanders had to be called to bring her round.

Kip describes Alex as "a good guy", and although they won't admit it, the indications are that they belong to his coven. Sanders instructed them on their act to make it more authentic, and consecrated the sacrificial sword that Kip uses.

As to their authenticity and how far the act is a gimmick, the group insist that they were interested in black magic to begin with. Says Kip: "What gets me is that when so much work has gone into this - hours and hours of research - people disregard that and put it all down to sensationalism."

Press hostility would, however, eventually persuade Black Widow to move away from a theme based upon the occult. Two more albums followed - *Black Widow* (1971) and *Three* (1972). They both proved to be more commercial but lacked the strengths of *Sacrifice* - leading to the band splitting up. Kip Trevor moved into music publishing and settled in the leafy suburbs of Surrey.

The pinnacle of Widow's career remains that occasion in 1970 when they played at the Isle of Wight Festival and found themselves sharing a bill with the Doors, Jimi Hendrix, Joni Mitchell and many others. Estimates of the attendance figures vary between 100,000 and 500,000 people. British Rail charged each of them ten bob per return ticket for the ferry crossing - netting a total of £750,000 in fares. The concert (with tickets priced at £3) turned into an unexpected 'freebie' for some music fans, as those who were camping outside of the arena were able to watch and listen from nearby East Afton Hill. Nigel 'Pop' Portman, at the time an apprentice carpenter from Corby, says that he revelled in being there. Nigel: "I went with a couple of mates and had a great weekend - getting pissed, forgetting all about dovetail joints and chilling out to the music. It was brilliant! What we heard was worth everything we went through - and that includes the cold night air and the dew-fall. We went as ordinary, fare-paying freaks to listen to the music, see some friends and get to know each other better."

An 'excited' Marie Nelson and friend had also travelled down from Corby - in great anticipation of seeing, for the first time, some of their idols performing live. It wasn't the experience that she'd hoped for. Camped on the hillside with half a million other rock fans, the debauchery, drunkenness, drug abuse and violence soon had them scampering to a local hostelry for refuge. Marie said: "It was horrible and we were scared to death. In addition we were so far away from the stage that it was a waste of time!"

Brian 'Herbie' Coyle remembers being seconded to a Royal Navy undercover drug patrol at the festival. He recalls having a 'great weekend jolly' and later being amused at the newspaper stories detailing the arrests that had been carried out by the patrol (who, incidentally, were dressed as hippies.) Brian: "One of those we nabbed was a chap who'd chatted up a Wren - a big fat bird who was really gross. He kept insisting that she was beautiful - so naturally we assumed that he had to be high on drugs! Another guy was picked up for selling pills at £1 a time, but it turned out that they were only aspirin!

As regards the music I thought Family was the best group there - they played *Weaver's Answer*, *No Mule's Fool* and all that stuff. Terrific! The folk group Pentangle were really good as well. They had a girl singer who always sat down when she was on stage. I don't know why she did it - a gimmick I suppose. Anyway, at the Isle of Wight she stood up. Fans of the band obviously didn't approve though - because they heckled her to sit down again. Guess you can't win!"

Following their sojourn with Shanks & McEwan, 'Big C' Smith and 'Big Ted' Foster went their separate ways. Smith decided to try his luck at yet another building site - this time a housing estate near the Phoenix pub. The site (which was being constructed by Firman's of Peterborough and was

Above: A bemused member of Rockingham Forest Wheelers cycling club ponders the meaning of Corby's much talked about abstract mural. Although no one seems to know what happened to the controversial frieze, what is known is that a decade later Grammar School teacher Anthony Parsons (right) offered to create a replacement for it. Alas his generous offer was declined by the powers-that-be (who once again failed to recognize the cultural value of modern art!)

still in its early stages) was being run like a prison camp, under the watchful eye of a miserable, snarling, sour-faced ganger called Charlie Harper. Clive recalled: "Charlie, together with the majority of his gang, was from the outback - i.e. places like King's Cliffe and Uppingham. It was obvious to me that he didn't like Corby, or its people - and that included both the Jocks and the Welsh!"

Bearing that in mind, it came as no surprise, therefore, that despite his best efforts Big C always managed to fall foul of his boss. On the bonus side, Clive remembers that a large part the summer of 1970 (on what turned out to be his longest ever 'working holiday') was spent *in* the Phoenix - rather than working on the Phoenix site. Clive: "There was an element among the Corby lot who would disappear into the pub as soon as it opened, and then would reappear hours later, fighting and arguing amongst themselves. No wonder Harper hated Corby! Most of the crew opted for a lunchtime session in the pub (e.g. a couple of pints and a game of darts) then they'd head back on site to find a hole in which to hide for the afternoon!

SINGERS WARNED BLACK MAGIC ACTS DANGEROUS

Could conjure up 'she devil' says top witch

ON STAGE every night Corby pop singer Kip Tre-vor is stripped to the waist and whipped . . . then as a terrifying highlight to his black magic pop act he holds a mock sacrifice, enacting the ritual of stabbing a naked girl before his horrified audiences.

So realistic is Trevor's act with his Black Widow group that he has been warned by the self-styled King of the European Witches, Mr. Alex Saunders, that he may "open the gates of hell and conjure up a she-devil."

Mr. Saunders—who recently appeared on a top television show to talk about the growing black magic cult and how it is spreading into pop music —has told the group that they are dabbling in something they do not understand.

American contract

But Kip, whose mother lives at 1 Bancroft Road, Cot-tingham, in

knife, which he believes ma once have actually been use in Black magic ceremonies.

There is also a seduction scene.

The girl has become frightened by the group plung ing deeper and deeper int the supernatural that she ha quit and returned to college study—and Black Widow no have to hire models to tak part in the sacrifice numbe when they go on stage.

In an interview with "Evening Telegraph" spoken Kip, who has well known in Corby circles for several years "We formed Black about six months ago.

"Three of us h

'On stage every night Corby pop singer Kip Trevor is stripped to the waist and whipped... then as a terrifying highlight to his black magic pop act he holds a mock sacrifice, enacting the ritual of stabbing a naked girl before his horrified audiences.'

There was one old Irish fellow who drove Harper to distraction - a pipe-layer by the name of Hughie Brown. Old Hughie would delegate all the tasks for the day (usually to me) and then make himself scarce - normally around opening-time. He'd whisper: 'If anyone's looking for me - tell them that I've gone to get some fag papers'. Four hours later Hughie would return, give me a bollocking for sitting around all day, point out a few examples of poor jointing in my pipework, and then stagger off in search of a taxi to take him to the Cardigan Arms.

An exasperated, Harper decided to move him to another site on Occupation Road, where they were working on a block of flats, however, it came as no surprise to learn that he only lasted for about three days there - as it was just across the road from the Welfare Club!"

With old Hughie gone, it wasn't long before Big C was exposed as the dastardly pipe-laying fraud that he really was. Harper was to swing the axe again - and this time it would be Big C's head that would roll!

During the afternoon of the fateful day, Big C had watched a couple of brickies building a wall and had marvelled at the "brilliant way" in which they had started at opposite ends and then met perfectly in the middle. Unfortunately, on hearing the hooter sound for the afternoon tea break, rather than walk round the structure, Clive chose to step over it and in doing so accidentally caught the wall with his knee. Sadly, he wasn't to know that at that precise moment, he was bringing about his own (as well as the wall's) premature downfall!

In the event, Big C's earlier appreciation of the bricklayers' feat counted for nothing with Harper - or with the brickies themselves, and Clive remains convinced that it wasn't just his pipework that let him down that day. He is of the opinion that in Harper's eyes the lethal combination of: (a) his being of Welsh descent, (b) coming from Corby, and (c) knocking down a wall, most probably sealed his fate - resulting in him having to catch an earlier than usual United Counties No. 291 (West Circular) bus home!

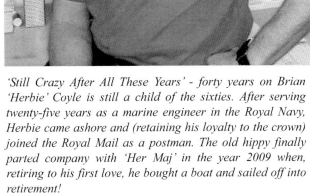

'Still Crazy After All These Years' - forty years on Brian 'Herbie' Coyle is still a child of the sixties. After serving twenty-five years as a marine engineer in the Royal Navy, Herbie came ashore and (retaining his loyalty to the crown) joined the Royal Mail as a postman. The old hippy finally parted company with 'Her Maj' in the year 2009 when, retiring to his first love, he bought a boat and sailed off into retirement!

Thanks to his numerous forays into the Phoenix pub, Clive discovered that it was different from any other Corby boozer - in that it possessed an underground bar. The Barrel Bar (as it was called) was cramped and had very poor air-conditioning. It was a lounge/music-room and, at the time, was considered to be quite a popular haunt for local bands to practice in. However, as the years went by it would gradually fade from the minds of Corby pubgoers.

Of rare vintage in the Barrel Bar was the flamboyant stage act of Pat Lavin, which (with Lavin in the guise of his alter ego Harry Garter) could be said to be bordering on camp.

The young singer was born in Bannockburn in Scotland - a short distance from the site where in 1314 Robert the Bruce defeated the English Army. He moved south with his family when the local pit closed and his father was made redundant. Growing up in close proximity to the famous battleground must have instilled a little of Bruce's spirit into the painfully reserved Scot - for after much deliberation he revealed his 'braveheart' by agreeing to try out for a band (new to the Corby music circuit) who were looking for a vocalist.

Who would have believed that shy Pat Lavin (the fresh-faced lad pictured centre with his group Privy Seal) would rapidly morph into one of the most outlandish front men in the business? L-R: Malcolm Watt, Mick Timmus, Pat, Ricky Devlin and Pete Dyne.

This took place halfway through the 1960s - when Pat was learning his trade as an apprentice welder in the Engineering Shops at B.S.C. His habit of warbling while he worked soon caught the attention of two of his workmates, Malcolm Watt and Pete Dyne, who were in the process of forming a band. Alerted to young Lavin's vocal ability, the more than impressed industrial talent-spotters managed to persuade an uncertain Pat to attend an audition at the town's Silver Band Club.

"When they asked me, my first reaction was to say no," admitted Pat, "but when they insisted, I eventually agreed and said that I'd see them there. As things turned out, I bottled it and didn't turn up!" Fortunately, Malc and Pete were not to be put off by Lavin's reluctance - at work the next day they offered him another chance. This time, however, they insisted on picking him up en route to the club.

Pat's audition proved to be a success, and so with Mick Timmus on bass guitar and Ricky Devlin on drums, the group that was to become Privy Seal was complete. However, early rehearsals were a test of nerves for Pat. He says: "I was mortified in case anyone came into the hall when I was singing - I even had my back to the entrance door! In fact I was so self-conscious that, if anyone did come in, I would stop and refuse to continue until they had left."

Architecturally, the Festival Hall Complex was viewed by many of the locals as a white elephant - later contenders being the Rockingham Triangle Football and Athletics Stadium, followed by Rockingham Speedway. N.B. Although strictly speaking, due to a trade-off involving Kirby Hall (brokered by Corby Borough Council and its Oundle counterpart) the race circuit officially falls within the jurisdiction of East Northants Council.

THE WAY WE WERE: (as at March 31st 1970) The population of Corby stood at 49,680. British Steel Corporation employed 12,490 male and 802 female workers. Other firms in the town employed 6,304 male and 5,553 female workers. Corby Development Corporation and Corby Urban District Council between them rented out a total of 12,489 houses (with a further 585 dwellings under construction) whilst there were 1,042 privately-owned homes and 25 more under construction. 3,796 domestic garages were available for rent with 342 under construction. The Development Corporation's annual income from domestic housing rent was £1,167,120. On the health front Corby had 1 diagnostic centre and 1 maternity unit. There were 13,530 pupils attending schools in the urban district and 202 full-time, 887 part-time (day) and 785 part-time (evening) students were enrolled at Corby Technical College. We were entertained in 1 Civic Centre and 34 halls. Our taxes paid for 1 Public Library and 1 Technical Library. Our souls were soothed by 17 churches and our thirsts quenched at 17 public houses and 2 hotels. We slept safely in our beds courtesy of 1 fire station, 1 police station and 1 magistrates' court. Finally we were laid to rest in either of two cemeteries or 1 parish church graveyard.

Pete Dyne: "Getting Pat Lavin to join us completed our line-up. We learned around sixteen songs - which we had to repeat to fill the night out. Our first booking, which was at a church hall in Oundle, was remarkable only for Pat playing the whole show with his back to the audience! Although he suffered terribly with nerves in the beginning, once he overcame the jitters he went on to become one of the best frontmen around. He was a really charismatic character."

Pete Dyne began his career in 1965 by standing in for a few nights with a band called Gemini Five. Pete: "In my opinion, the seminal moment for the group came when we were booked to play on Sunday nights at Kettering Granada, during the interval between films. The front rows would be packed with screaming girls - which we all thought was great! I don't suppose it was because we were particularly brilliant; it was just the norm in those days - if you were in a band it gave you extra appeal. That was the real spur for me to form a band, and my mate Malcolm Watt was just as keen."

Privy Seal was managed by the irrepressible Basil Barnard. "One thing about Basil," Pete remembers ruefully, "he wouldn't allow any of the girls that we fancied to get on his bus. However, on the occasions when he hired it out to us, we got round this inconvenience by arranging to pick them up around the corner from the venue!"

A Privy Seal engagement which still gives Pat Lavin 'the shudders' is the one where they went on stage as the supporting act to Cliff Bennett and the Rebel Rousers (a group of British rhythm & blues stars who were appearing at RAF Cottesmore.) Pat: "I was in night school, at Corby Technical College, when Basil walked straight into the class and told the tutor that he needed me for a booking at Cottesmore. I went weak at the knees! - as it would be the first time that we'd be playing with a big 'name'. The rest of the boys, who were waiting for me in the minibus outside, were all excited. It transpired that the support band for Bennett had dropped out at short notice and so the agent had contacted Basil for help. I remember Cliff Bennett's look of relief when we turned up and started taking our gear out of the bus. He obviously feared that he might have to do the whole show on his own. One of the numbers that we had been rehearsing was Cliff's *One Way Love* - but even so, I was in a bit of a panic at the thought of playing it in front of the original artist. I must have done all right though, because he congratulated me for making a decent effort"

All bands harbour hopes of hitting the big time, of being booked into prestigious venues and of being in a position to demand 'riders' such as crates of booze, grub, groupies, or maybe even an oxygen tent manned by three foxy ladies! In 1970 that kind of lifestyle was just a pipedream for Privy Seal, so who can blame them for jumping the gun one night and helping themselves to a bag of frozen sausages from the kitchen of Dorothy's Niteclub in Cambridge? Pete Dyne remembers the occasion all too well, saying: "The bangers were carefully stored under a seat in the van and then promptly forgotten about. It wasn't until we discovered them, two weeks later that we found out where the horrible stench had been coming from. Basil wasn't amused!"

After Johnny Cash had paved the way for them, back in the 1960s, prison concerts became 'de rigueur' for many artists. In fact two of the finest albums to come from 'The Man in Black' (*Live At Folsom Prison* and *San Quentin*) were recorded behind bars for CBS.

Thanks to a prison warder who drank in the Phoenix pub and who set up a gig for them at Gartree High Security Prison, Privy Seal were soon to follow the trend. Pete Dyne: "Entering that place was a strange experience, and when they closed the gate behind us it felt really scary. It was nerve-racking! Pat said that he was tempted to paraphrase that famous line from the song *San Quentin* - but somehow 'Gartree, I hate every inch of you' was a bit too corny!"

Bob Gowen also had a spell with Privy Seal. He recalls that the Boston Gliderdrome (where local bands often provided support for big name acts) was one of his favourite venues. Bob: "William Bell was on one night when we were there. He'd had a hit with Judy Clay entitled *Private Number*, and was a real live Stax legend.

Unfortunately, that night he was suffering with a sore throat and only managed to struggle through about four numbers before retiring. We thought at the time there was something strange about him - then a couple of weeks later we read in a Sunday newspaper that a William Bell impostor was doing the rounds and conning everybody!" Pete Dyne: "We also played on the same bill as the Ronettes - who were still a strong pull, despite not having had a hit record for a few years. I've got a lasting memory of walking into the dressing room and being startled at the sight of Ronnie Spector, the lead singer, who was standing there in just a yellow basque. She was stunning! My mouth dropped open - but Ronnie didn't even bat an eyelid!"

Having served their time, Privy Seal left prison rock where it belonged - behind bars. Lavin and Dyne were paroled and (with brothers Mick and Tony Haselip, and ex-Pacifics' drummer Johnny Heron) went on to form Magnetic Storm. In next to no time, however, they had transformed themselves into Golden Fleece. Pat: "We made some records and Tony Blackburn actually played one of them on his radio show. It was called *Something Keeps Calling Me Back* - a Northern Soul-type number with Lilian Grimley and Cathy Kilgannon on backing vocals."

Johnny Heron, one of a long line of drummers, can boast a grandfather (James Cameron) who played with the Cameron Highlanders in Scotland. His Uncle Jimmy was the drummer for the popular 1950s/60s bands, the Vigilantes and the Phantoms, and (keen to maintain the family tradition) his nephew Cameron plays drums with the Grampian Pipe Band. Johnny's own career started in the early sixties, at the age of fifteen, and he can list numerous bands

Having been introduced to the guitar at the age of eleven (an old acoustic instrument which they mastered with the aid of Bert Weedon's 'Play In A Day') brothers Mick and Tony Haselip went on to enjoy forty years as respected performers on the local music scene. Evolving into a tremendously talented bass player, Mick started gigging with local bands from the age of sixteen (and continued to do so right up until his tragic and untimely death in 2003 - the victim of a brutal murder.) His brother Tony still plays guitar on a semi-professional basis and has no plans to retire in the immediate future.

on a CV covering a period of forty years. His brother Jimmy, however, has always been content to act as a 'sub' - filling in (often at the last-minute) whenever someone has been short of a drummer. Brian Heron is another member of the family to make his mark on the local music scene, but unlike the rest of them, must have been tired of all that drumming - he opted to play the bass guitar instead!

In June 1970 executives of the Bell Fruit Machine Manufacturing Company were forced to deny that some of the figures on their one-armed bandits represented members of the Royal Family. Newspaper reports had claimed that a scantily clad woman (depicted as part of a circus finale scene on one of the company's new machines) resembled Her Majesty the Queen. This followed a story about another of their machines, which was said to feature a horsewoman, complete with riding-habit, who looked just like Princess Anne. The Nottinghamshire firm had received a deluge of complaints from various prominent members of the Establishment, e.g. the Duke of Bedford, Lord Arran and Mr. Tom Iremonger, Conservative MP for Ilford North.

In response Mr. Allen Payne (a director of Bell Fruit) had this to say: "The first machine was produced two years ago, when Princess Anne did not even look as she does today. She may have grown to look like it since, and I suppose it does look a bit like her, if you look at it long enough. The latest machine includes a figure which people say looks like the Queen, but the figure in question is only half-an-inch high and is not the main feature."

Lily McGuckin of Fineshade Grove, a regular player on the Rangers Club's 'bandits' commented: "That Mr. Payne's got a cheek saying that Princess Anne has grown to look like a horse." Although her friend, Margo Paterson, pointed out that Payne hadn't actually said anything of the kind, Lily vowed that she wouldn't use the machines in question "at least not until they promise to remove those offensive daubings."

Later the same month the lollipop ladies of East Kilbride in Lanarkshire won their fight to end a period of intense personal embarrassment. The previous summer they had been issued with waistcoats that were fitted with flashing amber lights at chest level, and the ladies claimed that the unfortunate positioning of these lights had caused them acute embarrassment and made them the butt of rude remarks by passing schoolboys and workmen. Following a climb-down by the local authorities, replacement waistcoats were issued - only this time the flashing lights were on the shoulders. Mother of three children, thirty-three-year-old, Mrs. May Campbell said that although she and her colleagues were still on the receiving end of unwanted remarks - "One young lad called me a Dalek" - the new uniforms were a vast improvement. "The lights can still be seen quite clearly," she said, "but it's not at all embarrassing." It was agreed that the original waistcoats would still be issued to male road-crossing attendants in the town. As Mrs. Campbell pointed out to the local press, "Our male colleagues are quite capable of dealing with cheeky youngsters!"

On the local sports front, Corby Town Football Club were playing in Southern League Division One and were proving to be way ahead of their time by securing the services of overseas players. John Singlehurst, the chairman of the club, had taken over from Dr. John Devine in July and had been successful in orchestrating deals that would result in the Danish football stars: Benny Nielson, Aage Hansen and Fritz Ahlstrom, coming to play in England.

Singlehurst announced his intentions and ambitions for the Steelmen during his first press conference, saying, "I see only one pathway for the Steelmen over the next three or four years - into the Football League!" He qualified his prediction by adding, "The support of the Corby community will be essential in achieving that aim." The new signings proved that he was a man on a mission. Twenty-five-year-old Ahlstrom (who was also a sports reporter at that time for the leading Danish newspaper *Politiken*) will be remembered by the Occupation Road faithful for scoring with a header - whilst wearing glasses - in a game against Gravesend and Northfleet. He still reflects on his time with the Steelmen but doesn't see it all through rose-coloured spectacles. Corresponding in 2005, Fritz revealed how he became one of the first overseas footballers to play in England: He revealed: "I flew into Heathrow on Saturday, 28th November, 1970 and was driven by car (John Singlehurst's Jaguar) to Corby, where we arrived at the Occupation Road ground approximately one hour prior to the 3p.m. kick-off. In the souvenir programme, they showcased both Benny Nielson (No.9) and me (No.10) - however, Benny couldn't make it. Having played for Denmark the previous Wednesday, in a World Cup qualifier against Belgium, he had been invited by Sparta Rotterdam to discuss a transfer. In the end he signed for the Belgian First Division club Cercle Brugges KSV.

I played all ninety minutes against Gravesend. We were losing 1-0 when I equalised after seventy-five minutes. Jimmy Jardine (a young Scot who had been 'reduced' to substitute to make space for me) was quite upset about it, however, he came on after sixty-nine minutes. Four minutes after my equaliser, I made a pass for Jimmy to score the winning goal for the Steelmen - making us friends instantly. After the game I returned to Heathrow and from there to Denmark, but promised to come back. I did so, together with Aage Hansen, a nineteen-year-old midfielder and team-mate at AB (Academic Boldclub) who had accepted to replace Benny. Regretfully, I only played one more match for Corby - a cup game (which, as far as I can remember, we drew after extra time.) The reason for returning home so quickly was that we were not given the accommodation promised. Aage and I had to share a small bedroom, for example. He stayed for some months and did very well, and then he was joined by another talented Danish player, Fleming Osbeck, from Kastrup Boldklub.

Fritz Ahlstrom (friend to Corby Town's Jimmy Jardine and Sir Alex Ferguson) hung up his 'shooting glasses' in 1971. He later went on to become manager of Brondby and Senior Media Officer for UEFA before retiring in 2008.

How come we joined Corby? John Singlehurst did some business in Denmark and asked his contact at the company if it was possible to recruit one or two Danish players during the winter break in Danish football. The owner of the company knew one of the football writers at *Politiken* and he asked me if I would give it a try. By the way, Aage made it to the Danish Under 21 team, but never to the national team. However, he was good enough to be signed by and to play for the Belgian First Division clubs, SC Lokeren and Royal Antwerp for several seasons. Today Aage is working for AB in rather different roles - principally as the first team's assistant coach. Benny is also back in Denmark. After an excellent career with Cercle Brugges KSV, RWD Molenbeek, RSC Anderlecht and AS Saint Etienne, he now works as a players' agent. He was in the RS Anderlecht team which beat FK Austria Wien 4-0 in the Final of the UEFA Cup Winners Cup, at Parc des Princes in 1978. He also made twenty-eight appearances for Denmark, scoring seven goals in total."

What's on the box? Not a lot - according to this 'Evening Telegraph' television and radio schedule for December 1st 1970. Looks like a case of four channels and early to bed (every night!)

Fritz Ahlstrom was appointed Press Officer of the Danish Football Association in 1987. He left in 1991 in order to take over as General Manager of Brondby, but, unfortunately, a disagreement over the sacking of Morten Olsen (Brondby's coach) led him to quit the club also. In 1995 Fritz was offered the post of UEFA Senior Media Officer - where he worked until his retirement in 2008.

A weekend visit to a pen-friend in Manchester turned into the trip of a lifetime for seventeen-year-old Christine Beaver from Corby, when she was lucky enough to meet up with football idol George Best. Forty years on, the avid Manchester United supporter still has strong recollections of the day. Christine: "I had a pen pal called Lynn at the time - who lived in Wytheneshawe in Manchester, and whose parents actually worked at Old Trafford.

Christine Beaver standing beside the sporting heroes on her bedroom wall. Unfortunately the Corby teenager wasn't very pleased about the black eye that she herself was sporting!

They used to sell match tickets for the games and the match programmes. Anyway, it was Lynn's mum who told us that George Best owned a boutique in the city. She also explained to us just how to get there and told us about a few other places where he used to hang out. Armed with that knowledge, on the Friday Lynn and I set off in search of George - not expecting for one minute that we would find him.

When we arrived at his shop and looked through the window, Lynn said excitedly: 'There he is! C'mon Christine - let's go in'.

Before we knew it, we were both inside the boutique and were face-to-face with George Best. He asked us our names and where we came from. He also asked which team we supported. I was in a state of shock and found my self completely tongue-tied. There was I - talking to the footballing genius whose photographs covered my bedroom walls.

On the Saturday we went to a reserve game at Old Trafford, in which Bobby Charlton and Denis Law both played - having been out of first team action due to injury. On the subject of injuries, the only thing to mar what was for me a truly memorable day, was when I walked into a lamp-post and got a black eye! As we were making our way around the stadium prior to kick off, Lynn suddenly shouted 'Look! There's Denis Law!' As I turned round to try and get a glimpse of our king, I also neglected to watch where I was going and walked smack bang into the offending lamp-post. Within minutes I had a huge shiner!

After the match had ended I phoned my mum and dad to tell them that I'd met George Best, and this prompted my dad to notify the *Evening Telegraph* about my escapade. When one of their reporters knocked on our door on the following Monday and asked to

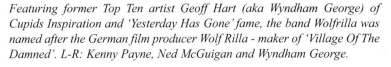

Featuring former Top Ten artist Geoff Hart (aka Wyndham George) of Cupids Inspiration and 'Yesterday Has Gone' fame, the band Wolfrilla was named after the German film producer Wolf Rilla - maker of 'Village Of The Damned'. L-R: Kenny Payne, Ned McGuigan and Wyndham George.

take a photo of me, I was mortified because the black-eye was still very much in evidence. Looking back, it was a fantastic weekend for a football-mad teenager - and certainly one that I just couldn't have imagined when I set off from Corby on that Friday morning."

Despite several setbacks, Corby's Progressive Music Concert was a huge success. The event, which took place in December and was promoted by Dougie King and his friend Tom Haworth, attracted an audience of more than seven hundred people. Fat Mattress and Emerson, Lake & Palmer were originally booked to perform at the show but, as Tom Howarth explains, things didn't exactly go according to plan. Tom: "Things were going so well that we really thought we were the kiddies! Then we received a phone call saying that ELP had cancelled - and we realised with a jolt that we were still only small fry. The agency told us that we could have T. Rex (who were just making it big at the time with *Ride A White Swan*) and that seemed fair enough, until the day of the show, when their road manager informed us that they wouldn't play - or even take their gear out of the van - until they were paid the full amount both up front and in cash. They wouldn't accept a cheque. I explained that although we hadn't sold many of the £1 tickets up to that point, we were expecting a big crowd to turn up and pay at the door. Unfortunately, they weren't having any of it and I spent the rest of the afternoon racing around in a panic - trying to get hold of the £150 that I was short of. To cap it all, the first thing that Marc Bolan said to the audience, when he came on stage, was that he was sorry that they'd had to pay so much to get in!"

Also appearing at the concert that night were Blodwyn Pig and an Irish folk duo called Tir Na Nog, but the unenviable task of opening the show was left to local outfit Wolfrilla (made up of Wyndham George, Ned McGuigan and Kenny Payne.) The band performed both sides of their forthcoming single *Song For Jimi/Kangaroo* which was scheduled for release, on the CBS label, the following January.

Reg Civil celebrates fifty years of 'cutting it' in showbiz. After spending three years working as a professional artist with the Lynton Boys, Reg went on to open the Kettering dance school responsible for nurturing the youthful talent of local lad Jim Dale. On the night of Reg's special anniversary 'do', Rothwell born Dale (by this time a hugely popular all-round entertainer and star of 'Carry On' film fame and the Broadway stage) paid tribute to his early mentor via telegram from New York. Sadly Reg passed away a few years later in January 1978. He was sixty-four years old.

A fortnight before Christmas Anthony Roye, the long-suffering impresario of the New Midland Theatre Company, finally brought down the curtain on his Corby adventure by announcing that his 'dream of creating an East Midlands theatre empire in the town' was coming to an end. Claiming that he was over £15,000 worse off and that he was leaving with just a suitcase to his name, Roye's parting shot was aimed at the town's planners as much as at the apathetic public (with whom he was 'appalled' because of their very visible lack of support - evident in the small numbers attending his productions). Anthony said: "to a certain extent the town centre is fine. It has a pub, an expensive hotel, one-class shops and an excellent Civic Centre entertainments complex, but in some respects

Corby is not a community in the traditional sense. There is no high street or main thoroughfare along which visitors, or indeed residents, travel on their way to other parts of the town. This lack of foresight by the planners prevents potential customers from gaining knowledge of what is taking place in the town. What is more, for half of the week the town centre is in darkness after 5.30p.m. - during the autumn and winter months. Until the area is lit up and made to look and feel more welcoming, the Civic Centre will remain a white elephant."

The Diddymen celebrate another trophy win. L-R: Back row - Brian Hollywood, David Black, Bob Parker, Stevie Lattimore (face obscured), unknown, Colin Took and Alan Brooks. Middle row - Duncan Robertson, John 'Mugs' Murray, Ian Fulton, Johnny Morrison, Terry McBlain, Derek Reeves. Front row - Alec 'Fudge' Redmond, Rod Bailey, George Bradshaw and Tommy Geoghegan Snr.

Also in December, Corby's jazz fraternity went into mourning after it was reported that Albert Ayler (the famous tenor saxophonist) had taken his leave to perform at the 'the big free-form gig in the sky'. The news came from across the Atlantic that thirty-four-year-old Ayler's body had been fished out of New York's East River. Bob Crawford, Corby's pre-eminent saxophonist, described Albert as being 'the most primal of the free-jazz musicians of the 1960s'.

Immediately after hearing the grave news, John Sandy (a committed 'modernist' and ardent admirer of Ayler's unbridled style) talked via the transatlantic telephone link to Mr. John Litweiler, Director of the Jazz Institute of Chicago. Following their conversation, he revealed: "Mr. Litweiler was of the opinion that there was absolutely no ambiguity about Albert's music. He didn't flirt with western techniques of construction - or seek harmonic principles as Coltrane did. Ayler's horn was simple, emotional and wild.' I have to concur that never before - or since - has there been such naked aggression in jazz. His albums *Spiritual Unity* and *Bells* received critical acclaim such as 'bringing a new flavour to jazz' and 'exhibiting a wild primitive feeling'. They show him advancing the improvisational notions of Coltrane and Coleman into abstract realms - where timbre, not harmony and melody, are the music's backbone."

Ayler reputedly once said: "I must play music that is beyond this world." After appearing to jump from the ferry that was carrying him to the Statue of Liberty - he was finally where he wanted to be!

Avon's Magnificent Seven tour guides line up outside Corby Civic Centre in their smart designer uniforms. Left - Right: Ingrid Mitchell, Janice Smith, Maureen McDonald, Pat Gowing, Carol Norman, Jackie Wiseman and Jackie Armstrong.

On New Year's Eve the Diddymen assembled once more at the Raven Hotel and, crammed into an overcrowded bar, sang again their ribald 'Diddy' songs, swigged Ansells Mild from their two-pint mugs and reflected on a year that was about to be consigned to the history books.

It had been a year during which Corby had celebrated its twentieth anniversary as a New Town, the future of British Steel as a major player in the steel industry had been underpinned (or so it

- HAND MADE SUITS
  Made in seven days to your own design for around £20

- WE SPECIALISE IN...
  SUEDE AND LEATHER
  in all our Shops, including Wellingborough

Stockists of BOYS' & YOUTHS' FASHION CLOTHING

WE LEAD —
  OTHERS FOLLOW

The County
SUEDE & LEATHER
CENTRE
is at
HORSEMARKET,
KETTERING

D.ROADNIGHT

Gloucester Place, Wellingborough : Roadnight's
Corner, Gold Street, Kettering : Horsemarket,
Kettering : High Street, Rushden : Corporation
Street, Corby

WE'VE GOT THE MIDLANDS COVERED

Roadnights were acknowledged throughout the county as being the leading outlet for up-market, trendy clothing - at a time when quality off the peg and made to measure fashions were not readily available.

'WE'LL DRIVE TO MEXICO BUT WE WANT SPONSORS'

TWO local men are planning to take part in the gruelling 16,000 mile car rally to Mexico being organised by a national newspaper. But first, they need firms and individuals to back them to the tune of £2,500.

The men are Mr. Philip McLaughlin, of 268 Studfall Avenue, Corby, and Mr. Robin Ellis, of 45 Oakway, Wellingborough.

They hope to start from Wembley in Mr. McLaughlin's Ford Galaxy on April 19 on the first leg of the six-week rally, and arrive in Mexico in time for the World Cup.

Starting with them will be at least 105 other cars, many of them from teams sponsored by the world's major car firms.

"But I think it is anybody's rally, and every car that even finishes will have done very well," said 25-year-old Mr. McLaughlin.

Mr. McLaughlin works for the Northampton engineering firm of J. C. Cowley Technical Services Ltd., of which Mr. Ellis is manager.

They are hoping that their own firm will give them money towards the trip, and that others locally might like to support them.

"We would put their stickers on the car, and it would be good advertising for them, especially if we should win," said Mr. McLaughlin.

BORSTAL FOR GIRL WHO TOO JUMPER[S]

A 20-YEAR-OLD girl was for Borstal training whe appeared at Northam shire Quarter Sessions terday and pleaded gui shoplifting.

Joyce Adam, of no abode, pleaded guilty stealing two jumpers £5 5s. from F. W. Wool and Co. at Corby on Ja 17.

Mr. N. R. Page, coun the prosecution, said sh in breach of a two yes bation order made at mouth Quarter Sessio June last year.

Mr. Page said Miss and a man were seen i worth's. She put two carrier bag, an

Phil McLaughlin appeals for £2,500 from sponsors, to jump-start his plans to drive the 16,000 mile 'Daily Mirror' London to Mexico World Cup Rally.

seemed) and 'Big C' and 'Big Ted' had sought new horizons. 1970 had also seen Britain's electrical manufacturers exporting a record £591 million worth of goods, 15 per cent more than the previous year. The UK yearly inflation rate had hit 5.9%, a gallon of four-star petrol had been selling at 34p (6s 8d in old money) and the average house price had soared to £4,975. It was a year of innovations, during which the World Trade Centre in New York was completed and the barcode (for use in the retail trade) was introduced. Meanwhile, on the music front, things were beginning to take a new and more aggressive direction. Returning to local matters deemed newsworthy, the *Evening Telegraph* reported the 50th anniversary in showbiz of Reg Civil from Kettering (whose pupils had included the internationally acclaimed Jim Dale.) Avon Cosmetics was also celebrating - this time the opening of its new premises in Corby. Seven of the company's famous tour guides were pictured outside the new building; wearing outfits specially designed for them by Roadnights of Kettering. We also read about the three Corby men with itchy feet - who revealed some rather ambitious plans. Phil McLaughlin announced his intention to drive to Mexico in a car rally, whereas Bruce Summers and Andy Sullivan laid out their plans to travel around the world. On a sad note, there would be no great life adventure for William Lumley of Westminster Walk in Corby - in March of that year William was burned to death in a tragic accident in the coke-ovens of British Steel.

All in all, 1970 was best summed up in the words of Dana Gillespie (winner of that year's Eurovision Song Contest) who sang *All Kinds Of Everything*.

Chapter Two 1971
Steel Waters Run Deep

On January 2nd, 1971 Corby's hogmanay celebrations were curtailed when news filtered through from Ibrox stadium that sixty-six football fans had been killed (and a further two hundred injured) during a hotly-contested Old Firm derby between Rangers and Celtic. As the day wore on it became apparent that the casualties had been sustained during the chaos that followed a late equalising goal by Rangers.

The disaster was to impact on many households in Corby - leaving stunned families fearing for the safety of loved ones who had made the trip to Scotland. First reports suggested that the fatal crush (which took place on Stairway 13) started to develop when hundreds of Rangers fans began to stream out of the ground after Jimmy Johnstone's 89th minute goal for Celtic. Victory for the Hoops had seemed inevitable, and then in injury time fate intervened - Colin Stein scored for Rangers, causing a huge roar to erupt from within the stadium.

According to eyewitnesses, many fans tried to climb back up the stairs - only to collide head-on with those who were descending, and although rescue workers arrived at the scene within minutes and attempted to force their way through the crowds, unfortunately, most of their efforts were in vain. One survivor described the maelstrom from his hospital bed, saying: "I was making my way out of the stadium and down the stairs, when suddenly everything seemed to stop." He continued: "The lads at the back just kept coming forward down the stairs. I went down with the rest of the crowd - who were being pushed and pulled onto the ground. Everyone was struggling to get out, suffocating. It was essentially a fight for survival. After ten or fifteen minutes I was dragged out by a policeman and brought to hospital by ambulance."

Michael Bloomfield (a cockney lad who was living in Corby at the time) witnessed events at close quarters. Michael had made the journey up to Scotland with his friend Neil McLean and a coach-load of other football fans from the Corby Rangers Supporters Club. Aged twenty and a supporter of Celtic, he was on his first ever trip north of the border. Michael recalled: "It was the very first 'Old Firm' game that I'd been to. I was wearing my Celtic colours and badges just to wind up the Rangers fans. Most of those on the bus were my friends and it was all very cordial. We were looking forward to the match and in general having a good time and a booze-up. Once I was inside Ibrox, I was very impressed by the place and thought it was an excellent stadium. Not for one minute did I think I would be in any danger - in those days all football stadiums had the traditional high terracing with crash barriers. The game had been exciting, tense, and with a great atmosphere. Celtic were leading 1-0 and there were just minutes to go, so we decided to make our way out of the ground (Neil, his brother Sammy and myself.)

Being Rangers fans, the McLeans were bitterly disappointed with what we assumed would be the final result. Suddenly, a massive roar went up and I turned around - along with hundreds of other fans

The 'Alpine' Stairway 13 in Ibrox Stadium, Glasgow - scene of terrible tragedy. In the immediate aftermath of the catastrophe many Corby families would spend anxious hours worrying about loved ones who had travelled to the game. The above photograph illustrates just how dangerously steep the staircase was.

- intending to go back up the stairs to see what had happened. Neil and Sammy were about six or seven feet away from me at that point - when big Colin Stein scored his last minute equaliser.

Abruptly it became a stampede and people were rushing forward in an attempt to escape, whilst others were trying to get back in. Some fell and were trampled underfoot as people started to climb over each other. Bodies were lying on the ground and getting trodden on - but I couldn't do anything! The screams and the crying were awful! I was lucky because if I'd turned back just a few seconds sooner, I'd have been caught up in the mêlée. By a stroke of good fortune, I was swept along on a human tidal wave which carried me straight out of the stadium to safety. I survived!

Looking back through the gates, from the

Life-long Rangers supporter James 'Maxie' McCafferty retains his ticket for the fateful match at Ibrox Stadium as a poignant reminder of the day. Sixteen months after the tragedy, on a bittersweet night in Barcelona the Corby football fan would witness another (albeit less traumatic) incident involving the famous Glasgow club.

safety of the street, I could see the total bedlam on the stairs. Badly shaken, the three of us made our way across the road to Sammy's parent's home, where news footage of the scene was being broadcast on TV. We just sat there feeling numb - the reality of what had happened didn't sink in at first, and we didn't really know the extent of the fatalities till later."

Meanwhile back home in Corby Michael's parents were frantic with worry and feared the worst. His sister Sharon said: "We heard the awful news on the television. My dad, Bill, was ill at the time with chronic bronchitis (a legacy of his years spent working in the Sinter plant at the steelworks - where, ironically, he was a Health and Safety officer.) His condition was exacerbated by the whole situation and the awful fear that gripped the family. In fact it was all too much for my mother and she collapsed because there had been no word from Michael. To cap it all, Mum and Dad were convinced that they had seen him on the TV news - lying on a mortuary slab!

Typical of young lads who are away from home with their mates, Michael didn't think to get in touch to let us know that he was safe. It wasn't until he walked through the front door, the following day, that wc knew for sure that he was alive."

Michael: "Next day, everyone on the bus home was very subdued - most of us were suffering with delayed shock. I can't recall if anybody from Corby had relatives amongst the victims.

When I got home I got a right telling off! My mum did her nut because I had failed to let her know that I was safe. Looking back I realise that it was thoughtless of me, however, I had witnessed scenes of such an appalling nature that I suppose my mind was elsewhere.

I had been looking forward to that trip for weeks. Sadly, it ended in such wretched circumstances that I was traumatised for a long time afterwards. Later on I suffered from flashbacks and nightmares - which eventually led me to seek counselling."

Many years later Craig Smith from Livingston, near Glasgow, recounted the story of the frantic fight for life put up by his father and two uncles when they found themselves trapped in the crush halfway down the 'Alpine' stairway No. 13. He recorded his memories of that day in a harrowing letter which was subsequently displayed on a Rangers-related website. It told of the part that his father, George Alexander Smith, had played in helping to save the life of his own brother - and of the dreadful price that he had paid for his unstinting courage.

Craig recalled: "My father, his brother John and brother-in-law Alex had been standing in the Rangers end. After the final whistle they made their way up the terracing towards stairway No. 13. As they got nearer to the top they could feel the crowd getting tighter. People behind were pushing them on, over the top, towards the stairs. Uncle John noticed the worried looks on the faces of the people surrounding him and realised something was wrong. Over they went on to the stairway - forced on by the press of bodies from behind.

Halfway down the stairs John was lifted off of his feet. Alex had somehow managed to reach safety by climbing over the fence at the side of the stairs. My dad pushed John over towards the fence, where men were pulling people clear of the crush. As Uncle John scrambled over the fence he recalled looking out on a sea of terrified faces. It was at that point that he realised people were dead. He turned to look for my dad - intending to pull him to safety. However, just as John reached out for him, Dad was swept away by the force of the crowd. Uncle John could only watch as his brother, my father, died upright - the life squeezed out of him.

Later that evening my mother answered the door to find my uncles standing there. They said that they had lost George at Ibrox - he was dead. My father's brothers were paralysed with shock and who could blame them? Anger followed when it came to light that two people were killed on the very same stairway in September 1961, eight were injured in September 1967 and there were a further twenty-four injuries in January 1969!"

Alick Buchanan-Smith, Scottish Minister for Home Affairs, called for an immediate inquiry into the tragedy. Though this proved to be inconclusive, it was suggested that a supporter, tripping on his way down, could have triggered the horrific chain of events. Unlike most public venues of the time, Scottish football stadiums didn't require safety certificates - even though they were able to hold as many as 100,000 supporters. The aforesaid inquiry (together with the Wheatley Report of 1972) resulted in the introduction of the Safety of Sports Ground Act of 1975, which at long last made safety certificates mandatory.

As January 1971 drew to a frosty close, the forthcoming 'Decimalisation Day' cast an aura of uncertainty over the general public and in particular over the normally 'sharp as a button' clientele of the Open Hearth in Corby. On that day decimal currency would replace the imperial monetary system that was in use at the time. Overnight the 240 pennies to the 'pound in your pocket' would be equivalent to 100 new pence. Confusing? You bet!

In the run-up to the big event, the government had distributed conversion tables - hoping that the nation would quickly get to grips with the new money. On implementation, however, problems soon became apparent throughout the country - some of the population (especially the elderly) couldn't make head or tail of it!

On the eve of 'D Day' the price of a loaf of bread was 1s. 9d. (9½p), twenty cigarettes cost 6s. 2d. (31p), a first class stamp cost 7d. (3p) and a pint of milk - a bob (5p). Mars Bars were a tanner (2½p), a colour TV licence was £11 and the average price of a three bedroomed house was £6,500. The change over to decimalisation would soon start to nudge prices upwards.

Experiencing life in the front line, on that momentous day, was Graham Reilly. Serving behind the bar of the Open Hearth, Graham was forced to bear the brunt of the anger expressed by disgruntled customers. Cyril Milligan was a typical example. When asked for 'twelve and a half pence' for his pint of Star Light, Cyril made the conversion into old money and bellowed: "Star Light was only 2s. 3d. yesterday! Today you're asking me for 2s. 6d. It's outrageous!"

More evidence of 'decimal inflation' was to be found in the EWSR canteen of the tubeworks. Here the price of a bag of chips had jumped overnight from a tanner (sixpence) to five new pence. It didn't take long for mathematicians in the canteen queue to work out that this was the equivalent of a shilling - double the price. What made matters worse was the fact that the portion was only half the previous size!

Cyril Milligan (who had a reputation for being a shrewd gambler with a knack of winning 'real money' on the horses) was most uncomplimentary about the new decimal coinage - likening it to chocolate money. Wonder where he got that idea from?

Jimmy Wishart (a crane driver in the 6 inch mill) having purchased a bag of chips, looked at his diminished lunch in disbelief and asked. "What's this?"

Nora Sweeney, the stony-faced assistant, replied: "That's the new size."

"Fill the bag up!"

"I can't" said Nora.

When the situation at the till threatened to get out of hand, the canteen manageress (affectionately known as 'Big Maggie') intervened - in an effort to restore calm. She said: "We're under strict instructions to use the new bag size and to give the correct portions - so that'll be five new pence please, Jimmy." For Wishart it was the straw that broke the camel's back. He protested: "Hang on there! Five new pence - that's a bloody bob! You're not on!"

His workmate, Joe Bremner, was observing the encounter and exploded with fury. "Stuff your chips *and* your 'Kate and Sydney' pies!" he snarled angrily.

As accusations that the canteen was fleecing its customers began to be levelled at Maggie and her staff, amid the mounting chaos Alex McLeod (a shop steward in the EWSR) initiated a walkout, followed by a warning that the canteen would be picketed until normal service was resumed - and at the right price! News of the stand off spread rapidly throughout the steel complex but, surprisingly, it took another two days before a compromise could be reached. When placards calling for a boycott were put up outside the canteen, a meeting between management and workers was hastily arranged (the upshot being that the price of a bag of chips would go down to three new pence, the new bag size would be retained and Big Alex would apologise to Big Maggie for calling her a fat cow - which, as a matter of principle, he only agreed to do after being threatened with the sack!). After a five-day token absence Alex returned to the canteen and, to a background of cheers, apologised to Maggie, saying: "I'd sooner make love to you than fall out with you!" Good sense prevailed and Maggie 'n' Alex became friends once more.

In the meantime, over in Kettering things were not going down too well at a meeting of the Town Health Committee. Councillor Mr. R. Cross and Councillor Mrs. King had just attacked the Borough Council's decision to make adjustments to its coin-in-the-slot machines in the town's public lavatories, in order to enable them to take the new (extremely small but lightweight) half-pence piece. The King/Cross alliance had been forged out of a desire to facilitate the passing of a motion - in favour of the more user-friendly 1p piece. During the meeting Councillor Cross voiced concerns over the length of time it was taking to complete the conversions. He also made reference to the amount of revenue that was being lost. In response, the Borough Surveyor gave an assurance that the new locks would be fitted within weeks.

A still dissatisfied Mr. Cross reminded the surveyor that when the order was first placed, he had pointed out to him that it was almost impossible for a manual machine to be operated with the new half-pence. He said: "We would have got these locks much sooner if we had decided to convert them to use a penny."

In support of her fellow councillor, Mrs. King interjected: "These days, a half-new-pence is an unrealistic price to pay to spend a penny, and, in any case, there are already signs that the half-pence will not last long as legal tender!" The Borough Surveyor was unwilling to be brow-beaten and told her that because some of the work had already been done, to alter the decision again would almost certainly incur greater conversion costs.

When it was discovered that the new half-pence piece wasn't heavy enough to operate the locking mechanism on the toilet doors in Dalkeith Place, Councillor Cross of Kettering Borough Council was said to have complained "There's been a distinct lack of movement on the part of our suppliers." His fellow councillors agreed, saying that the firm 'needed a good shake'.

Councillor Mr. M.M. Thomson reported that there had been no acts of vandalism in the lavatories since they had been made free of charge. In spite of that, however, he thought that it was a bit stiff to expect the council to change its mind. He said: "The decision should stand" - and so it did.

Coinciding with the currency make-over, Fleet Street's *Daily Mail* was also given a face-lift. Beloved of female readers, the broadsheet was to become an even more attractive proposition for them, when its format was changed to a more manageable tabloid size. It was a stratagem that had previously failed to save the *Daily Sketch* (one of the nation's favourite daily newspapers.) The Sketch's demise had left a hole in the market that would never really be filled - despite a number of valiant attempts.

Also creating headlines that week was Idi Amin, Major General of Uganda. The former Ugandan Heavyweight Boxing Champion (1951-60) had taken advantage of Prime Minister Milton Obote's absence from the country, in order to mount a bloody military coup. After seizing power, Amin appointed himself President and quickly became known as one of Africa's most brutal and feared dictators. When the despot later declared himself to be King of Scotland (professing to have served with the Black Watch Regiment) many of Corby's Scottish ex-pats considered his claims of Caledonian ancestry to be dubious - to say the least!
"Not on my watch", protested Tam Burns (a retired fireman from Kilmarnock.)
"If he's the King of Scotland - then I'm the Queen of Sheba!" mocked an incredulous Oona Campbell. Her cannie sister-in-law, Maggie Green, declared resolutely: "I'll reserve judgement until I see what the gallus pretender has under his kilt!"

Officials at the Corby Town Supporters Club took a leaf out of the 'Danny La Rue Entertainment Guide' by booking the first ever professional drag artist to appear in the town. David Lang, their entertainments secretary, said that he anticipated that the act on February 7, 'would create quite an interest locally.'
Taking place that February was a dinner, at the Talbot Hotel in Oundle, which was for members of Corby's long established Yorkshire Society. Mr. A. E. Cripps, the society's treasurer, told the *Evening Telegraph*: 'It's the highlight of the year - a night when we can all get together over a nice meal and have a good moan.' (N.B. Fifty whingers were in attendance!).

"Where, oh where are the carefully crafted and imaginative pop songs of the 50s and 60s - i.e. *Be Bop A Lula, Tutti Frutti, Splish Splash* and *Giddy Up A Ding Dong*?" complained Mick McColgan, a frustrated baby boomer of Occupation Road in Corby. Mick's criticism was aimed squarely at the plethora of middle-of-the-road music (with its banal and lyrically inane songs) which had in recent months blighted the Top Twenty record charts.
One group who embraced the genre to such an extent that they called themselves Middle Of The Road, achieved fleeting stardom with the song *Chirpy Chirpy Cheep Cheep*. Mercifully, its follow-up (*Tweedle Dum Tweedle Dee*) proved to be a really 'dumb' idea and the band went back to where they had come from - obscurity!

1971 gave rise to a new type of solo performer - the singer/songwriter. Classic examples of this type of artist were James Taylor, Van Morrison and Joni Mitchell. Their music would feature in *The Old Grey Whistle Test* - a new BBC2 rock programme which aired for the first time that September. Its host, 'Whispering' Bob Harris, was a softly-spoken former Police cadet and *Time Out* journalist from Northampton. Much lampooned for his trademark laconic enthusiasm, Harris was considered at the time to be the epitome of the understated television anchorman - but in reality was merely a throw-back to the days of 1950's BBC Radio, where modern jazz was studiously dissected and picked over by Bob's introspective predecessors. In addition, those artists who were otherwise denied regular exposure on television (such as the Sensational Alex Harvey Band, Stone the Crows and the J. Geils Band) also found themselves being showcased.
For members of the 'literati' of rock, Bob's comatose style quickly became essential TV viewing, enabling the 'Whistle Test to achieve audience ratings that would compare favourably with those of *Ready Steady Go* at its zenith.

The unusual title of the programme was inspired by the grey-suited doormen who worked at the music publishing houses of London's Denmark Street. Harris revealed: "It was a tin-pan alley phrase from years ago. When publishers received the first pressing of a record, they would invariably play it to the 'old greys', and any song that they could whistle - after having heard it just once or twice - was deemed to have passed the old grey whistle test."

One artist who definitely would have passed the 'old greys' test was Rod Stewart of the Faces (a band who were born of chart-toppers the Small Faces.) Stewart, and the band that he fronted, were among those booked by landlord 'Big Bob' Knight to play at the Nags Head in Wollaston. An added attraction at this heavily attended Friday night bash came in the form of the Radio 1 disc jockey John Peel, whose duties included 'covering' the door and stamping the hands of the punters as they entered the venue.

From the late 1960s to the early 1970s the Nags Head at Wollaston played host on a weekly basis to the best up-and-coming bands and to a succession of Radio One DJs. Big Bob Knight, disc jockey and landlord (not to mention the brains behind the pub's huge success) relates: "Don Planner and I started running the discos in our spare time - because the shoe factory where we worked was on a three-day week and our earnings had dropped. I only used to do the Nags on a Friday and Saturday, but then one night the landlord told me that he was leaving and said that he thought Don and I should apply for the licence. We took his advice and one of the first things we did as tenants was to start up a 'blues disco night' in the downstairs lounge. On the first night there were only about five people there, however, the following week the punters were spilling out into the yard because they couldn't get in! It was then that I made the decision to move upstairs." Soon after that Bob started booking Radio One DJs to appear at the pub. He said: "We had Dave Lee Travis, Noel Edmonds, Paul Burnett and then John Peel."

Good judgment and a helping of good luck led to quite a few scoops for the new promoters on the block. Former Nags Head DJ Steve Hadjuk recalls one group in particular. Steve: "They were a band called Black Cat Bones - the forerunner to Free - who were on as the supporting act to Alexis Korner. Alexis had already played at the Nags on two or three occasions before then, but I can remember him ringing in advance to say that this time he would be bringing along a band in which his friend's son played. He said that they had a record coming out and that they needed to rehearse. It turned out that the lad was guitarist Paul Kossoff and his father was the actor David Kossoff."

History tells us that the original Bones line-up didn't last long. Paul Kossoff left, along with drummer Simon Kirke, to form a new outfit around singer Paul Rodgers. The only thing that they were lacking was a bass player - and that's where Alexis Korner stepped in. Korner put forward the name of Andy Fraser (his daughter's boyfriend) who had just been released from John Mayall's Bluesbreakers.

Over the years much debate has ensued over the group's actual debut. While some claim that Free played their first ever gig at the Nags Head in Wollaston, Andy Fraser confirmed personally to the authors of this book that the band (who had world wide success with such classics as *All Right Now* and *Wishing Well*) performed together for the first time at a pub of the same name - but in Battersea, South London. Andy: "It was more of a rehearsal really. We were playing upstairs in the pub, whilst Alexis was downstairs celebrating his 40th birthday with a large crowd of people. He definitely thought we had something and so he brought the party up to watch us. It was Alexis who gave us the name Free At Last (which was the title of one of his albums - and a handle we thought was naff!) It was also through Alexis that we were offered a contract by Chris Blackwell of Island Records - a guy who immediately wanted to change our name to the Heavy Metal Kids. We said 'No way!' and argued the point until eventually a compromise was reached and we shortened our name to Free."

Playing under the new name, the band would return to Wollaston on two or three subsequent occasions and were a great draw. Steve: "I remember them playing *The Hunter* and thinking they were fantastic. When their first album *Tons Of Sobs* came out, I managed to get all of them to sign my copy. It's still one of my most prized possessions."

As time went by more and more people flocked to the Nags Head on Fridays - making 'The John Peel Night' a massive hit. When transport became an issue for those travelling to and from the venue, Knight took the matter into his own hands. Bob explained: "United Counties wanted to stop running the bus here from Wellingborough, because some of the kids were making a nuisance of themselves on the way home, so in order to prevent that from happening, I said that I would install a bouncer to keep them in order. As that entailed sending out a car to bring him back, in the end it made more sense to buy a bus of my own - a pink double-decker!

When John Peel started appearing at the Nags, he and I immediately hit it off as friends - in fact he loved it so much that he stayed there for four or five years." Far from just showing up, playing a few records and then going home again, John became involved in every aspect of the running of the show - even plugging the Nags every week on his radio show and in his *Melody Maker* column.

Steve Hadjuk: "The reason why John liked Bob so much was because he wasn't in the least bit starstruck. Mind you, back then Peel wasn't the cult hero that he became in later life - he was merely a relaxed guy, milling around with everybody, who'd stand at the top of the stairs at the Nags and stamp your hand as you went in. Although he was just one of the gang to us, as far as Bob was concerned, he'd become one of his closest friends.

Bob: "Peely was a genuine bloke. As we had three bedrooms he'd come and stay the night at the pub, and then the next day he'd either go back to London to do his radio show, or else go up to Liverpool to see his beloved 'Reds' play."

WOLLASTON PARISH COUNCIL

NAGS HEAD
First referred to in 1787 as Mr Lucy's Hostelry, this pub was known as The Nags Head until 2003. In the 1970s and '80s entertainers such as U2, Free, Edwin Starr, Rod Stewart and The Faces, The Who and John Peel appeared here on their way to international stardom.

AD 2007

Pictured in its heyday - the Nags Head at Wollaston. Situated between Wellingborough and Northampton, this once-popular music venue was recently deemed worthy of one of the blue plaques commissioned by 'Enjoy England' (formerly the English Tourist Board.) As part of the England Rocks campaign, it commemorates (amongst others) the appearance in May 1971 of Rod Stewart and the Faces. Surprisingly, the tablet fails to mention Big Bob Knight - the man who made it all happen. Obviously Bob's was a 'Face' that didn't fit!

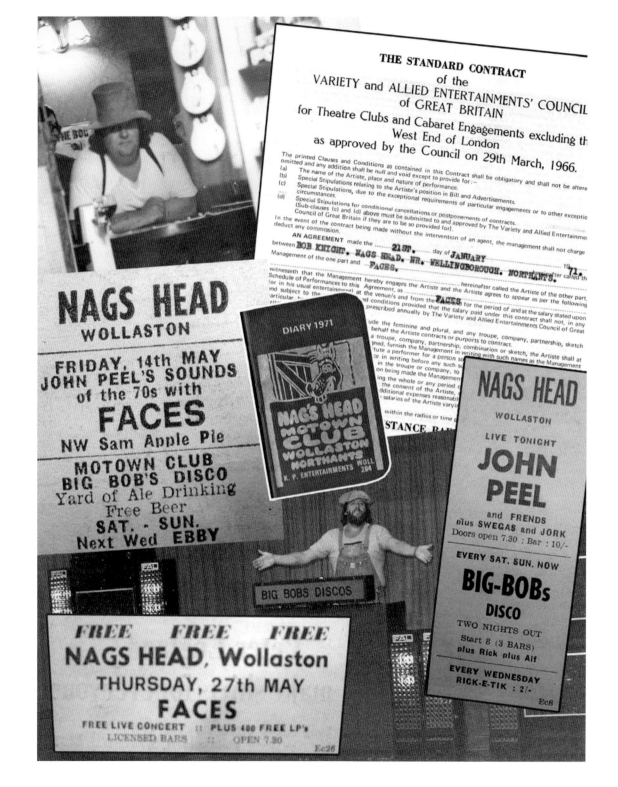

THE STANDARD CONTRACT
of the
VARIETY and ALLIED ENTERTAINMENTS' COUNCIL
of GREAT BRITAIN
for Theatre Clubs and Cabaret Engagements excluding th
West End of London
as approved by the Council on 29th March, 1966.

The printed Clauses and Conditions as contained in this Contract shall be obligatory and shall not be altere
omitted and any addition shall be null and void except to provide for:—
(a)   The name of the Artiste, place and nature of performance.
(b)   Special Stipulations relating to the Artiste's position in Bill and Advertisements.
(c)   Special Stipulations, due to the exceptional requirements of particular engagements or to other exceptio
circumstances.
(d)   Special Stipulations for conditional cancellations or postponements of contracts.
(Sub-clauses (c) and (d) above must be submitted to and approved by The Variety and Allied Entertainmer
Council of Great Britain if they are to be so provided for).
In the event of the contract being made without the intervention of an agent, the management shall not charge
deduct any commission.

AN AGREEMENT made the ....21ST....... day of JANUARY ...., 19....71..
between BOB KNIGHT, NAGS HEAD, NR. WELLINGBOROUGH, NORTHANTS.
Management of the one part and ....FACES,.......

NAGS HEAD
WOLLASTON

FRIDAY, 14th MAY
JOHN PEEL'S SOUNDS
of the 70s with
FACES
NW Sam Apple Pie

MOTOWN CLUB
BIG BOB'S DISCO
Yard of Ale Drinking
Free Beer
SAT. - SUN.
Next Wed EBBY

DIARY 1971

NAGS HEAD
MOTOWN
CLUB
WOLLASTON
NORTHANTS
K. P. ENTERTAINMENTS WOLL 204

BIG BOBS DISCOS

NAGS HEAD
WOLLASTON
LIVE TONIGHT
JOHN
PEEL
and FRENDS
plus SWEGAS and JORK
Doors open 7.30 · Bar : 10/-

EVERY SAT. SUN. NOW
BIG-BOBs
DISCO
TWO NIGHTS OUT
Start 8 (3 BARS)
plus Rick plus Alf

EVERY WEDNESDAY
RICK-E-TIK : 2/-

Ec8

FREE   FREE   FREE
NAGS HEAD, Wollaston
THURSDAY, 27th MAY
FACES
FREE LIVE CONCERT :: PLUS 400 FREE LP's
LICENSED BARS :: OPEN 7.30
Ec26

72

It was through Peel's connections that the Nags was able to acquire the services of top acts such as: Medicine Head, Uriah Heep, Audience and Skid Row (featuring the relatively unknown Gary Moore). Every Thursday thru Sunday legions of rock fans headed for the outpost that was the 'in place' - and whichever style of music was on offer, they could be sure of a great night out.

Another group to make an early appearance at Wollaston was Brewers Droop (who at one time numbered Mark Knopfler of Dire Straits amongst their ranks) but it was the visit paid by Rod Stewart and the Faces that would remain planted in the memory of those who frequented the Nags Head at that time.

Above: A telegram sent from the Faces' management company (confirming the group's rescheduled appearance at the Nags) promises that free albums will be given away on the night. Renowned for his business acumen, a wily Bob miraculously conjured up four hundred albums for his 'Evening Telegraph' advertisement instead of the fifty mentioned in the original dispatch.

Over the years numerous theories have been put forward as to why the group suddenly pulled out of a booking on Friday, May 14, 1971 - only to return on Thursday, May 27, to play a free live concert. Some say that Rod Stewart was suffering from a throat infection that night, whilst others claim that he was too inebriated to perform. Keith Anderson from Corby (a Wollaston regular) remembers the star turning up late that night. Keith added: "He fell out of his car - pissed as a newt! John Peel had a right go at him. He told Rod that he was out of order and pulled the show."

Although he was only twenty-six-years-old, by 1971 Stewart was already a veteran of the music business and had been singing professionally since the early sixties (featuring in several different bands.) His first stint in the recording studio had been as a harmonica player on Millie's 1964 hit single *My Boy Lollipop*. Later on he teamed up with Long John Baldry to play in Steampacket and then in Shotgun Express, and after this Rod joined the Jeff Beck Group. The Faces were his last stepping-stone on the road to international stardom, and although *they* may have been saying *Stay With Me* - Rod had other plans. A solo career beckoned (one which he would eventually launch in spectacular fashion with his own composition - *Maggie May*.)

The person most likely to know what really happened that evening is Bob Knight. Bob: "It was John Peel who originally asked Rod Stewart to play; Rod was a friend of his and agreed to do it as a favour. The contracts had been signed on January 21, and at lunchtime on the day of the gig, their equipment arrived - in an articulated lorry! There was a mountain of it. In fact only about 10 per cent was actually set up on stage, because that's all there was room for! So there we were - with the bands kit ready and waiting, the fans assembled in their numbers and Peely standing at the door with his stamp in his hand. The atmosphere and the sense of anticipation was incredible. As for the Faces? They were nowhere to be seen!"

Alan Crawford from Corby can remember the cloud of disappointment that descended on all of those present. Alan: "The build-up to the gig was exhilarating, the level of expectation amongst the crowd immense - then suddenly, rumours started going round, saying that the band weren't going to show up. We waited and waited, and then eventually went back downstairs into the pub - feeling angry and frustrated. You wouldn't have thought that an event as big as that could take place in a village pub in the heart of Northamptonshire - and in the end, it didn't!" What should have been the greatest night in the pub's history, ended in bitter disappointment.

Steve Hadjuk helped John Peel to carry his records to the car that night. Steve said: "Just as we were loading them into his car boot, a set of headlights pulled into the car park. Inside the vehicle, a white Rolls-Royce, sat the Faces. John blew his top. I'd never seen him lose his temper the way that he did that night. He bawled at them: 'This is my friend's place - and you've let me down!' The wretched looks on their faces said it all. John continued to give them a tongue-lashing for a few more minutes - and then he got in his car and left.

Billy Gaff (manager of the Faces) got involved and so did their record company. Everyone agreed that the only available date for a re-run was on Thursday, May, 27, and Gaff said: 'We'll do it for free.' John couldn't make it that night, as it coincided with his radio show - so it was down to me to stage manage the affair. It was fantastic!"

Always the diplomat, Bob Knight says that he's not really sure why Rod and the Faces failed to make it for the original show. He prefers to give them the benefit of the doubt and says that at the time he just assumed that there may have been some confusion over the pub's opening times. Steve Hadjuk, on the other hand, believes that it was simply a case of the band getting lost en route. The last word however must go to Bob's wife (who was probably nearest to the truth!) When interviewed in 2009, Judy Knight said matter-of-factly: "They were all stoned".

Whatever the reason for the group's no-show, all parties were confident that the rearranged gig would go ahead. Steve: "Once we'd agreed on another date, we tried to confine the news just to our regular customers - because if it had been advertised, we'd have been swamped. John also wanted it to be kept low-profile. I don't think he even gave it a plug on his radio show."

Bob Knight: "By six o'clock that night the car park was teeming with fans - we had more than we could handle! Naturally, the first to be admitted were those punters who had bought tickets for the aborted show, and even though - as on the previous occasion - the group's kit was there and was set up, I couldn't stop biting my nails. When the Faces finally arrived the place just went ballistic! We couldn't believe that we'd got them there!"

Steve Hadjuk: "You couldn't move upstairs. The audience was right up close to the band and it was virtually impossible to get to the bar - which was right at the back of the room. It was the first time that I'd ever seen a band take what they called a 'tea-break' in the middle of a set! Rod Stewart shouted to the roadies to pass them a crate of beer forward and then asked for the lights to be put on. He then ordered thirty pints of beer for the fans at the front. I distinctly remember him promising to pay for them later - which of course he never did! Next thing, punters began passing pints down over people's heads to the guys at the front, and everyone enjoyed a drink whilst the band chatted to them. After about ten minutes or so, Rod said: 'Is everybody happy? Good. Now let's get the lights down

again!' At that the band kicked back in and played the remaining sixty-plus minutes of their set."
The night was a massive hit and those who were there had the time of their lives - with the added
bonus of being able to 'hang out' with the band. Steve Hadjuk recalls: "It was really awesome.
The show ended at around 11.30p.m. - which was late in those days - and afterwards we all sat around
in the lounge having a drink and keeping up with the Faces. They were fantastic - they just came right
in and started signing autographs and giving away albums. You can tell how relaxed it was because
later on that night I spotted Ronnie Wood sitting in a corner picking his toenails!"

*The Nags Head Omnibus Company's 'Disco Special'. On disco nights Big Bob's pink double-decker picked up
eager punters from Irchester, Rushden, Higham Ferrers and Wellingborough, ferrying them to the Nags for
8p.m. At the end of the evening it would depart the venue at 11.30p.m. sharp. Bob also used the bus to take
members of his Motown Club on day trips to Skeggy and on the occasional shopping trip to Northampton -
where he had a special dispensation to park it in the United Counties bus station.*

Hadjuck (who was by then working for Phonogram Records) remembers meeting Rod Stewart again
a few years later, when he attended a conference at the Crick Hotel in Northampton. Steve: "It was
the first time that I'd been at an event of that nature and I felt a bit self-conscious amongst all those
men-in-suits. Anyway, I was on my own at the bar when I suddenly spotted none other than Rod
Stewart - standing with a group of businessmen who were on the other side of the room. When Rod
saw me he gestured that I should come over and join them. At first I thought he was pointing to
someone else, but then I realised that he meant me and when I walked over he said, 'Don't I know
you from somewhere?'

The only thing I could think of in reply was, 'The Nags Head, at Wollaston?'

'Yeah. That's it' he said, and then went on to introduce me to his group of friends - telling them what a great night the Faces had when they played at the Nags. There was plenty of friendly banter and (although I was keen to say something) I never let slip that Rod hadn't paid for the three-dozen pints he'd ordered that evening! Later in the conversation he crowed, 'Big Bob Knight's the only guy that I've ever worked for - for nothing!'

I interrupted: 'I'm sorry to have to tell you Rod but you've got that wrong.'

'How come?' he enquired.

'Actually it was the other way round - you paid Bob for the privilege of playing there. Two hundred and sixty quid to be precise!'

Stewart looked surprised and shook his head in disbelief, and so to clarify the situation I said, 'Ask your ex-manager if you don't believe me - it was Billy Gaff who signed the cheque!' (The Faces' management company had paid Knight the money in compensation for the group's failure to turn up for the first gig).

To his credit, Rod (who is renowned for his reluctance to part with money) saw the funny side and burst out laughing. And when you think about it - in a roundabout way he actually did pick up the tab for those drinks!

Towards midnight when the event at Crick was drawing to a close, in typical Rodders style he produced a football out of nowhere and invited us all to an impromptu game of football on the hotel's pitch 'n' putt course." Rod lost out there too - as the team I was playing for won the match!"

Not everyone who frequented the pub at Wollaston harbours pleasant memories of the 'Big Bob Experience'. Pete Marshall from Corby (a big Rod Stewart fan) remembers an altogether different side to the Nags. Pete said: "John Chapman and I went over to Wollaston on the first night that the Faces were meant appear. When they didn't show, the management announced that everyone with a pass-out stamp on their hand would be able to get their money back - so Chap and I stumbled back up the stairs to collect ours. We were about to make our way back down to the pub bar, when suddenly I realised that I'd lost my wallet. I turned to go back in, but Big Bob and one of his DJs were barring the door. When I told Bob that I'd lost my wallet - and was only going back in to look for it - he swore at me. Then, completely without provocation, he punched me in the face! As I reeled backwards I bowled John over (he was standing right behind me) and we tumbled downstairs - ending up in a heap at the bottom. We were both too drunk to argue our case, and so I just looked at Chap and said indignantly: 'There was ten bob in that wallet!' Because his foot was stuck in the banister and he couldn't get up, John merely shrugged his shoulders and offered me a cigarette, saying: 'Never mind. Have a No 6' (which was the 1970's equivalent of a Woodbine.) Looking back, I suspect that the reason why they took such a dislike to us was because we were from Corby!"

Nigel 'Pop' Portman was at the Nag's on the night when Uriah Heep played. Pop said: "The upstairs room was packed to the rafters and the doors were closed. I was part of the overspill of customers who swarmed into the ground floor bars and had to settle for a good piss-up instead!" He added: "Among the Corby contingent was a lad called Vic Beleschenko - who usually drank at the Rockingham Arms pub. Pop: "Anyway, when the landlord's wife was collecting the empty glasses that night, she bent over the table in front of Vic, and he couldn't resist the urge to pinch her bottom. As you can imagine, she let out such a scream that it caught the attention of her husband. Bob was standing over at the bar and was chatting to a group of his henchmen when he heard her squealing. He was over in a shot and stood there growling and threatening retribution. I must say, for the size of the guy, Mr. Knight couldn't half shift. He was a formidable sight. Needless to say - there was no more bother from us that night!"

Sneaking out of the pub at the end of the night (with their eyes in the back of their heads - for fear of being 'jumped' by Bob's heavies) the Corby lads returned home feeling somewhat dispirited. They all were of the opinion that it would be a good idea to give Wollaston a miss for a week or two!

Pat Devlin (who was a market trader in Kettering back then - but used Corby as a base) has vivid memories of the Nags Head. He also remembers many other popular venues in and around the county where live-music was on offer. Pat: "My mates and I would drive over to Wollaston from Corby, hoping to see groups that we'd either read about in the *NME* and *Melody Maker*, or heard on *The John Peel Show*. We'd each have a couple of pints and then we'd climb up the steel staircase on the outside of the Nags - in order to get to the room where the bands played.

Although the stage was only about the size of a kitchen table (and the toilets often overflowed) the atmosphere was terrific. The majority of the bands that we saw never got further than their second album. Except for the odd mention in *Record Collector*, many of them are now long forgotten.

When I think back to those days, the Nags at Wollaston wasn't the only good venue around - we used to go to the Railway Hotel at Blisworth (which is where we saw Deep Purple.) In addition to that there was the Tin Hat in Kettering and a place in Market Harborough called the Frolicking Kneecap, where on Sunday afternoons you could see bands like Black Sabbath and Jethro Tull performing. The Kneecap later changed its name to the Lantern and on Saturdays featured all-night Northern Soul - that is until the building was commandeered by a tyre-fitting company!"

The Raven Hotel in Corby re-opened its doors in April - following 'extensive refurbishment' (i.e. - a new steak bar and lounge which had been 'tastefully festooned in the Spanish style'). Landlord Douglas Swain and his wife Edna were delighted with the alterations, claiming that they were "el supremo" and should satisfy the customers "no problemo".

On that very same night, just around the corner from 'Little Spain', Corby Town Football Club was hosting a 'Grand Opening Spectacular' to launch a sponsored charity walk in aid of Corby-Sport (which it hoped would raise around £20,000 for the cause.)

In an Occupation Road ground that was almost full to capacity, the evening's entertainment included a challenge to test the knowledge of 'Memory Man' Leslie Welch. Mr. Welch was a veritable encyclopedia of sport but he was certainly up against it with the Corby crowd. For example, the question posed by John Black (Who plays centre half for Airdrieonians F.C.) had him stumped right away!

In recognition of his having 'fathered' the town of Corby throughout twenty-one years of 'tremendous expansion', Henry Chisholm, Chairman of Corby Development Corporation, received a knighthood in the Queen's New Years Honours List. Sir Henry was self-effacing in his acceptance of the tribute, saying: "I feel this is an honour for Corby, something we can all take modest pride and satisfaction in." A keen sailor, the former chairman of DCONSA (the Departmental Committee on Organisation of Naval Supplies with the Admiralty) also said that he hoped to celebrate the 25th anniversary of the Development Corporation by opening Corby's new boating lake - an amenity set in the heart of the town's woodland which would offer a natural picnic area, small café, rowing boats for those with a leaning towards the outward-bound, plus an abundance of fish for anglers to tangle with. (Given time it would also attract migrating wild geese, swans, coots - and the odd pram!)

Corby folk were again under attack in the press for failing to support the town's leisure amenities - in particular the much maligned 'white elephant' that was the Civic Centre. However, Corby's 'canny philistines' (Who were used to being described by local journalists as 'apathetic and cultureless') remained unmoved. Kelvin Glendenning, Chairman of Corby Urban District Council's Civic Amenities Committee, was defensive. He said: "Compared to five years ago, bookings for the Civic are way up. When the massive alterations that are being carried out are finished, there will be more bar space, more catering facilities, more toilet blocks and more lifts. I am sure it will encourage more people to hold more functions there." Glendenning's assurances didn't appease Mr. Corbert Bond of Carron Close. Corbert observed: "It's just more empty promises, more flights of fancy and more pie in the sky. If you ask me, Mr. Glendenning might do better investing in castles in Spain!"

With the public fast losing confidence in his Amenities Committee, Glendenning played his ace card by announcing that the Scaffold (a Liverpudlian group who were famous for their folk music and

Pictured: An artist's impression of the proposed Boating Lake.
Below: Work begins on the long-awaited public amenity - despite fears that it might become 'over-commercialised' and turned into another Wicksteed Park. Mr. Henry Chisholm, the Corby Development Corporation's chairman, said: "We hope that the lake will be more like the Serpentine - very picturesque. With the woods in the background it will make an ideal picnic spot."

Corby's new boating lake — an artist's impression.

We don't want a 'commercial' lake — corporation

CORBY Development Corporation have expressed fears that the town's planned boating lake will be turned into a Wicksteed Park.

The corporation, who launched the plans for the lake, hoped the amenity would be more like the Serpentine.

And they don't like the idea of turning it into a commercial enterprise.

Mr Henry Chisholm, corporation chairman, said too much noise would be created if it became like Wicksteed Park, and the diagnostic centre and maternity unit nearby would be affected.

"When we thought of providing this gift for the people of Corby, we intended that it would be a woodland lake with birds nesting on the islands and a few of the larger types of boats. We envisaged a Serpentine, not a Wicksteed Park," said Mr Chisholm.

Mr Chisholm made this point at a meeting of the corporation and the urban council's joint policy committee.

The corporation are building the lake, pavilion, picnic area and other amenities on the site at a cost of £60,000. Corby council are also contributing towards the scheme by providing the boats and part of the landscaping cost.

Mr A. T. Bardsley, Director of Technical Services to the council, said that as the building on the site had to be manned the project must be turned into a commercial enterprise to offset wages and running costs.

Thirty boats are being put in the lake by the council and more will be added if there is a demand for them. There will be 3½ acres of water and the lake will be 100 yards long. Boats will range from children's paddle boats to rowing dinghies and twin-seater canoes.

The site is off Cottingham Road near the diagnostic centre, and Mr K. Glendenning, chairman of the civic amenities committee of the council, said: "The lake should look very picturesque when it's completed.

"With the woods in the background it will make an ideal picnic spot and we are sure that the people of Corby will appreciate and make use of it.

poetry) were pencilled in for February 7, and that Judith Durham of the Seekers would be appearing in concert that March. Kelvin may have worn the smug smile of the self-satisfied over his Civic Centre master-stroke, but it soon became apparent that his troubles were far from over - the St Brendan's Club announced that they were planning to stage a haggis eating contest on the same night. In addition, the contest (which would be open to all-comers) was to be filmed by Anglia Television for transmission later in the year.

Also making news was the assertion that Corby had become - despite a very obvious lack of neon! - the Las Vegas of Northamptonshire. In March a report had been published which revealed that the town had an unmistakeable addiction to gambling (or to be more precise - bingo!) 'Corby's invisible industry is big business' the report claimed. It went on to portray Corby as 'needing bingo like a heart needs blood!'

The Scaffold concert turned out to be hugely successful and delighted the Merseysiders themselves almost as much as it did the audience. John Gorman admitted to having a slight twinge of apprehension before the show and said that it was because the group were going to try out some new ideas and material. After their performance he was more upbeat, saying: "It appeared to go down quite well - which was rather swell." All in all the group put in a thoroughly decent performance. Accompanied by an appreciative audience, Scaffold rounded off the evening in great style with a rousing rendition of the aptly titled *Thank You Very Much*.

Following a brief sabbatical Anthony Roye (Corby's former 'Mr. Theatre') surprised everyone by resurfacing in Kettering in order to take over operations at the Central Hall. The move provoked a local journalist to ask: "Does he seriously believe that cultured Kettering will recoup his Corby cash?" - a reference to Roye's claim that he had lost a substantial amount of money as a result of his entrepreneurial endeavours on behalf of the town.

When in 1970 the first Tory government since 1964 came to power (with Prime Minister Ted Heath at the helm) it had a clear and unmistakeable strategy - to curb wage demands and cut public spending. To this end Margaret Thatcher, the Education Secretary, started the ball rolling by announcing the end of free school milk for children. The first test of the government's new pay policy came in January '71 when, encouraged by the Cabinet, Post Office managers sought to impose a pay cut on their 230,000 strong workforce. It was an act calculated to destroy workers' morale and force the postmen to walk out on strike. In total the handling each day of an estimated 35 million letters and 500,000 parcels was affected.
Heath's ministers were of the opinion that the moderate Post Office Union would be unable to stick it out for more than a week or two - as it didn't have a strike fund. It came as a nasty shock to them, therefore, when after a week of industrial action the Cabinet heard that Tom Jackson, the leader of the post workers' union, was 'coming under pressure from militants fortified by promises of financial assistance from other unions'.
The strike (which began on January 20,) even made the headlines of the *Evening Telegraph* when it was reported that John Mason, a thirty-four year-old postman from Rushden, was shot in the back with a .22 air rifle. When he was interviewed at Kettering General Hospital, the injured man complained "So much for public support!" It was believed that the shot had come from the direction of the grassy knoll outside Sainsburys supermarket!
A mass march on the 29th of the month attracted one hundred workers from around the county to convene in Corby. They joined the town's postmen in a parade which started at the Labour Club, passed through the Town Centre and then proceeded up the hill towards Studfall Green. As they passed the Rockingham Arms they were confronted by a group of wisecracking inebriates who were perched on the pub's perimeter wall, and there were shouts of 'Where's my Giro?' The bibulous scallywags then treated everyone to a hilarious a rendition of the Carpenters' current hit *(Wait a*

minute) Mr. Postman! In response to such blatant Mickey taking, Joe Riddoch (one of the Corby postal workers) somberly unfurled a banner bearing the demand 'WHAT ARE WE WAITING FOR? - A DECENT WAGE INCREASE!' emblazoned across it. After a quick 'about turn' and a round of applause from the Rock's hard up clientele, the marchers then headed back to the Town Centre for a meeting in the Festival Hall.

Ray Moffatt had only just started working at the Post Office when the strike was called. Looking back at events he remembers: "We were promised financial aid from other unions but the only help we received was from Welsh and Yorkshire miners who kept us going with food parcels.

Corby—it's Britain's Las Vegas

CORBY IS IN THE grip of a giant gambling fever—and when the chips are down its the town's second biggest industry. And with Corby's weekly stake on horses, dogs and bingo soaring into thousands of pounds—£25,000 is estimated to cross the ten Corby bookie's counters every week—all sorts of people are hitting a surprising jackpot.

Big business - or just a harmless flutter? No one could accuse Arthur Pitcher, Managing Director of the Stardust Club, of attempting to bring Las Vegas style gambling to Corby. Pitcher's only crime was to name his new club after a famous hotel/casino in that same city. As usual (in matters relating to Corby) the story was inflated out all of proportion by the local press.

We were otherwise skint and starving for the duration - although some of the local shops did their bit to help. I remember Pipe's Bakery, in the Market Square, giving us preferential treatment over the pigs by donating the previous day's bread and cakes for half price. It all helped!"

By the end of February a weakening Industry Minister, Robert Carr, reported to his colleagues that the seven-week-old strike was still remarkably solid, adding: "Maybe we were over-ambitious in the wage reductions we were trying to achieve." By coincidence, just as Carr was beginning to waver, on March 8, the postmen returned to work. It had been forty-seven days since their walk-out and many were unhappy with the decision to abandon the strike. Their reward - for enduring nearly eight weeks of financial hardship and strife - was the promise of 'an official inquiry' to decide their pay settlement.

The long-term prospects for steelmaking in Corby were again under discussion when W. H. Crawford (one of Corby's top steelmen) laid it on the line, saying: "The golden key to Corby's future in steel is a happy marriage between unions and management with no industrial strife. Serious strikes and pay demands without productivity could wreck Corby's hopes of keeping its head above water and plunge to the depths any chance of competing with the forthcoming deep water coastal ore ports.

CORBY LEADER

NORTHAMPTONSHIRE ADVERTISER SERIES   ELIZABETH STREET, CORBY. Tel: 3505.   FRIDAY, JANUARY 15, 1971.   6d. (2½p)

Corby's future . . . SPECIAL

Storm clouds gathering

CORBY PEOPLE are watching with growing alarm as the storm clouds gather over the town's industrial scene—and many are sure that their future, and that of the town, is now in a critical balance.

No one is running to the lifeboats—but some young folk warned this week that they are ready to pull out if the going gets any tougher for them and their children.

But at the other extreme... Their comments range from far Corby people say the a despairing "Corby is town's earnings are so much finished... dead..." to the optimistic pithy. They have defined... chin-out statement shattered some storm... like "This town will still be and they will ride this one here in 100 years."

Mrs. Joan O'Neill of 5 Bar... Their reaction... entered... Square, was one of the too. Square, was one of the for a special 'Corby Leader' desperate ones. "My husband was carried out to gauge was out of work just after as nearly as possible the Christmas. He was a labourer hopes and fears for the town on a building site and he just as that a steel chief des... can't get a job anywhere else arrived recently as "make or now. It's six years since he break year" was last out of a job.

"I think Corby is finished— I just don't see a future for the town at all. And what future is there for the young-sters here... I don't see any."

"With all these big fac-tories running down, paying people off and making them redundant there doesn't look to be much future at all. I think this might become a question of making the push. I think we will go eventually."

Mrs. O'Neill, a young mother with two girls aged nine and seven, added: "Five years ago you could have got a job here just like that, but not now. There is nothing for the adults here, so what is there for the children grow-ing up."

Mr. John Graham, aged 58, came here as a young man in 1935. He has seen the town fight its way out of similar situations—and remains con-fident.

BETTER

He said: "There have al-ways been these sad stories about Corby's future—and the town has always come

THIS IS YOUR TOWN, YOUR FUTURE, AND THIS IS YOUR NEWSPAPER. WHY NOT USE IT AND LET US KNOW WHAT YOU FEEL.? WRITE TO THE LEAD-ER, MARKING YOUR LET-TER "FUTURE OF CORBY," AT 36/38 ELIZ-ABETH STREET. WE'LL PAY A GUINEA FOR THE BEST LETTER PRINTED. "THE FUTURE OF COR-BY SPECIAL" SEE CEN-TRE PAGES FOR THE COM-PLETE PICTURE.

Mr. John Powell, aged 33, of 50 Weston Walk, Corby, married with four children: "We need more industry. Things should be better in ten years time. I hope so for Corby's sake."

Brian Diver, aged 29, of 9 Corby Road, Cottingham, mar-ried with three children: "I hope the future is good. We have to think for the best. I can't see Corby coming to a sticky end."

Miss Agnes Simpson, aged 19, of 13 Barnley Square, Corby. "It doesn't look too good for Corby with Golden Wonder laying off all those people and the other people out of jobs, too."

Workers in mass demo

MANY of Corby's main fac-tories lost at least three hours production time on Tuesday when their workers joined the mass march and rally against the Government's proposed In-dustrial Relations Bill.

About 800 trade unionists

pm. After waiting outside the factory for an hour they went home and a day-night-shift did not go in either. Work resumed at 6 am on Wednesday.

At Golden Wonder no production was lost. The trade unions claimed

many women. Inside the hall, the total number swelled to about 800 who loudly cheered their leaders on the plat-

Contd. on page 2

MR. WILLIAM Firth, well-known in Weldon as a far-mer and councillor, died sud-denly on Sunday morning, aged 72.

Mr. Firch of 9 Church Road, Weldon, was taken ill at his home on Saturday and died the following morning at St. Mary's Hospital, Ket-tering.

In January 1971 Brian Diver graced the front page of the 'Corby Leader' with his comments that Corby was a great place in which to live. "Despite all the uncertainty relating to the town's future, I still have confidence in the town and would not wish to live elsewhere. I firmly believe that the years ahead will be good for my kids." Thirty-nine years later Brian (who worked as a self-employed baker until his retirement in 2008) has no regrets about his decision to stay put and still insists that he wouldn't want to live anywhere else!

Corby Works lost £2 million profit through industrial disputes last year. The Steel Corporation's plan is for the bulk of steel production to be centred at coastal sites - with the biggest tonnage of steel being produced there. Corby's would be marginal tonnage of a specialised nature. A strike would have a serious effect on Corby's long-term future."

Following hot on the heels of Crawford's warning came the news that in Corby there were more people out of work than at any time since the war. Figures revealed indicated that there were eight hundred men and women without a job, plus a further one hundred and ten under-18s are jobless. (3.2 per cent of the town's population.)

It soon became evident that Corby was facing an industrial crisis. The crunch came when Golden Wonder Crisps announced one hundred and fifty redundancies to add to the job losses already made known by Lancashire Steel and Aquascutum Ltd. What the relevant authorities didn't realise at the time was that the challenge to bring new industry to the town would prove to be an uphill struggle.

After his brief flirtation with the building industry, Big C returned to BSC - this time to work in the Lancashire Steel Plant. Clive: "I was determined to land myself a constant day job, therefore, when the incumbent 'Bog Ore Assistant' suffered a heart attack and I was offered his job, I jumped at the chance. I later found out that nobody else wanted it - the work was nauseating and sometimes dangerous."

Being less than charmed with his new position, Clive soon began looking for alternative employment and decided to make the trek over to Kettering 'in order to suss out what was on offer at the Primecut Foods meat processing factory.' That line of enquiry didn't last long though. Clive said: "Standing for eight hours a day and stirring a large kettledrum-like pot of bubbling steak and kidney - wasn't very appealing." So it was back to the Lancs for Big C, where he spent his days cleaning out gas tanks (a task slightly less odious than cooking with kettledrums!) and where there was the occasional period of hair-raising excitement thrown in. Clive: "There was always a risk that escaping gas would ignite (which it frequently did) affording me the opportunity to fulfil every young boy's dream - that of being a fireman! For me, the upside of being a 'B.O.A.' - apart from the chance to get my hands on the fireman's jacket and helmet - was that there was a complete lack of managerial supervision. As long as the gas tanks were cleaned out, no one seemed to be interested in what I did during my working hours. It didn't take me long to work out that it took less than ninety minutes to complete my chores - leaving me with approximately six hours to kill. Mind you, that was a void which I helped to fill by sinking a few pints in the White Horse! At around eleven o'clock, I'd climb through a hole in the perimeter fence and spend long, leisurely lunchtimes in the bar. Then, when it was about half past two, I'd go back to work - just in time to show my face before clocking off!

Inevitably, one day I was confronted by a patrolman who had spotted me. The next morning I was up before the manager on a charge of leaving the premises without permission. I vehemently denied it and feigned all knowledge of the hole in the fence. Of course the manager threatened to fire me, however, due to the imminent closure of the plant, a transfer to the EWSR was already on the cards and was probably the reason why the matter was dropped - and also why just a few weeks later I was included in the first batch of Lancs' employees to be redeployed!"

More bad news was thrust upon Corby workers when British Steel Corporation announced a cutback in production. Those at the top blamed the 'drastic industrial recession' for the severe slump in orders for steel and tubes. It was a crippling blow for those employees who literally 'lived' in the steelworks working double and even treble shifts. Fraser McNeil (a slinger in the CW Mills) protested: "This is a near-nightmare scenario for me. Without extra shifts, how am I going to fund my proposed sheep-dog training facility?" Fraser was regularly admonished by his workmates for habitually working 'doublers'. They'd say: "Watch out for the dog when you go home, Frazer! Lassie might think that you're an intruder and take a lump out of your leg - that is if you ever decide to go home again!" Thick skinned Frazer remained unabashed.

Tony Lombardi who was a displaced person (or in the vernacular of the time 'a D.P.') was well known for routinely disregarding company guidelines regarding the dangerous but not uncommon practice of working too many hours. On one occasion he was marched out of the EWSR by a patrolman and ordered to go home - because management had discovered that he hadn't clocked out for three days! It turned out that (on successive shifts) each time a charge-hand came round and asked for men to stay on at work, Tony raised his hand. A foreman eventually found him slumped in a washroom - fast asleep!

Groundwork, repairs and general cleaning within the BSC complex were carried out by a group of labourers known collectively as Charlie Dunne's Gang (formerly Ramsey's Gang.) It was the type of employment for which there was an endless supply of vacancies and which was ideally suited to those who were between jobs or seeking work of a temporary nature.

Indeed, when home on leave from the Merchant Navy, Tommy Steel from Corby regularly took advantage of this convenient and readily available job opportunity. Tommy: "The 'work' was actually a bit of a joke. There tended to be a very relaxed and convivial atmosphere within the gang - at least

Pictured bottom: The main entrance to Golden Wonder Crisps Ltd. in Corby. Over the course of two decades several hundreds of shift workers passed through these gates as they hurried to clock on for their shift on one of the company's busy production lines. Top: Sue Beaver (Miss Golden Wonder 1971) helps to promote a competition offering a rubber kayak as the first prize. Only one lucky customer would find the elusive winning voucher contained in his or her packet of crisps. When the factory was later destroyed by fire, investigators refuted claims that it was the work of a sore loser!

among the Corby contingent - on account of the fact that we knew we were only there to cover for absentee production workers or to fill in during holiday periods. Any work that the gang did around the complex was incidental to that."

On weekend shutdowns we would regularly be dispatched to the Ore Crushing Plant to carry out routine maintenance - a euphemism for cleaning up. Starting at 1p.m. on a Saturday and ending at 6a.m. on a Sunday morning, the shutdown shift was an attractive proposition for a young man on the lookout to earn some extra beer money - it was highly paid and didn't involve much hard graft! For us lads from the Raven, however, the Ore Crushing Plant held an even greater appeal - once on site there was no proper supervision and we were simply left to our own devices. Needless to say, we soon found better ways to spend our time. One of them was staging re-enactments of World War II!

First of all we'd smuggle in over the brickshed fence our seven-pint 'caskets' of Ansells Bitter - (or 'Diesel' as it was commonly called in those days.) and then, after stashing it away in the basement, we'd gather to listen to the gaffer's instructions. To our credit, we'd begin the shift by dutifully sweeping and cleaning the plant, but it didn't last long - after an hour or so of half-hearted effort we'd lose interest and drift down to the unlit basement. This was where the real action would take place! (There would be no sign of the gaffer, as by that time he would be safely ensconced in the 'Old Legion' and would be having a pint, or else he'd be taking a nap in the engineering shop's cabin - a haven for column dodgers!) Meanwhile, armies gathered in the gloom of the Ore Crushing Plant, waiting to commence battle. Before this could happen, General Corbert Bond and his adversary General Mick Matson, would - with stiff upper lips to the fore - be engaged in the process of taking turns to draw names out of a hat, as a means of selecting 'conscripts' for their respective armies.

For ammunition we used balls of clay which had fallen from the conveyor belts transporting lumps of iron ore. They were already shaped into perfect rounds, had the consistency of plasticine and could often be as large as a tennis ball (ouch!) Although most of the lads who participated in the basement battles were hardened veterans, there would always be a few rookies who, predictably, would retire quickly to the Blast Furnace canteen - discouraged after being targeted repeatedly by the more experienced combatants.

Troops were required to be agile, fearless and to have eyes in the back of their heads (preferably cats' eyes - to enable them to see well in the gloomy depths.) A high pain threshold was also mandatory - at least until enough beer had been sunk to provide an anaesthetic that was capable of masking the intense pain derived from being struck by a heavy clay ball!

When the recruiting process was complete and adequate supplies of ammunition had been stockpiled, the normal order of events was that both sides would retire to opposite ends of the labyrinthine basement. At a pre-set signal both armies would advance upon each other (with carry-outs to hand!) Stealth was of the utmost importance in these matters as an early strike from the enemy could prove very discouraging to a sober infantryman!

It was extremely hot down in that subterranean vault and in the early days we wore only jeans and T-shirts (not the best of combat gear!) When you took a hit to the head or the body - Boy did you know about it! As the 'campaigns' wore on, experience taught us that, in spite of the heat, it made good sense to cover up - so eventually we started to wear safety helmets, goggles and other protective equipment. After all war might be waged for several hours within that deep recess which housed the workings of the giant ore crusher.

When finally we became battle-weary (i.e. fed-up) following our Stalingrad ordeal, we'd hop over the fence behind the old bricksheds and make for the West Gate car park - where our cars would be parked in readiness for a quick getaway to the pub and a well earned pint! After that, the evening was spent at leisure in the Raven bar, playing several games of table football (to relax us and to help recharge our batteries!) and then it was back over the fence to the Crushing Plant - for a swift inspection of the 'night's work'. There was nothing left for us to do then but follow the example set by the ganger and seek repose for the rest of the shift!

Those bricksheds certainly came in handy. I remember one occasion when late on a warm July night a gang of us from the Raven decided to climb over the fence with a carry-out. What's so ridiculous is the fact that we weren't even working that weekend! Inside the sheds there were gaps, between the pallets of bricks, where you could sit, hide, sleep or party in comfort - and that's just what we did! John Hamill worked there for a time and I can remember him sniffing the air one morning and saying to me, 'I'm sure somebody had a party in here last night'. He was bang on the nail! That night we'd staged a floodlit Scotland v England match until 3 a.m. and then we'd staggered home to bed. By 6 a.m. I was back in there my only concern being where to find the best place to kip down and sleep off a hangover!

Following Ted Heath's announcement that the New Town of East Kilbride was to be established in Lanarkshire, Ken Farnham, President of the Corby Chamber of Commerce, warned: "The way things are going, there could be a 'wagon train' of Scots leaving Corby for fresh opportunities in Scotland." Already alarmed by the lack of job prospects in the town, Ken was keen to know if the government intended to help unemployed Glaswegians to return home.

Steelworkers were also being lured to West Germany - by the promise of a weekly wage of £60. A company called J.G. Engineering International Ltd. (of Hillingdon in Middlesex) was running a recruiting campaign on behalf of a tubemaking plant near Dusseldorf, and was offering to fly workers to Germany free of charge and to guarantee them a flat in which to live. In addition, the successful candidates' holidays, sick pay and medical expenses were to be included in the package.

Adding to the woes of the British Steel Corporation, the Corby Secondary Modern School For Boys, situated in James Watt Avenue, lodged a complaint regarding the 'unacceptable levels of pollution' coming from the nearby Sinter Plant. Jack Allanson, the school's caretaker (and as a consequence the person on site most likely to be affected by the pollution) protested: 'I've had enough of struggling daily with the dust and smoke discharged from the steelwork's chimneys. Having swept up the dust and cleaned all the grime off of the classroom walls, I find that within hours I have to start all over again. It's a vicious circle - a bit like working in the Sahara desert! Books are being ruined, desks are soiled and the pupils' uniforms look as though they've been washed in Brand X.'
When Jack decided to start a petition, Mr. Morgan from the English Dept., Mr. Talbot from the Art Dept. and the school's Headmaster, Mr. D. J. Wright all pledged their support - a surprising development considering that the four men had worked together at the school since the 1950s and had never before commented publicly on the problem. Prompted by Allanson, the headmaster drafted an accompanying letter which was then posted off to Sir Geoffrey DeFreitas, MP.
Back on the brush, the caretaker was resolute regarding their intentions, declaring: "We intend to kick up a fuss and force BSC to reduce this pollution which is spoiling the school environment!"
In response to Jack's outburst, a spokesman for BSC admitted that the smoke was indeed coming from the Sinter Plant. Furthermore, he gave an assurance (to both the school and to nearby residents) that when a proposed modernisation scheme for the plant was completed, the nuisance would be eradicated.

Elsewhere in the country, health fears were also dominating conversation - this time the subject being the smoking of cigarettes and its inherent dangers. In a newly published report, the Royal College of Physicians issued the following warning: 'If current habits don't change, by the year 1980, 50,000 deaths will occur annually through lung cancer.' As was to be expected, those who enjoyed the odd fag… or ten, were scathing. Glyn Cummings of Corby's Nags Head spoke for many when he said: "I'll die happy then, not miserable!" In the wake of the report, Wills Cigarettes 'Pacemakers in Tobacco' continued unashamedly with their latest sales promotion campaign - a special offer for twenty Embassy Regal cigarettes at their 'biggest ever value', of 2s.6d.
Another firm hoping to benefit from increased advertising was Watneys (the Brewery which owned the Nags Head in Corby) whose marketing department decided to try and raise the profile of one of their longest selling ales, by changing its name from Red Barrel to the trendier sounding 'Red'. Despite much media hype, the more discerning beer drinker remained unimpressed and the campaign

made little impact on sales figures. The problem lay in the fact that the beer was simply overrated - it was the type of bland, innocuous tipple that led to the formation of CAMRA (the Campaign for Real Ale).

The Open Hearth (another Watneys pub) became a favoured haunt for CAMRA recruiters when the brewery's latest brand of pale ale was introduced. According to seasoned beer drinkers at the pub, the brew (called Star Light Bitter) was best described as 'maiden's water'. Star Light failed to impress anyone - and least of all Bill Quinn (who divided his drinking time between the Raven Hotel and the Hearth). Bill claimed that the only stars that he was interested in were the ones that he saw after a night on the Raven's Ansells Bitter!

Willie McEwan was another of the Open Hearth's customers who had strong opinions about weak beer. Having been given the all-clear from his doctor to start drinking again in moderation, Willie informed the barman that he had been advised, however, that it would be preferable to drink water for a while. "Give me a pint of Star Light!" he ordered.

Any takers? Win Smith (barmaid at the Open Hearth) faces an uphill struggle to convince her customers of the merits of Watneys Red.

At Corby Magistrates' Court, Alex Burton of Malton Walk (a thirty-year-old, vending machine operator) was fined £2 for stealing eggs from the British Steel Corporation. Burton pleaded guilty to stealing two-and-a-half dozen eggs valued at 8s. 9d. The court heard that a security officer had found the defendant's bicycle - parked out of bounds and with a bag of eggs hanging from the handlebars. When questioned, Burton explained to the patrolman that he'd taken the eggs in lieu of meals that he was entitled to when working a nightshift. To the dismay of the defendant, magistrates of the court were not disposed to thinking along the same lines!

Also in court were two neighbours from the Exeter estate who had been apprehended by a policeman on Panda Car duty. The officer had become suspicious after spotting that the back end of their Vauxhall car was scraping along the road. When called upon to give evidence, Police Constable Bob Dibble said: "The vehicle came to my attention whilst I was on duty in Everest Lane. Upon closer inspection, I found that the car's heavily-laden boot was filled with coal. Their explanation - that they

Except for the beer, the Open Hearth on Studfall Avenue remains pretty much the same today as it was in the 1970s. According to some of the pub's regulars, barrels of Watneys Red were great for making table lamps - but little else!

had found it by the side of the road - was in my estimation a bit lame, and so I decided to investigate further. It later came to light that the two men 'found' the coal in the BSC plant." Both men admitted stealing £4 worth of coal and were fined £10 each. "Excellent work Dibble!" said Police Sergeant McCormack, in praise of his subordinate.

At Kettering Magistrates' Court a man was charged with attempting to break into an allotment hut in Desborough. John Gray, an itinerant worker of no fixed abode, claimed that he was in fact looking for his yellow budgie, when he was challenged by Percy Jobson (the owner of the allotment.) Martin was fined £15.

In Paris Edward Heath and President Georges Pompidou of France concluded protracted talks by announcing that the way was now open for Britain to join the Common Market. Across the English Channel the issue of Common Market membership was causing a great deal of angst, especially amongst the country's steelworkers. Dr. Robert McIntyre, the celebrated spokesman for the Scottish National Party, expressed the concerns felt by many, when he said: "Our steel industry is already under threat as a result of London centralist control instigated by the Labour Government and

continued by the present Government. In the Common Market any future development would be under the control of the European Iron and Steel Community - and the prospects would be dire indeed." Sentiments aired twelve months earlier by Sir Geoffrey DeFrietas, the MP for Corby!

Away from that summer's industrial strife, Mick Jagger of the Rolling Stones married Bianca Perez Morena, in a glitzy showbiz affair that would elevate Jagger to the rank of A-list celebrity. The wedding (which took place in St Tropez) coincided with the Stones' release of *Sticky Fingers* - arguably their finest album.

On a sadder note, one of the world's original rock 'n' rollers died. Gene Vincent had suffered with ill health for years - his weakness for alcohol playing a major part in his early participation in the 'Mortal Coil Shuffle'.

Robert 'Mull' Muldoon (centre) was fortunate enough to meet not one but two of his idols - without setting foot outside of his home town. Firstly Gene Vincent shared a 'Massie-burger' with Mull (from the mobile food van belonging to John 'Jack' Massie) following an appearance at the Welfare Club. Then in May 1989, on a visit to the Willow Room Denis Law happily shared a few footballing memories with his biggest fan.

John Black, a great fan of the rock star, recalled the night when Vincent played at the Welfare Club in Corby - back in 1963. John: "Brian Dowell of the Size Seven booked him - along with Sounds Incorporated (who backed many of the visiting American stars when they toured this country.) Robert 'Mull' Muldoon and I tried to gain admission to his dressing room at the end of the show but were prevented from doing so by two very large bouncers who, incidentally, were brothers of the boxer Jack Gardner. At that point I conceded defeat - but somehow Mull managed to find his way in. He later described to me the sad and sorry state the singer was in. Mull said: 'Although Gene was pissed and in a foul mood, he still shouted "Hi Mull" when he saw me.'

Yeah right! I said. Nevertheless, Mull persisted: 'I've met him three times before. He knows me.'

Unimpressed on the night, I had to eat my words a couple of days later when Mull produced a photograph of himself and Gene, in the Welfare Club dressing room - both of them chewing on large hamburgers!"

Roy Young (a keyboard player and one of Vincent's chums from his Hamburg days) was looking to recruit a saxophonist for his band, following the departure of Howie Casey. The latter had once been a member of Derry and the Seniors - who in 1960 became the first British group to play in that city (predating the Beatles by several weeks.) In 1976 Howie, a Liverpudlian, would team up with Paul McCartney for the Wings world tour - having posed a few months previously, with other luminaries from the

"IT'S PERHAPS NOT THE BEST PLACE TO PLAY IN, BUT IN HERE AT LEAST MY BUM NOTES GO DOWN THE PAN!"

world of showbiz, for the famous front cover of the groups groundbreaking album *Band On The Run*. Through his London music connections, Young was able to make contact with Corby ex-pat Ricky Dodd - who was living in Chiswick at the time, and was working as a session musician on Rolling Stone Bill Wyman's latest project (the production and recording of a debut album for a band called Tucky Buzzard.) Ricky was also playing the occasional pub gig and meeting up with his old friend, the ex- Midnighters' guitarist Adrian Holland.

Having moved south from Corby in the mid-sixties, Holland was now entrenched in the suburbs of Reading. Ade says that he can remember an incident perfectly encapsulating Rick's bizarre sense of humour. Ade: "During a session in the very small bar of Wokingham's Bush Hotel, Ricky was asked to 'tone it down a bit' as the bar staff couldn't hear what the customers were ordering. True to form, Ricky walked into the Ladies toilets and played the rest of the set from there. He only emerged to find out what the next number was!"

Dodd joined the Roy Young Band just in time to be included on their next single, *Grannie's Got A Painted Leg*. After that they headed off to the continent for a tour of music festivals which would keep them busy throughout the early years of the 1970s.

Young says that the British tour that he did with Chuck Berry was one of his most interesting experiences. Roy: "The pair of us flew up to Glasgow for a concert and when we were walking through the terminal, on our way to collect our bags, I noticed about fifty photographers in the arrivals area. Chuck turned to me and said, 'Roy, put your best foot forward - we're about to be photographed.' His jaw then dropped and he spluttered a few choice words when our too cool walk took us straight past the photographers and they paid us no attention at all! They were too busy loading their cameras in readiness for the person right behind us - world champion racing car driver Jackie Stewart, who was returning home after winning a major circuit race."

Berry had previously borrowed Roy's band when playing at the Lanchester Arts Festival (an event held at the Locarno Ballroom in Coventry - under the auspices of Coventry University.) Pink Floyd had been the headline act and Slade, Billy Preston, Chuck Berry and the Roy Young Band were the support. Before his death in 2006 Ricky Dodd described exactly what it was like to work with Berry. He related: "Chuck was the most obnoxious and arrogant person that I ever had the misfortune to play with. Before the show started, when we went to his dressing room (in order to find out what we would be playing, in what key and so forth) we were greeted by one of his heavies who asked us what we wanted. We told him that we were Chuck's backing group and wanted to have a chat with him. All of a sudden there was a big yell from behind this fellow. It was Berry - telling us, in no uncertain terms, to 'get the hell out of here!' We were absolutely raging and decided there and then to get our own back by playing the very worst that we could. We devised a plan in which drummer Ronnie McIntosh disconnected his bass pedal and guitarist Owen McIntyre would 'forget' to plug in. As for me, I would just go through the motions - hardly making any sound at all. When Berry came on stage that night (playing *Maybelline* and doing his duck walk - all that crap!) he turned round and shouted to us 'I can't hear the bass, man!' then 'I can't hear the drums.' We carried on regardless, trying to suppress our glee. Although it was an awful performance from us, we made him look and sound like garbage. It was sweet revenge!"

In May the Roy Young Band released another single, on the MCA label, entitled *Wild Cherry Wine*. Shortly after that they left for a tour of Germany - as the supporting act for Deep Purple. Roy recalls that the trip wasn't exactly without its troubles. He said: "One night I was invited (along with Ricky Dodd and the rest of the tour's entourage) to a pre-show dinner at a German restaurant, and by the time we arrived there we were all starving. On entering, we encountered a table that was laden with a variety of different breads and a huge dish of butter. Never the type to stand on ceremony, we all just ploughed in! After about fifteen minutes the proprietor appeared - a huge German woman. Her voice was so loud and piercing that she reminded me of Adolph Hitler, hectoring his followers in one of his wartime rants. She announced: "Zer vill be a twenty course dinner. I am going to lock zee door and you vill not leave here until you have eaten every piece of food. You are all too thin, or - as you say in England 'skinty' - therefore you vill be fattening up!" (she was of course unaware that we had filled up our bellies with the bread). Meekly, we sat down at the dining table - feeling like a bunch of cowed school kids.

When she went to the kitchen to oversee the food, Ian Gillan said to me "Let's unlock the door and skedaddle!" The thing was - none of us dared to move. Within minutes 'Mrs. Hitler' was back with two courses (which wasn't too bad) but it was when the third course arrived that we started to worry - because we realised that there were still another seventeen to go! Ricky made the suggestion that during her next trip to the kitchen we should draw straws - to determine which one of us should tell her that we didn't want any more to eat and that we'd like to leave (and pretty Schnellish!)

Unfortunately, when the fourth course arrived our courage rapidly deserted us, and so (resigned to our fate) we made a valiant effort to tuck in. As we did so our hostess stood behind us, banging on the table and urging us to 'Come along! You vill eat, eat…EAT!' It was a good thing that the local promoter could see - by the colour of our faces - that his pampered rock stars were in trouble, and without further ado he informed her that if we ate any more, then there probably wouldn't be a show that night!

As we arose from the table and prepared to leave the restaurant, we all had this phoney smile on our faces. Ricky thanked our kind Frau for the wonderful time that we'd had, and, of course, for the incredible food. In response, she systematically lifted up each of us in a big bear hug, shook us and thanked us for coming to her restaurant. We looked at each other, as if to say 'Who's going to be the first one to puke?' Luckily, no one did - we all survived to take part in the show alongside Deep Purple, East of Eden and Savage Rose (a Danish band co-founded by Alex Reil - one of Europe's most influential jazz drummers. A fact which impressed jazz fan Ricky no end!)"

Holding court that March inside a 'lively' Corby Trades and Labour Club, was the panel of the popular BBC Radio Four programme *Gardeners Question Time* (chaired by question master Frank Engelman.) For the occasion, local green-fingered enthusiasts had turned out in their numbers - each of them eager to quiz the team of experts on matters horticultural. Many of the audience posed questions relating to the plethora of slugs which was plaguing the flowerbeds of the town. Paddy Johnson from Lindisfarne Road had this sorry tale to tell. Paddy: "I have a pinky-coloured plant - an *Ajuga reptans Atropurpurea* - which the slugs hardly seem to bother with; whereas the brown one (*Braunherz*) they love and have nearly destroyed. They also appear to be disinterested in my geraniums and haven't bothered with the *Festuca Glauca* or the *Lavatera* - which I find rather odd as I've noticed that they have eaten Denis McBlain's next door. They like daffodil leaves, once the flowering has stopped, and they've killed all my *Primulas*. As a result I am now concentrating on growing plants that they don't like."

Audrey Spiers of Stuart Road was almost tearful: "I very nearly lost my *Christmas Rose* to these monsters, but managed to deter them by smearing petroleum jelly round the edge of the plant pot - which so far seems to be working and the plant is looking pretty healthy again. I noted Mr. Johnson's comments about his *Ajuga* escaping the attentions of the little blighters, but, unfortunately, ours have been attacked by both slugs and snails. Climbing up brickwork doesn't seem to be a problem for them either - I've even found them in my two window boxes. I'm desperate."

Alan Murphy of Westfields Road adopted a more aggressive stance: "It's comforting to hear how other gardeners are dealing with the slug problem. As for myself? I am constantly slug-flinging - which I feel could become a new sport. I hate them! I have even found one on my cat!"

Tam McGillivary of Cupar Crescent, who was a Labour Club regular and rather uninformed (horticulturally speaking) was observing the proceedings from the rear of the hall. Clutching his pint of IPA, he scoffed: "That's a bit harsh pal! You should take a look at my garden - it's like a jungle. It's a veritable holiday camp for slugs! The wee beasties are nae problem. Live and let live I say!"

Tams words of wisdom brought this admonishment from Paddy Johnson: "Tam, you wouldn't be saying that if you had an *Ajuga*. Get away back into the bar - ya big eejit!"

At this point Frank Engelman called for a short break (by all accounts to avert a potential case of 'on air' fisticuffs!). He needn't have worried though. "Anyone fancy a game of darts?" asked a mischievous Tam as he departed the hall.

By June the strike waged in Corby by fourteen hundred blastfurnacemen (linked to their 35 per cent pay claim) was beginning to have a throttling effect on other parts of the works. Owing to a slump in orders, the Open Hearth had already been out of action for several months and this gave rise to fears that the Rolling Mills and Strip Mills might face the same fate - resulting in more lay-offs. An editorial in the *Evening Telegraph* warned that the strike could have a disastrous effect on a town where over 80 per cent of the male population worked (either directly or indirectly) for B.S.C.

The writer behind that theory wasn't the only person predicting a devastating outcome - but this time it was concerning the future of the planet. Dr. S.R. Ayre of Leeds University's Geography Department had issued the following edict: "The human race is facing extinction because of over-population. People may destroy the planet's remaining fertility in a vain bid to survive." Addressing the British Association, Dr. Ayre explained that he was worried that the human race might ultimately find itself in the position of animals like the lemming (i.e. driven to commit suicide en masse - as a result of neurosis spreading amongst the group due to overcrowding.) Another analogy proffered by the academic cited the case of laboratory bacteria - killed by its own waste products after failing to die of starvation. He also suggested that, from the perspective of the animal world, the human race is representative of a pest of the worst order - it uses up irreplaceable resources and produces relatively indestructible waste.

In concluding what, with hindsight, was a remarkably perceptive speech for its time, Dr. Ayre estimated that "three more doublings of the world's population could easily happen over the next one hundred years, but little more than three doublings of the world's food supply is theoretically possible - even assuming that the whole Earth was managed as a unit, with no major mistakes."

In June 1971 St Cecilia became the first Corby band to gain a Top Twenty hit, with a catchy little number entitled *Leap Up And Down (Wave Your Knickers In The Air)*. The song was penned by the group's bass player, Keith Hancock, who says that he was inspired to write it on his return from a holiday spent on the east coast of Britain. Keith: "Les Smith and I had rented a cottage in Norfolk - which is where we met some French girls. Anyway, during the time we spent with them the phrase 'leap up and down, wave your knickers in the air' came into my head (maybe I was being optimistic!) and for some reason it must have lingered in the back of my mind".

SPAIN'S BLUE PENCIL

SPAIN is hotting up its censorship actions against foreign-recorded discs whose lyric content is felt to be "lewd." Following the ban of Mungo Jerry last week, Slade and St. Cecilia have had their latest singles – both of them hits here, although the St. Cecilia disc has run into a spot of bother with the BBC – banned by the Spanish authorities.

According to the authorities there are "lewd" lyrics on the 'A' side of St. Cecilia's single, "Leap Up And Down (And Wave Your Knickers In The Air)" and on the 'B' side of Slade's single, "Get Down And Get With It," which is titled "Do You Want Me."

St Cecilia. The hit-making line-up: L-R: Les Smith, Ricky Moss, Keith Hancock and John Proctor. Kneeling Graham Smith.

A week later, when I was back at work in the Plug Mill office, I phoned Ricky Moss (who was clerking in the Blast Furnaces office on the other side of the Works) and I said to him: 'This morning I'm going to write a song that will be a hit record - it's called *Leap Up And Down!*' Ricky just laughed at me, but, nevertheless, a couple of hours later I phoned to tell him that the song was ready. It was a few days before the rest of the band got to hear it, and then (when they'd given it the thumbs up) we started featuring it in our stage act. *Leap Up And Down* got such a good reception from the fans that we quickly decided to make a demo of it - so we booked time at Derek Tompkins' Beck Studio, in Wellingborough."

The recording session went very smoothly and resulted in St Cecilia exiting the studio with a product that they felt certain would be snapped up by some enterprising record company. It had a lovely brass sound on it - 'really raucous and ballsy' - and it also had what they thought was a great bass line. The next step was for their management to send out the demo to the various record companies - however, because of its lyrical content, they all seemed reluctant to take it on. Guitarist John Proctor: "Wherever we played the song people would ask us if it was available on disc, and so we eventually started selling individually cut acetates for £1.50 a time. That was a huge amount of money at that time - in 1971 a 7″ single normally cost only 35p. It was also enough to convince us that a record deal would prove lucrative.

At some stage Jonathan King heard the song and, recognising the potential appeal of its inherent humour, decided that he could make it into a hit record. He subsequently arranged a recording session for us at the Marquee Martin Studios, in London's Wardour Street, where we re-recorded our song along with its absolutely dire 'B' side - *How You Gonna Tell Me*. (The latter was provided by King himself, in a shrewd business move to ensure that he would reap equal royalties if the record was a hit.) Surprisingly, Jonathan informed us that he didn't care for the bass line, insisting that it sounded too similar to the Beatles' *Ob La Di*. Although Hancock didn't agree with him - he changed it all the same. As a result, we felt that all the guts had been taken out of the recording. It changed the sound altogether. To make matters worse, we never even got the chance to have our say regarding the final mixing. As soon as the recording session was over, we had to rush off to the South coast for a booking later that night.

Derek Tompkins at the console: A pioneer record producer, Derek worked with a number of local and international artists. He also played host to Andrew Oldham (the former manager/Svengali to the Rolling Stones) who brought down a band from Liverpool to make a recording at the Wellingborough studios. Derek recalls that Oldham spent the entire session quaffing wine and, as a result, was carried out 'legless' to his Rolls Royce at the end of the day!

the 50 RECOR... MIRRO...

singles

1	1	6	CHIRPY CHIRPY CHEEP CHEEP Middle Of The Road		RCA 2047
2	5	5	CO-CO The Sweet		RCA 2087
3	2	5	DON'T LET IT DIE Hurricane Smith	Columbia DB 8705
4	3	7	BANNER MAN Blue Mink	Regal Zonophone RZ 3034
5	4	8	HE'S GONNA STEP ON YOU AGAIN John Kongos		Fly BUG 8
6	7	8	I'M GONNA RUN AWAY FROM YOU Tami Lynn		Mojo 2092 001
7	6	10	I DID WHAT I DID FOR MARIA Tony Christie		MCA MK 5064
8	10	8	JUST MY IMAGINATION Temptations	Tamla Motown TMG 773
9	19	3	BLACK AND WHITE Greyhound		Trojan TR 7820
10	9	7	LADY ROSE Mungo Jerry		Dawn DNX 2510
11	12	11	PIED PIPER Bob and Marcia		Trojan TR 7818
12	11	4	I DON'T BLAME YOU AT ALL Smokey Robinson & Miracles	Tamla Motown TMG 774
13	16	5	WHEN YOU ARE A KING White Plains		Deram DM 333
14	18	4	ME AND YOU AND A DOG NAMED BOO Lobo	Philips 607 3801
15	15	14	KNOCK THREE TIMES Dawn		Bell BLL 1146
16	22	2	RIVER DEEP, MOUNTAIN HIGH Supremes/Four Tops	Tamla Motown TMG 777
17	17	3	MONKEY SPANNER Dave and Ansel Collins	Technique TE 814
18	26	2	TOM-TOM TURNAROUND New World		RAK 117
19	14	11	I AM... I SAID Neil Diamond		Uni UN 532
20	15	11	HEAVEN MUST HAVE SENT YOU Elgins	Tamla Motown TMG 771
21		2	GET IT ON T. Rex		Fly BUG 10
22	23	3	(AND THE) PICTURES IN THE SKY Medicine Head		Dandelion K19002

album

1	1	63	BRIDGE OVER TROUBLED WATER Simon and Garfunkel		CBS
2	2	6	RAM Paul and Linda McCartney		Apple P...
3	6	13	MOTOWN CHARTBUSTERS Vol 5		Tamla Motown STM...
4	5	10	STICKY FINGERS Rolling Stones	Rolling Stones C...
5	4	14	TARKUS Emerson, Lake and Palmer	Island I...
6	15	2	MAGNIFICENT 7 Supremes/Four Tops	Tamla Motown STM...
7	4	3	FREE LIVE! Free		Island IL...
8	10	15	SPLIT Groundhogs		Liberty LB...
9	9	64	ANDY WILLIAMS GREATEST HITS		CBS
10		1	LOVE STORY Soundtrack		Paramount SP...
11	11	11	OVER AND OVER Nana Mouskouri	Fontana ST...
12	11	22	FRANK SINATRA'S GREATEST HITS Vol 2		Reprise RSL...
13	9	11	SYMPHONIES FOR THE SEVENTIES Waldo De Los Rios	A&M AML...
14	14	6	SINATRA AND COMPANY		Reprise RSL...
15	12	7	MUD SLIDE SLIM AND THE BLUE HORIZON James Taylor	Warner Bros WS...
16	25	2	SOUND OF MUSIC Soundtrack		RCA SB/RB...
17	18	22	LED ZEPPELIN II		Atlantic 58...
18	22	12	AFTER THE GOLD RUSH Neil Young		

Public Opinion

Knickers to old Auntie Beeb!

COME off it, B...
Fancy banni...
hit pop song...
TV because it...
tions the comm...
everyday w...
"knicker...

In that...
have a ma...
up" sessio...
sexy plays...
sary four-l...

Can I ju...
word on th...
Fronts.—Mi...
(aged 17)
Essex.

nig...
hav...
and go down...
protest against the decisio...
They will be waving poste...
and banners with knicke...
to bring the point home
the BBC," said Ken.

This is the first big brea...
through for the group, a...
manager Ken Cox hopes...
will be in the top ten...
next week.

Alex Gordon our
columnist writes:
Cecilia should be rub...
their hands with glee...
that BBC have f...
fallen into the trap...
banning their mor...
little song about knick...

JIMMY SAVILE

Sorry, just too broad!

POLICE stations...
some odd phone ca...
one of the oddes...
have been last Th...
telling them that...
of mainly young...
had besieged the...
gates of Tele...
...and were...

Pop dead? knickers!

POP MUSIC, according to Saint Cecelia, is about the only thin...
isn't dead.

"We'd like to play heavy music," says Ricky Moss, "and we'd al...
to play our own songs more, but no one wants to know. You get a...
name in our part of the world—Corby in Northamptonshire—and th...
are deserted. Pop is the only thing that packs them in. People co...
dance and have a good time."

With "Knickers" still waving, Saint Cecelia have already record...
follow-up.

"It's totally different from "Knickers," which we'll admit we didn...
very much," they say. Their astonishment in finding the great J. ...
made them sound so raw and thin was only matched by their f...
astonishment at finding the record a hit. And even Jonathan King ...
he doesn't like it much...

...e protest at BB...
...pop song ban

...week
Irate fans left Corby this
morning complete with
banners and posters for
their protest against the
BBC this afternoon. They
plan to present a pair of
knickers to the director
general with the words "St.
Cecelia now in the charts
why not on Top of the
Pops."

The BBC has banned the
record from television because they consider it in bad
taste although it has been

widely plugged on Radio
One particularly by house-
wives' favourite Jimmy
Young.

But manager Ken Cox
said: "The record is not in
bad taste at all, it is merely
a fun record and it is mad
to think anything else.

"Over 100,000 pop fans
have bought the record to
put it into the charts and
now the BBC are depriving
them of the right to see the
group appear on TV.

"The ban came late last

From left: Kathleen Langley, Anne Aldice, Betty Hewitt and Linda Ru...
think of the BBC ban on their favourite group before setting...

Jonathan King secured a deal for us with Polydor Records and then three weeks later we were summoned to their offices to hear the finished product. We were distraught. It sounded awful - when compared to the original demo - but there was nothing we could do about it. Looking back on the whole affair, I sometimes wish that we had recorded a cover version of *What Have They Done To My Song, Ma?* (Melanie's big hit of 1971) as a response to King's interference."

St Cecilia received a boost to their bid for chart success when Peter Jones reviewed *Leap Up And Down* in his 'New Singles' page in the *Record Mirror*. Jones stated: 'This is blatantly commercial and could easily make it. Pretty straightforward stuff, at a breakneck tempo, and the frequent use of the word 'knickers' is no hardship. Could click.'

Proctor recalls: "Unfortunately, it labelled us as a sort of dirty picture-postcard band. Although Polydor released the record in April 1971, it was a struggle to get airtime on the radio. The lyrics appear tame now - but back then they caused us a problem."

The opening verse of *Leap Up And Down* was:

> *I once knew a girl who was very, very shy,*
> *Who never ever seemed to catch anyone's eye,*
> *She hit on a theme that made all the boys stare,*
> *She leaped up and down and waved her knickers in the air.*

Bringing his considerable resources to bear, Jonathan King promoted the record relentlessly. When interviewed in *Reveille*, during July of that year, he explained what it was that had captured his imagination. King: 'When I set out on this road, I decided that my own formula for success was to be different. My formula is so different that when producers hear my product - it stands out. They programme it and the housewives who listen have to notice it. 'Knickers' is a perfect example. When I first heard the song it made me sit up - so I guessed it would have the same effect on others. It was ghastly, but different. It had a common, catchy, bouncy, enthusiastic quality - rather like a seaside postcard.' King's views were not shared by a prim Auntie Beeb and DJs such as Tony Blackburn who refused to play a song about knickers on his Radio One show. It therefore came as a surprise to everyone when Jimmy Young eventually decided to give it a spin. Entering the charts at number 49, on June 19, of that year, the record received the following review in the 'New To The charts' column of the *NME*:

> *'That little number advising the ladies to jump about waving their undergarments is*
> *in the NME chart for the first time at number 28. It's another production from that*
> *man behind a million hits, Jonathan King. According to bass player Keith Hancock,*
> *"We did it to shock people. Everywhere we played, we found the audiences in a kind*
> *of coma, hypnotised by the so called progressive groups. When we performed, we*
> *really shook them up and we found we could sell the acetates around the ballrooms.*
> *A copy fell into the hands of Mr. King. And the rest is history, as they say.'*

John Proctor: "The BBC refused to let us perform the song on *Top Of The Pops* - which was a huge blow! A coachload of our fans made the journey from Corby down to London, in order to protest outside the BBC studios - but to no avail." The Beeb would not to be swayed. Mel Cornish, the producer of *TOTP*, stated: "I simply made an editorial choice to leave this number out of the programme, bearing in mind the time it went out and the very young audience we attracted. I just didn't think it was appropriate."

Adrian Rudge (a spokesman for Polydor Records) spoke out against the ban, saying: "The programme is supposed to reflect public taste but if *Top Of The Pops* are not going to use this song, somebody is acting as the arbiter of public taste - namely Mr. Cornish. He is also denying the group their right to appear."

Though generally scorned by the music establishment (and despite St Cecilia's own reservations) *Leap Up And Down* remained in the British charts for over three months that summer - peaking at No 12. Decades later Keith Hancock defended his lyrics, saying: "The word Knickers may have been saucy twenty years ago - but not now. In retrospect, the publicity that we gleaned from the ban worked wonders for the platter's sales, however, we five lads from Corby were distraught that we weren't going to be on the telly!"

They say that out of adversity come fifteen minutes of fame. John Proctor can certainly identify with that. John: "Suddenly St Cecilia was in demand and playing one-nighters all over the country. We supported established acts on the Top Rank circuit such as the Alan Price Set and the Sweet. Of course, all this meant saying goodbye to our day jobs and turning pro. We employed two roadies (Jim Smith - a bass player who had worked with numerous local bands, and Dougie Wilson - a local DJ and former Butlins Redcoat) who drove the equipment to the venues and set it all up while the band followed in Ricky's car. The group made a point of always being at the venue by mid-afternoon - for a sound check - and then we'd retire to the local hostelry for a bevvy or two! That autumn a mini-tour of Scotland gave us some great nights in Hamilton, Hawick, Ayr and Dunfermline. I loved every minute of it - the travelling didn't bother me at all."

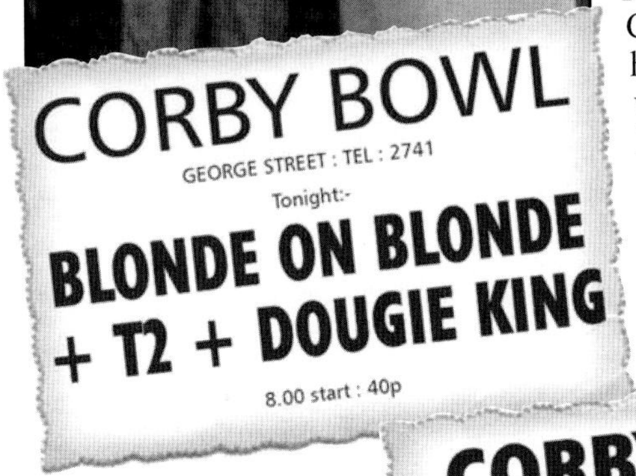

In June 1971 Corby Bowling Alley was taken over by Hamblin Leisure Services Ltd. and renamed the Stardust Club (Arthur Pitcher, the managing director, had been on holiday in Las Vegas and took a liking to the name after visiting the Stardust Casino.)

Music at the club was provided by Dougie King and Tom Haworth's 2001 Discothèque (this time the name being inspired by the film *2001: A Space Odyssey*.) Tom: "We were thirty years ahead of our time!"

Tom would eventually climb the managerial ladder at the Stardust. Dougie continued to make a name for himself as a quick-witted and affable disc jockey. Manager Cliff Smart, spotting King's undoubted potential, quickly recruited the talented DJ to head up the entertainment side of the business. With folk nights and progressive music nights laid on (not to mention his own disco show which was on four nights of the week) Dougie soon had the punters flocking in.

CORBY BOWL
GEORGE STREET : TEL : 2741
Tonight:-
BLONDE ON BLONDE + T2 + DOUGIE KING
8.00 start : 40p

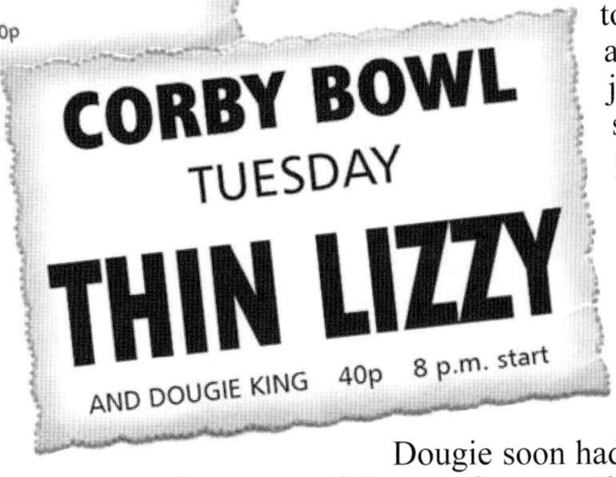

CORBY BOWL
TUESDAY
THIN LIZZY
AND DOUGIE KING   40p   8 p.m. start

Top: Dougie King pictured on his wedding day with bride Marilyn (nee Alderman.) Although he was undoubtedly 'bowled' over by his new wife, domestic bliss failed to quell the young DJ's enthusiasm for his highly successful Tuesday Rock Night at the Corby Bowl.

A revamp of the premises saw the opening in September of its 'Jailhouse Boutique' (which was launched with the enticing offer of a chance to win four free dresses - to be given away during the Dougie King Show.) 'Friends, Romans and Stay-at-Homes, a chance to enjoy yourselves!' promised the Big Man. Another enticing feature of the refurbishment was a Lunch Bar Restaurant which served three course meals for just 30p.

DLT. Dave Lee Travis made the most of his visit to the Stardust Club in Corby. His rider for the night? - scotch pies of course!

An ambitious Cliff Smart predicted that the Bowl would become Northamptonshire's leading entertainment centre and that big names would be appearing on a regular basis. The folk nights proved to be very successful. Peggy Seeger and Ewan McColl guested on the inaugural night in October and were followed by Noel Murphy and Hamish Imlach. Just as successful were the 'Tuesday Rock Nights' at which top groups (including Chicken Shack, Van der Graaf Generator and Medicine Head) appeared. Even Thin Lizzy played the Stardust twelve months prior to hitting the big time with *Whisky In The Jar*. Corby guitarist John Grimley has special memories of that night. John: "I remember that Dougie Martell was the DJ on the night and Phil Lynott asked him if there was anywhere that he could get hold of a plectrum - as he'd lost his.

Dougie suggested to their roadie that I might be able to help. I said 'Sure! But you'll have to give me a lift in your van - I live just up the road.' When we got back to the club I went into the dressing room with four or five different plectrums and found Phil Lynott in the process of rolling a spliff. For a moment he panicked - but the roadie explained that he had nothing to worry about. In the end I sat there and shared it with him!"

Over the years the Stardust also booked several Radio One disc jockeys (costing the club between £100 and £150 a time.) Tom Haworth: "The best one without a doubt was Johnny Walker. I recall Johnny inviting me to join him in a charity game of tenpin bowling. He wasn't that bothered about the money - he just fancied the challenge. He even gave me a fiver tip before he went off at the end of the night. Most of the DJs who came to the club had appeared earlier in the evening at Bailey's night club in Leicester. They would come over to Corby for a quick and easy hour - i.e. without any gear, records or anything. They used our kit. Of course all the consoles were different to those that they normally worked with, therefore I spent half the night sitting beside them and putting the records on for them while they signed autographs and gave away Radio One paraphernalia. Dave Lee Travis was the most miserable. He once turned up in a pink Cadillac De Ville that was twenty feet long and had personalised number plates that read '1 DLT'. He insisted that we post a security guard in the car park to watch over his pride and joy for the duration of his visit. He also demanded Scotch Pies as a rider - he'd obviously been to Corby before!"

With the complex rapidly becoming the county-wide success that Cliff Smart had predicted, in December 1971 (under the banner: 'A new Night Spot - with A Big Scene Atmosphere!) the Exclusive Club opened on the premises. It was the forerunner of what would later become one of Corby's most infamous drinking dens - Shafts. Late night revellers had never had it so good!

July 1971 saw the town of Corby swamped by an estimated 15,000 visitors. This figure included umpteen coach-loads of Glaswegians (on a fortnight's vacation during the annual Glasgow Fair) who spent the first weekend of their holiday, basking in two days of glorious sunshine as they enjoyed Corby's 4th Highland Gathering and Tattoo. Held on the Welfare Club's recreation ground, the event featured pipe bands and highland dancing - which immediately made the visitors feel 'right at hame'. Unfortunately, on the Sunday drama unfolded when a makeshift grandstand collapsed (due to a stanchion giving way at one end of its five-tier construction) causing fifty people to be sent tumbling down onto the grass.

Press coverage of the collapsing spectators' stand at the 1971 Corby Highland Gathering. Miraculously, no one was seriously injured as a result of the incident.

Although only six of them were injured as a consequence, dozens of others were left dazed and in a state of utter confusion. Luckily, representatives of the St John Ambulance Brigade and the Red Cross were already in attendance at the event and were able to reach the scene quickly to offer assistance. Spectator Jim Ogilvie later told of his concerns regarding the robustness of the stand. He said: "When I saw big Tam Elder take his seat I thought to myself - this thing's never gonna last." A co-worker with Tam in the steelwork's Morgan Mill, Mr. Ogilvie turned out to be quite justified in his fears, as Mrs. Elsie Thomas of Station Road (who had been sitting alongside him) appeared to agree that they were not without foundation. She told a newspaper reporter: "When I saw Big Tam getting on as well, I thought to m'sel, - here we go. It was like a boat rocking and then all the planks gave way!"

Speaking on behalf of the St John Ambulance Brigade, a Mr. Farr, commented: "There were bodies lying everywhere - a jumble of people. However, it looked worse than it really was. It was fortunate that athlete Geoff Capes (displaying his strength and setting a new record of over 60 feet in the Shot Putt) and his fellow international, Jim Watt (setting a new record by tossing the 56lb weight to a height of over 14 feet) were performing nearby." His thoughts were echoed by Jim Porter of Wellandvale Road. Jim mused: "Aye, the big fellas were handy - they got their weight behind the rescue effort and soon 'putt' things right!" An official inquiry into the near-disaster later absolved Big Tam of any blame - it revealed that the collapse was caused by a defective fixing bracket.

With rescue efforts disrupting events in the main arena, elsewhere in the grounds the crowds were being entertained by members of Her Majesty's Armed Forces. Teams of army gymnasts showed off their skills on the trampoline, whilst a Royal Artillery motorcycle team also provided a welcome distraction with its marvelous displays of derring-do - including forming a human pyramid and riding through a tunnel of fire. Not all were impressed though. One smart alec piped up: "Watching Jimmy Cramp racing up and down Studfall Avenue on his BSA is more fun." The complainant? Cramp's drinking buddy - Pat McGeechie. (Jimmy Cramp was well known in the town for performing daredevil antics on his motorcycle - earning the British Steel tour guide the sobriquet 'Crasher Cramp'!)

Away from the main arena was a Living and Leisure Exhibition that was packing them in. The British Steel Corporation's own stand claimed to offer something for everyone - 'from tableware to tubes'. Henry Miller from Stanion revealed that after buying a set of salt and pepper pots for his wife Ruby, he'd then treated himself to some RHS (rectangular hollow section) made in the CW (Continuous Weld Plant - where he was a foreman.) "I might make myself a market stall and start selling condiment sets," joked Henry.

Also present at the Highland Gathering were officials from the Corby Development Corporation. They were hoping to use the event as a vehicle for selling some new houses on the recently constructed Lincoln Estate. Offering a £50 discount as an incentive to buy over that weekend, CDC staff were forced to field scurrilous comments that the inducement was only being made available because they couldn't get rid of the houses. (The award-winning housing estate had been the subject of fierce local criticism because of its 'characteristic maze of warren-like alleyways'. Indeed, many on the estate feared that it would inevitably become a haven for drug-takers and layabouts).

With the exception of the collapsing stand fiasco, all had been fun and games at the Welfare Recreation Ground - that is until opportunistic thieves (who had been on the lookout for easy pickings) spoiled the party by stealing three hampers and nine bottles of red wine from a van parked outside the Raven Hotel. "Bang went the picnic," groaned the vans owner, Mrs. Annie Knight. Whoever the thieves were, they obviously had huge appetites as they rounded off their ill-gotten feast by helping themselves to five pork pies from Dewhursts the butchers!

Two weeks later Celtic Football Club announced that they wouldn't be put off by the events at the Recreation Ground. In May they had ordered 37,000 feet of tubular steel from BSC Tubes Division in Corby - to be used in the construction of a massive new grandstand (as part of a £1 million facelift at the club). On hearing the news about the faulty stand, a spokesman for the Glasgow football club said: "We are not worried by the collapse of the grandstand at Corby and have every confidence in the quality, strength and longevity of the tubes that we are buying."

Above: Jim 'the Big Clunk' Smith and partner Lesley Hourd enjoy a trip to the 2003 Reading Festival. Jim's son Darren - a bass player like his father - was performing there that year as a member of Corby heavy metal band Raging Speedhorn. Interestingly, retired schoolteacher Lesley once stepped out with Paul Kossoff of Free. Lesley: "We did date for a couple of months, but ultimately I couldn't put up with his drug-taking and unreliability and was forced to dump him."

Throughout their short career as a 'novelty' pop band St Cecilia enjoyed some unforgettable experiences - e.g. the night at the Belfry golf course near Sutton Coldfield. John Proctor explained: "We were headlining that night - supported by a local rock 'n' roll band. Imagine our surprise when, completely out of the blue, the Move's Roy Wood and Jeff Lynne joined us on stage for our last set. Another high was appearing in many of the teen magazines of the time. We were fortunate enough to have articles and photographs in *Romeo*, *Mirabelle*, *Valentine* and *Jackie* - publications which sold in huge numbers during the 1970s." Keith Hancock: "Fame at last! Looking back, I'm sure that there was more than a little resentment towards us felt by some of the older, more established bands in Corby. Many of them were smarting over our sudden 'leap' to prominence. Although nothing was ever said to me directly, one could sense that certain people were thinking - it should have been me!" John Proctor says that it was around that time that he developed a keen interest in hypnosis. He added that whenever he got the chance he would try out his newly-acquired skills on his fellow band members - sometimes with catastrophic results! John: "Jim Smith was my best subject as I could put him in a trance very easily. One night when we were about to play R.A.F. Alconbury, I put him under while our equipment was being set up. Shortly afterwards he disappeared back into the van and, apparently, the next thing he was aware of was waking up at a set of traffic lights in Peterborough! When he had regained his senses Jim returned to the airbase, grabbed me by the throat and threatened to pulverise me. Of course, everybody else thought it was hilarious!"

Jim Smith was originally born in Finedon, but attended Wellingborough Grammar School and it was while he was a pupil there that he and some schoolmates formed what was to be his first band - the Phantom Five. Their first performance took place at the Lyric Cinema in Wellingborough, where they performed in front of five hundred screaming youngsters. Jim recalls: "The kids from school completely drowned us out. It was just as well really - cos we could barely play a note! As we were still learning, we were having to make it up as we went along!"

Jim's next band (the Felix) consisted of Randall Pybus, Bob Streathers and Malcolm Hart (brother of Barry Hart who played with the Q-Men) who all lived in the Kettering/Burton Latimer area. Jim: "We gained experience by playing regular Saturday and Sunday night gigs at the Ex- Serviceman's Club in Lloyds Road, Corby - along with the Jimmy Scales band (a combo featuring Bill 'Dozy' Clarke on drums, Jim's wife Sandra on piano, sax player Bob Crawford and accordionist Bill Beadie) That was a great education. What characters they were!

Dozy was always ready for a laugh; he'd come out with things like, 'my wife gave me a plate of peas tonight and I mixed some ball-bearings with them - so if I fart, you'd all better duck!' One of his party pieces was to take out his false teeth and drop them into his pint!

Bill was another one who loved the ale. He'd start the set by telling us to 'follow this' and off he'd go on his own. We had to try and catch him up - playing the same thing as best we could. As the night wore on (and he and Dozy got more and more inebriated!) it became a virtually impossible task to stay with them. Although the pair of them could be a real nightmare, the nights were great fun and the club was always packed."

As the 1960s drew to a close, in addition to his work at Nene Valley Caravans, Jim Smith filled his time by 'roadying' for a couple of bands from Kettering. They were Gideon's League and Natural Gas. The latter's drummer, Graham Smith, went on to play for St. Cecilia.

Jim Smith: "When I joined up with St Cecilia I worked as a full time roadie for them - on a wage of £20 per week. Dougie Wilson, the acting sound engineer was in charge of the mixing desk - which had about four knobs to twiddle! - whereas I was mainly involved in repairing anything that broke, i.e. amplifiers, guitar strings etc. The band performed all over the country and would often work four or five nights a week. Our schedule was so hectic that we'd travel to places like Sheffield, Glasgow, Nottingham, Penzance… all in a matter of days! Despite people sneering at them, in reality St Cecilia was a top rate outfit and the group surprised a lot of critics."

Jim went on: "Some people thought that the song wouldn't do them any favours and couldn't believe it when *Leap* raced up the charts, however, the band had hidden depths and were able to cover such material as the Stones' *Honky Tonk Women* and also tracks from the progressive rock band, Yes. The harmonics that they produced on numbers like *Beyond And Before* were brilliant. They'd spend four or five days rehearsing each new song - until they got it exactly right."

Ricky Moss: "The reason why we put in that amount of practice was because people expected you to be able to play really well if you'd had a hit record. They thought you'd be as skilled, musically, as groups like the Marmalade - who'd been at the top for years."

'Maybe pop music is taking itself too seriously', suggested the *Melody Maker* in July. It continued:

> *'If so, the tendency is reflected in record sales. St Cecilia's 'Leap Up And Down' is typical. Its droning lyrics and limp melody have little to commend them, unless in the context of a reaction against the droll complexity and pretension that constitutes the worst of 'progressive' rock. Essentially it's a fun record.'*

Hitchin' A Ride! During the 1960s and 1970s the Volkswagen Type 2 van proved to be a popular mode of transport with pop groups. Unfortunately, once their equipment had been loaded there wasn't much room left inside. It would appear from this photograph of Kettering band Felix that there were some unlucky band members who were occasionally obliged to travel alfresco! Pictured L-R: Cats on a hot tin roof - Randall Pybus, Malcolm Hart and Jim Smith. Standing: Bob Streathers 'pawses' for thought before taking the wheel.

Pictured: In 2003 Bill Beadie - a true Corby 'legend' - demonstrates his accordion skills at a family gathering attended by L-R: Son Robert, Bill, friends Joe, Dylan and Diane, plus granddaughter Eva. Bill (who came to Corby in 1955 and married here in 1957) was a popular entertainer in the local pubs and clubs up until the year 2006. He says that these days he spends most of his time in the company of his extensive family of 6 children, 11 grandchildren and 1 great-granddaughter.

John Proctor: "We didn't pretend to be great musicians - or singers for that matter. I'd even flunked an audition for Gideons League, having failed to impress Jimmy Pollock with my attempts at *You've Lost That Lovin' Feeling*. With hindsight that was a good thing though - in the absence of a singer who could carry a song, we concentrated instead on becoming a harmony group and would spend hours practicing. It was hard work but the end result was that we became what I considered to be one of the best harmony groups around. Funny thing is, if we'd had a lead singer like Mick Quinn or Gideon, we probably wouldn't have taken off."

In his review of the band's performance at Barberella's in Birmingham, *Melody Maker* columnist Denis Deatheridge, perhaps summed up the feelings of the majority of the entertainment media towards the band.

He wrote:

> *'They didn't exactly get everybody up waving their knickers around in the air but they succeeded in making the title of their current hit seem like something from a Sunday school song book compared with some of their material. 'The Girls From Roedean' was introduced by lead singer Les Smith as "a filth spot". By the time they'd got through this drawn-out routine featuring drummer Graham Smith in drag, no one*

was likely to dispute the accuracy of this description. It all seemed innocent enough at the start as pianist Ricky Moss, top hat aloft, led the band into 'Nutrocker'. They also put across 'Delta Lady', 'No Matter What', 'Joy To The World', and 'Travelin Band' with a healthy vitality. Perhaps they should have saved the smut for the next stag do!'

Leap Up And Down was one of that summer's most popular records and was being played everywhere, despite being denied an airing on British TV and Radio - St. Cecilia would have to wait another fourteen years for that privilege. (In 1985 they were invited to take part in a BBC television production called *The Time Of Your Life*, hosted by Noel Edmonds, which was similar in format to the once popular *All Our Yesterdays*. John Proctor: "The show's producer contacted me and explained that they were going to showcase the year 1971 and wanted to know if it would be possible to reunite the band for a one-off performance. With the exception of Ricky Moss - who was unavailable - we found ourselves sharing a bill with round-the-world sailor Chay Blyth and former Prime Minister Ted Heath. Although none of us wanted to get together as a band and go back out on the road in an attempt to relive past glories, there was one good thing that came out of it - Graham and Keith formed a duo called the Wright Price and made a record entitled *Come On Down*.")

The fifth Corby Arts Festival got under way on Saturday, July, 17. With local MP Sir Geoffrey De Frietas (resplendent in a pinstriped suit) ascending the Festival Hall stage, crashing some cymbals and then proceeding to deliver the opening address. As the audience waited patiently for the appearance on stage of the famous Tamla Motown star Jimmy Ruffin, followed by Ashton, Gardner and Dyke (who had just had a hit with *Resurrection Shuffle*) and a pop group called Madrigal, Sir Geoffrey attempted to amuse them with an impromptu hip shaking jig. He told the baffled onlookers: "I'm supposed to do a short song and dance routine, however, as I can't sing, a wee dance will have to do!" Applause rippled around the hall as he 'boogied-on-down' - the volume increasing substantially when he promised: "This festival is going to be the best ever, but next year will be even better still - because that's the spirit of Corby!"

Appearing in the Ashton, Gardner and Dyke line-up was Howie Casey - the man whom Ricky Dodd had replaced in the Roy Young band. Many years later Howie had this to say of the late Ricky: "He was a lovely guy and a great sax player. It was so sad when he died - he was one of the guys from those days who became a victim of the substance. I've seen so many go before their time because of drugs. I managed to stay clear of that side of things - even during the Hamburg days with the Seniors, Kingsize Taylor and the Beatles. I was lucky.

I remember playing in Corby with Tony Ashton's band - at the time of *Resurrection Shuffle*. It was basically Roy Young's brass section thrown together for a few shows - in order to cash in on the success of the record. It was a strange gig. I remember us being introduced to the mayor and his wife, who were very polite and who had laid on a huge buffet for us. I can also remember thinking - how come there are so many Scottish accents in this town? I checked it out later and discovered about the steelworks and the immigrant thing in the 1930s. I was fascinated because in a lot of ways Corby seemed reminiscent of Liverpool."

The only disappointment on the opening night of the festival was when Radio One DJ Johnny Walker failed to turn up. Jimmy Ruffin (whose *What Becomes Of The Brokenhearted* proved a massive hit) excited the female members of the audience enough for them to race down to the stage and try to touch him. Backstage a breathless Jimmy espoused: "The people here are beautiful - really responsive. I feel we had something going."

Seventy-two-year-old Louise Page (aka Corby's own songwriting granny) also had something going. Mrs. Page from Deene announced that she was learning to play the guitar. She said: "I'm forming a new group called Granny's People which will be made up of senior citizens from the town. In addition to writing most of our material, I will also play lead guitar. Our first performance is scheduled to take place at the Ernest Wright House in Corby."

Death of talented musician

A MUSICIAN who once shared a stage with Jimi Hendrix and Chuck Berry has died aged 57.

Ricky Dodd died on Sunday at Blackpool Lady Victoria Hospital following a long illness. Born and raised in Corby he became well known in the area during the 1960s and 1970s for his talent for jazz music.

While many of his friends were listening to the Beatles, Mr Dodd's love of jazz lead him to play the saxophone

During his career he also played with the Roy Young band and appeared at Ronnie Scott's jazz club in Soho, London, when he was only 15.

He was also an accomplished session player counting Dave Edmunds and Bill Wyman among his credits.

Although Mr Dodd moved to Fleetwood, near Blackpool five years ago, he had many friends in Corby.

Corrie Grey, of Epsom Walk, said she would miss Mr Dodd's friendship.

"He was a fantastic musician, but there was much more to him than that," she said. "He was a lovely person. A lovely soul."

Mr Dodd was following a family tradition for music, as his father Fred had

■ TALENTED – saxophonist Ricky Dodd played with the legendary Jimi Hendrix, right

been a professional drummer.

Clive Smith, of Teesdale Road, Corby, said: "Rick's death came as a great shock even though he had suffered with ill health for the last few years.

"I was in regular contact with him and like all his friends, am deeply saddened that he's gone.

"Rick was a really wonderful person with a great sense of humour, and a true local legend."

Mr Dodd's funeral will be held today at Carleton crematorium, near Blackpool.

Saxophonist Ricky Dodd. After his musical career took off Ricky found it difficult to settle again in his home town. Highly respected (particularly in jazz circles) he delighted audiences all over Europe, and although a troubled man, he never gave up fighting his personal demons right up until the end. (Ricky died in May 2006 at Fleetwood near Blackpool).

Louise's last song *Walking Home Together* had received a glowing response from no less a music critic than former Prime Minister Harold Wilson. Louise proudly declared: "It's the second song that I've sent to Harold and his wife Mary - the first was *Prayer Of Peace*". She added: "I received a letter of thanks in which they both said that they had enjoyed the tune." Louise had once sent a copy of one of her songs to the American astronaut and first man on the moon, Neil Armstrong. It seems that Granny Page was once more aiming for the stars.

Seen warming up for a gig at Ernest Wright House is multi-talented local grandmother Mrs. Louise Page. Senior citizen Mrs. Page looked more than happy to demonstrate her 'wicked guitar chops' for the photographer that day. (What's the betting that she was yet another proud owner of Bert Weedon's 'Play In A Day'?)

When the English Sinfonia Orchestra took to the stage (conducted by former Corby Grammar School teacher Neville Dilkes) it was hoped that after seven days filled with music and drama, the festival would go out with a bang. Unfortunately, because the Festival Hall was only a third full, the event didn't so much explode - as fizzle out like a damp squib!

In an effort to boost attendance figures, the orchestra's repertoire had been selected with great care and treats such as *Beethoven's Fifth Symphony* (arguably the most famous piece of music in the classical firmament) and *Grieg's Piano Concerto in A minor* had been included. The organisers had anticipated their hand-picked programme of popular classical fare would appeal to Corby's musical hierarchy and thereby maximise their chances of attracting a substantial audience. Regrettably, box office receipts did not bear out their reasoning.

The Sinfonia began with a lightweight opener, Bizet's suite *'Jeux d'Enfants'*, and was followed by Grieg's *Piano Concerto*. After the interval came Elgar's *Serenade For Strings* - a piece in which Ronald Thomas and his fellow violinists displayed 'a rich range of texture and an evenness of tone' (even if it failed to strike a personal chord with the music critic from the *Corby Leader*!)

At a later date, when they'd had sufficient time to review the over-all success of the festival, the organising committee made it known that the future inclusion of the symphonic element was in doubt and would henceforth come under intense scrutiny by those in authority. It was a depressing end to what should have been Corby's cultural masterpiece.

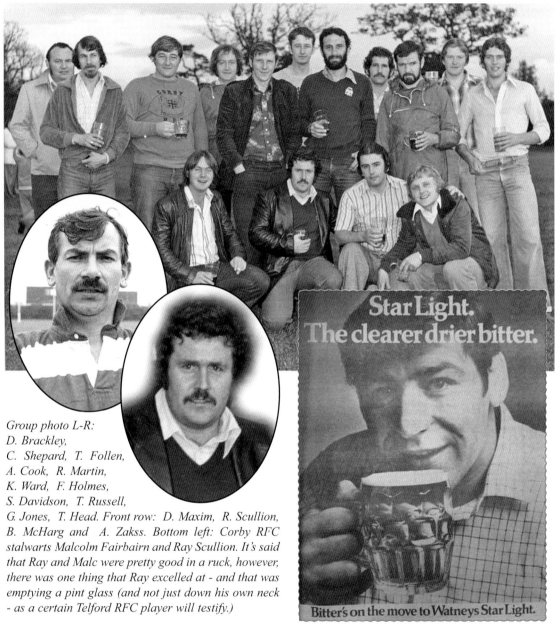

Group photo L-R:
D. Brackley,
C. Shepard, T. Follen,
A. Cook, R. Martin,
K. Ward, F. Holmes,
S. Davidson, T. Russell,
G. Jones, T. Head. Front row: D. Maxim, R. Scullion,
B. McHarg and A. Zakss. Bottom left: Corby RFC
stalwarts Malcolm Fairbairn and Ray Scullion. It's said
that Ray and Malc were pretty good in a ruck, however,
there was one thing that Ray excelled at - and that was
emptying a pint glass (and not just down his own neck
- as a certain Telford RFC player will testify.)

Star Light.
The clearer drier bitter.

Bitter's on the move to Watneys Star Light.

According to the *Corby Leader* music critic, the lack of support for the ESO may have been due to its relative youth (the orchestra had only been in existence ten years.) Those who came off worst from the musical non-event were the thirty small firms constituting the Corby Industrial Group. They had been persuaded to back the concert to the tune of several hundred pounds - and lost the lot!

In 2010 local postman William Easton (a Rangers supporter, Elgar fan and budding historian) recalled the night of the concert. He said: "I attended all of the Corby Arts Festival events and have to say that they included some great nights of blues, jazz and folk music, however, my favourites were always the classical evenings. They often featured the Halle Orchestra. It was most disheartening when the

English Sinfonia's performance of 1971 failed to capture the imagination of the public. Personally, I'm a big fan of Elgar and Grieg. Not many people are aware that the latter is of Scottish descent - his great-grandfather fled Scotland after the Battle of Culloden to settle in Norway. For all I know, he may even be a relative of the former 'Gers captain, Big John Grieg. If they were here today, the Arts Festival organising committee would no doubt be saying: "If only William's enthusiasm could have been shared by more of his townsfolk!"

Apart from laying claim to a crack darts team in the 1950s, in the decade that followed, the Open Hearth pub had become nothing more than an afterthought for passing trade. It came as a surprise to many when during the summer of 1971 all that changed and it became the central point of activity for all that was 'happening' in Corby.

Aided by Corby Rugby Football Club (which had relocated its headquarters from the White Hart) Alan Smith, the landlord of the Hearth, had transformed the Watneys' alehouse into the busiest pub in town. As he himself had been a founding member of the Rugby Club and an established front-row player since 1958, Alan always extended a welcome to visiting teams after a game.

The visitors not only added colour to the evenings, but, more often than not, were keen to join in with the customary singsongs, party games and high jinks. A favourite on these occasions was the game of Dam Busters - in which contestants (with a 10p coin wedged between their buttocks) would attempt to manoeuvre themselves over a series of hurdles in order to reach the winning post and drop the coin into a pint of beer! All this was to the accompaniment of three dozen watching rugby players humming the well-known theme tune to the film *The Dam Busters*.

From time to time things got out of hand - as happened one Easter Monday when a side from Telford visited the pub. The atmosphere turned sour when Ray Scullion, (Corby RFC's court jester) poured a pint of Star Light over an opponent's head. On reflection, maybe it wasn't Ray's clowning around that caused the Telford player to take umbrage - perhaps it was the taste of a very flat and unappetising pint of Watneys!

Tom Black (or 'Big Tam' as he was more widely known) was a mountain of a man who stood 6ft. 6ins. tall, weighed 15st. and sported a mane of jet black hair - styled in the type of carefully coiffured D.A. that was favoured by the Teddy Boys of the 1950s. In fact he bore more than a passing resemblance to the cartoon character Bluto (Popeye's old adversary.) After being asked to stay away from the Pluto - where he'd developed a habit of upsetting people - Tam became a regular in the bar at the Open Hearth. The big fellow was fond of a game of 'arrows' and became accustomed to demanding unrestricted access to the dartboard - which, on account of his stature was rarely denied him! Wally Maguire remembers one night at the Pluto when he and his pal Mick Boyle were warming up for an Evening Telegraph Cup match in which they were due to partner each other. He says: "Big Tam walked in, got himself a pint from the bar and sat down near the dartboard. After a minute or two he began complaining that we were hogging the board, so we explained that we had an important game coming up that night and needed all the practice that we could get. Before we realised what was happening, Tam had got up on his very large feet, grabbed the dartboard and threw it straight out of the window. 'If I can't play, then nobody's playing!' he growled."

Even when Tam found himself a new watering hole - things didn't always run smoothly! One night when he was finishing off a game of darts whilst waiting for a taxi to arrive, he shouted over to the barman: "Hey Graham, stick a couple of pies in the microwave for me to take away." Although Graham Reilly heard the order, he completely forgot about it as he was busy pulling pints and engaging in friendly banter with the other regulars - that is until the taxi turned up and Big Tam yelled, "Where's my pies Reilly?" Stifling a giggle, quick-thinking Graham pulled a couple of frozen chicken pies out of a box and stuffed them into a bag. Tam grabbed them, flew out of the door and disappeared into the taxi. The next night an extremely irate Tam burst through the bar door to confront Graham. As he chased the startled bartender through to the Smoke Room he roared: "Reilly, you swine! Those pies nearly broke my bloody jaw. You owe me for a new set of false teeth!" Fortunately for Graham the big man later accepted his apology.

The Nags Head in Corby: Seen to the right is the entrance to the Stagecoach Lounge. Back in 1973 the new lounge guaranteed excitement and entertainment from the many talented performers who passed through its doors. Licencees Jimmy and Ann Tibbs promised 'a warm welcome and wholesome food' to accompany them.

'Time stands still for no man' as the old adage goes, and no matter how successful Alan Smith had been as the landlord of the Open Hearth, the brewery was still not satisfied. Despite tripling the takings since his arrival at the pub in late 1967, Alan found himself under considerably pressure to agree to plans for an extension to the Lounge - with the aim of making room for more people on disco nights. Once he had given the go ahead for building work to begin, the pub had to be closed temporarily - causing a knock-on effect for Bip Wetherell (i.e. his 'take' was affected.) This prompted the young DJ to start up another disco in the Shire Horse - marking yet another step up the entrepreneurial ladder and helping to lay the foundations for what would become his locally renowned leisure business. The Nags Head in the

WATNEYS

OPEN AT LAST!
The 'New Look'
NAGS HEAD in
High Street, Corby

incorporating The Stagecoach, an enlarged music lounge featuring

★ Live Entertainment ★ Discos ★ Country and Western
★ Facilities for private parties and weddings, etc.

PLUS — The NAGS BAR. Yes, this is the re-decorated, re-furnished public bar where wholesome hot and cold pub grub lunches will be served at the bar.

There's always a warm welcome from Jimmy and Anne Tibbs.

A Watney Mann House

109

old village was to be his next venue. Given a free rein by Jim Tibbs (the licensee) and with three discos on the go (not to mention his participation in Granite - an 'eight piece sound explosion' based on the American outfit Blood, Sweat and Tears) Mr. Bip was suddenly a man very much in a hurry! Granite was in fact an amalgam of former Marylanders' jazzmen (Jake Pressley, Ron and Dick Kirk) added to the talent of several other local musicians - i.e. Bob Gowen, Bob Grimley, Jack Murphy and Bip himself. The band came into being following Pressley's determination to sculpt his very own jazz/rock fusion, after hearing and being inspired by Chicago's *25 or 6 to 4* (a track which Bip often played down the Nags.)

When Jake first sounded out Wetherell, he discovered that he too was enthusiastic about such a project, so without further ado they quickly assembled a band and hit the road. Jake: "Bip had many talents. Apart from his organisational skills, playing the guitar and the keyboards, he also fancied himself as a songwriter. We actually made a series of demos of his songs, however, he then wanted us to play them at the gigs - and they were awful!"

Bob Gowen: "Jake was regarded as the band's leader and he proved to be just that. We were about to go on stage one night at RAF Lakenheath when the management informed us that the bar was closing for the night. Jake promptly told them that if the bar was to shut then that would be the end of the show - insisting (quite rightly) that when we'd finished our spot we would want a drink. Unfortunately, the Yanks wouldn't reconsider - so we packed up and came home!"

Brothers Stuart and Jim Irvine (who later would become well known with Alias John Smith and Scenestealer) recorded one of Bip's songs at Derek Tompkins' studio in Wellingborough. It was called *Funky Funky Party*. When Bip played it to Mick Harper, the latter helped him to get in touch with Ray Connolly - a well-known music columnist who had worked with the Beatles and who at that point in time was managing a band called Gonzales. Bip: "Instead of my record, Ray decided to release a number called *Haven't Stopped Dancing*. It went straight to the top of the charts. That was that - *Funky* was scuppered and became another of my celebrated near misses!"

Alias Smith and Jones aka Dennis Priddy and Geoff Williams.

Nowadays Jim Tibbs runs a successful holiday homes business in Florida. Recalling his days as the landlord of the Nags Head, he said: "After moving from the Spittlemore (a small corner-pub in Coventry) in order to come to Corby, in 1971 my first wife, Anne Culpin and I took over the Nags from Jumbo Macallian. Jumbo was a nice Irish guy who ran the pub with an iron fist - albeit in a velvet glove! That was the only way in those days! After that Jumbo moved to the Candle and once more deployed the iron fist - only this time minus the glove!

Meanwhile, back at the Nags, Anne and I decided to put on some music. We tried everything from disco to live groups. This was in the Assembly Rooms, as they were called. The old lounge at the back was never used. We did have a television room (until someone stole the TV!) which later became the entrance to the revamped lounge - Stagecoach.

There were a number of local groups and societies that regularly used the Nags - such as the Buffs. The Royal and Ancient Order of Buffalo's (or as jazz singer George Melly once said 'that mysterious proletarian version of the Freemasons') used to hold their meetings and dances there. The German and Austrian Club did likewise. Around this time, Hugh Murphy joined me behind the bar. Hugh and I had worked together in the Detail packing department of the tubeworks. He had also stood as best man at my wedding. We worked together for quite some time at the Nags and then Hugh left to become head barman at the Civic Centre - where he remained for many fruitful years.

Michelle and Paul (our children) were both born at the Nags Head. It was nothing for them to be lying in their carrycot - behind the bar of the old function room! I think they liked the disco as it seemed to put them to sleep. I remember once trying to promote a dance on Thursday nights and booking a band from Leicester - called Choice. Although they played every Thursday for quite some time, I didn't really feel that it was working out and so we parted company. A few months later they changed their name to Showaddywaddy and had a hit single shortly afterwards. Story of my life!"

Lykes of Witch. L-R: Barry Monk, Corrie Gillies, Tony Paul and Paul Willis plus unknown saxophonist. Former band members have no recollection of the mystery musician - in fact no one can remember a saxophone player ever having featured in the band. Is this a case of collective memory loss, or is the guy in the photo a ghostly apparition (the lykes of witch they will never meet again - or will they?)

Appearing at Corby Civic in August 1971 were the Groundhogs. Led by 'blues' man Tony McPhee and with a best-selling album, entitled *Thank Christ For The Bomb*, this unit of British progressive rock merchants were considered at the time to be one of the hottest bands around.

The audience was left more than a little disgruntled, however, when the Hogs wound up their set after barely an hour. Word soon got round that the concert had been curtailed because the support act (a band called Trapeze) had failed to turn up. Matters took a turn for the worse when a brief apology, delivered by a spokesman for the Civic, was met with a round of boos. Three-hundred belligerent, foot-stomping concertgoers were not in the mood to be short-changed and when their demands for an encore were rebuffed by management, the mood inside the hall became even more menacing. Chants of 'We want our money back!' began to reverberate around the room. Meanwhile the Hogs, convinced that their gear would be put at risk if things got out of hand, decided to remain on stage. An official pleaded for calm and commonsense and requested that people 'please leave the building - the show is over.' This was greeted with a torrent of abusive language and the foot-stamping grew louder.

Eventually the police were called and an officer appeared on stage to order everybody out of the hall. Unfortunately, he was soon told where to go! When one indignant fan climbed up on stage to challenge him, the unsympathetic copper simply grabbed hold of the interloper and tried to push him back into the crowd. The officer's rough-handling of the situation only served to further incite what was fast becoming an angry mob (they were threatening to take matters into their own hands if he didn't let go of his victim!) Luckily, in the end the voice of reason prevailed and the policeman complied with their demands. Then, with the excitement over, the crowd made their way out into George Street and headed for the various town centre pubs - where they regaled each other with their tales of bravado or simply reflected on the dramatic end to what should have been a fantastic gig.

Although 'the Tank' was an apt choice of nickname for Ron Atkinson in his days as a football player, he was also known as 'Bojangles' because of his penchant for ostentatious jewellery and his flamboyant sense of dress.

The events of the night most definitely shaped the opinion of one man - Tony McPhee never visited the town again!

Another musical act to appear at the Civic Centre that year was Kenny Ball and his Jazzmen - who were met with rapturous applause at the end of the show. Over in Wellingborough the Johnny Dankworth Quintet blew them away at the Jazz on the Rails Club (which was housed inside the British Rail Working Men's Club.) It was a busy venue and regularly attracted the best of that particular genre. In contrast Johnny Duncan and the Blue Grass Boys performed at the club the following week and were ably supported by Corby's Ray and Ann Brett. Also holding their own in this illustrious company was a zany Northampton outfit called Horace M. Smith and his Jubilee Serenaders. A familiar act at the Open Hearth, their home-grown brand of Bonzo Dog Do Da Band - type humour went down a treat with the Corby clientele.

In November a combo by the name of Alias Smith and Jones comprised of (ex-Size Seven/Cascade guitarist Dennis Priddy and ex-Crusaders vocalist Geoff Williams) made their debut before a packed audience in the new cabaret lounge at the Open Hearth. Their name had been taken from the popular TV series based on the film *Butch Cassidy and the Sundance Kid* - featuring Paul Newman and Robert Redford. That night a highly polished performance from the Corby duo gave Prohibition (the folk/bluegrass band from Bedford who were the main act of the evening) something to live up to. Rising to the challenge, the headline act thrilled the crowd - providing a terrific start to Alan Smith's new venture. The Hearth landlord was delighted by the way in which his customers had responded and promised that there was a lot more to come. Smith was true to his word and over the next four years the Open Hearth became synonymous with first-rate live entertainment and gave punters who were unable to travel to Bailey's (a well-known nightclub in Leicester) the chance to enjoy an evening's cabaret on their own doorstep.

Former Manchester United player Alex Dawson signs for Corby Town FC - witnessed by the club's chairman, John Singlehurst (left) and vice chairman Morris Lee.

Despite the opportunities provided by pubs like the Open Hearth, semi-professional entertainers relied mainly on local workingmen's clubs for the bulk of their work. A typical weekend might see the 'Works' in Kettering boast Bobby Leroy and his Rock and Roll Revival on a Friday night, and Mr. Toad at the piano on Sunday night, whilst Nicky ('England's Banjo Champion') would be guesting at Raunds Working Men's Club.

One of the busiest bands of the year was the Lykes of Witch. Enticing the punters with their promise of 'an eerie night with...' they appeared alongside the famous Hillsiders from Liverpool, at a Wagon Wheel Country Music Club 'do' in Wellingborough. A week later they were performing at the Raven in Corby. This time it was as part of a programme advertised as: 'Tonight at the Pit - the listen with Plop Show - starring the fantastic, lovable, Plop!' (Plop being the resident DJ - Pete Robb).

In October Mungo Jerry came to Corby Civic Centre. Advance publicity described them as playing 'blues, rock and skiffle in a carefree manner'. The next big name to appear there was Matt Munro on November 7. Local fan, Willie Byers, described Munro as 'the cream of British crooners'.

In 1971 struggling Kettering Town Football Club appointed Ron Atkinson as their new player-manager. Ron, aged thirty-two, had previously engineered lowly Oxford United's promotion into the Football League and his acceptance of a three-year contract with the Poppies was viewed by observers of the game as a route to even greater managerial success for him. Back then few would have predicted that this flamboyant character would eventually manage Manchester United, Atletico Madrid and other world-famous football clubs.

THAMES TELEVISION LIMITED
'OPPORTUNITY KNOCKS"

YOU ARE INVITED TO ATTEND AN AUDITION AT.

The Royal Angus Hotel, St. Chad's Ringway,
Birmingham 4.

ON SUNDAY 27th JUNE 1971   AT...2.00 p.m.......

Please bring this card with you.
If you require our pianist to play for you, it is
essential that you bring copies of your music with
you. Your act must not be longer than three minutes.

We look forward to seeing you.

                                    ROY MAYOH
                                    Producer/Director
Please notify Thames Television, Teddington, Middx.
(telephone 977-3252) if unable to attend, quoting
above date and time.

Billy Mathieson, who was the drummer for Sharon and the Strangers, says that this page from his scrapbook reminds him of an 'opportunity missed' because he can't recall ever having attended an audition for Hughie Green's popular ITV talent show. Derek Cowie (one who does remember the event) says: "We were on the same set of auditions as two guys who were called the 'Duelling Duo'. Although their act was really nothing more than a bit of straightforward swordplay between the two men - they made it on to the show. Maybe if we'd spun a few plates or did a few bird impressions whilst trying to escape from a block of ice, Hughie might have put us through to the next round!" L-R: Jimmy Gourlay, Maureen Gourlay, Billy Mathieson and Derek Cowie.

'Big Ron' or 'Bojangles' as he was affectionately known, would become one of television's best loved soccer pundits. He was famous for his idiosyncratic way with words (often referred to as Ronisms or Ronglish) however, this would ultimately land him in hot water with the media and in April 2004 led to a very public fall from grace over a perceived racist remark.

Corby Town F.C. pulled off the 'signing of the summer' by recruiting former Manchester United and Preston North End centre forward, Alex Dawson. The new signing made an immediate impression on the clubs supporters by flattening Kettering Town's former West Ham United goalkeeper, Colin Mackleworth, in the first few minutes of a game at Rockingham Road. Understandably, fans of the Poppies were outraged to see Dawson standing with arms outstretched (in a gesture of feigned innocence) whilst listening to the referee reading him the riot act. The Black Prince had arrived!

Notwithstanding the arrival of the new player, all was not well at Steelmen H.Q. and a humiliating defeat by Irthlingborough Diamonds (in the First Qualifying Round of the F.A. Cup) brought things very much to a head. After a game played in front of a very disappointing home crowd of five hundred and sixty six people, supporters gathered to demand the resignation of Chairman John Singlehurst, and the immediate sacking of manager Derek Race. Norman Cameron, the chairman of the supporters' club, was scathing when he said: "There has to be a reappraisal, we can't just keep pumping money into the football club. The manager and directors are destroying the club!"

Dawson, the son of a Grimsby trawlerman, had been a professional football player at United since May 1957. One of the famous 'Busby Babes', he was once described by a sportswriter as 'the Red Devils' bull-necked battering ram'. Fortunately for Alex, he was not selected for that fateful European Cup tie in Belgrade - from which so many of his team mates were never to return. On a happier note, Alex went on to create footballing history by entering the record books as the last player to score a hat-trick in an F.A. Cup semi-final - a feat which (at the time of writing in 2010) has remained unchallenged for over half a century.

His achievement dates back to a 1958 fixture which saw Manchester United play Fulham in an FA Cup semi-final replay at Highbury (just seven weeks after the Munich tragedy.) The whole of the country, it seemed, was willing the decimated Manchester club to make it to Wembley. In the aftermath of Munich, Alex Dawson became a first-team regular and the eighteen-year-old scored against Sheffield Wednesday in the famous Cup victory that took place immediately after the disaster. Then came his record-breaking hat-trick in the semi-final against Fulham.

Now in his seventies, Alex (who lives in Rothwell) remembers: "Highbury was just a mass of thick mud that day and that was just the way I liked it! It was a bit misty too. I scored with a header, a left-footer and then finally a right-footer. The best of the three goals was the first one - a diving header. Although no one has scored a hat-trick in a semi-final since that day - a couple of players have come close.

After we'd beaten Fulham, we went on to play Bolton Wanderers in the F.A. Cup Final at Wembley. In that match I played on the right wing against Bolton's left back, Tommy Banks. I was told that he said: 'You can't put that little baby in to play against me!' Alas there was to be no fairy tale ending to what had been a traumatic season for United as Bolton won the game 2-0 after two controversial goals from Nat Lofthouse.

Dawson's best spell for the Red Devils would come during the 1960-61 season (when he notched twenty goals in thirty-four matches) however, the arrival of David Herd signalled that the Black Prince's days at Old Trafford were numbered. He signed for Preston North End and featured in their F.A. Cup Final side of 1964, then later went on to play for Bury, Brighton and Brentford. Alex ended his footballing career by playing for the Steelmen at Occupation Road.

Corby Town F.C.'s on-field reputation came under fire in 1971 following a Midland Floodlit Cup tie in which they entertained (and were defeated by) Nuneaton Borough. Trouble flared when fifty Steelmen supporters invaded the pitch during the game and forced the referee to bring proceedings to a temporary halt. David Pleat, Nuneaton's player/manager, was far from amused. He complained

Pictured: Corby's preferred mode of transport - the black cab. The ubiquitous Hackney cab was often to be seen cruising 'tree-lined boulevards' - or in this instance Occupation Road. Its route in this particular photograph takes the cab past Charles's off-licence (popular purveyors of Liquorice Wood - or Spanish Wood as it was also known.) The shop was the place where schoolkids could buy a quarter of 'Kay-lie' (phonetic spelling) or, if they were older, their daily 'fix' of a single woodbine cigarette. Footloose teenagers would then pop along the way to Martin's chip shop/café to listen to the jukebox, or take a leisurely stroll down Occupation Road to Tipaldi's on nearby Rockingham Road.

afterwards: "It was a disgrace! The Corby supporters were disgusting throughout the match - chanting obscenities at our players! I have some brave men in my team but even they were desperate to see the end of the game. It was so bad that I felt like taking my players off and giving Corby the points. To make matters worse, £60 worth of damage was also done to our coach. I intend to lodge a complaint because I fear for other teams having to come here." In defence of his supporters, Morris Lee (the newly-elected chairman of Corby Town) denied that there were any problems. He claimed: "Mr. Pleat has blown this up out of all proportion!"

Overreaction was also a criticism that could have been levelled that year at FIFA (football's world governing body) for issuing a worldwide ban on the signing of local amateur player Crawford Potter. Having taken a three year sabbatical in the Australian state of New South Wales (where he had been playing for a side called Corinthians) on his return home Potter had hoped to continue his career with Corby Gainsborough. Rightly or wrongly, however, the Australian side was under the impression that they were entitled to a fee for his transfer. "Outrageous!" was the response from Robin Richardson, the manager of Gainsborough, who pointed out that the Corby side were precluded from entering into transfer situations because of their strictly amateur status. Unfortunately, it transpired that Corinthians had the backing of the Australian authorities - who absolutely refused to issue the necessary international clearance certificate. That being the case, FIFA insisted that they had no option but to sanction the worldwide ban on Potter, and to that purpose, informed all football associations that 'under no circumstances should Crawford Potter be allowed to play'. There the matter rested for several months.

In May, only five days after clinching the League championship at White Hart Lane (when they beat their North London rivals Tottenham Hotspur) Arsenal Football Club completed the double with a 2-1 win over Bill Shankly's Liverpool, in the F.A. Cup Final at Wembley. They were only the second team in the 20th century to achieve this.
Another of Arsenal's big London rivals was Chelsea. The Stamford Bridge side (whose line-up included Peter Osgood, Ron Harris and Charlie Cooke) gave the capital something else to shout about when they beat Real Madrid 2-1 in the European Cup Winners Cup Final in Athens.
Looking back over the year's events, although 1971 had begun tragically with the Ibrox Stadium disaster, in the aftermath Corby's footballing community put their individual allegiances aside to form the joint Rangers & Celtic Fund Raising Committee. The initiative saw Catholic and Protestant football fans joining ranks in an effort to raise money for the families of the dead and of the injured.
In May the citizens of Corby had seen the appointment of the town's first dog catcher - which happened to coincide with the live appearance at the Nags Head of the group named Ken Dodd's Dad's Dog's Dead. Another first was the placement in the local newspapers of advertisements for taxis - from firms looking to rustle up trade in the economic downturn. (This was in a place where the majority of people had become more accustomed to jumping into a taxi than to waiting for the bus!) Visitors to the town were invariably surprised to discover such widespread use of this mode of transport, however, even the townsfolk themselves would have been bemused to learn that statistically Corby boasted more taxis per head of population than any other conurbation in Europe!

Above: Bob the dog (owned by Margaret Wilson of Westfields Road) proves to the rest of the neighbourhood hounds that he was no 'feartie bum'! Although the swings, sand pit and slide are long since gone (as are the steelworks in the background), it's said that on a warm summer's evening faint echoes of Bob's excited bark, as he descended his favourite slide, can still be heard in that part of the Wessie..

Chapter Three 1972
Communication Breakdown

As the 1970s wore on it became apparent that the emergence of the mobile discothèque onto the local pub and entertainment scene, was slowly but surely sounding the death knell for traditional acts such as the guy playing the 'old Joanna' on a Saturday night (and most likely murdering a good tune like *I Belong Tae Glasgae* into the bargain!)

As discos flourished, many of those bands who were playing in order to make a few extra pounds (or even to carve out a career for themselves in the business) became increasingly disenchanted. Indeed it seemed that live music was in danger of disappearing altogether from the average public house. A climate existed where there were just as many young lads harbouring aspirations of 'making it' as a disc jockey as there were those who dreamed of playing guitar with their favourite band. Furthermore, their heroes were just as likely to be Noel Edmonds, John Peel (or even local DJ Dennis Taylor) as they were to be Eric Clapton and co. Dave Irving was inspired by Dennis after noticing the T-Shirt that he was wearing at a wedding reception - it bore the slogan 'Dennis Taylor Star of TV' emblazoned across the chest. When an impressed Dave quizzed Dennis about his TV appearance, Taylor replied with typical wit: "My mother spotted me in the crowd on *Match Of The Day*!"

The Sunday night disco was becoming increasingly popular. Young people who were fed up of listening to *Songs Of Praise* and to Harry Secombe belting out gloomy hymns, lounged in their armchairs as they waited restlessly for the pubs to open at 7 o'clock. Jam-packed every week with sweaty and excited punters, Sunday nights at the Open Hearth absolutely 'rocked'. It was a place where Slade's *Take Me Bak 'Ome* thundered, Clapton's *Layla* cooled it a little and then Bowie's *Gene Jeanie* revved it up again. They were exhilarating times for a generation liberated by low unemployment and regular wages - a generation who swilled down Snakebites, Carlsberg Hof and pints of Brown and Mild.

Corby's Sealed Beams Club, Rangers Club and Silver Band Club (which still gave houseroom to live bands but tended to squeeze them in between bingo sessions) were equally packed to the rafters - as were Kettering Workingmen's Club, the Windmill Club and the North Park Club. The doorman at the North Park Club was 6ft 7in. Noel Rayson a gentleman who was affectionately known as 'Big Noel'. These days the term 'local legend' is far too easily bandied about, but it is entirely justified when speaking about former shoe factory worker Rayson (who became involved with the entertainment business through his association with many of the most prominent clubs in Kettering.)

Born in Kettering in 1929, Noel grew up to be a big but amiable lad - in fact one of the most instantly recognisable figures in the town. He can remember, from his childhood days, when World War II bombers used to circle overhead as they prepared to land at the airfield in nearby Grafton Underwood. Even more exciting was the occasion when a German fighter plane crashed on the Rothwell Road. Noel: "The plane was coming down, in the area where the Beeswing pub is, when suddenly one of the crew baled out and landed in my uncle's garden - right in the middle of a row of brussel sprouts! The other crew member flew on, dumped a load of incendiary bombs in a field and then he too jumped out - leaving the plane to crash further on. It eventually came down very close to where the Woodland Hospital now stands. My mates and I cycled out there to try and find the wreck and, hopefully, a few souvenirs. This we did (I took a few scraps of shrapnel which I had for years) but not before a copper came along and gave us a good telling off. 'You could have got yourself killed!' he scolded.

Now and again we would bike over to Grafton Underwood to watch the allied bombers taking off and landing. I remember there being a massive pile of soil at the end of the runway - the purpose of which was to prevent aircraft from overshooting. Anyway one day when a gang of us lads were hanging around, a lorry drove past and its wheels accidentally clipped the mound - causing several boxes of

oranges to fall from the vehicle and scatter all over the road. Naturally, we jumped off our bikes and stuffed as many as we could into our jackets and jumpers - that is until the driver chased us away!"

After the war Noel went to work at Frank Wright's shoe factory. He also helped out at the slaughterhouse in Bath Road (loading up the lorries with meat for distribution to W. B. Wright's Butchers and the neighbouring towns and villages.) Humping carcasses around also enabled him to keep in trim for his favourite pastime of boxing. Noel explained: "One day one of the guys bet me that I wouldn't be able to pick up and carry two sides of beef into the lorry. I did it - no problem! Another day Mr. Wright asked me if I could help out Rothwell butcher Tommy Austin - whose lorry had broken down. I loaded and unloaded two lorries that day! That night I was

As discos began to flourish, local DJ Dennis Taylor (seen here in his customary Ben Sherman shirt and braces) was in the vanguard of all things 'hip' on the local pub and club scene.

due to box in the Central Hall, however, by the time I had got home and had washed, changed and ran all the way up there - I was knackered! Even so, I only lost the fight on points. The guy wasn't able to put me down!"

In 1957 Noel became Entertainments Secretary at the Town Band Club on Rockingham Road. He took over the job just as a music craze called skiffle was starting to take off. Noel: "The club was dying. A little old fellow called Freddie Pell used to sit on the door and made it his life's work to make sure that everyone who wasn't a member was turned away. The club was full of old men playing dominoes and cards, so when I decided to put bands on it transformed the place and punters were soon coming from all around the county to watch and dance to the Blue Diamonds from Market Harborough, the Size Seven and the Hepcats from Corby, the Keystone Skiffle Boys from Kettering - plus all of the American airbase bands. Kettering's skiffle bands bought their washboards and broom handles from Tinker Smith's ironmonger's on Rockingham Road, and the tea chests were acquired from Cobley's greengrocer's in Regent Street. From time to time I'd step in and play the tea chest or get up and play harmonica if a group was short on manpower."

It was Rayson's job to be on the lookout for new acts for the Kettering club; he even travelled as far as London to scout for talent. "It was a good excuse to visit the 2 Is coffee bar in Soho," said Noel. "That was the place where it was all happening in the mid 1950s. The ceiling was so low that I had to bend almost double to avoid disturbing the natty middle parting in my hair! I can remember watching Harry Webb singing there (before he became better known as Cliff Richard) and I also saw Reg Smith - prior to his transformation into Marty Wilde. The Big Bopper (*Chantilly Lace*) also turned up once. He was wearing his huge ten-gallon hat. I'd never seen anything like it! Of course there was no chance of getting the likes of them to come up to Kettering, however, a few years later I did meet up with quite a few of them when they appeared on the Granada package tours. That was when I was involved with providing the cinemas with doormen - including my old mate Terry Page. They used to say: 'Terry Page hits them in the face, Big Noel hits them in the ribs!'

When rock 'n' roll films such as *Rock Around The Clock* and *The Girl Can't Help It* were doing the rounds and were causing mayhem (due to the rowdiness of over-excited youngsters) there was never any trouble in Kettering because I put members of the Town Band Karate Club in the cinemas. Any prospective rabble-rousers were warned that they'd be turfed out quick-style if they started any nonsense!

I organised the Granada's first live performance by a pop band. It featured a young group called the Red Cats, who played on a Saturday morning for the kids. The Granada's manager, Rex Smith, saw how well it went down and got the idea that it might work with the adults. Pete Downing helped Rex to get things off the ground (he was managing the Size Seven at the time and had all the contacts.) I was the voice behind the curtain who introduced the bands, saying something along the lines of 'Tonight, ladies and gentlemen, we present to you the Size Seven!' (or whoever else was on.)"

Noel Rayson was the instigator of what would later be classed as 'a disco' in the Town Band Club, playing records when the bands were having a break. "Anybody who brought along a record got in for sixpence, and if they didn't - it cost them two bob," said Noel. He added "Apart from anything else, it saved me from having to buy the records!"

Because of the disparate mix of local lads, Jocks from Corby and Yanks from the bases, it was inevitable that evenings would often end in a brawl. Nevertheless, this didn't prevent the Town Band Club from becoming one of the most popular clubs in the Midlands. Noel: "The American servicemen and women travelled over from Alconbury and Molesworth to support their own bands (e.g. the Molesworth Rockets and Texas Rangers) but the funny thing is, people seem to think that this only took place during the rock 'n' roll days, however, I can recall them coming regularly to Kettering during the war years. The Yanks would park their army lorries alongside the wall in the Market Square and then swagger down to the pubs and clubs to impress the local females with their

Committee men: A dapper Noel Rayson and Bert Silburn are pictured during the 1950s. Noel was heavily involved in plans for the revamping of Kettering's Town Band Club.

money, chat and chewing gum. This of course caused the local fellows to take umbrage and there would end up being a scuffle. Many a time the American military police were called in to sort things out. A fearsome-looking sight they were too - they'd turn up with their white helmets, white bands around their middle, white gaiters, pistols in their holsters and armed with truncheons! They weren't afraid to use them either - they'd tear into their own men with abandon and would batter them!

Anyone who wanted to become a member of the Town Band Club (and later the North Park) first had to get past me - and if I thought that they looked like troublemakers then they wouldn't get in. I once threw a bloke out of the Town Band - literally! He landed on a copper who was standing outside. I said to myself 'that's buggered it' but then simply apologised to the policeman, picked him up and dusted him down. Sometimes, when two guys were fighting, I would grab the pair, shove them into what used to be the billiards room and shut the door. I'd say to them, 'if you want to kick the daylights out of each other - do it in there and then knock on the door when you're finished!' After a while they'd come out - covered in blood, shirts torn and with black eyes. I'd tell them to go and clean themselves up and then shake hands as if they meant it. Then I'd let them back in!"

Known to the locals as 'Skull', Tommy Cullen (an associate of Rayson) was an equally familiar face on the Kettering club scene. Noel remembers one occasion when, completely unsolicited Skull decided to leap up on stage and sing with the band that had just come on. Noel: "Tommy could be quite a handful! Although he was short in stature, he had a reputation for being lethal with his fists and with his head. Nevertheless, friend or not, I had to haul him off the stage that night!"

Art Elmore (also an acquaintance of Noel) was another one who was more than capable of taking care of himself. A middleweight boxer of some repute, he worked the door at Kettering's Drill Hall - which had been a popular dance venue since the early 1950s when it played host to the likes of the Roy Fox Big Band and Humphrey Lyttleton's

Noel Rayson pictured in December 2004 attending a North Park Club reunion.

Jazz Band. In addition to being a doorman, Art drove buses for United Counties and was regularly seen at the wheel of the infamous 11.30 p.m. 'last bus to Corby'. Noel: "Because of all the fighting on board, Art would routinely stop the bus at Barford Bridge, and make the troublemakers get off. He said that it was mostly the Jocks and the Irish who caused the trouble. 'Buggers used to make an awful mess!' he'd say."

Rayson himself was no stranger to Corby. He says that he used to come over to the Raven Dance Hall during the time when Fred Winstone and Tommy Murray put on the dances there. Noel: "Fred used to run a weekly raffle where one of the prizes was always a bottle of whisky. They used to say that he fixed it so that one of his mates would win it and then hand the bottle back to him. That bottle of whisky must have been recycled, as you might say, for weeks on end!"

The Tartan Combo. L-R: Bob McAuslen, Jack Stewart, Tommy Smith and Alistair Sinclair. Over the years spanning 1972 – 2006, the much-loved entertainers 'plaid' at innumerable local functions. (Sadly, the year 2009 saw the death, at the age of sixty-five, of drummer Tommy Smith.)

Back in the 1950s and 60s the Stag and Pheasant in Kettering served as the starting point for many of the early evening's revellers. It was especially popular with the Corby contingent because the United Counties bus stop was just opposite - and also because of its extremely potent home brewed scrumpy! Noel Rayson recalls that the landlord of the Stag (which was on the same road as the Town Band Club) used to put a piece of meat into some of the scrumpy mix, in order to establish when it would be ready for consumption. "If the meat turned green - the cider was ready!"

Around that time Tommy Steel was a regular visitor to the Kettering pubs and clubs. He says that he has vivid memories of both the Stag and the scrumpy (which he described as being raw, flat and capable of blowing your head off!) Tommy: "The pub was a dive really. The landlord carried a spanner with him all the time and, if there was any trouble, would use it to belt people over the head. His wife was just as bad. She was a big woman and she wasn't afraid of anybody. She carried a spanner as well! In a way, I suppose that she was ahead of the times - she liked to place copies of *Playboy* magazine around the bar. That really was extraordinary for a pre-sixties pub. The landlord used to carry up the scrumpy from the cellar in a big jug - it looked like soup! The first time I drank it I ended up with stomach cramp and was left bent double. For a few hours I wasn't even able to go to the toilet unaided. It was painful and embarrassing - but not half as sore as those spanners!"

When a fifty pound note was handed in at the Corby branch of Barclays Bank, Mr. L.A. Partridge, the Assistant Manager, told the *Evening Telegraph*: "It was the first time that we had received such a note. It was larger than the £5 and coloured white with a blue pattern. Although we thought it was genuine, just to be sure we sent it to Head Office for verification."

The note turned out not to be counterfeit. It had been issued by the Northern Bank of Eire in 1943 and was still legal tender. It appears that the person who unearthed it (and who chose to remain anonymous) was clearly blessed with 'the luck of the Irish'!

Turgid rock 'n' roller Chuck Berry had his final British hit in 1972. A novelty record called *My Ding A Ling*, it was famous for its double entendres and went to number one in the charts. In June the oleaginous Berry was the headline act at a Wembley Stadium summer bonanza - appearing alongside Jerry Lee Lewis, Little Richard, Bo Diddley and several other 'not quite bona fide' British rockers. The later group included the self-styled Screaming Lord Sutch who, in the company of four naked ladies, strolled audaciously up Downing Street in order to publicise his presence at this illustrious gathering of rock 'n' roll's aristocracy. Supposedly intent on briefing Prime Minister Edward Heath about the forthcoming *London Rock 'n' Roll Show*, the only thing that Lord Sutch succeeded in doing was getting himself and his glamorous companions arrested and subsequently charged with indecent behaviour.

On the day of the show Wembley played host to the largest coming together of Teddy boys that had been seen in Britain since the late 1950s. Joining the throng inside the stadium were brothers John and Dave Black, and their friend Roger Johnson, who were all from Corby (and all resplendent in their draped jackets, drainpipe trousers and brothel creeper shoes.).

Dave Black says that it was Little Richard's performance that stands out in his mind. He explained: "Richard began his act by rattling off three or four of his most famous songs and, at that point, we all thought that he was terrific. Unfortunately, after that he seemed to find God. He began cavorting about the set with his arms in the air, exhorting the audience to repent their sins. As the rock and roll star lurched about the stage, shadowing his every step were half a dozen of the smallest human beings that I had ever seen. They were gaudily-dressed, formidable looking creatures who appeared to be acting as his bodyguards.

The stage had been erected at one end of the stadium and was about twenty-five feet above the level of the pitch, and when the American singer teetered on the edge of it (as he tried to 'commune' with his 'congregation') the midgets linked hands and formed a knee-high daisy chain around him - in a feeble attempt to prevent him from falling, or, as he was obviously out of his mind on drugs, to stop him taking a swan dive onto the ground below.

In stark contrast to what was fast becoming a pantomime, was the sight of Mick Jagger sitting on stage - reclining imperiously against a grand piano as he sipped a glass of whisky (which was recharged at regular intervals from an optic-sized bottle standing on the piano lid.) From his grandstand view of the proceedings, Jagger was observing the almost surreal spectacle with an air of indifference - watching a famous rock star mentally disintegrate in front of the vast Wembley crowd. After about thirty minutes of his raining fire and brimstone on the bewildered audience, Richard was finally escorted from the stage by members of the St John Ambulance Brigade (presumably 'The Almighty' had heard enough!) followed closely by the attendant midgets. A few minutes later he was loaded into the back of a waiting ambulance with its blue lights flashing and spirited away, one suspects, to the nearest hospital or loony bin.

On a personal note, it had been great for me to watch a performance by one of rock 'n' roll's true innovators (if only for the few short minutes of those opening songs) however, when I later looked back on the day's events, I was both shocked and saddened by what I had witnessed."

With the exception of the retro showcase at Wembley, 1972 was the year of glam rock (a largely British, high-energy type of music that was predominantly dependant on showy, theatrical effects.) The most famous exponents of the trend were T. Rex, David Bowie and Gary Glitter. All three acts consolidated their commercial success by appealing to an increasingly younger pop audience (known as 'glitter kids'.) Their stage acts were characterised by the stars flouncing about in effeminate attire, make-up and platform soled boots. Also making it big in the pop charts back then were Roxy Music, Dr. Hook and Mott the Hoople - who each had their own distinctive brand of rock and country music.

In direct contrast, the record charts of the time also featured strongly the fabricated offerings of a group known as the Partridge Family. Although they didn't actually exist as a real band, or indeed a real family, (being the product of an American TV show about a fictional pop group of the same name) they spawned a craze known as 'Partridge Family mania'. Despite the nature of the band and the lack of depth to their music (which could only be described as 'bubblegum pop') record sales soared.

Classic albums such as Pink Floyd's *Dark Side of Moon*, David Bowie's *Ziggy Stardust* and Neil Young's *Harvest* strengthened the belief that all was not completely lost in the mishmash of mediocrity that represented pop music of the day.

In February former Beatle Paul McCartney made a surprise appearance at Nottingham University - playing his first live performance since 1966. McCartney's new band Wings (which had been cobbled together from old pals, family members and pet dogs) got off to a flying start in front of a hall full of Students Union members who had paid 50p apiece to get in. Proceeds from the gig were later shared out amongst the band in the back of a van. The pets had to settle for a bone!

Elvis Presley was also in the news. As a tribute to the 'King of Rock and Roll', Highway 51 South in his adopted hometown of Memphis, Tennessee, was to be renamed 'Elvis Presley Boulevard'.

Eight years after President de Gaulle of France had blocked the UK's entry to the Common Market, on May 21, 1972 Prime Minister Edward Heath and President Georges Pompidou of France announced that they had reached agreements that would pave the way for Britain to join the European Economic Community. On January 22, (amid fierce opposition from both members of his own and the Labour Party) Heath signed *The Treaty of Brussels*. He had earlier promised that this would not take place without 'the full-hearted consent' of the nation, however, when the House of Commons passed the *European Communities Bill* with a less than overwhelming mandate (309 votes for, 301 votes against) hearts didn't come into the equation.

Very much against this perceived betrayal was Mrs. Mary Phipps of Corby who managed to persuade over 3,000 housewives and shopkeepers to sign a petition (bound for 10 Downing Street) putting forward a case for staying out of Europe. Mrs. Phipps was alarmed at the prospect of soaring prices and urged: "We must do all that we can to stop the Government from taking this fatal step. There will be no turning back if we go into Europe, and we will all suffer the consequences. Prices are high enough as it is - and they are bound to increase in leaps and bounds!" Mr. Heath and the Labour leader Harold Wilson (who had also received a letter from Mary) were courteous enough to afford her a reply - 'thanking her for her interest.' Shortly before Heath put pen to paper he was drenched in black ink by a woman protester (not Mrs. Phipps incidentally) and forced to take refuge in a lift so that aides could tidy him up.

Many people were against us forging closer ties with our European cousins - for fear of losing our national identity, sovereignty and control of our own destiny. "We're an island, we don't need Europe!" proclaimed Tommy Elder who was a twenty stone veteran of the Battle of the Bulge.

Joining Europe did have some benefits though - it allowed for free movement of labour and unrestricted access to people living in the E.C. To the Romanies amongst us, the prospect of spending a few months working in a bar in Spain (or Italy - if that was your fancy) came as excellent news.

On the debit side, British companies would face fines if the European Commission considered they had broken EEC rules on free and fair competition, and although the UK would be eligible to receive payments from the European Social Fund and the European Investment Bank, the downside was that there would be an obligation to contribute to the Community budget. Export duties were to be abolished on coal being transported from Great Britain to other Common Market countries and it would no longer be permitted to negotiate for new independent trade agreements with other member states. Understandably, all these new regulations quickly became the subject of much (and often heated) debate within the pubs of Corby. On January 2, whilst sipping their shandies in the Smoke Room at the Welfare Club, Maggie Green and Oona Campbell listened with great interest as their husbands debated endlessly over the pros and cons of entry into Europe. Maggie eventually turned to her pal and declared: "I expect we'll be going tae the Common Market for our tatties and neeps noo?" Britain may have been heading for Europe but in January her government was heading for trouble when the threatened miners' strike over wages became a reality. At their Annual Conference in 1971 the NUM had decided to seek a 43 per cent pay rise and had voted to take industrial action if their demands were not met. That being the case, the National Coal Board's offer of a derisory 8 per cent was rejected out of hand, leading to miners all over Britain downing tools (which resulted in the closure of 135 pits in South Wales alone.) As the strike got under way picket lines took up position in the first instance outside power stations which were fuelled by coal. There was then an escalation which saw the picketing of other stations (irrespective of their sources of energy) and that of other major users of coal. Adding fuel to the fire, the dockers pledged support for their comrades by refusing to unload the coal from ships coming into port.

MRS. MARY PHIPPS, the Corby woman who was so incensed at the Tory "mini-budget" that she started a petition, has now handed more than 1,000 names to her MP, Sir Geoffrey de Freitas.

Sir Geoffrey called at her home, 8 Butterwick Walk, on Christmas Eve to collect the petition personally.

He told her: "I think it was a great effort."

Mrs. Phipps collected the names on the petition single-handed because she was so angry at the budget, rising costs and Britain's proposed entry to the Common Market.

Said Mrs. Phipps: "He was very nice. He is going to give the petition to Mr. Heath and said he would do what he could to see that something was done about it."

Mrs. Phipps has already written to the leaders of both the major parties, Mr. Harold Wilson and Mr. Heath, complaining about rising prices and the cost of living.

Mrs. Mary Phipps - the Corby woman who made it her business to petition against Britain's entry into the Common Market. (In light of recent events, Mary's concerns over what the European adventure might hold in store appear to have been somewhat prophetic).

In February the Government declared a state of emergency and a 3-day working week was introduced in order to save electricity. Although the Central Electricity Generating Board announced that homes and businesses would be without electricity for up to nine hours a day, in the event many factories and businesses were forced to close because of the shortage of power. Claims that 1.2 million workers had been laid off - provoked the headline 'MINERS' STRIKE TURNS OFF THE LIGHTS'. As a precautionary measure, Imperial Chemical Industries (one of the largest companies in the country) gave a week's notice to its 60,000 weekly-paid staff.

Production at Corby's steelworks was also under threat - as the shortage of coal raised the possibility that up to 1,000 men might have to be laid off. In addition, a previous agreement negotiated between the unions and management (in which 9,500 manual workers were guaranteed a minimum weekly wage) had become null and void due to the 3-day week. Released from this obligation, BSC would now only pay the men for 'actual hours worked'.

Several departments in the Tubeworks, notably the seamless tube Plug Mill, were hit badly by the inevitable fall in orders and by the ensuing loss of overtime. On the positive side, however, BSC was advertising vacancies for thirty clerks - in connection with the planned move from Glasgow to Corby of the Commercial Department of the Tubes Division.

Although the UK in general may have been faced with the prospect of power cuts and general industrial unrest, in the Rose of the Shires village life continued in much the same way that it had always done. For the people of Gretton the most pressing concern was over whose responsibility it was for trimming the hedgerows - and more pertinently the one at Pick Playing Field.

During a Gretton Parish Church Meeting, a tense situation was swiftly defused when it was announced that £62 had been donated to the Parish Council by the trustees of Gretton Allotments Charity, and that arrangements had been made for the cutting of the hedge in question. Anxiety was also voiced over a locked gate, a broken stile and an overgrown footpath - all of which had been discussed and promised attention at a previous meeting.

Dougie Martell and Tom Howarth are seen out and about promoting Corby Bowl's top-draw(ers) attraction St Cecilia - their trio of helpers no doubt suppressing an urge to 'Leap Up And Down'! Pictured second from right is Katie Boyle from Corby. Unfortunately, the names of the other two young ladies in the photograph remain a mystery. Perhaps they found their 'brief' encounter with fame to be too embarrassing and forbade the reporter to take down their particulars!

This page from the local evening paper reflects the wealth of entertainment available at the working mens clubs in the towns and villages around Corby.

Located in the Village Hall, Gretton Women's Institute was thriving. As well as attending a full calendar of meetings and events throughout the year, the group travelled widely and had visited many interesting places in pursuit of excitement and adventure. Mrs. C.W.C. Woolston (their President) gave a detailed and very amusing account of the trip to Greece which she and three other members had taken. Mrs. Frobisher was perceived to have blushed when the group heard how she had rebuffed the attentions of an over-familiar barman who was in the employ of one of the many tavernas at which they had sought refreshment. The Rev. F.W. Beaver, Vicar of Gretton, showed slides from the trip and all present agreed that they were riveting.

Tea was then served by Mrs. H. Canning and Mrs. G.H. Wilson, along with some delicious scones that had been baked by Mrs. Oliff, caretaker of the Rectory. Next on the agenda was a session of community singing - accompaniment provided by Mrs. Doris Thompson.

The only thing to mar the evening had been the enforced cancellation of a planned talk on the subject of chocolate - the speaker being indisposed due to haemorrhoids. "It's terribly disappointing but we hope to reschedule for a later date," said Mrs. Woolston.

On Valentine's Day members of St Cecilia made a rare appearance in their home town. Dougie Martell, the booking agent for Corby Bowl, forewarned fans that "this is the only chance Corby people will have of seeing their heroes this year". Working with Dougie on the promotion was Tom Haworth. Tom's main recollection of the whole thing is of 'walking around the town's Market Square - handing out paper knickers to advertise the performance!"

After the success of *Leap Up And Down* (their debut single of the previous year) the band was in great demand. Lead guitarist John Proctor: "We travelled the length and breadth of the country throughout early 1972 - sometimes in ever decreasing circles. On a mini-tour of Wales we spent a lot of time driving around with absolutely no idea of where we were going - thanks to the Welsh Nationalists painting out the English road signs and turning the signposts round. In some cases they had removed them altogether! Having said that, we usually managed to get to the gigs eventually!"

Corroborating John's account, newspapers of the era report that eight members of the Welsh Language Society were tried at Swansea Assizes for plotting to steal and destroy English road signs. In addition, following an unsuccessful attempt by the accused to have their case heard in Welsh, two women in the public gallery were thrown out of court for reading aloud from pamphlets and chanting 'Justice for the Welsh language!' (They were later jailed for three months for refusing to agree not to interrupt the case.)

John Proctor: "One booking particularly sticks in my mind. It was after a long journey north that we arrived at a rather scruffy miners' social club and were told that we would have to make do with the Gents toilet as there were no dressing room facilities available. Following a quick inspection of what turned out to be a real hellhole, we decided that we would probably die a slow and torturous death if we were to change in there - so we hatched a plan. After doing a sound check we sloped off to a nearby pub for a few beers, arriving back at the club just as the audience was being seated. Then, in full view of the assembled crowd, we took to the platform and proceeded to wash, shave and change into our stage outfits!"

The band sparked even more controversy during a Hunt Ball at Tiverton in Devon. While they were singing *Leap Up And Down, Wave Your Knickers In The Air* - one of the ladies in the hall did just that! The *Daily Mirror* (no less) reported:

> 'Sporty types roared with approval, but not all were amused. Local councillor Bill Jones complained: "I've never seen anything like it in my life! This quite attractive lady of about twenty-four took off her knickers. My wife and I will think twice about going to a Hunt Ball again."

Two weeks later (having heard about the high jinx at the jointly run Stoke Hill Beagles and Devon Foxhounds Hunt Ball) Tiverton Council Property Committee turned down a request by the Tiverton

Staghounds Hunt to hold a dance in the Town Hall. Bill Jones, the Hunt's spokesperson, pointed out to the committee that no one had ever waved their knickers in the air at any of their dances. "Our last Ball was a very well-behaved affair."

During that time when St Cecilia was out on the road, Keith Hancock and Ricky Moss were being encouraged to write more songs. Keith: "We went back to Beck Studios on several occasions to record demos. I had a couple of songs - one of them another saucy number called *The Village Bicycle*, Ricky had a novelty number called *He's A Collector* and John had written a skiffle-style song called *Don't Want Women, Don't Want Wine*. The recordings for these numbers took place in one single eight-hour session in September 1971. We decided that John's number would make an ideal choice for the lucrative Christmas market and went on to record the master copy of it at Polydor Studios - complete with clinking glasses and a singalong party atmosphere. Ricky's song *He's A Collector* was chosen as the 'B' side and was recorded at Beck Studios. It was produced by Derek Tompkins. A release date was tentatively set for mid-November, but, unfortunately for us, Polydor had other priorities and our 'Christmas single' was delayed until January 21st!"

Don't Want Women, Don't Want Wine made the 'breakers' on its first week of release. The *NME* reported:

> *'With all due respect, many people were attracted to their recent hit by the 'forbidden fruit' aspect of its lyric. Auntie BBC shouldn't have anything to frown about with this new one. It is however, a tremendously happy affair which looks set for healthy sales.'*

Despite its encouraging exposure in the music press, '*Wine*' unfortunately evaporated as soon as it hit the air waves. John: "Ricky and I were still writing and decided that the next single needed to be another controversial one. We came up with a ditty which we felt could be an anthem for the fast-growing women's liberation movement. It was called *C'Mon Ma, Burn Your Bra!* When John Peel reviewed the disc in the music press, he pointed out that it established us as an 'underwear' group rather than an underground group! The three of us then wrote a number for the 'B' side, called *How Come* (featuring a flute passage from Ricky) and went off again to Beck Studios to record them. I can remember Derek Tompkins listening to *How Come* and declaring it to be b-b-b-b-bloody d-d-d-delightful!"

In 1965 Ken Cox, a 32-year-old from Stamford, began his career in the music business by becoming the manager of Hedgehoppers Anonymous (the RAF band who had a hit record with *It's Good News Week*.) It was around this time that he first teamed up with Jonathan King - who was also in the charts with *Everyone's Gone To The Moon*. Ken moved into the agency side of the business in 1968 and then returned to management in order to take charge of St Cecilia's affairs and those of a number of other bands in the area.

After a lifetime in the entertainment business Dougie Martell is one of the best placed people to share memories of life on the road with St Cecilia. Today a successful entrepreneur who lives in the Manchester area, Dougie believes that (in common with so many other artists in the spotlight) the band was ripped off. Dougie says: "St Cecilia only received two per cent of the royalties for recordings of songs that were written by Keith Hancock and Ricky Moss. *Leap Up And Down* was a great production with its full brass section included, but when Jonathan King decided to tone it down or - in his words 'desimplify it' - it sounded crap. That is in comparison to the original acetate. Then there was the issue of the record's lyrics - which I have to admit were a bit rude. The BBC refused to give *Leap* airplay because they considered the words to be too contentious, however, in a roundabout way that only served to give the number more publicity. It was even a big hit abroad - reaching number three in Greece and Cyprus, number ten in New Zealand and twenty-three in Australia."

The follow-up to *Don't Want Women* - was released on April 21, 1972 Everyone connected to the band thought that *C'Mon Ma, Burn Your Bra!* would be a real smash.

To promote their new release St Cecilia spent a day on a photo shoot in London's Carnaby Street, accompanied by two well-endowed ladies (brunette Della Mancini and blonde Brandy de Franck) who were predictably waving their bras in the air! In addition, manager Ken Cox felt that it would make good sense, publicity-wise to send a copy of the record to Germaine Greer - a leading protagonist of the Women's Liberation Movement. His thinking was that the band might get a big push at the American market because the movement was rooted in the States. As things turned out (despite all the optimism and the hype) apart from raising a few eyebrows *C'Mon Ma, Burn Your Bra!* flopped.

Gary Glitter (real name Paul Gadd) appears at the Corby Bowl in July 1972. The diminutive singer and self-proclaimed 'King of Glitter' had in a previous pop incarnation also used the name Paul Raven. At Corby that night he certainly hit the headlines - and not for the last time, as things turned out.

As the year progressed it became apparent that not only was the writing on the wall for St Cecilia - it was daubed in indelible ink! The bookings were starting to dry up, money was tight and the constant travelling was becoming a chore rather than an exciting adventure. Although in June they supported the Sweet on a ten day tour of the Top Rank circuit, the band's time in the spotlight was fast running out. Dougie Martell left to pursue his own career and in the autumn the band split up. Keith Hancock went to work for Ken Cox at Dawn Promotions. He then started his own agency called Keri Enterprises - which enjoyed its fair share of success over the following decade. The agency looked after the interests of some of the best of the local bands (e.g. Alias Smith and Jones, Buzzard, Teaser and Chrome Molly.) It also handled several other successful acts from the Midlands, including an up-and-coming comedian called Lenny Henry. Keith: "We arranged three tours for Lenny. They were mainly at RAF bases and working men's clubs. In the beginning he was on a grand a week for seven shows, but that soon went up to a grand and a half. Lenny was a phenomenal performer and character. Another star attraction on the books was Linda Grant - an ex-policeman who had undergone a sex change. Linda had an unusual talent for getting tunes out of all different types of utensils. She'd amuse the audience by playing a kettle, the tube from a Hoover vacuum cleaner and even a plant pot! It sounds ridiculous - but she made a living for a while and became quite well known after appearing as a regular on the Esther Rantzen TV show *That's Life*."

Fresh from topping the charts with a mammoth hit record, Gary Glitter made a chaotic appearance at the Corby Bowl - amid scenes reminiscent of Beatlemania. In the excitement of it all, three young girls were crushed as the hysterical audience surged forward to salute their new idol.
Reporting the event, the *Evening Telegraph* ran the following headline: 'Frenzy! Glittermania hits Corby Bowl.' The report continued:

> *'Fans went berserk and the show was brought to a premature close as the audience became uncontrollable. Young girls were screaming as Gary rocked the stage with his act and the whole atmosphere was electric. The 28-year-old rock singer with the silver clothes was comparatively unheard of six months ago. Today, his hit record 'Rock and Roll, Parts 1 & 2', is near the top of the hit parade. His concert at Corby was only the fourth he has done in this country. Until now he has worked in Germany. Before Gary went on stage his voice was cracking and he was worried that he wouldn't be able to sing at all. At the end of his performance it was hard to hear him - and yet for nearly two hours he talked to fans in his dressing room, letting them try on his stage gear, and signed autographs. At 28 - an age at which most pop idols see their star begin to wain - Gary is just starting out on his career. But the glitter and the silver clothes, the way-out dancing and flashing light isn't all gimmick. "It's the way I am," said Gary. "I've always worn these clothes and I've been doing this act for ten years. The thing that surprises me is that it is me and the group who has helped revive rock and roll and that the fans are as mad about the music now as they were in the fifties." Although married for a short time when he was nineteen, Gary has no ties. "I really don't have time to spend on girls and it would be unfair to them as I am moving from one town to another nearly every day."*

There to witness this most glittering of occasions was a group of young Corby lads who were about to embrace glam rock culture to the max. Ian Easton, Ray Moorey and Dave 'Louie' Lewis were so impressed by Gary Glitter that they began to make regular shopping trips to London's Carnaby Street in order to buy clothes like his. Ian: "I spent a fortune on gear, buying a silver top hat and matching pair of silver high-heeled boots (which I struggled to stand up in - never mind walk in!) Ray and Louie had equally bad taste, meaning that the three of us looked like something out of a circus! We didn't care though - we thought we were the bee's knees! We even started our own 'Glitter Disco'. Our debut night was at a York Trailers dance and I can remember that we were all wearing this gaudy garb. Quite what the punters made of us I'm not sure! Anyway, I decided to do the first stint of the night, but when it came to it - I completely froze. My tongue dried up. Ray called to me from behind the curtains: 'Say something! Speak between the records!' he implored. It was no good though - I just wasn't able to. To make matters worse, we weren't aware that the microphone was switched on and that everyone could hear us. Ray was calling me every name under the sun and the air was absolutely blue! It was so embarrassing. When we reflected upon the evening afterwards, we all came to the same conclusion - we might have been crap but we certainly gave everybody a good laugh!"

After a less than brilliant start the boys were soon given the opportunity to learn the ropes from seasoned DJs Ian 'Robbie Stewart' Eccles and Dougie King. This led to a number of relatively straightforward bookings which they hoped would set them on the road to fame and fortune. With Easton's stage fright no longer posing a problem (he was too much of an extrovert to allow it to come between himself and his audience!) the future was looking rosy. However, spells as the resident DJs at the Maple Leaf and the Phoenix Barrel Bar (interspersed with an assortment of wedding bookings) was as good as it got!

Ian's favourite band at the time was Mungo Jerry. He says that when they came to Corby he couldn't resist the chance to go and see them. Ian: "Dressed-up in all of our glam gear, Ray Moorey and I approached the entrance to the Civic - only to be turned away by the doorman. The thing is, just as this was happening the man himself pulled up right next to us in a big limo. 'Hey Mung' I shouted to him, 'this geezer won't let us in. We're your biggest fans - in fact your record was the first one I ever played at our disco.' At that 'Mungo' stared at us and replied 'My name's not Mung, it's Ray Dorset.' As neither Ray nor I were aware of this fact, we just stood there open-mouthed. Dorset then said 'Come with me' and gestured to us to accompany him inside. As we strolled in past the doorman, I noticed that he was equally open-mouthed!"

Alan Crawford was also in attendance at the show and recalls: "Mungo

Pictured Left: Former 'Glitter Kid' Ian 'Ike' Easton's got his suitcase packed and is about to go in search of a Ziggy Stardust reunion concert. Right: Although it looks like he eventually found one, reliable sources reveal that it was merely the 2002 Corby Carnival!

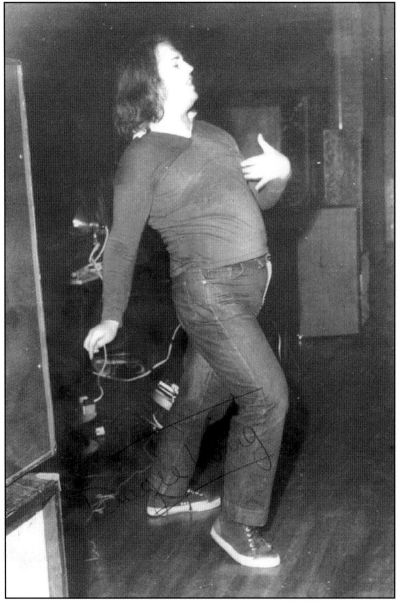

Jerry was basically a jug band who played stomping-type stuff. The trouble was if they were having an off-night it could sound terrible. It was the Green Abbotts (who later changed their name to the Racing Cars and went on to have a couple of big hits) who were the supporting act that night. The Abbotts came on stage, played a lively set and got everybody going. They were so good in fact that Mungo Jerry had their work cut out to follow them. Maybe it was just a case of their lead singer, Ray Dorset not being in the mood - but they were awful! The audience started jeering and booing them, and then next thing Dorset walked off the stage in a huff - leaving the rest of the band looking more than a little bemused!"

It was around that time that Dougie King was operating his own mobile roadshow and was travelling and performing all over the Midlands. During a show at Husbands Bosworth he met Paul Graham - a DJ from Leicester. Graham was involved with Radio Free Leicester (a land-based pirate radio station) and within weeks Dougie had clambered aboard to join him in plundering the airwaves (i.e. broadcasting

Dougie King strutting his stuff during a Kingswood School disco. Obviously a great fan of cartoon character Tweetie Pie, Dougie enjoyed nothing more than singing along to his signature tune of 'I Tot I Taw A Putty Cat!'

without authorisation) in what was the Big Man's first - albeit illegal - radio gig. Enthused by the Leicester experience, and having heard that Radio Caroline was set for a relaunch aboard the good ship *Mi Amigo*, Dougie set sail for Holland - imbued with a determination to chance his luck with the famous pirate radio station. Alas, he'd left it too late - his berth aboard *Mi Amigo* had already been taken by some other seafaring disc jockey.

The miners' strike lasted the best part of six very long and hard weeks before the bargaining between an unyielding NUM and the Government could reach a satisfactory conclusion. The picketing was then called off, the lights were switched on, and the miners became some of the highest earners within the working classes.

The future of Corby's steelworks, and, of more significance, the steel industry as a whole, was brought into sharp focus again when a television broadcast by Lord Melchett, chairman of the British Steel Corporation, informed the nation of BSC's plans to produce more steel using fewer men. Melchett said: "There will be fewer jobs in every steel town; almost all will have to prepare themselves for changes, large and small. Even areas of large investment will not be excluded." This in turn prompted Corby's trade unions to propose a public meeting at which fears of steel closure could be discussed. "There are thirteen thousand anxious workers who want to know what the Government's plans are," declared Andy 'Law' Black (a former shop steward in the Bessemer.)

Corby MP Sir Geoffrey DeFreitas and his counterpart for Neath in South Wales, Don Coleman, were quick to respond - delivering a message of hope in which they suggested reasons why Corby should be able to face down any imminent shake-up of the industry with confidence. Their reasoning went as following:

1. Corby shouldn't be compared to Ebbw Vale - where 4,500 jobs (half of the workforce) were to be axed.
2. Corby steelworks was sitting on top of an ore field.
3. The town was in an ideal position, geographically, to supply the requirements of the huge Midlands industrial area.
4. BSC had invested a massive amount of capital in Corby and there was a higher quality of labour available in the town.

Sir Geoffrey was of the view that 'Corby had 'fine people and a fine future'. One hopes that included in all those fine people were the residents of Stephenson Way who had complained about the pollution spilling out from the steelworks. Mrs. Annie McSkimming, who had served on Corby District Council for over seventeen years, maintained: "The fact that many people in the town have recently switched over to either smokeless fuel, gas or electric heating, in an effort to cut down on pollution, appears to be a waste of time - because the grime and smoke has formed a permanent blanket over the whole area. Dust covers the house, inside and out."

As a last resort, she had been forced to call out the

Councillor Annie McSkimming of Corby. Annie was the driving force behind a campaign to pressure BSC officials into cleaning up their act regarding pollution which for decades had blighted the Lloyds housing estate.

Chief Health Inspector, Mr. G. Waterworth, who said that the problems were due to fog trapping the particles and not allowing them to blow away. One of Annie's neighbours, Mrs. O'Sullivan, was equally exasperated. She revealed: "People are having difficulty breathing in the smoggy conditions. I moved here to get away from the London smog but this is much worse". In a show of solidarity, Mary Watson added: "Dust gets in your eyes, mouth and throat. We seem to be fighting a losing battle."

Mr. Waterworth responded: "Council officers and BSC officials have detected a rise in dirt".

Attempting to reassure the residents, he then said: "We are carrying out investigations. A new plant being built to handle sinter should be in operation in the near future".

Another person to share Sir Geoffrey's sentiments regarding the people of Corby was Father Dan Cronin of St Brendan's Church on Beanfield Avenue. At a presentation to commemorate his having completed twenty-five years of service to the community, a representative of Corby District Council said of him: "Father Dan has been the driving force behind the building of four schools, a church and presbytery, and a social club. He has said mass in Wimpey and Shanks & McEwan building site huts and has travelled to Brigstock and Weldon camps to preach to the exiles who came to Corby to work in the steelworks. He's the longest serving clergyman in town."

Father Cronin (who left Bedford in 1946 to come to Corby) told all those present that on his arrival in the town he had been fascinated by the sight of the Corby Candle. He recalled: "The greatest thing about Corby is the kindness and generosity of the people. It was a frightening experience coming to Corby from an old town like Bedford. I was amazed when I first stood on the Rockingham Road Bridge and looked across at the Blast Furnaces."

Attempting to follow in the footsteps of St Cecilia was a young band whose name Sunoko had been borrowed from a brand of petrol advertised in a motoring magazine. Chris Ashby (aged 14) on lead guitar, Steve Everett (aged 15) on drums, Kevin Monk (aged 14) on rhythm guitar and lead vocals, plus David Dewar (aged 12) on keyboards, were all desperate to get out on the road with their music - despite the fact that three of them were still at school. Andrew Dewar (their manager and David's dad) made it clear to them, however, that nothing would be allowed to interfere with either their schoolwork or with any homework that they'd been set.

Steven Everett: "I was fourteen years of age when, in March 1970, I came down from Glasgow to live in Corby. About a year later,

Canon Daniel Cronin: A hugely popular figure, Father Cronin served as a priest at Our Lady of Walsingham Roman Catholic Church in Corby from 1946 to 1956, and at St Brendan's from 1956 until his retirement in 1992. During his early days in the town 'Father Dan' travelled the world seeking donations towards the cost of building St Brendan's Infant and Junior schools. He was also instrumental in raising funds for the construction of the Our Lady and Pope John Secondary Schools, the St Brendan's Church, presbytery and Catholic Club in Beanfield Avenue, plus the St John Ogilvie Church in Copenhagen Road. It is a measure of the man that (in a remarkable gesture) he felt moved to march in front of the Protestant Orange flute band that travelled down to London to campaign against the closure of Corby's steelworks. Canon Cronin eventually left the town in 1997 and (at the age of ninety-three) passed away on November 24 2009 at a nursing home in County Cork, Ireland. His legacy lives on in the town he called home.

my sister Christine informed me that a new band was looking for someone of my age to join them on drums. She said that the only stipulation was that the successful candidate had to have his own drum kit. There was no mention about an ability to play them! When Christine told her boyfriend Pete Ashby (who was the lead guitarist's brother) that I owned a set of drums - within a few days I was offered the job.

For the first eighteen months I managed O.K. with them (the drums) in spite of the fact that they were only a practice set that I'd bought for £10 from a friend at Kingswood School, however, as time went by I came to the conclusion that I'd need something more professional if I was going to have a real stab at working in the music business. To that end, my mum and dad signed the hire-purchase agreement for a full Sonor drum kit and I paid for it.

When we started out I couldn't play very well, and so I'd practice by drumming along to Beatles songs - as they had a simple beat. Prior to our debut at the British Legion in Darley Dale Road, we used to rehearse at Rankine House and the St John Ambulance hall, and it was during that time that we found ourselves being influenced by the music of the Lykes of Witch (from whom we were receiving tuition on how to play our instruments.) After that first appearance we played at many venues in the area, including the Sealed Beams Club, Labour Club and Rangers Club. We also got a lot of bookings for wedding receptions. My favourite venue though was the Beehive Club in Islip - where I'd get the chance to play a drum solo at the end of each night (cheered on by the audience!)"

Above: An image that portrays confidence and excitement about the future. Starry-eyed hopefuls Sunoko smile happily for the camera. (L-R: David Dewar, Steve Everett, Christopher Ashby and Kevin Monk).

With the four aspiring musicians growing in both confidence and proficiency, they soon had their eyes on the next target - which was to appear on television. An optimistic Steve Everett told the *Evening Telegraph*: "We have already written to *Junior Showtime* to enquire about an audition. We hope to hit the top but realise that it will be some time yet. We are all young - so we've got plenty of time. If we appear on television, then our next aim will be to make a record. Being young does have its drawbacks though. Most people think because of our ages we can't be much good, and tend to laugh at us - until they hear our music and realise we are not fooling around. We take our music seriously. Alex Beale - a sixteen-year-old friend of ours - has even started writing songs for us. In return, we are teaching him to play guitar." (Alex, who was one of Andy Dewar's workmates, would later join the band).

Andy's main role was to look after the financial side of things and make sure that the band's equipment and other expenses were paid for. He was equally upbeat about their prospects and told the *E.T.* "We are getting quite a few bookings to play the local clubs. Everywhere they play, the audience seems to enjoy them. I think they can certainly make it."

Make it they did - but only to the final round of a talent contest organised by Corby Town Supporters Club. In front of a Festival Hall audience of more than five hundred people, Sunoko gave an

Popular Corby singer Ray Ritchie. Part-time performer Ritchie took early retirement from his main employment (as a sales executive with a replacement window company) to move abroad to the holiday island of Cyprus. Assured and professional in all of his undertakings, Ray now spends his time doing what he considers to be his 'real' job - entertaining people.

admirable performance on the night but were overshadowed by several acts with considerably more experience than them. The winner of the contest was established crooner Ray Ritchie - whose take on Dean Martin's *Volare* and *That's Amore* not only stole the limelight but also brought a touch of Vegas to the event!

The runner-up was Bobby Civil, an impressionist from Kettering, who attracted tremendous applause with his rendition of Ken Dodd's *Happiness*, and in third place was yet another classy act - local folk-singer June Creighton. June put in a very polished performance of Dylan's *Just Like Tom Thumb's Blues*.

Creighton was, incidentally, one of the driving forces behind the local folk-music scene which had been growing steadily since the late 1960s. To begin with, a group of enthusiasts used to meet up at the White Hart public house, however, at a later date they relocated to the Nags Head. June said: "They were good days for trying out new songs, meeting other artists and making lots of new friends. A member of St Cecilia introduced me to their agent (Ken Cox of Dawn Promotions) which gave me the opportunity to take my music to a broader audience. I've sung in every RAF club in the land, on a floating nightclub on the River Thames - and even in Kettering Cattle Market! For a while I had my own show on London's Capitol Radio and on Liverpool Radio, and for a couple of years I also helped to organise the Corby Arts Festival 'Folk Nights'. Talent contests were popular back then and it was on account of winning one at Northampton's Salon Nightclub, that I received a recording contract and a silver disc."

In the 1980s June was the licencee of the Plough in Caldecott. In her words 'when it was a spit and sawdust pub!' It was there that she introduced a hugely successful Wednesday night folk evening. June recalled: "If you weren't there by six o'clock, then you couldn't get in. All types of artists used to play there - people would just come in and sing their tales. We became widely known and received letters and phone calls from folk artists throughout the country who wanted to appear."

Around that time the BBC was making an historical drama called *By The Sword Divided*. Based upon events that took place during the English Civil War, the series was filmed on location at Rockingham Castle near Corby and starred Sharon Maugham, Jeremy Clyde and Malcolm Stoddard. If the timing had been right, it might also have featured June Creighton. June: "Glen Allen - another fine local artist - popped down to the Plough one day and told me that he was doing a series of 'walk-ons' up at the castle. He asked if I'd like to come too, as I was a member of Equity and this would have been another avenue for me to explore. Unfortunately, coming so soon after the birth of my baby daughter, I had to decline the invitation." Rockingham Castle proved to be an ideal location for the BBC production. Explaining the damage to the buildings by cannon fire, Commander Michael Saunders-Watson, R.N. (the castle's owner) said at the time of filming: "It was one of the ruins that Cromwell knocked around a bit during the battle between the Royalists and Parliamentarians." He went on to say that the castle had been in the family since 1530 and that re-enacting the famous battle had been marvellous fun.

There was a certain irony in the fact that June Creighton turned down the opportunity of a TV appearance, as elsewhere in Corby there were others who would have jumped at the chance. Unfortunately for the band Sunoko - they never did hit the big time, and in late 1973, despite achieving success in other local talent contests, split up when Alex Beale and the Dewars decided to leave. Steve Everett explained: "The main reason why we split was because we didn't have a driver, whereas when we started out Tony Ashby (another of

June Creighton. Folk singer June (another from the stable of Ken Cox and Dawn Promotions) had a long and varied showbiz career that was buoyed by the experience of appearing at a floating nightclub on the River Thames.

Chris's brothers) and his dad Albert shared it between them. We'd sally forth with our high-top transit van loaded up with equipment, musicians and girlfriends - not to mention the Pink Floyd blasting out of the rear speaker! To put it simply, we were just a bunch of fresh-faced school kids who were determined to make a name for themselves. It was a shame, therefore, that we had to pack it all in as the signs were there that we were making progress. I remember thinking that it was great being a schoolboy and playing rock music in all these clubs, (Having said that, I must emphasise that Andy never let us drink anything but soft drinks). As far as I know, no other member of the band, apart from me, went on to play as a solo artist or in any other band."

In 1995 David Dewar died in tragic circumstances. He was aged thirty-five. His father Andy passed away four years earlier, at the age of fifty-nine, from a multiple sclerosis-related illness. Jill Dewar (Andy's widow) still lives in Corby. As for the others - Alex Beale gave up singing, Kevin Monk settled down to marriage and family life, Chris Ashby left town and hasn't been seen by his family for many years (and so probably is unaware that his parents have both since died) and Tony Ashby

Seen here are the picturesque village of Rockingham and (at the top of the page) Rockingham Castle. Dating back to the time of William the Conqueror, the castle on the outskirts of Corby affords a magnificent view over the Welland Valley, encompassing five different counties. It was also the setting for the 1970s BBC historical drama *'By The Sword Divided'*.

now runs a barber's shop in Corby's Everest Lane.

Steve Everett: "I recently visited David's mother and we talked about the old days - about the group and Mr. Dewar. When we said our goodbyes she handed me a CD which had been copied from an old audio tape. On it were recordings of Sunoko rehearsing in what I believe was Rankine House. We can be heard laughing and joking with each other as we rehearse the harmony parts for *American Pie*. The recording took me back down memory lane to that time thirty-five years ago when we were four schoolboys who were intent on pursuing a career in pop music. It's the only tangible record that remains of us kids striving to learn the trade which we all fervently hoped would lead to a successful career in the entertainment business. On the tape we come across as being full of hope and eager to learn. The bullish tone in our voices indicates a sense of earnestness about what we were doing. Sadly, like many thousands of hopefuls before us, the dream didn't work out for Sunoko."

After the band's demise, Steve was joined by his brothers Alan and Brian ('Budgie' Everett) and the three of them formed a new group called Myrth - which later became Psycho. Although John McHarg and Phil Dyne were regular members of the group, over the years (in order to cover for absences - such as the time when Steve broke his leg in a motorcycle accident) they employed the likes of brothers John and Bob Grimley, John and Jimmy Heron, and Tony Haseslip.

Another band in which Steve played was the Neutrons. When contacted in early 2009 fellow band member John Bentley (who has been living in Charleston, West Virginia for the past twenty years) spoke about those early days and of how his career in the music trade has rewarded him with a lifetime of memories. Nowadays, working as both a guitar dealer and a musician, John, said: "I grew up in Corby and played in a number of local outfits when I was in my teens. Steve Everett was the drummer in the first real gigging band that I joined. I was almost fifteen-years-old and I think he was about eighteen. The band was called the Neutrons and was a spin-off from Sunoko. As far as I am aware, we were the youngest working band in Corby at that time. I was encouraged by my parents to be a musician and experienced the local club scene at an early age. I never felt I was too young to be doing this sort of thing - to me it all seemed like fun and a free ticket to the good life. While I was out at night playing my music and learning about life (i.e. pints of beer and girls!) I'd think about my pals from school who were at home watching TV and doing their homework."

It appears that the Neutrons bombed and after that John Bentley met up with Harry Thomas and the two of them put together a band called Boot Z. John: "As I recall, we wanted to name the band Boots, but somehow a 'Z' got put on the end - instead of an 'S'. Harry was a generation older than me and my school friend Roy Muir, so he and Malcolm Wright generally made sure that we got to and from the engagements - although I can remember making many trips in taxi-cabs and in my dad's car. Harry eventually purchased an old ambulance that we converted into a 'bandwagon' (complete with hippy-style artwork.) We performed as a band, at most of the local clubs playing all the hits of the day."

Boot Z lasted for a year or two and then after some changes in personnel called themselves the Variations. The line-up included not only John Bentley, Harry Thomas and Malcolm Wright, but also John Dolby and Barry Hart. Although still only seventeen-years of age, Bentley held his own as the band's bass player until a promoter offered the group a chance to work in Spain. John recalled: "They considered that I was too young to go - hence I stayed home in Corby while the rest of them travelled to the Iberian Peninsula."

A couple of years later an opportunity arose for John to play professionally with a band called Cheat (whose members were from the Kettering and Northampton area.) John: "We went to Germany and for a few months had a great time playing the American military bases. Then suddenly disaster struck - the engine of our Ford Transit van gave up the ghost and we couldn't afford to replace it. So that was the end of the band! It was with great reluctance that we all came home, however, a week later I was amazed to receive a phone call from my agents in Germany, Karl Herman Entertainment, informing me of a vacancy within a band in the Manchester area. They were called Aquarius and were due to travel to Germany for a six-month tour but were without a bass player. They asked me if I wanted the job and (having said that I did) the following day I boarded a train to Manchester to meet

Aquarius and to rehearse with them. After three days of eight hour practice sessions, I returned to Corby for a couple of days and then left once more for Germany, where I ended up doing the six-month tour - plus a two-month extension."

On his return to England John felt that it was time to try something different and so he decided to

The group that was described in Malcolm Wright's scrapbook as - the infamous 'play anywhere - anytime - for anything' Boot Z. L-R: Ricky Muir, Harry Thomas, Brian Gillies, Malcolm Wright and John Bentley.

form a new band. This one featured drummer Steve Short, Stuart Neal (former member of Snake) and a keyboard player from Northampton who was named Stan. They did a few local gigs but were soon working for Mecca Entertainment of London - who arranged for them to travel to Denmark to play at a night-club in Copenhagen. John said: "We worked an amazing six weeks without a night off - playing eight half-hour sets each night, between the hours of 10 p.m. and 6 a.m. in the morning. There was a full-time DJ who played records in the thirty-minute intervals between each set. On weekends we played an extra set because the club was open until 6.30 a.m." Needless to say this was a very tired but a very tight-sounding band.

After Copenhagen they went home to England for a few weeks rest before their next tour (which, for Bentley, involved yet another trip to Germany.) "We were called the District Attorney - a crazy name but one to which the Yanks could relate." After playing with them for a few months John decided to call it quits. He felt that it was time to return to England and marry his American girlfriend (now his ex-wife) and start a family.

He lived in England for four years before emigrating to the USA. Speaking of his life in the USA,

John said: "I was eventually drawn back into the music business and have been a guitar player here in Charleston for more than twenty years. I've been with a local three-piece band called Rhapsod for approximately fourteen years now. We still play two or three times a month in the local area - mostly at weddings and private parties etc. I've paid my dues in the entertainment venues over here and have just about seen and done it all - from honky-tonk bar fights to playing big concert venues with famous entertainers. I owe a lot to my mother and father, Reg and Joan Bentley, who are now deceased. They allowed me the freedom and the opportunity to develop as a musician, instead of forcing me to do something else."

Malcolm Wright's story began in 1970 - at a time when he was a shy, unassuming lad who played drums just for fun. Inspired by his favourite rock group Deep Purple (and in particular their drummer Ian Paice) he says he bought his first set of drums from Billy Mathieson. Malcolm: "Well, I gave him a down payment of £20! Back then I had no aspirations of becoming a professional musician - because I didn't have the nerve to play live."
That was all about to change though, as one day in October 1970 John Hanvey turned up at his door with a proposition. Malcolm: "John was a singer and guitarist of whom I knew but had never met. He had been playing in a semi-professional capacity for many years and was therefore somewhat of a veteran at the game. Anyway, John informed me that he and his brother Terry had been performing as a duo but needed someone to accompany them on drums - and preferably by Saturday (which was only three days away!")

During a break in gardening Malcolm Wright takes the opportunity to get in some practice on the drums (after all, the skinsman for John, Terry and Malk did shell out twenty quid to Billy Mathieson for the privilege.)

Wright says that he was taken aback when Hanvey suggested that he join them and that his first reaction was to decline. Malcolm: "I explained that I only played drums for my own amusement and that I'd never played in front of an audience before. I admitted to him that my knees were knocking at the very thought of it! Hanvey wasn't easily dissuaded though and tried to encourage me by saying that I'd be O.K. on the night. Finally, despite my reservations, his persistence did the trick and I found myself agreeing to go along with the scheme, and when Saturday came I somehow managed to

Chris Ashby & Kevin Monk of Sunoko

survive the ordeal - in fact the punters didn't seem to notice whether I was any good or not! At the end of the evening John and Terry thanked me for my effort and I thought that was the end of it. A couple of days later, however, they were back at my house and were asking if I'd be willing to do a booking at a club in Burton Latimer. At that my knees started knocking all over again! John and Terry must have noticed because they started to butter me up, and in the end persuaded me to give it another go. Shortly after that the job became mine on a permanent basis." As he grew in confidence, Malcolm eventually plucked up courage to ask the brothers whether his name might be included on the bill. In the creative process, 'John and Terry' then became a very imaginative 'John, Terry and Malk'.

It's Saturday night at the British Sealed Beams Club on Rockingham Road in Corby and trouble is brewing. The guy on the left is thinking: "I've paid 60p for two tickets to get in here tonight and I reckon I've been fleeced. The girl on the right says to herself: "Cheapskate! I thought he was taking me to Bailey's to see the Three Degrees. Talk about having the wool pulled over your eyes!" Meanwhile, in the background an unsuspecting Golden Fleece attempt to please at least some of the audience! L-R: Dewi Toleman, John Grimley, Pat Lavin, Johnny Heron (obscured) and Pete Dyne.

Malcolm: "I look back at that period as an apprenticeship which stood me in good stead when the opportunity later arose for me to join Boot Z - and after that the Variations." Reflecting on his time with the Variations (who later changed their name to Spyglass Hill), Malcolm spoke about what should have been the 'trip of a lifetime' - the chance for himself, Barry Hart, Harry Thomas and John Dolby to fulfill a three-month engagement on the Costa del Sol in Spain.
Malcolm: "We worked our butts off. It was great fun, but absolutely knackering. It therefore came as a huge shock when at the end of the tour we discovered that there was no money to pay us. John Dolby (not one to take things at face value) threatened to throw the band's purser into a nearby dock. Anyway, that episode brought another chapter of my musical career to an end.
Looking back to the weekend prior to our departure for Spain, an incident took place which very

nearly put paid to the trip altogether. It followed a farewell 'booze up' on the Friday night and involved two of our friends - John and Jimmy Heron."

Jimmy Heron takes up the story; "We were up at the Labour Club when John Dolby told us that he was having a little get together at his place in Weston Walk - which is near the Phoenix. So, while John and Malcolm were sorting out some business to do with the trip to Spain our John and I went on ahead with the carry-out (several cans of Party Four and a bottle of vodka.) We drove to the flat and parked up, and then we decided that we might as well make a start on the swally while we were waiting for the others to arrive. Next thing we knew, five grebos had turned up. When I asked them what they wanted, one of them replied that they'd heard that there was a party going on in the neighbourhood. I responded by asking whether any of them had been invited, and when they said that they hadn't, I told them all to clear off - which they didn't take too kindly to and started swearing at me. In the end, I got out of the car and started laying into them. Just at that moment John and Malcolm turned up and asked me what was going on - so I fired into them, demanding to know what had kept them so long (we'd been waiting for over an hour).

With the five would-be gatecrashers complaining about my behaviour, a woman then came out of a nearby house and started screaming that she had seen everything and had called the police. Then it was the turn of an angry Malcolm to berate me for causing trouble. By then I'd really lost it - so I belted him as well! Malk went down, holding his ribs and gasping for breath, so the woman disappeared into her house and was on to the emergency services again - this time for an ambulance. Unfortunately, I hadn't meant to hit Malcolm so hard and I could see that he was genuinely in pain. Soon after that the police arrived and got out of their cars. When they asked who'd started the trouble, 'Neighbourhood Watch' started to scream 'It was him - he's mental! I know him and he's a loony!' I began to get worried (I was already on a suspended sentence for assault!) so I asked John to back me up and say that I had only acted in self defence. I said that the other guys had started on me - after all there were five of them! For a while it was pandemonium. The ambulance men were putting Malk on a stretcher, the woman was still shouting and bawling, the five guys were still moaning and, in the midst of it all, stood several completely bewildered looking policemen!

After a time the police gave up. They just screwed up their notes and left. The funny thing was - just as Malk was being carted into the ambulance (wearing an oxygen mask to help him breathe) my brother Johnny remarked, 'It's a shame about Spain.' (a reference to the forthcoming trip.) Malk obviously overheard the remark, and when it dawned on him that he might miss out on three months in the sun, he literally jumped off the stretcher and shouted, 'Hey, I'm not that bloody bad!' He must have thought that I'd given him a smack so that I could replace him on the trip! We have often had a good laugh about it since."

Playing regularly on the East of England cabaret circuit and at the surrounding airbases was a band called Golden Fleece - made up of Pat Lavin, Pete Dyne, Johnny Heron, John Grimley and Dewi Toleman. Pat Lavin says that he has some alarming recollections of one concert in particular. It was the night when they were booked to support Kenny Ball and his Jazzmen at an RAF base near Lincoln. It was also the night which effectively marked the end of Golden Fleece. Pat Lavin: "The booking came about through an officer's wife who had seen us play at St Neots. I can remember the evening getting off to a bad start because, when he found out that we were from Corby, Kenny Ball started slagging off both us and the town. He claimed that the place was full of drunken, violent yobs - all that kind of stuff. (I think he must have had a bad gig here at some time or another!) Naturally, we defended the town and told him that he was talking a load of rubbish. We said that Corby was no more violent than any other frontier town. Anyhow, we kicked off the night in the Officers Club - and then Kenny's band took to the stage after us. We were then supposed to play another set before they came on again for the finale, but during our break an argument erupted among members of our band when a speaker got knocked over. It was weird how something that trivial could deteriorate so rapidly into a violent confrontation. There were even a few seconds of utter madness during which a knife was flashed and I ended up bloodied and bruised. Eventually the police were called and I was taken to hospital to get my wound cleaned up. The officers in the club weren't very happy about what had taken place. Come to think of it - neither was Kenny Ball!"

John Grimley strikes a nautical pose. Three years after relinquishing his duties in the Royal Navy (courtesy of a 'sub' from his brother Bob) John appears reluctant to shake off his seafaring image. Seen here on a virtually traffic-free Occupation Road, Grimley appears to be giving an impersonation of cartoon hero Popeye the Sailorman. (However, to this day J.G. denies that he was on his way to the nearby 'Wessie' for an assignation with Olive Oyl!)

During the course of the 1970s John Grimley was steadily building a reputation for himself as one of the 'hottest' young guitarists around. In 1969 he had left school to begin work as an apprentice car mechanic with Wards Garage in High Street, Corby - which is where he encountered fellow employee and keen guitarist John Dolby. Having played with several of the local country and western bands, Dolby was able to pass on some words of wisdom to John. He said: "You'll never make any money in this place. It's only at the weekends when you work outside your house doing 'home jobs' that you'll make any bread." Already dissatisfied with his weekly wage of £4 (when some of his pals were earning up to £17 in their factory jobs) John soon heeded Dolby's words and handed in his notice. He then proceeded to work in a succession of factories before opting for a career in the Royal Navy (signing up in September 1971.)

John: "Yeah, I had thoughts of seeing the world and learning a trade, however, (although I spent six months at *H.M.S. Sultan* - the Marine Engineering Training School in Portsmouth) the only time I went to sea was on the Gosport ferry! It didn't take long for me to realise that I wasn't cut out for a life on the ocean waves, and so I persuaded my brother Bob to stump up the £20 to buy me out - which shows that we weren't always fighting!" The release certificate stated: *'Discharged from Active Service - 6th January 1972. Free to take up civil employment forthwith'*.

The 1970s' songwriting team comprising L-R: Robin Goodfellow, Pete Dyne and John Grimley. In this hastily shot publicity still, the three local singer-songwriters attempt to present an air of brooding intensity (in keeping with the image adopted by so many pop stars of the time.)

From a very early age John had harboured aspirations of becoming a drummer, however, when his father brought home from work one day an old battered acoustic guitar - the nine-year-old was promptly hooked, and after weeks of nursing very tender fingertips was able to master the *James Bond Theme*. John then concentrated on learning to play some of the tunes that were being produced by guitar 'greats' like Hank Marvin and Eric Clapton.

When he reached the age of eleven John Grimley played in public for the very first time. He and school friend John Mowatt entered a talent contest at the British Legion club and performed a number called *Sha La La La Lee* by the Small Faces. Although the youngsters won their heat, they unfortunately went no further.

At thirteen years of age Grimley joined his first 'proper' band. It also included Gary Carson on bass and Graham Smith (later of St Cecilia) on drums. The band had the typical 1960s name of Tangerine Fantasy and performed regularly in schools and youth clubs. John: "We played all the pop stuff but I was always more influenced by the music of Eric Clapton or people like Peter Green of John Mayall's

Bluesbreakers, which (even if we could have managed to do a decent job on) still wouldn't have gone down very well in venues like the British Legion!"

By 1969 John had become a well-respected, self-taught guitarist and backing vocalist. He was much sought after by local bands who wanted him to join them or to fill in for vacancies. Very often he would be the only schoolboy in the line-up - as was the case when he linked up with Jimmy Pollock, Bob Gowen, Bip Wetherell and Jack Murphy (a team of seasoned semi-professionals) to play for Gideon's League. John Grimley: "It was a great experience - travelling up and down the country in the back of a van, playing the gigs and having the crack. I really felt like a junior when I was with those guys, as they'd been doing it for years. I must say though, they looked after me right up until I eventually left school at Easter in 1969."

Speaking of his time with Gideon's League Bob Gowen said: "Basil Barnard was in charge of the bookings and transport. He'd been doing it for years with a number of bands - including Pollock's Freemen. Occasionally (and only because he trusted me) Basil would allow me to drive his yellow Commer minibus. However, one night when we were playing in

William Mathieson - aka Billy Biro. Following a disastrous debut gig (in which his talents as a stand-up comedian were laid bare) Billy quickly ditched his 'pen' name and signed off as a Corby gag-man.

Peterborough, Bip pestered me until I gave in and let him have a go at driving it. So how did he repay me? By driving it straight into a pillar in the underground car park - scratching the whole side of the bus! I then dreaded having to face Basil and tell him what had happened - so in the end I lied to him by saying that a lorry had done it and driven off!"

Jim Pollock, former singer with the Freeman, was fronting his own band with Gideon's League (which also included Robin James, Sally Butters and Bob Grimley.) Together they released a 7" single called *Did You Know You've Got Your Face On Upside Down*. It was a Robin Goodfellow and Steve Fearn composition on the Parlophone label and was coupled with *You've Got A Mind Of Your Own*. The backing track was recorded at London Weekend Television Studios (assisted by members of the Juicy Lucy and Keef Hartley bands) and the vocals of Pollock, Butters and Grimley were later added at Beck Studios in Wellingborough. Although Goodfellow had been writing songs for over five years when the contract with Parlophone arrived, his latest offering was to receive a somewhat mixed review in an *Evening Telegraph* article which read as follows:

> *'It is one of those infuriatingly daft songs that you feel you should hate, but somehow you wind up singing the darned thing in the bath, and as St Cecilia proved with their 'Knickers' hit - discos are not averse to a nutty song which will get the crowd singing along.'*

Though ultimately failing to make any headway against the dross which was flooding the charts back then, the record did receive plenty of support from Radio One and from Tony Blackburn in particular. Eventually settling in London, Jim Pollock carved out what he deemed to be 'a comfortable living'. This revolved around playing in some of the capital's top hotels with the Tony Evans Big Band, and writing material for a number of prominent artists (e.g. the Creation).

Feeling that a change of direction might be in order, Billy Mathieson (former drummer with the Phantoms and the Midnighters) decided to try his hand at stand-up comedy. As a result of this, within weeks Billy found himself on the same bill as a pair of strippers and making what could only be described as an 'ignominious' debut.

Corby band Auction. Left to right in ascending order: Jim Smith, Derek Cowie, Reg Knowles, Mick Harper and Billy Mathieson. Yet another band with high hopes of climbing the 'stairway to the stars', the 1960s' music scene veterans put in an ultimately unsuccessful bid for fame and fortune.

Billy: "I decided to give it a go after speaking to a few 'so-called' comedians who told me that they were earning the same amount of money as the bands on the local cabaret and club circuit. As I figured that I could do that too, I asked my agent Glen Allen to fix me up with a booking, but not one in Corby. So what does Glen do? He gives me a stag-night at the former Boys Club on Cottingham Road in Corby!"

As he made his entrance on the big night (in front of an audience of Corby Locomotives Football Club players) Billy, dressed to impress in a dinner jacket and bow-tie, sauntered up to the microphone and introduced himself as Billy Biro. "That's my pen-name" he quipped. Unfortunately, his cover was blown immediately, when a member of the audience shouted "That's Mathieson!" causing everyone to start hissing and booing.

Billy: "The next thing I knew was that some of the Loco players (Davy Norman and his pals etc.) were up on the stage, divesting me of my expensive penguin suit. Under my breath, I said to myself, 'This is not supposed to happen!' However, consummate professional that I am, I decided to carry on regardless. Little did I know that I would end up stark naked! Then to chants of 'Off! Off! Off!' the Loco's 'back four' literally carried me out of the door and dumped me on the lawn!" For weeks after that I wouldn't walk round Corby unless I was wearing a balaclava and shades. To cap it all, the two strippers that were on that night were also crap - they were booed off as well!"

It was a traumatic debut but one made all the worse by the promoter's dissatisfaction with his 'star turn' - Mathieson had £20 deducted from his fee. Billy: "Although I argued that I was supposed to get £100, the promoter was straight and to the point. He said, 'You were shite! Take it or leave it!' So that's how my 'stand-up' career came to an abrupt end. After that I stuck to drumming!"

Billy got back in the groove by joining up with Derek Cowie, Ted Ward and Mick Harper (who were old friends of his) to form Auction - a band which would become increasingly popular as the Seventies wore on. Reminiscing about that era Billy said: "There was one occasion, when the band was booked to play at the Rangers Club, that we aborted the engagement before it had even begun. We had all set up our gear (except for Derek - who was having trouble tuning his guitar) when, suddenly, a

Peter, Paul and Egbert. A popular act on the 1970s' local cabaret circuit, the quartet were all former members of the Senators (Rothwell's most durable rock group.) L-R: Ian Wade, Pete Daniel, Roy Smith and Dave Mitchell.

member of the committee came up on stage and said: 'Right. You've got two minutes. If you haven't started by then, you'll only get half the money!' I said to him, 'In that case we're not playing!' We then got all our things together and walked out - leaving the place in uproar and the committee man looking like a haddie! It's strange how things turn out, because that little episode led to regular employment for the group and an unexpected change of fortune for the Open Hearth pub. We went to the Open Hearth afterwards for a drink, Alan Smith (the pubs landlord) asked us what was up. He listened while we related the story and then said 'Why don't you play here?' We didn't need time to think about it - Alan's proposal sounded good to us. That was how the cabaret nights started up down there."

As it happened, Smith had been toying with the idea of providing a cabaret venue for some time. With the disco scene fading at the Hearth (due to competition from its rivals - i.e. the Shire Horse and Nags Head) and with the opening in January of the Maple Leaf pub in Canada Square, he had reached the conclusion that live music in the form of a cabaret night was the obvious way to go. Furthermore, Alan felt sure that he had spotted yet another gap in the market - and one that could easily be remedied.

For those who had tired of discos but preferred going to a pub rather than to a nightclub, Alan decided to introduce basket meals of chicken or scampi. He was of the opinion that the chance of a bite to eat would enhance the atmosphere of the evening. Having provided an extensive menu for his lunchtime customers, Smith was already a dab hand in the field of catering and planned to do all the cooking and serving himself. His midday clientele consisted mostly of sub-contracting central heating installers (part of a small army working in the town on a major council house central heating programme of the time.) 'Sausage, Chips 'n' Beans' was an Open Hearth speciality - with 'Pie 'n' Chips' coming a close second.

The cabaret nights rapidly became so popular that tickets often sold out within a few days of going on sale. There were regular appearances by the likes of Auction, Scenery (a Northampton band who belted out some fantastic harmonies) and Kettering's Peter, Paul and Egbert (featuring frontman Roy Smith - a former member of the Senators.) Arguably the best of the rock and roll singers in the locality, Bobby Leroy also packed out the Hearth. Not all the bands who performed were great though, and there were undoubtedly some nights when they proved to be a distinct disappointment. On these occasions Alan Smith would leave the business of 'sorting them out' (i.e. paying them) to his sidekick Tommy 'Skull' Cullen. Having worked for years as a doorman at the clubs in Kettering, Skull was well-versed in such matters and had a reputation for getting straight to the point. There was one night when a band from Lincolnshire had been on and had played very poorly. When they asked Tommy how well he thought they had gone down with the crowd, he tersely delivered the verdict "You were Cat!"

"Cat? What does that mean - good or bad?" enquired the singer.

"Cat!" Tommy repeated, "Cat malodeon!"

Still none the wiser, the vocalist asked Tommy to explain again.

"It means you were shite!" Tommy enlightened the perplexed performer.

There were no let-downs of that kind in store for customers of the Nags Head in Corby Old Village - they were very well catered for. Predominently country and western fans, this audience were treated on a weekly basis to the talents of Patsy Powell and the Playboys (the pub's resident artists who hailed from Coventry.) Ken Harris, the group's bass player, remembers: "Corby was such a great audience - the crowd was well-informed, appreciative and receptive. We may have played all over the country, however, in our opinion the Nags had by far the best atmosphere." Coming from an act who had toured with all the big names (including America's Slim Whitman) and who had appeared at many of the major venues, this was praise indeed for the Corby nightspot and its patrons.

Stetson-wearing Jimmy McDougall, of Lincoln Way in Corby (who claims never to have missed a 'country night' down the Nags) says: "It was a great night out. We'd sing along to all of the country favourites, let ourselves go and have a right old time." Jimmy says that he often tried to persuade his wife Sadie to accompany him to the Nags, however, his attempts were always met with a polite 'No way!' Then one night she finally relented.

Sadie: "Jim had been going there on his own every week. When at last he managed to drag me away from the Rutland bingo club, I became one of the converted - a real devotee. Regardless of that, it was also a good excuse to keep my eye on him!"

Cat malodeon! Tommy Cullen's facial expression conveys his thoughts regarding yet another 'cat' performer at the Open Hearth.

Situated on Corby's award-winning Kingswood estate, in 1972 the Maple Leaf pub in Canada Square was about to become a venue for several thriving sports teams - i.e. football, darts and dominoes. Although a sense of pride in their neighbourhood seems to have evaded at least some of the area's residents back then (an eye-catching ornamental pond had to be filled in after council officials became fed up with having to arrange for trolleys and stolen bicycles to be fished out of it!) Tony and Glenys Abbey, the pub's new licencees, were quick to enthuse about their new environment. In a joint interview the couple, who had recently moved from Coventry to Corby, said: "We heard that Corby was a rough-and-ready place but we have met some lovely people. They really seem to respect the place and we have had no complaints about damage to the pub since we came. We believe that bright and pleasant staff, ready to welcome our customers by being happy, really does create a good impression." Unfortunately, not all of the 'Leaf's clientele were met with the aforesaid bonhomie. Alan 'Scouse' McGahey took umbrage with one of Mr. Abbey's barmen for being what he deemed a 'sour face'. Each time he ordered a pint McGahey insisted on addressing the perceivedly sullen barman as 'Smiler'. It wasn't long, therefore, before the latter responded by telling him that, if he didn't like it, he knew where he could go! This prompted the Liverpudlian to grab him by the throat and attempt to pull him over the bar. Subsequently barred from the premises and forced to find a new watering hole, Scouse, pre-warned staff at the Open Hearth "I like a smile with my pint!"

Another altercation which involved customers from the Maple Leaf occurred when their domino team clashed with one from the Open Hearth in the Wednesday Night Domino League. The Hearth's team boasted players of such calibre as that of wheelchair-bound Jack Rothe, Patsy Goodall, Cyril 'Smiler' Smith and Cyril 'Snuff' Milligan. The two Cyrils were regular partners in the game and were often the butt of some good-natured ribbing from their teammates. Smith had a tendency to grin like a Cheshire cat when he saw the game going his way - which gave rise to suspicions that he was giving signals to the short-sighted Milligan. Routinely accused of cheating, the pair remained remarkably sanguine about the insults (if anything they led to Smith grinning even more broadly!) As for Milligan - his response, although good-humoured, would without exception be unprintable!

Also a member of their team was recently-retired steelworks guide Jimmy Cramp. Nicknamed 'Jason King' because of his remarkable resemblance to the hugely popular television sleuth of the day, Cramp had started work at Stewarts and Lloyds in 1934, and in 1959 had become the company's official tour guide. Despite 70 per cent of the company's visitors coming from overseas, word had it that Jimmy was never short of something to say to them - and more often than not it would be in their own language. Such was his dedication to the job that (from the comfort of his extensive home 'library') he would study phrase books and learn about the countries from which his customers had travelled. It was during his spare time (at work presumably?) that he was able to hone the skills that would enable him to become an integral part of the Open Hearth's championship-winning domino team.

The dispute at the Maple Leaf arose because the Rothe/Goodall partnership had also been accused of giving each other signs regarding which domino to play. It culminated in a situation where the pair had to be forcibly restrained after challenging their opponents to step outside. WNDL administrators were left feeling dismayed by the adverse and unwelcome reports which the fracas received in the local press. Concluding its report on the game with (one suspects) tongue-firmly-in-cheek, the *Evening Telegraph* had this to say:

> '*Darts and dominoes have long campaigned to be included in the Olympic ideal and if the standard of the local leagues are anything to go by, then there is a valid claim. After all, if something as trivial as synchronised swimming deserves consideration then darts and dominoes most definitely do as well.*'

It was extremely unlikely that Jack Rothe and Patsy Goodall would take their places that summer alongside the all-time greats who would grace that pantheon of sporting excellence known as the 20th Olympiad. The nearest they would get would be when they, like millions of others around the world, became glued to their television screens, watching in disbelief as horror engulfed the athletes' village in Munich.

The 1972 Olympic Games should be remembered, principally for the remarkable achievements of some of its sportsmen and women. Who can forget the record number of seven gold medals amassed by swimmer Mark Spitz, or the almost as impressive tally of four golds collected by seventeen-year-old Russian gymnast, Olga Korbut?

CANADA
SQUARE

Located alongside its soon to be filled in ornamental pond is the Maple Leaf pub in Canada Square.

Veterans of the Open Hearth dominoes team. L-R: Jimmy Geekie, Percy Horn, Johnny Watson, Jimmy Mullen, George Nater, (with trophy) Jack Rothe, John Eames, Cyril Smith, (kneeling) Dennis Fieldhouse, Tommy Cox and unknown.

Even that precise moment when Northern Ireland's Mary Peters collected her winners medal for the pentathlon holds a special place in the nation's collective memory. Sadly, these feats were completely overshadowed when Arab extremists broke into the Olympic Village and, in scenes of carnage which ripped the heart out of the Games, shot dead two Israeli athletes and took nine others hostage. The gunmen demanded the release of several Palestinian prisoners who were being held in Israel and also a safe passage for themselves out of West Germany. After seventeen hours of negotiations they and their hostages were transported to a military airport at which a shootout then took place. Fatalities included all nine of the Israelis plus a German policeman. Five of the eight-man Arab gang also died. The brutal images remain printed indelibly in the minds of those who watched the dramatic events on television screens around the world.

Guitarist Graham Henderson, who had become disenchanted with life in BSC's Wagon Shops, decided in September 1972 to head for the Antipodes. Now living in Melbourne, on a visit to Corby in June 2007 he recalled: "I was actually in the air when all those dreadful things were going on at the Munich Olympics." Regarding his pursuit of another way of life Graham (better known as Hendie) said: "I was looking for adventure, I think. Besides that it seemed like a lot of people were leaving the UK at that time. Funnily enough, I had little idea of what to expect down under - I just decided to go for it. As it turned out - I got married and divorced twice! I've had a good life though and don't regret anything.

I have a daughter living in Swansea and my eldest grandson is a heavy metal drummer. My other two children live in Adelaide. I still play guitar and over the years have performed a few times as part of a duo and at the occasional party. I once met up with Helen Stewart (an old friend from the days when we were teenagers and used to hang around Studfall shops.) Helen married over here and has got three sisters here in Australia. Ex-Corby Town footballer Willie Armour is another expat with whom I've met up since coming to Oz - and ex-Steelmen John Fyffe and George Flecknor. They went to New Zealand first and then on to Adelaide to play football. Then there was Johnny Robson - who used to play drums in a 1960s band called the Legal Matter. John was originally a pipefitter in the steelworks. His brother Billy, another former steelworker, also lives over here. Billy was a pretty big guy who rode around on a bike. The last I heard was that Fyffe, Flecknor and Johnny Robson were all in Adelaide - and that Billy had a puncture!"

16 DEAD—BUT THE GAMES CONTINUE

ALL NINE Israeli hostages seized by Arab commandos in the Olympic village were killed in a gun battle between the guerrillas and West German police at a military airfield.

Also shot in the battle at Fürstenfeldbruck Airport were four of their Arab guerrilla captors and a policeman, bringing the total number of deaths to 16.

Gun battle terror

Urgent

Graham Henderson - Guitar wizard of Oz. Former Rhubarb Tree member Graham is seen here revisiting his roots during a trip home from Australia in 2008.

When Graham Henderson left these shores he carried with him a wealth of memories. He says that he would often regale his new-found friends with stories of 'life on the road' during his days with the Pacifics, Blue Magnum and the Rhubarb Tree. One of his most treasured memories is of a concert in Leeds. Graham explained: "On the bill were Status Quo, Jefferson Airplane - and lots of other big names. Our group, the Rhubarb Tree, was last but one of the twenty acts due to perform. While we were waiting for the concert to get under way, we were tuning up when suddenly my 'B' string broke. It was just my luck - because I didn't have a spare one. There were stages all around this huge warehouse building and another band was tuning up on the one alongside us. Pointing to them, our lead vocalist Mick Quinn said: 'Try that fuzzy-haired guy over there for one'. So (shy, dumb seventeen-year-old that I was) off I went to ask this fellow for a string. When he gave one to me, I offered him ten bob (50p) in return. 'Don't worry about it' he responded, in a deep, gravelly voice. I toddled off feeling very relieved - I only had ten bob in my pocket! Back with the rest of the boys, I started to put the string on my guitar when Woody (John Woodward - our drummer) came over and said: 'Do you know who that guy was?' to which I replied 'No'. It was in fact Alexis Korner - the doyen of British blues!"

Henderson went on to tell another tale. Graham: "After a performance at RAF Wittering, we were packing our gear into the van when Mick Quinn decided that the table and chairs in our dressing room would be ideal for his new dining room. (Mick had just become engaged to his newly-pregnant girlfriend and intended to set up home with her). So, after we'd loaded the equipment, we put the table and chairs in on top and we set off. I remember it was a real pea-souper of a night (cold, foggy and damp) and our van was full to bursting-point. It had a cargo of ten people, a set of drums, set of amplifiers, six chairs and a table! None of us had taken much notice of how we had gotten into the base and so consequently we took a wrong turning and couldn't find our way out. The next thing we knew, we were being chased by MPs (military policemen) in patrol cars with their blue lights flashing. Naturally, we immediately assumed that they were coming after us for the furniture, and so we threatened to throw Mick and his contraband goods out of the back door. However, the reason why we were being pursued soon became very clear to us - we were on the runway and were surrounded by Harrier Jump Jets!"

Former Corby Town F.C. players George Flecknor & John Fyfe are seen holding aloft the Corby Sunday Streets League championship trophy.
It wouldn't be long before the footballing pair embarked on a professional soccer career in the Antipodes.

Graham Henderson was a product of Corby Boys Secondary Modern School in James Watt Avenue (where he was enrolled after failing his eleven-plus exam.) Hendie says that many a newcomer to the school would spend the preceding long summer holiday in fearful anticipation of the notorious initiation ceremony that involved pupils being thrown down the banks. Although 'the banks' were really nothing more than a grass slope on the Telfords Lane side of the school, as far as the wide-eyed eleven-year-olds who were starting their first year at 'the big school' were concerned, they might as well have been the side of a mountain! At the beginning of each Autumn Term, 2nd Year boys would lie waiting in gleeful anticipation of the chance to inflict upon others the sense of terror which they themselves had faced just twelve months previously. Scared of being singled out (for what they equated to a Jackie Pallo body-slam) the new boys would cower in doorways and bike sheds as they waited anxiously for the nine o'clock assembly bell to ring.

It was a time-honoured ritual that nowadays would be classed as bullying and would not be tolerated. Indeed, back then it gave rise over the years to numerous instances where young lads were in receipt of broken bones as a consequence of being hurled down the slope by three or four older boys. Graham Henderson was one to join the long list of casualties. Having dislocated a shoulder at his initiation ceremony, Hendie spent the first few weeks at the Boys School with his arm in a sling. As luck would have it, there was no long-term damage and he was able to take up playing the guitar and become a member of the Hangmen (the name of the school band.) On leaving school Graham pursued his musical ambitions by playing in various other bands, whilst at the same time chiselling out a career for himself with a carpentry apprenticeship in the steelworks' wagon shops.

Backs to the future! Pupils line up in the playground of Corby Boys School circa 1953. In the background Stewarts & Lloyds steelworks threaten to spill out over Telfords Lane. Although the majority of boys pictured were destined to work in the steelworks, Alec 'Popsie' Gibson opted for a career in entertainment and achieved success in the music and film industries. Alec is seen here at the head of the fourth line from the left.

In the summer of 1972 the introduction of 'hot pants' (a new fashion in ladies clothing) raised the temperature of just about every red-blooded male in Corby. Local DJ Dougie King described them as being 'delicious'. He explained: "You get sick of seeing the girls running about in long coats during the winter months. It's nice to see their legs again when spring comes around."
Mr. Edward Thompson, a retired steelworker, took a different view. Edward said scornfully: "They're a disgrace! I don't include hot pants or mini-skirts among the joys of spring. I think they look awful and they show too much." The overall view was best summed up by babe-watcher John Wilson of Westfields Road. John mused: "In my opinion, spring just wouldn't be the same without miniskirted dollies!"

Another introduction guaranteed to set tongues wagging was that of Corby's first traffic warden. Although when interviewed prior to donning his yellow cap of office, former steelworker Walter Greenhill was described (contrary to popular stereotype) as being 'human after all!' The article went on: 'There appear to be no horns sticking out of his head, no heart of stone cold stare and no sadistic streak'. It didn't take long for all that to change though - Walter soon gained a reputation for being a hard-nosed and unsympathetic character. Clive Smith (who was by then driving taxis for a living) was less than amused when one Friday afternoon he was booked by Walter, for parking his front wheels over the zigzag lines of a pedestrian crossing opposite the Civic. Clive: "I pulled up outside the taxi rank and because it was full, hung back for a minute while the other cabs moved round to pick up fares from the queue. Whilst I was waiting, I suddenly decided to nip out of my cab and into the newsagents to buy a Mars Bar. It was a spur of the moment kind of thing. As I did so, Walter, who had been lurking in a doorway, crept out of the shadows and began writing a parking ticket. I couldn't believe it. After all, at this point I'd hardly set foot on the pavement. 'You must be joking!' I shouted at him, and when he asked for my name I told him where to go. 'I was only getting a Mars Bar,' I explained. Unfortunately, it was of no avail - Walter just repeated calmly 'Name and badge number please?' At this

Mini skirted Margaret Martin and her friend Helen McPhie are pictured on a trip to the seaside resort of Great Yarmouth. Margaret (whose marital name is Leaker) says that she and Helen hitchhiked there in order to attend a disco that Dougie King was putting on in one of the town's major venues. She remembers that prior to the event the girls had great fun running along the promenade with one of Dougie's voluminous shirts held aloft between them - billowing in the sea breeze. Joining in the fun, the amiable DJ chased after them.

point I really lost it and called him a 'blinkin' jobsworth'. Next day the police came to my door and read out Greenhill's report. Everything that I had said to him was written down on it. Even the police had to laugh - but it didn't stop them fining me £20!"

Another incident involving the traffic warden took place in the car park of the Rockingham Arms pub. It was there that Walter, whilst bending over to check the tyres of a vehicle belonging to Peter Murphy, that he received an almighty kick up the backside that propelled him forward and caused him to bang his head on the bonnet. When asked in court for *his* version of events, Murphy told the magistrate: "I thought he was slashing my tyres!" Unsurprisingly, the defendant received a £60 fine. Andrew Hunter of Sheffield Walk in Corby also received a fine from the Magistrates' Court. On this occasion it was a £2 penalty for riding his bicycle along a footpath. Despite having been stopped earlier on and ordered to dismount, Hunter had chosen to ignore the advice of WPC Margaret Ridout and had later climbed back onto his bike. The policewoman (who had been following Hunter in her Panda car) then cautioned him.

At the hearing Hunter denied the offence. He claimed that it would have been impossible for him to ride a bike as he'd only recently had a calliper removed from his leg, plus, the affected limb would still have been too stiff. Hunter's plea of not guilty was dismissed.

At the same court session an appearance was made by Gerald Dawson of Kingsthorpe Avenue, who (as a result of a purge on motoring offences) had been charged with driving his moped without due care and attention. The magistrates heard that Dawson had been spotted driving his vehicle - whilst carrying a ladder on his shoulder! He pleaded guilty to the offence and was fined a sum of £3.

In an attempt to revive his flagging career, Kettering balladeer Barry Noble decided upon a very unusual course of action - he persuaded the *Sun* newspaper to sponsor a competition in which readers would be invited to think up a brand new name for him. Mike Nevard, the editor of the music page, made the following pitch to the public:

Can you NAME A POP STAR!
You could win £100.

'Here's a chance to play a super name game and take a hand in shaping pop history. It's exciting, it's fun and it could win you a fantastic prize of £100, PLUS a dream night out in London, all expenses paid. All you have to do is to rename a pop star. A real singer called Barry Noble. At present he is a successful performer on the club circuit, but Barry is ambitious - he wants to be a star like Gerry Dorsey, Terry Nelhams or Clive Powell. Dorsey, Nelhams, Powell? These are of course Engelbert Humperdinck, Adam Faith and Georgie Fame. Without their name changes, would any of us ever have heard of them? The image builders doubt it. In selling a pop artist, an intriguing, memorable label is reckoned to be of prime importance. That's why Barry, who at 26 has good looks, and a big voice, wants a new name. And we want you to find one.'

Readers wishing to compete were instructed to study a photograph of Barry and 'let your imagination do the rest.' Barry: "We received suggestions from over 12,000 entrants to the competition, however, they were all so bad that I decided to carry on with my own name. It was a nice bit of PR though!

In 1972 a single of mine called *Mary Put The Lights Out* was released on a small label by the name of Plexium. I wrote both sides to it and Derek Tompkins came down to London to do the production. Although it was played on the radio a few times, it didn't get an airing on TV at all.

Later on I made three singles for Supreme Records (based in Antwerp in Belgium.) They all had radio play but not big sales. Luckily I had a good name on the cabaret circuit and made a living in the Seventies by doing night clubs in the UK alongside Bob Monkhouse, the Barron Knights, the Platters, Eartha Kitt and Larry Grayson. I also did theatre shows and worked at the Derngate in Northampton twice - with the Tremeloes, the Fortunes, Larry Grayson, plus Frankie Howerd. I remember Frankie wearing an extremely ill-fitting wig, and believe it or not - his manager/ boyfriend wore something similar. I thought it was hilarious.

I also worked in Zambia for a month, doing hotel cabaret. On several nights there were fully armed members of the Patriotic Front rebel army in the audience - which I found off-putting, to say the least! Fortunately they enjoyed my act and so I survived to do the show for a Commonwealth conference in Port es Solam, Tanzania. I sang for the final time on TV in 1979. It was on *The Datsun Show* in Singapore, and I was accompanied by a forty piece orchestra. From there I went on to Bangkok and Thailand - where I sang at the Hilton Hotel for a month. 1979 was also the year when I appeared alongside the French star Juliette Greco, at the Atlantic Ball in the Savoy Hotel, Madiera."

Throughout the 1970s, both midweek and at weekends, hundreds of Corby football fans travelled the length and breadth of the country to watch their favourite teams in action. One such fixture took place on the September 18, 1972 - a testimonial for the Manchester United and England forward Bobby

Charlton. Played against Celtic Football Club, the match drew a crowd of 60,538 supporters to Old Trafford (the largest ever recorded for a match of that nature.) Corby's representatives were, not untypically, late arrivals to the occasion - owing to the fact that several of the buses carrying them to the game had broken down en route. Don Gracey, a passenger on the bus that had set off from the Shire Horse pub, recalls the motorway being littered with the 'crocked' convoy of vehicles belonging to Flanagan's of Corby. Don said dryly: "Old Murt's coaches didn't enjoy the best of reputations in town!"

In May of that year a party of twenty-eight Rangers F.C. fans travelled from Corby to Barcelona, in order to support their team's quest for honours in a European Cup Winners Cup Final against Moscow Dynamo. Although the football match would end in victory for the Scottish team, it was also a game destined to end in farce and affray. James Whyte (the Supporters Club secretary) had in fact warned beforehand that trouble would flare up if any of the Rangers fans were to make disparaging remarks about religion or General Franco. Unfortunately, his words of wisdom proved to be spot on though, thankfully, none of his party was involved throughout the day in any of the ugly scenes that took place on the streets of the Catalan capital, or in the violence that erupted at the end of the match itself. With hindsight, the event was bound to end in conflict - after all, Spain is a Roman Catholic country. It was inevitable that the barrage of insults and abuse that was being exchanged (between the Rangers fans, who were being urged on by Catalan Nationalists, and the local militia) would result in an explosion of tempers at the final whistle. When fighting broke out and the uncompromising Spanish police set about belting anyone and everyone with batons, the planned pitchside presentation had to be cancelled.

Although 'The Sun' newspaper ran a competition to find a new name for Barry Noble, in the end the Kettering balladeer opted to retain the one he already had (and under which he continued to perform on TV and cabaret circuits throughout the world.)

Instead, the Rangers skipper John Grieg had to settle for collecting the hard earned trophy in the team's dressing room. It marked a miserable end to what should have been a glorious chapter in the history of the famous Scottish football club. To make matters worse, Rangers had to suffer the ignominy of being banned from Europe for two seasons.

The *Daily Record* described the events as follows:

'It was like a scene from a bad Western movie - the baddies were the winners. This was the night Scottish football went mad in a neutral city which is now aghast. Thousands of Rangers fans turned the club's greatest victory in Europe into a sordid unruly riot. A crowd from Scotland of nearly 25,000 tried to show Europe that they were the most loyal supporters in the world - and emotions, helped on by drink, took over with the craziest result football has ever seen. What should have been the pay-

off for the fans, who had arrived in 60 chartered planes, buses, cars and on foot, was turned into a total shambles. It should have been a carnival night. The Spaniards will long remember the visit of the Rangers fans. The sight of hordes of them racing out to attack a baton-charging line of the police struck a new note in hooliganism. Most humiliating of all was the riot police having to escort both sets of players back to their hotels ten miles away from the stadium. The hooligan supporters who invaded the pitch should have been sent back home on foot - and shunned when they got home.'

There were many fans, however, who claimed that the Spanish police themselves were to blame. Robert Miller of East Kilbride said: "A handful of Glasgow police would have sorted it out in a few minutes - without half the fuss and bother", whereas Norman Durham of Dennistoun deemed: "The Spanish police were brutal!"

In the aftermath of the game, as Barcelona returned to normality recriminations were rife. Arrested fans appeared in court - facing charges relating to fighting and assault. Others were sent home by train but, if they were unable to stump up the fare, had their passports impounded at Dover.

In the meantime, back in Scotland members of the winning squad were greeted at Prestwick Airport by legions of adoring fans. Decked out in team colours and wearing sombreros, they had turned out in force to give their heroes an unforgettable (not to mention raucous!) reception. 'The noise was deafening' reported John Cameron of the *Daily Record*.

Nearly four decades later, speaking from Corby, James 'Maxie' McCafferty gave his own slant on the events that took place in Barcelona: James: "I like to think that after the Ibrox tragedy (where on the January 2, 1971 sixty-six people lost their lives) Rangers became inspired to win more honours - a sort of 'Rebirth of the Blues' if you like. In that respect, winning the European Cup Winners Cup on May 24, 1972 was a fitting tribute to those who died.

I remember that we arrived in Barcelona around dinner time and checked into our hotel. Most of us then went shopping for souvenirs and to have a drink. We left the hotel at 7.00p.m. and headed for the Nou Camp stadium - where we were due to play Moscow Dynamo at 8.00p.m.

At the match we had a great first half in which Colin Stein and Willie Johnston put us 2 - 0 up, and then within minutes of the re-start Johnston scored again to make it 3-0. After that we seemed to lose our concentration - conceded a goal with half an hour to go and another with just three minutes of the game remaining. Somehow we managed to hang on to our lead though, and the final score stood at 3-2.

Everyone was overjoyed and a number of fans ran onto the pitch to share their excitement with the players. The Spanish police interpreted this as a threat against them and retreated to the other side of the park. They then decided that a baton charge was in order and started clubbing our supporters. At this stage I went down to the pitch - but only to attract the attention of the Red Cross. This was for one of our fans who was on his back with his head split open. Both before and after the game we'd had great rapport with the local people - some of them even joined in our celebrations.

The next day I went down to the beach to do a spot of sunbathing and my wallet and passport were stolen. Because of this, when I got to Barcelona airport I was refused permission to board my flight. I wasn't alone - there were quite a few of us in the same predicament. We were forced to spend thirty-six hours in the airport, whilst waiting for clearance to leave. Eventually, they put all the stranded Rangers supporters on the last flight out. It was the one which was carrying all the travel couriers who'd supervised the various charter flights. We took off at 5.00a.m. on the Saturday morning and landed back in the UK at Prestwick Airport which is near Glasgow. I was skint and absolutely knackered but somehow managed to get on a bus that was going into Glasgow. Although I was penniless and three hundred and fifty miles away from Corby, I was at least on home soil. As luck would have it, in the city centre I bumped into some friends from Corby (who were in Scotland for the home international football match against England) and they were able to lend me enough money to make my way to the home of some other friends of mine in Glasgow. I even got there in time to

It may well have been unjustified in this particular instance, but a cartoon published in the 'Daily Record' the following day decries the darker side of British football in the seventies.

watch the game on television. My friends from Corby were members of the Pluto's Scotland International Club and had travelled up to Glasgow by coach. When the organisers of the coach trip offered me a lift back with them on the Sunday, I was more than happy to accept. Even better, on the way home (courtesy of my hosts) I was wined and dined regally. I eventually reached home at 1.00p.m. on the Monday morning, and although I was rather the worse for wear, I have to say that I was eternally grateful to a number of very kind-hearted people.

In January 1972 Fleming Osbaek (18) and Aage Hansen (20) were two more Danish footballers to sign for the Steelmen. Announcing their arrival, the club's chairman, John Singlehurst, claimed that they would prove to be invaluable additions to the club. And they might well have been - had they hung around long enough! For like their fellow countrymen from the previous year, Osbaek and Hansen discovered that they couldn't handle the culture shock. A job in the Coke Ovens, digs in the Church Army hostel… what more could they ask for?

This was a markedly low period for a football club that found itself shorn of support and inspiration. Even a request for a £2,000 grant from Corby District Council (to improve facilities at the Occupation Road ground) was overwhelmingly rejected - despite support from Councillor Ricky Docherty who said: "The club is a very important part of the community, giving people in the town relaxation and enjoyment." Council Leader Kelvin Glendenning added in agreement: "A successful club would help publicise and improve the town's image. The money would help enhance the club." Councillor Jimmy Kane chipped in: "More people should go along and support the club," whilst Arthur Morgan was vehemently opposed to it. "There aren't sufficient people going along to justify the expenditure of council", he commented. Tom Sykes said that he would have given them £10,000 if it had been ten to fifteen years ago 'as football was then an attractive proposition'. However, in an attempt to explain his misgivings, he continued by saying that 'now this sort of football is doomed. It is on the way out and just about finished. It is only supported by bingo and raffles.'

More bad press was heaped upon the club when Tommy Hadden (widely regarded as a popular choice of manager) was abruptly dismissed in a phone call that had been taken by his wife! A spokesperson for the Steelmen tried to explain that Mr. Hadden hadn't been at home to take the call and therefore a message had been left for him. Whatever the truth of the matter, it was a disgraceful way to treat a man who had been a stalwart of the club for over twenty years. The former Airdrieonians and Stirling Albion full back had signed for the Steelmen in 1952, played for them for the next eight years and became their manager in 1962. He had then gone on to lead the club through one of the most productive and successful periods in its history. Having already been dismissed back in 1968 in a similarly insensitive manner (on that occasion in favour of former Rangers and Scotland captain Eric Caldow) Tommy had been tempted back to reclaim the helm on a temporary basis when the club found itself without a manager in the midst of one of its

James 'Maxie' McCafferty - Barcelona veteran and former Corby Exeter F.C. Full-back. Maxi played amateur football with distinction for many years.

all too frequently occurring crises. To make matters worse, his long-time friend Don Johnson (who was a trainer at the club) had this time also received his marching orders - leaving a very bitter taste in Tommy's mouth. "Don has been at the club for nineteen years. The least they could have done is give him a testimonial," he protested.

Unbelievably, just a few days later the Steelmen approached Hadden to ask if he'd consider taking on the secretary's job. "No chance!" was Tommy's curt reply. The club's next choice of manager was Ken Burton (the England Youth coach.) Ken had been responsible for guiding Rothwell Town Football Club towards the very pinnacle of its footballing achievements - a famous victory over Peterborough United, in the Northants Senior Cup Final, which had earned them the coveted status of 'giant-killers'. As a bonus, Burton brought with him Jimmy Kane, Rob Clark, Gordon Hall and John Fyfe - some of Rowell's finest players and, Corby lads one and all.

THE TARTAN ARMY (CORBY BRANCH)

Above: Former Corby Town manager Tommy Hadden. Tommy suffered the ignominy of being sacked as team manager of the Steelmen, only to be offered (within hours) the job of club secretary. Was that a sideways move - or just a 'route one' balls up?

Crawford Potter's nine-month battle to play amateur football again finally came to an end when a 'kangaroo court case of soccer oddity' (of which he was the subject) officially closed its files. Having been cleared to play by the referee, a victorious twenty-six-year-old Potter stepped out on the field for a UCL clash between Isham and Corby Gainsborough Reserves. Although the centre-forward had played for Gainsborough three-and-half-years prior to that, he had then taken up a job offer in Australia, and it was whilst there that he signed a contract with Corinthians to play professional state soccer in New South Wales (scoring thirty of a tally of sixty goals in his last season with the club.) Unfortunately, as Potter's wife was unable to adapt to life down under, the couple returned home to Corby in July 1971, and when a chance had presented itself for Crawford to link up again with his former Gainsborough outfit, Corinthians stepped in and demanded a transfer fee of 500 Australian dollars - the equivalent of £195.65p in sterling. The problem lay in the fact that under FIFA regulations the club was not permitted to pay and to make matters worse, the F.A. had issued instructions to all clubs that the player could not be signed until the cash wrangle with the Australian Soccer Federation had been settled. (Willie Middleton, Gainsborough's assistant manager) was quoted as saying at the time: "We immediately took up the case with FIFA. They met in Pakistan only last week and have decided to instruct Corinthians to drop the matter. In fact, moves have gone through in such a way that we have acquired Potter on the original terms that we wanted. If any professional club wants to sign him they will have to pay the Australian club 500 Dollars - such would be the case if Corby Town wanted him. As long as he remains an amateur, Potter is completely in the clear."

John Purdie, the secretary of Gainsborough F.C., had the final word on the matter. John said: "The F.A. supplied Potter with a 'K' registration permit form which I had to fill in and send back. The formal club signing-on was completed this afternoon by the referee - the only man who was able to do it within the twenty-four hour deadline." Antipodean adventurer Crawford Potter later left the Corby outfit to turn professional. It was a case of the southern hemisphere's loss becoming Corby Town F.C.'s gain (and then Irthlingborough Diamonds' and Stamford's etc.)

'Please Don't Leave Me!' ran the *Evening Telegraph* headline one July day in 1972. Sadly, that's the way it had to be for Peterborough United's reserve goalkeeper, Dick Dighton, who left his bride of just thirty minutes in order to play in a Watney Cup 1st Round match.

Speaking outside the Nags Head in her home town of Corby, his wife Janice (nee Kelly) told reporters: "I was upset when I heard that Dick would have to leave the reception early, however, we're married and that's the main thing. I suppose it's just one of the hazards of marrying a professional footballer." Dick, who had been a Posh player for two years, had only been notified on the previous night that he might be required as a replacement for the team's regular goalkeeper. Fortunately, Clive Smith (Dick's best man) had promised the groom that he would perform all necessary duties in the absence. When Dighton arrived back in Corby at around six o'clock that night (having picked up a hefty pay packet for playing in the 6-5 victory over Blackpool) he was met with an increasingly nervous best man. Clive Smith was beginning to worry about just how far into the night his responsibility might stretch!

Harbouring ambitions to transform Corby Civic Centre into one of the most prominent entertainment venues in the Midlands, Ross Jones (general manager of the complex), announced that a host of stars had been booked to appear there during the coming year. These included Harry Secombe, Frank Ifield, Alan Price together with Georgie Fame, Chris Barber, Yehudi Menuhin and others.
"The massive 1,400 - seater Festival Hall will be used to its fullest capacity," promised Jones. He added: "Dinner dances will be held on three Fridays a month. The cabaret on January 14, features Raffles, a pickpocket, who is amazing. He takes things off people so easily. Status Quo also appears on February 10. As you can see, we are trying to cater for everybody but it's very hard to get people to leave their armchairs and televisions these days."
In the event, the Quo concert (which was a sell-out) proved to be a very lively affair. Guitarist Francis Rossi had spent the night winding up the crowd with a steady stream of insults - provoking them to reciprocate with that same measure of robustness that one would expect from a typical Corby audience!
In direct contrast to this, the Operatic Society's production of *The Desert Song* was a complete disaster and ended up sustaining losses of over £600. It was a bitterly disappointed spokesperson, Mr. Dumican, who complained: "The show ran all week and apart from the opening two nights (on Friday and Saturday when about 900 turned up) the rest has been a waste of time".
Although operettas are generally considered to be less serious than operas - because of the comic and sometimes farcical nature of their plots, *The Desert Song* managed to provide steelworker Cyril Smith with a level of amusement over and above that normally associated with this somewhat satirical storyline. Cyril says that when he spotted his pal Wilf Woolmer (who collected glasses at the Rockingham Arms) dressed as an Arab and singing in the chorus at the back of the stage, he laughed so hard that his teeth fell out!
In the meantime, many of the younger elements in Corby felt that shows like *The Desert Song* didn't really appeal to the majority of people in the town (their reasoning being that only a select few would attend events of this nature.) On the back of this, complaints began to resurface regarding the 'lack of anywhere decent to go to' in the town, so Helen Baxter, a local newspaper reporter, decided to investigate. Helen challenged herself to try and have a fun weekend out in the town - with the aim of reporting back on her findings. While it was not an out-and-out damning indictment of Corby's nightlife, Helen's article did suggest that the town tended to be rather on the dull side. She revealed that there was a choice of seventeen pubs and umpteen licensed clubs, for those who drank, and in addition 'with a quick sex change operation I could gain admittance to Corby Bowl's stag night, could dance myself to a shadow at the Nags Head, Shire Horse, Corby Bowl and Open Hearth discos, freak out at the Bowl's heavy night - to the sound of the Idle Race - or take part in the rock 'n' roll revival show with Bobby Leroy at the Open Hearth. But if I wanted a drink after twelve o'clock I'd have had it. Why does everything shut down at midnight?" Ms. Baxter's final conclusion was that 'apathy prevails in the town'.
Maybe she was right - as around that same time it was announced that the Rutland Cinema would no longer be screening films on a Saturday morning (effectively bringing to an end a tradition which had lasted for more than thirty years.) Arthur Pitcher, the general manager of Hamblin Leisure Services, revealed that the concept was being transferred to the Civic Theatre. What's more, he infuriated interested parties by announcing that the entrance fee would be increased from 5p to 10p - due to the cost of hiring both theatre and films. Arthur countered: "We will continue to make a loss - but it was never designed to make a profit".

FAREWELL
– AFTER
THIRTY
MINUTES
MARRIAGE

PLEASE don't leave me!
But that's the way it had
to be on Saturday after-
noon when Peterborough
United's reserve goalkeeper
Dick Dighton left his Corby
bride of just 30 minutes to
play in a football match.

He left his wife, formerly
Miss Janice Kelly, of
Handcroft Court, at Corby's
Nag's Head on Saturday, to
play in the found of
the Watney

Said Ja
set when
would hav
ception
marri
in

Goalkeeping groom Dick Dighton is congratulated by Best Man Clive Smith.

It may well have been part of a long-term plan by local government to relocate all leisure and entertainment facilities of that nature to the blossoming Town Centre. "Corby will become the super shopping centre of the 70s for this area when phase 1 of its new town centre is completed by the end of the year," claimed the Development Corporation. "This is good news and should put an end to housewives moaning that there's nowhere to shop in Corby. Big names like Sainsbury's, John Menzies and Halfords are in the frame to grab one of the forty new units. A state-of-the-art multi-storey car park, alongside the new Jerry Lewis Organisation double cinemas, will also open on the day after Corporation Street closes for traffic."

Although there were poor attendance figures for the majority of shows that were put on at the Civic, the Peter Sarstedt concert of 1972 turned out to be particularly disappointing. Peter may have wondered *Where Do You Go To My Lovely?* but Oona Campbell and her pals were not on hand to tell him that it was to the ladies darts night in the Rangers club!

Even folk singers Jimmie McGregor and Robin Hall (sharing a bill with comedian Hughie Ferris who amused those present with his impressions of Andy Stewart and Eartha Kitt) were only able to command a small audience with their show *A Wee Drop Of Scotch*.

The Annual Corby Arts Festival was opened In July by Commander Michael Saunders-Watson - the castellan of Rockingham Castle (a popular tourist attraction, place of historical interest and source of much local pride.) In an enthusiastic speech to those people who were gathered in the Civic Square, he said: "This is the 6th festival and I hope there will be many more. There is the sort of entertainment here that you would not find anywhere else in the country. Corby really has nothing to worry about." The vice-chairman of the local Council spoke next. Councillor Willie Mawdsley said: "It was with some trepidation that Corby District Council decided to sponsor the very first festival. At the time we had little idea that it would become an annual event in the town."

The RAF Association (Corby Branch) Festival Dance got proceedings off to a flying start, and was followed on the Sunday night by David Kossoff's *A Funny Kind Of Evening*. It was a show which certainly lived up to its name - the small but appreciative audience were left in stitches after listening to two hours' worth of hilarious stories and jokes from the entertaining Mr. Kossoff.

The first Late-Night session of the week featured Steve Lane's Famous Southern Stompers - an immensely popular choice who were applauded by the crowd for 'giving a good account of their jazz ability.' The Late-Night sessions in the Willow Room were always popular because many of the punters revelled in the smoky, beery atmosphere of the venue. The next act up was brass-rock band Granite - consisting of Corby's Dick Kirk, Bip Wetherell and Jake Pressley, playing alongside others from as far afield as Bedford and Leicester. This eight-piece musical ensemble (who had spent the Easter week that year playing concerts in Corby's German twin town of Velbert) had the room positively rocking with their 'funky soul' sound. They were one of only a few rock groups in the country at that time to boast a brass section comprising of tenor sax, trombone and trumpet. Although they were heavily influenced by the American group Chicago, Granite's repertoire also included many soul and Tamla Motown numbers.

Appearing at the festival's Blues Night was a band which had been strung together by two stalwarts of the British Blues scene - Bob Brunning (the original bass player with Fleetwood Mac) and Bob Hall (Savoy Brown's keyboard player.) The Brunning Hall Blues Band's set consisted mainly of original material and came as a surprise to those who had been expecting the customary John Lee Hooker and Muddy Waters riffs. Tony 'Smythe' Smith, a

Above: Cast members from Corby Operatic Society's production of 'The Desert Song' are happy to pose for the camera (including Wilf Woolmer on the right.) Although content with his new theatrical role, Rockingham Arms 'pot man' Wilf was more normally associated with the line "Last Orders Ladies and Gentlemen!"

blues enthusiast from Corby, was well and truly impressed. "It made a change from the *Dust My Broom* and *Hoochie Coochie* stuff. Really cool!" he gushed.

The festival may have gotten off to a slow start as regards audience numbers, but by the end of the week Harry Maddams, Chairman of the Arts Council, admitted that he was delighted with the way things had worked out. He said: "This year's Arts Festival came in like a lamb - with poorly attended shows, but roared out like a lion - with a capacity audience for the Halle Orchestra. The numbers attending at the start of the week were disappointing, particularly for the Yonty Solomon and Thomas Gentry piano concert. We were expecting them to attract a large audience but less than a hundred turned up".

Corby group Granite prepare for a 'hard' slog out on the road. Their travels were to take them far and wide. L-R: Bip Wetherell, Jake Pressley, Roger Buckby, Bob Grimley, Bob Gowen (on drums), Dick Kirk and Ron Kirk. Keyboard player Bip Wetherell remembers: "Elaine and I were married on a Saturday and spent the night at the Piccadilly Hotel in London. The following morning we joined the rest of the band and set out for Germany in a Transit Van."

In a town where bingo, darts and a little flutter on the gee-gees (especially the ITV Seven - a fiendishly difficult accumulator) were still high on the leisure activities agenda, Harry may have overestimated Corby's appetite for culture on the grand scale. A Fellow of the Royal College of Music, the aforementioned Yonty had enjoyed a distinguished global career - his extensive repertoire including the complete Bach 48 Preludes and Fugues. Speaking from his lofty position astride a barstool at the Rockingham Arms pub, Jimmy Plunkett said: "That's all very well", but can he throw a good arra?"

An amusing tale that made the front pages of the local paper that year revealed the plight of the piranha fish with no teeth. Bob Tyler (secretary of the Corby Aquarist Society and owner of the unfortunate piranha) was distraught on finding out that his pet fish Pirie would have to learn to live without his gnashers following a collision with a rock in his aquarium. Bob explained that, in response to his advertisement for the services of a dentist who might be able to help, Mr. E. McAree of the Pytchley Court Dental Surgery had stepped forward to offer the injured party a check-up. "Looks like he's got gum disease" was his diagnosis, "I would have to recruit the help of a vet if I were to proceed with the treatment." Unfortunately for his owner (not to mention Pirie) the price of more than £100 to fit the piranha with dentures proved prohibitive. So after chewing the matter over, Bob reached the sad conclusion that there would be no new teeth for the gummy Piranha!

In October *The Wildest Show on Earth* came to town. With a wealth of acrobatic and juggling acts from Europe and North Africa on the programme, Circus Hoffman also boasted an assortment of animals from all over the world. Potential visitors to the circus were told that they would be able to witness the extraordinary prowess of a Herculean weightlifter who was able to carry the equivalent of six men on his shoulders. What they weren't privy to was the fact that (when he had completed his stint in the Big Top) that very same 'Colossus' doubled as the candy floss seller!

No false teeth for gummy piranha

CORBY'S famous pet, Pirie, the toothless piranha, will have to learn to live without his teeth.

For his owner, Bob Tyler, of 75 Occupation Road, Corby, says the cost of giving Pirie a set of false teeth is [...]

[...] ing Pirie false [...] be more than [...]

Mr. Tyler, who [...] of Corby Aqua- said: "The [...] hibitive. Pirie [...] £1 when I first [...] and now he is [...] worth much [...] terms than [...]

Pirie is being [...] ablets which [...] to his tank. [...] late—the re- [...] ank collision [...] es not mean [...] his public [...]

1972 saw the death of Joseph Arthur Rank - the man who had been unwittingly instrumental in providing the youngsters of Corby with what was probably the most influential and enriching establishment ever to grace the town - the Odeon Cinema in Rockingham Road. Born in Kingston upon Hull, J. Arthur became a devout Methodist who in 1933 began producing movies in order to spread the gospel - a crusade which would eventually lead to him being recognised as Britain's chief distributor of motion pictures. To the Corby kids of the 1940s and 1950s, the Odeon Cinema was undoubtedly a godsend. David Black, who as a child lived in nearby Gilchrist Avenue, recalls: "I practically grew up in the Odeon. It was draughty in the winter and the 1s. 9d. seats at the front of the stalls were of bare wood. Nevertheless, despite its spartan conditions, the Odeon became like a second home me - as it did to most of us kids. That was in the days before we had TV and I suppose the cinema was our window on the world.

My godmother was an usherette there and (thanks to her sneaking me in!) I was able to spend many a contented day and early evening watching the big films of the era. Even today, when I meet up with childhood friends we often reminisce about the magic that we experienced at the 'flicks' on the corner of Stevie Way. Personally, I'll never forget the thrill of watching that bit at the end of *Yankee Doodle Dandy* - where James Cagney tap-dances his way down the stairs of the White House. It's still my favourite moment from 'the pictures'. Thanks for the memory, J. Arthur!"

1972 was also the year in which Charles Atlas (the man who was undoubtedly at the forefront of today's obsession with the 'body beautiful') also passed away. Born in Italy under the name of Angelo Charles Siciliano, Atlas later emigrated to the United States of America. He was a rather delicate-looking youngster who, having suffered physical abuse at the hands of bigger and stronger kids in school, described himself as 'a pale, thin, and picked on youth, a truly 97 pound weakling'.

Drawing upon his observations of the big cats at the zoo and how they flexed their muscular bodies against the bars of their cages to strengthen them via the force of resistance, Atlas decided to develop his own method of body-building. He called the system 'Dynamic Tension' and was himself living proof of its effectiveness. In 1928 Atlas met businessman Charles Roman and together they founded Charles Atlas, Ltd. - a company which would make its name selling mail-order body-building courses. As the business expanded (along with the chests of half of the male population) Atlas became a hugely iconic figure. He earned the title of America's most famous muscle-man and retained it for the best part of the 20th century.

Back in 1963 Charles Atlas was the inspiration for three men who would become founder members of the Corby Barbell Club in Forest Gate Road. Mick Coleman, Francis McDermot, and Dave Morgan (all from Corby) were well known in the locality for having enjoyed a fair degree of success when competing for the Society of Amateur Weightlifters awards. With support from Norman Benn, the landlord of the Everard Arms, they were able to create at the rear of the pub a training centre for weightlifting enthusiasts.

After leaving Our Lady of Walsingham Roman Catholic School, Mick Coleman became a fitter in Stewarts and Lloyds. One of five children (the other four being Barbra, Martha, Therese and John-Joe - aka Banjo) he lived with his mother and step-father at the family home in Leighton Road, Corby. Mick later decided to join the Royal Marines and was sent to serve in Aden with 45 Commando.

On Wednesday May 29, 1968, Corporal RM 22525 Michael Patrick Coleman (26) of Corby, Marine Michael John Perry (20) of Wells, and Marine Percival Leonard Michael Newland (19) of Abercyon, Glamorgan, were all drowned when their boat capsized in Cawsand Bay near Plymouth.

On July 5, of that year, at an inquest into their deaths eighteen-year-old Marine Sheil (the only surviving member of the boat party) told the Coroner that on the afternoon of the tragedy nine marines had left Millbay Docks in a Royal Marine yacht. After going ashore in a dinghy, four of the men then went to Cawsand village - where they bought flagons of cider and drank about one pint each. Following the departure of the yacht, the young Marines visited the Ship Inn and then the Smuggler's Inn to have some ale. It was their intention to catch the bus back to Torpoint, however (as Marine Sheil informed the court) around 10p.m. they discovered that they had missed it. At this point they made their way down to the beach - in the hope of getting a boat back to barracks.

In response to a question from the Coroner, Mne. Sheil assured him that none of his companions was seriously under the influence of drink. He went on to say that the group had seen a small fibre-glass dinghy near the slipway, carried it down to the water and (because it had no oars or rowlocks) had taken an oar belonging to another boat.

Mne. Sheil described how the boat was low in the water because of their weight. He said that the tide was going out, there was no wind and that it was pitch black. After a short time the dinghy started to ship water and so they made a decision to turn back. Mne. Sheil explained: "It was off-balance as we turned and the water came in - but there was no panic as we could all swim."

Despite the efforts of local people and a massive sea-and-air rescue mission, the bodies were never recovered. The Plymouth Coroner, Mr. W.E.J. Major, recorded verdicts of accidental death on the three Royal Marines.

In a cruel twist of fate, as Mick Coleman and his three young companions fought for their lives in the treacherous waters off Plymouth Sound, two hundred and thirty miles east of Cawsand his favourite team Manchester United were celebrating an historic 4-1 victory over Benfica of Lisbon - in the 1968 European Cup Final at Wembley, It was a poignant irony that just when Matt Busby was laying to rest the ghosts of his Busby Babes (by delivering the prize that was so cruelly denied them in 1958) elsewhere the lives of another group of young men were being lost.

During the course of the year there were a number of significant (and some not so significant) firsts: Barclaycard launched Britain's first credit card to be followed later in the year by the Access card from National Westminster, Lloyds and the Midland bank. US *Billboard* Magazine published the first major article about the rapidly spreading social phenomenon known as disco.

The above newspaper collage depicts (top right) Mick Coleman and (bottom right) Francis McDermott - founder members of the Corby Barbell Club. The front page story on the left tells of the tragic events at Cawsand Bay that resulted in the deaths of three young Royal Marines - one of them being Michael Coleman.

Trevor McDonald joined ITN from the BBC World Service to become Britain's first black television newsreader. He later attained legendary status of a different kind - in the guise of newscaster Trevor McDoughnut (one of Lenny Henry's spoof characters on the children's Saturday morning show *TISWAS*.)

The *Evening Telegraph* reported that unemployment statistics for Corby showed that over 1,000 men and women were out of work and another 3,258 were on short time. Corby District Council announced plans to build seven hundred private houses on the designated Danesholme estate.

Mr. & Mrs. Tony Ashby, former licencees of the Maple Leaf pub in Corby.

In a move which would change forever the nature of shopping in Corby town centre, on August 11, 1972 Corporation Street was closed to traffic. (It was eventually paved over and a number of strategically placed benches were provided for shoppers to sit and rest their weary legs, examine the fast-diminishing supplies of cash in their purses or wallets or just sit and have a good chinwag with a passer-by!)

During December sweeping changes to the licensing laws were proposed by the Erroll Commission - the intention being to bring Great Britain into line with the continent. The report noted that although there was a decline in the number of U.K. pubs, off-licences appeared to be on the increase. It also foresaw a situation where the typical English café would end up serving gin and tonics alongside tea and crumpets. In addition, there would be more flexible licensing hours (e.g. from 10a.m. until 12 o'clock midnight) and the age at which young adults would be allowed to order a pint of beer would be lowered from eighteen to seventeen. The commission also concluded that it could see no reason why a sixteen-year-old should not be allowed to order beer, wine or cider to accompany a meal in a restaurant. The proposals received a lukewarm response from licencees in the Corby area. Tony Abbey, landlord of the Maple Leaf in Canada Square, said: "I think the age limit should be kept to eighteen. I don't feel that younger people are responsible enough to drink in pubs." His opposite number at Corby's White Hart pub agreed. George Tilley said: "We have enough on our plates as it is, in trying to keep under-age drinkers out of the pubs."

On October 4, Latvian glider pilot Indulis Ozols, of Constable Road in Corby, put forward the idea for a municipal airport. Indulis, a steel-worker, was confident that Britain's entry into the Common Market would ensure its success He said: "As the number of cars increase, people are going to be taking to the air rather than to the roads. With a bit of forethought and vision, it could put Corby on the map." A spokesman for the Development Corporation was less enthusiastic and put the damper on Ozols' idea, commenting: "It wouldn't be feasible with the mammoth expense that would be involved."

Sixteen members of the Irthlingborough Salvation Army Corps took part in a sponsored silence to raise funds for their annual Self-Denial Appeal. The period of silence was divided into two sessions. Each lasted ninety minutes and there was a break in between for refreshments and a good gab. The youngsters involved passed the time by painting and drawing. Five members of the group completed the full three hours and in doing so raised the grand total of £12.36. - and haven't stopped talking about it since!

Above: The hustle and bustle of Corby Town Centre on a typical Saturday afternoon in the 1970s. Below: Following its transformation into a pedestrian precinct, just a few weeks later Mrs. Brenda Jack (left) and her friend Cathy Berry (with Brenda's 19-month-old daughter Angela) are seen walking along a traffic-free Corporation Street.

In February sales of the Volkswagen Beetle motor car exceeded those of the Ford Model 'T'. In May the 'Don't Make A Wave Committee' (a fledgling environmental organisation founded a year earlier in Canada) officially changed its name to the Greenpeace Foundation.

Main box office attractions in 1972 were: *Cabaret, The Poseidon Adventure, Deliverance* and *The Godfather* (the latter winning the Oscar for Best Picture). The hit singles of the year were: *American Pie* by Don McLean, *Heart of Gold* by Neil Young and *Without You* by Harry Nilsson. The Christmas number one was an endearing rendition from Little Jimmy Osmond called *Long-Haired Lover From Liverpool*. Popular TV programmes to make an entry on our screens were: *Newsround, Mastermind, M*A*S*H, Emmerdale Farm* and *Are You Being Served.*

The end of the year saw the termination of America's Apollo moon missions - bringing to a conclusion the real life science fiction adventure that for almost two decades had captivated a worldwide audience. To this day the achievements of those pioneering astronauts have never been equalled. On December 7, 1972 Eugene Cernan, Harrison 'Jack' Schmitt and Ron Evans were the last crew to leave planet Earth for the moon, travelling aboard Apollo 17. The majority of people know that the first man to walk on the moon's surface was Neil Armstrong; they will also will be familiar with his famous first words that day, but how many can identify the last man to step foot on the moon - or his parting shot? The answer is that that distinction fell to Commander Eugene Cernan, who affirmed: "OK Jack, let's get this mother outa here!"

Good news on December 22nd 1972 - or just reinforcing the myth? This endorsement of the guarantee given by Mr. Peter Walker, Secretary for Trade and Industry, provided Corby's eternal optimists with the news that they'd been hoping for. Served up with their evening meal (courtesy of the 'E.T.') in truth the front page story contained a large slice of tongue (in cheek).

Chapter Four 1973
A Walk On The Wild Side

The news that Corby had been dreading arrived in February - in the form of a government White Paper. Within it John Davies, Secretary of State for Trade and Industry, outlined a ten-year strategy for the British Steel Corporation. Although Corby was on a list of steelmaking plants adjudged to have a 'limited future', the White Paper stressed that the town would continue to be a long-term major tube production centre and that there was every indication it would carry on making steel until at least the end of the decade. In consultation with all those concerned, a final decision on its future was to be taken over the course of the next few years.

The good news was that BSC was able to give confirmation that Corby would continue to be its headquarters and main production centre for tube making. Consequently, thirteen hundred new jobs were soon to be made available. The government appeared to be well ahead on the issue and had plans in the pipeline to 'cut hardship to an absolute minimum by giving redundant steelmen 90 per cent of their wages for two years while they undergo retraining etc.' However, there was no getting away from the fact that a huge question remained over the employment prospects of the 5000 people already involved in steelmaking at Corby.

It was against this background that Ian Baillie (a roving reporter for a Scottish national newspaper) made the following observations on a visit to Corby. He wrote:

> 'It is a tempting cliché to describe Corby's life blood as the red-hot molten metal flowing from the blast furnaces at the steelworks. Corby's fortunes are of the steel industry. The town's civic fathers bemoan the fact, the local MP bemoans the fact, probably the whole town regrets its utter dependence on the BSC but nothing, at least in the foreseeable future, is going to alter the situation.
>
> The people are made of stern stuff. They can take knocks and keep bouncing back. Within the next ten years the town is almost certain to take some heavy knocks - thanks to the government's 'rationalisation' of the steel industry. For 'rationalisation' read redundancies. For the majority of men and women working in Corby (read Scottish economic immigrants) redundancy is nothing new. Their background of the grim industrial history of central Scotland has prepared them for it. But not for them the sheepish acceptance of their fate. The people of Corby will fight any move to deprive them of their livelihood. They may not win but they will go down fighting. Perhaps it is their fighting spirit that has made it something of a 'black sheep' in Northamptonshire, the county of spires and squires. For the average Corby workers, especially the Scots, have little time for the feudal legacies of

Northamptonshire's squires and inherited privilege and inborn superiority that passes on to a lucky few. The people of Northamptonshire may accept the social divisions, the people of Corby, I believe, resent it and quite rightly so. There are those throughout the county who make patronising middle class fun of Corby. They look on it with disdain and regret. It represents progress. For here is no marketplace backwater regretfully contemplating the passing of the 19th century. Corby has vigour and bustling vitality. It is a town that is going places and the rest of the county will have to follow in its wake. It has made the rest of Northamptonshire sit up and take notice. From an insignificant village to thriving steel town and centre of the UK tube making industry - within forty years - is no mean feat. The people are generously friendly and open-hearted. A visitor could not wish for more kindness and hospitality.'

Unfortunately, 'kindness' was not an attribute that the former steward and stewardess of Corby's British Sealed Beams Sports and Social Club would choose to associate with those committee members responsible for his and her recent dismissal. The sacking had even caught the attention of the national newspapers, one of which ran the following headline: 'Pretty Margaret is no sour-puss!' It continued:

> *'Just a week ago Margaret Hegarty was an ordinary housewife with a full time job. Today she's had her picture in national newspapers, had a television crew knocking on her front door and people stop and stare at her in the street. Why? Because Margaret Hegarty is the woman at the centre of a 'no-smile' row.'*

Margaret and her twenty-seven-year-old husband Lawrence (who lived with their four-year-old daughter Tracey in Narvik Road, Corby) had been sacked from their jobs as steward and stewardess of the British Sealed Beams Club because the club's committee felt that they didn't smile enough and, more insultingly, that their faces didn't fit.

"In other words," said Margaret, "they're making me out to be a real sour-puss - which just isn't true! I'm a tall, slim, twenty-four-year-old brunette, with a ready smile for everyone." Originally from Birmingham, Margaret came to live in Corby at the age of fifteen. Before her marriage to Lawrence she qualified as a hairdresser, then in December 1972 (following the death of her father - who had been steward of the club since its opening two years previously) she and her husband took over at the B.S.B.C. After her daughter's dismissal, Betty Robertson, (Margaret's mother) continued to work behind the bar - that is until she too was given her marching orders. "Mum's going to have to find another job," lamented Margaret. "She can't live on her widow's pension".

Lawrence chimed in: "We were given a month's notice, and finish at the club on February 5. We must go where the work is, even if it means selling our house. As for the present situation - the atmosphere at the club is terrible. There's a lot of tension between the committee and the members. Mind you, we've found out who our real friends are!"

At the time, Margaret was of the opinion that the publicity she and her husband were receiving would help them to gain other employment. "People will know why we've been sacked," she said.

In the last week of January, with just a few days to go before the big heave-ho, the couple announced that not only had they taken up the matter with their solicitor, but that the regulars at the club had signed a petition demanding their reinstatement. "It looks like our future is still in the balance," said a hopeful Margaret.

After that last newspaper report, no one seems to know for certain quite what happened to Maggie and Larry. Bella Brodie claims to have heard on the grapevine that after leaving Corby they became tenants of the Laughing Cavalier hotel in Laughton, Leicestershire (or was it Grinton in Yorkshire?) and had introduced locals to the concept of the happy-hour!

To compound the pervading sense of gloom that was beginning to envelop the steelworks, BSC announced that Corby had just achieved its highest ever annual turnover - with 791,055 tons of tubes being produced in the twelve months prior to April 1973. "Exports played a big role," revealed Mr. H. G. Armitage, one of the directors. He went on: "I am absolutely delighted and this justifies the faith which many others and I have in the Corby operation."

An Action Committee (made up of trade-unionists and backed by Corby councillors) was set up in the wake of the White Paper. Its aim was not only to try and save the steelworks - where 6500 jobs were at stake - but also to attract a more diverse type of industry to the town. Councillor John Carr spelled it out: "Corby has been given a ten year lease of life to build a new industrial base." Councillors David Moon and Jimmy Kane agreed to back the action committee but stated that they believed the group would be ineffective if BSC did decide to end steelmaking in the town.

In June Corby's British Steel Tubes Division advertised two hundred and fifty vacancies. A spokesperson for the company revealed that three hundred workers had left in the months of February and March, adding that (as there was now a full order book) this constituted a shortage of manpower. The spokesperson went on to explain that many of the former employees had returned to Scotland, whilst thirty of them had simply returned to the dole queue. "Anyone interested in a job is guaranteed secure employment and at least £25.16 a week," he promised.

The same month Corby Council set in motion a recruitment drive which it hoped would attract workers from the London overspill areas. Pete and Yvonne Harvey were two such workers who, tired of their life in Enfield, were looking for a new start and a brighter future. They had little idea of how to achieve this until Peter (who worked for the Royal Mail) was delivering the post one day to Enfield's Labour Exchange and spotted a poster advertising just what they were seeking. He said: "Although I'd never worked in such an environment before and was doubtful, what caught my eye was the prospect of a well-paid job in the steelworks, the promise of a new house on a modern housing estate and good New Town leisure facilities.

'Come to Corby' was the title of a talk and slide show given by Corby Council. I went along as much out of curiosity as anything and saw pictures of the town and surrounding countryside. I heard about the new housing estates that were being built at Danesholme and Kingswood, the town centre that was being developed and the employment opportunities. It looked and sounded

Pretty Margaret is no sour-puss !

JUST a week ago Margaret Hegarty was an ordinary housewife with a full-time job

Above: Margaret -'if you like a smile with your pint, don't bother comin' in here'- Hegarty. Despite widespread press coverage and ensuing local jocularity, the majority of customers at Corby's Sealed Beams Club found Margaret and her smile to be highly appealing.

brilliant. After the show I put my name down for a coach trip to Corby, and a few weeks later had my first sight of the town. I was shown around the newly built council houses on the Danesholme estate and ended up queuing for a job interview in the British Steel works canteen. It was only when I went back a few weeks later with Yvonne, in order to have a proper look around, that I encountered 'the Scottish connection'. Yvonne and I were astonished to discover that most of the inhabitants talked with a broad Glaswegian accent. We couldn't believe it at first - we thought we'd slept over on the bus and ended up in Scotland!

Despite newspaper ads painting a picture of growth and prosperity within Corby, press headlines from July 1973 tell a completely different story.

The Development Corporation offered us a house in Taunton Avenue. We arrived to find that it was everything that they had promised it would be. It was new and clean - plus we had some terrific neighbours.

I started work in the EWSR on two shifts and (although I can't say I was too enamoured with the job) the money was better than what I had been getting as a postman in Enfield. I also became a member of the Welfare Social Club It was a great place at the time and had rock 'n' roll and big bands at the weekends.

There were also snooker tables and a bowls section. We loved it! Then one day when I was in the Town Centre Post Office, I noticed an advert saying 'Postmen Wanted'. I decided to apply and got the job. Moving to Corby was the best move of our lives." Peter Harvey was held in high regard by all who came to know him and proved to be a valuable addition to the postal service in Corby. He served as a postman in the town for over twenty years. Sadly, in 1999 Peter died after a long illness.

On what was by sheer coincidence the 29th anniversary of the D Day landings, on June 6, Mrs. Angus Maude, Chairman of the Transport Reform Group, launched an extraordinary verbal attack on the town of Kettering, likening it to the aftermath of a raid by Adolf Hitler. After touring the town with members of Kettering Civic Society, Mrs. Maude delivered the following bombshell: "Your town looks as if it has been the late subject of an attack by Adolf Hitler. If you had famine, the Black Death and the Great Fire of London as well, it couldn't look worse. I think it's shattering what your Labour representatives have allowed to happen to your nice old town." Mrs. Maude, who had been drafted in to discuss opposition to the proposed inner ring road for Kettering, added: "I am really appalled at the road plan. Kettering has never been a very handsome town but it still retains a good deal of its original street plan and fragments of its character."

The response to her comments was mixed. In defence of the proposals, Mr. C. Warburton said: "Kettering is a damn nice place. The ring road is a good idea and will be a big improvement for the town." Rik Butcher wrote in the *Evening Telegraph*: 'On the whole, Kettering is a jolly nice town. Maude's comments are twaddle, absolute twaddle! To be sure, Kettering isn't the loveliest place on earth - but equally it's not the ugliest!'

Standing on the Cottingham Road railway bridge, Stan Boulton introduces baby daughter Julie to the sights, sounds and smells of Corby works. Visible in the background of the photograph is the Stewarts & Lloyds gasometer that stood on the area of land near Lloyds Road and the Jamb. 1955.

In response to America's Christmas 1973 blitzing of North Vietnam, Stan Boulton (a local pharmacist and member of Corby District Council) joined the self-styled 'Peace Group' from Corby - which travelled down to London to mount a protest outside the American Embassy in Grosvenor Square. On New Year's Eve Stan sent telegrams from the group to both the Embassy and to President Nixon. They read as follows: 'You have mocked the season of peace and goodwill by your slaughter, through incessant bombing, of the Vietnamese people. You showed your power on Christmas Day. We appeal to you to stop forever.'

As a teenager, Stan (along with around 40,000 other men) had joined the International Brigade. Made up of volunteers from fifty different countries, its mission was to fight against fascism in Spain, and combatants from the U.K. were under no illusions regarding the views of the British Establishment towards them. (In 1937 the Foreign Enlistment Act had outlawed membership of such organisations, and from then on there had been a distinct lack of sympathy from the Government towards those who flouted this ruling).

Boulton followed the well-established path that had been taken by others before him - the boat train from London to Paris, followed by an escort to the Spanish border and a precarious night-time trek over the Pyrenees. After four weeks of basic training at a camp near Valencia, he was immediately thrown into the action and found himself helping to reinforce the Republican withdrawal over the River Ebro.

Rebels with a cause! Spanish Civil War veteran Stan Boulton (right) and his brother-in-arms Joe Norman attend a rally in London. 1975.

It was whilst serving in the Brigade that Boulton first met up with Joe Norman - another well-known Corby figure. Joe, a Communist Party organiser with the British Battalion, once described the hostile reaction which a group of captured brigadiers were met with during an encounter with a right-wing *Daily Express* journalist. "You'll all be shot," he taunted. Years later Joe would lament the fact that on more than one occasion, the reporter's spiteful words were to prove correct.

Statistics show that around a quarter of the Brigade lost their lives in the conflict (termed one of the bloodiest civil wars in European history.) On a pittance of seven pesetas a day, the men could hardly be described as mercenaries. What spurred them on was the realisation that if fascism in Spain wasn't defeated, then there would be a war in Europe. They were proved right.

Boulton was in fact a Mancunian who was born in the 1920s to a founding member of that city's Communist Party, and it was evidently his mother who exerted so profound an influence on her son's political views.

Stan moved to Corby in 1954. His first pharmacy was in Rutherglen Road, but he later moved to one of the shops on Gainsborough Road - opposite the Pluto. It was whilst there that Stan recognised a need in the the town for a better service for those women who were pregnant. He felt it was unfair that the nearest maternity unit was in Kettering, and with this in mind organised a petition on the subject - to be presented, at the House of Commons, to the Minister of Health. The 7,000 signatures it contained evidently were enough to convince the powers that be, as in 1961 a Maternity Unit was opened on the site of the Diagnostic Centre in Corby.

Stan was a regular customer at the Corby Candle pub, and it is there that he met up again with his old compatriot Joe Norman. Between them, the former brothers-in-arms hatched the idea of founding a Trades and Labour Club in the town, and it was mainly down to them that the Stuart Road club was indeed built and then in 1962 subsequently opened.

During his visits to the Candle, some years earlier Stan had also forged a friendship with Doctor Maxim and it was the latter who in 1958 assisted him in the formation of the town's first rugby club. Another of its co-founders, Alan Smith, recalled the first time that he encountered Stan Boulton. Alan said: "It was early in the 1950s - at the fairground behind the Cardigan Arms. As I was lining up my sights on the rifle range, I was aware of this little guy beside me who was carefully taking aim. Every time the girl on the stall turned her back, Stan changed his aim from the tin cans to the light bulbs and shot them out. He then looked at me mischievously and winked. He was as mad as a hatter! When I saw him a couple of years later, at a Corby Rugby Club meeting, I said to Stan, 'I know you - you're the chap who shot out the lights at the fairground!' Stan just looked at me and burst into laughter."

After a lifetime of fighting other peoples' causes, Stan Boulton died in the year 2000. In his obituary, he was described as being one of Corby's most senior ambassadors and activists. Paula Boulton (one of Stan's daughters) speaks proudly of her father. Paula: "His life had a real richness and I learned a great deal from him. Dad always championed the underdog and fought for what he believed in. As chairman of Corby CND, he took me along with him to the Aldermaston march in 1958, when I was aged two! It was the beginning of a lifetime of political activity for me. My father never talked about his experiences in the Spanish Civil War. If you asked him about it - he just seemed to go blank. It was as if he didn't want to remember. He wouldn't open up. He was a pacifist and a member of both Amnesty International and CND. Dad was also head of the Governors at Hazel Leys and Kingswood Schools - during which time he fought for the abolition of corporal punishment in schools. Every year he would make sure that a wreath was laid at the Corby War Memorial in honour of the International Brigade."

Keith Cooper (Export Sales Manager for Plaister & Hanger) reflects on the New Year message that he's just received from his counterpart in Holland - warning him about the perils of joining the Common Market. Judging by Keith's expression, he doesn't look too concerned about the future.

Biiiig mistake!

On January 1, the Union Jack was raised outside the European Commission Headquarters in Brussels, signalling Britain's entry into the Common Market. Prime Minister Ted Heath was unshakeable in his optimism, saying "an exciting time is just beginning. We can work together with our eight new partners and have a much brighter future of better jobs and a higher standard of living."

Although perceived by 'Johnny Foreigner' as being insular and largely unenthusiastic about the Common Market (and Europe in general) the British were in fact, holidaying on the continent in ever growing numbers, and were returning home with sombreros perched on their heads and straw donkeys tucked under their arms. There were also signs of a newly acquired taste for pasta, paella and pizza. In the supermarkets, German, French, Spanish and Italian wines were nudging their way on to the shelves, whilst continental lagers were also being viewed as a refreshing alternative by the erstwhile beer-swilling U.K. pub-goer. 'We're all Europeans now!' became the mantra of the British tabloid press.

Joining Europe was a monumental step which inevitably attracted a confusion of emotions. The manager of the Kettering haberdashery firm Plaistere and Hangar, revealed that he had received a tongue-in-cheek telex message on the subject from an associate in Holland.
It read:

> *'To the newest members of the Common Market, from members of eight years standing, expressing our most profound sympathies. When you perceive in future that the price of normal English water is suddenly higher than the price of an honest English beer in former days, then remember you're in the Common Market now.*
> *When your salary is growing and growing, but never reaches the rocket speed of price rises for food, so that every salary increase is making you poorer, then remember you're in the Common Market now.*
> *When your bread is becoming dearer and dearer because there is an extra price in it to support the silly, stubborn French cheesemaker who is making such a stinking ill-tasting cheese that he never succeeded in selling it, remember, you're in the Common Market now.*
> *Wishing you a happy and prosperous New Year, though you will indeed need some luck to survive the benefits of being a new member of the European Common Market.'*

For many Britons it was an opportunity to broaden their horizons and (taking advantage of the cheaper travel costs associated with the package holiday industry) they set about exploring for the first time the vagaries and delights of the Continent. Liverpool Football Club devotee Jimmy 'Knocker' Knox, whilst travelling to an away game in Germany, found himself aboard a ferry bound for the Hook of Holland. He and his friend were making the journey in order to support Liverpool F.C. in their quest for UEFA Cup victory over Borussia Munchengladbach - and what a cultural eye-opener it turned out to be for the former Crow's Nest 'greaser'! For starters, when they eventually reached Rotterdam railway station and stopped for a quick toilet break, on the way out they were accosted by a crabby old lady who was banging on a tray littered with coins (the inference being that they should donate a few guilders in exchange for use of the facilities.) Knocker took a dim view of the idea. "Let me tell you hen - where we come from it's only the women that have to pay!" he protested. This brief insight into English washroom formalities made not the slightest bit of difference to her. In fact it resulted in the lads being subjected to a torrent of Dutch invective and much fist-waving - especially when they declined to cough up and instead made a swift exit.

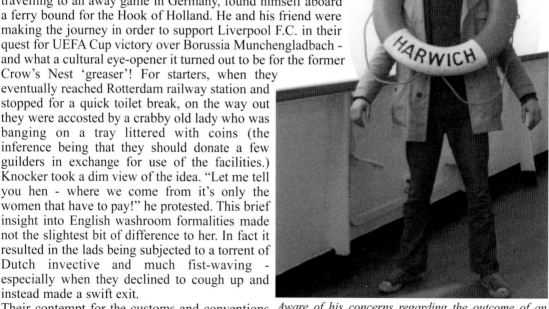

Their contempt for the customs and conventions of continental Europe failed to deter Knocker and his companions from pressing on with their journey, and although 'the Reds, lost the match in Germany by a margin of two goals, the team were

Aware of his concerns regarding the outcome of an important European match involving his beloved Liverpool F.C., Clive Smith's travelling companions and fellow 'Reds' insist that he wear something appropriate during the North Sea ferry crossing.

awarded the UEFA Cup on account of their 3-0 victory in the home leg. It was to be the famous Merseyside club's first ever European trophy.

The humble doughnut became the subject of widespread publicity in February 1973 when 'Doughnut Month' was celebrated throughout the UK. During that month doughnut makers all over the country went into overdrive.

The Queen Mother's visit to Corby in 1973 was the cause of great excitement in the town. Above: The royal visitor pays a house call to the home of her 'kinsmen' Mr. and Mrs. Torrance. Right: Flag-waving Rosemary McEwan (aged three) captures the spirit of the occasion perfectly.

One bakery in Peterborough even produced a double-jam doughnut (two blobs of jam instead of one) with the help of a new development on the market - the twin-prong jam injector (or 'jammer' as it was known in the trade.) Despite claims from The Doughnut Institute of New York that this small fried cake originated in prehistoric southwestern regions of the USA, another theory suggests that it crossed the Atlantic in the sixteenth century with early Dutch settlers who, on account of its greasiness, called it the 'olykoek' or 'oily cake'.

The ring doughnut came about when Hansen Gregory (a nineteenth century sea captain) was eating a doughnut whilst sailing his vessel through a storm. It is said that on a dark and squally night in 1874, his ship suddenly rocked violently and threw him against the wheel - impaling his cake on one of its spokes. Gregory admired the cake's new shape so much so that he ordered the ship's cook to make all future batches of his teatime favourite with holes in them. History reveals that doughnuts were even used as part of the war effort during World War I - when the Salvation Army would cook them in garbage pails and serve them on bayonets to US troops. Such was their popularity in the American trenches that US soldiers soon became known as 'doughboys.'

The newly constructed Queen's Square shopping precinct was officially declared open by Her Majesty the Queen Mother in April 1973.

April 1973 saw Her Majesty Queen Elizabeth The Queen Mother paying her second visit to Corby (in 1945 she had accompanied her husband, King George VI, on a tour of the steelworks.) On this occasion - a blustery day in spring - she had come to the town in order to declare open the £2.75 million extension to the main shopping centre. Oona Campbell, a spectator in the crowd, swore that at the end of the ribbon-cutting ceremony she heard the Queen Mum declare: "Right gentlemen, where is the nearest off-licence?" and that one of the attending local dignitaries replied: "Balls Brothers is just across the square Ma'am."

Chaperoned by Sir Henry Chisholm, Chairman of Corby Development Corporation, the royal guest and party then left by car for a tour of the town - dropping in for a chat "or does one call it a 'blether' here, Sir Henry?" at the Torrance household in Farmstead Road. David Torrance (who was then aged ten) says that he remembers the day very well. He explained: "Our house had been selected at random for the royal visit. The Corporation asked my mum if it would be O.K. and she said 'Yes. We'd love for her to come!' Some people in the neighbourhood thought that we must have been given new furniture for the occasion - even a new television - but that was just nonsense!

On the day, I looked on in disbelief as my younger brother Gary walked up to this little old lady and asked her, quite matter-of-factly, if she'd like a cup of tea. The Queen Mum smiled that toothy grin and replied 'Of course I would, young man.' I'll never forget that moment."

After the royal visit cynics were quick to ask: "Did the Queen Mother see the real Corby?" The *Corby Leader* gave its own view of the proceedings.

'Well it's all over - the excitement, bustle, uniforms and the crowds. Corby's day of triumph when the Queen Mum came to visit and give her blessing to the new shopping precinct has passed. The people have gone home, flags are furled, medals put back in their box and the Corinthian pub in Queen's Square can shed its temporary front of curtained windows'.

At least Her Majesty didn't go away empty-handed - having been presented (by Michael Gray - Director of Network Cinema UK) with a 'golden pass' to the new £185,000 Jerry Lewis Cinema complex. Gray informed the royal guest that the pass would grant her unlimited entry to any of the four hundred Jerry Lewis cinemas. He gushed: "It's only the second pass ever presented. The first was given to President Nixon".

At its Grand Opening later that same month, the cinema presented a twelve hour programme of Carry On films. In a bid to create 'a carnival atmosphere', Brigadier Hugh Hamilton released hundreds of balloons into the sky over Corby, and there to add the finishing touch to the ceremony were celebrity guests - Charles Hawtrey, Liz Frazer and Lindsay Marsh. - *Carry On Corby* had begun!

Unfortunately for fans of the big screen, the cinema was beset by teething troubles. After only two weeks the projection equipment broke down halfway through *The Godfather* (the epic gangster movie starring Marlon Brando) and caused a very impatient audience to start whistling and jeering out of frustration. The manager, who to his credit remained remarkably calm during this unexpected interlude, made his customers an offer which they couldn't refuse - he told them that a refund would be given to anyone who didn't want to wait for the projector to be repaired. In the event, while engineers attempted to fix the problem and get the show back on the road, many patrons regarded the operational hiccup as an opportunity to nip out for a quick pint in the nearby Corinthian public house!

For an audience previously unused to viewing in comfort, the plush interior of the new Jerry Lewis cinema complex was an added incentive for them to carry on coming!

Normal service was resumed after forty-five minutes of hopeful tinkering - enabling a thoroughly relieved manager to dispatch his assistant on a mission to round up the straying audience. Whilst making his way back to his seat, and on encountering the cinema boss standing in the foyer, a liquidly refreshed Ginger Graham passed the following acid comment: "We never had this problem in the Odeon pal!"

One of the premises in the new development was leased by Treasure Music. Paul Beard, the shop's manager, was not only an accomplished player of guitar, clarinet, keyboard and several brass instruments, but was also the highly respected leader of a local band. Music had been a way of life for Paul from the age of six (when he won a talent contest in his native London) and a year after moving to Corby with his family, in 1953 he joined the Corby Silver Band. By the age of fourteen Paul was playing trumpet with various local outfits, however, he didn't receive a proper introduction to playing in a dance band until joining the one led by Corby drummer Billy Clark. In 1957 the Paul Beard Trio was formed - comprising Paul, drummer Billy McHarg and guitarist Chris Newman.

Reflecting on the decline of live music in general, in 1973 Paul had this to say: "Despite the onset of the disco, there is still a tremendous demand for dance bands in Corby." He continued: "The emphasis is currently on pop - and the dance bands are moving with the times. There was some great music written in the 1920's and 1940's eras but many of today's songs will be evergreen." An enthusiast of both traditional and modern jazz, Paul was one of the first members of the Marylanders Jazz Band. He said: "I still get together with a few of them for an odd blow now and then."

In later years Paul became the Superintendent of a crematorium in Sussex. Trevor Wright (an old mate of Paul's and a fellow Marylander) remembers: "The last time I saw Paul was when I went to a funeral at Kettering Crematorium in 2004. I had no idea that he was back in the area. When I walked in the organ was playing softly and I glanced over to see who was playing it, Paul gave me a big wink. Catching up with him after the service, he informed me that he was now playing part-time at the crem' as well as performing in jazz venues around the county."

Also in the newly constructed Queen's Square was the Charlois café - an establishment where many of the town centre's career drinkers would congregate when the pubs had shut for the afternoon. Because of her heavy-handed approach to make-up, one of the waitresses there was nicknamed 'Leo Sayer'. (It was a reference to the clown's costume and painted face worn by Leo when he performed his song *The Show Must Go On*).

David 'Ginger' Graham - a regular customer at both Kettering's Granada cinema and its counterpart the Odeon in Corby.

A few feet away from what was the town's first escalator was a new record shop. Managed by local DJ Dougie King, it purported to be 'the only shop where one can peruse a selection of Howlin' Wolf or Muddy Waters albums!' However, (and much to the disappointment of the owner) this claim fell on deaf ears as far as Corby record buyers were concerned. Needless to say the shop soon closed.

Over at the Civic Centre a new Entertainments Manager was hired when Ross Jones left to become manager of a five star hotel on the Isle of Man. The successful candidate, Reg Campbell from Stevenage, said at a hastily arranged press conference: "I have a lot of failings but I suppose that is my big advantage. I have been an agent and have booked artists as well. So I should know what's going on. The amenities here are fantastic for a town of this size."

First to appear under the new regime was country artist Marvin Rainwater (of *Whole Lotta Woman* fame) and British backing group the Muskrats. It was said that Marvin had the audience literally 'leaping out of their seats with sheer enthusiasm' - a fact that impressed the singer no end. The husky, towering, half-Cherokee performer remarked later: "Larger audiences aren't usually as receptive or as friendly as the one at Corby".

The Market Square, Corby. Although local gossip has it that Balls Brothers off-licence (situated within the square) was patronised by the Queen Mum on her 1973 visit to the town, closer inspection of the official agenda for that day renders the notion to be completely 'off-piste' - in addition, the list of Royal Warrants of Appointments for that era confirms that the 'offi' was never awarded the right to display the Royal Coat of Arms!

Retaining the American theme, the Civic next presented a 'Country Meets Folk' evening. A group called Frisco (who had been voted most promising new country band of the year) went on stage first, followed by U.S. singer Suzanne Harris. After the interval it was the turn of former Hollywood star Tex Ritter - whose songs included *High Noon, Wayward Wind* and *Deck Of Cards*. Judging by the report from Tom Roberts, music critic of the *Corby Leader*, it appears that the veteran cowboy saved the show. A scathing Roberts wrote: 'The promoters should just have presented the second half and some of the highlights of the first. Before the interval Wally Whyton did his best, although Frisco and American Suzanne Harris were dull. Both lacked the hillbilly ambience.' Whether it was the

Local band Edition made regular appearances at Shafts nightclub. L-R: Malcolm Watt, Dave Dean, John McConnell and Andy Brown.

SHAFTS

(EXCLUSIVE CLUB) CORBY
GEORGE ST., CORBY
Tel. ☎ 2757

TONIGHT AND THURSDAY—
FREE BUFFET & DISCO
Girls admitted free all evening
9 pm — 1 am
FRIDAY—
DISCO 8 p.m.—2 am
SATURDAY—
Live Music from EDITION
plus DISCO 8 pm—2 am
SUNDAY—
DISCO
Standards of dress observed
Meals and Snacks always available
A MEMBERS ONLY CLUB

Cc25

convivial atmosphere, the drink, or the mere fact that Tex provided a welcome relief from the tedium of the first half, the crowd applauded and cheered each and every one of his songs.

One of Ross Jones's final duties at the Festival Hall was to serve on a panel of 'experts' who were judging a talent contest at the venue (the proceeds of which were to go towards the Queen's Silver Jubilee Celebrations Appeal in Corby.) This 1970's version of television's '*The X Factor*' was to prove a very sweet experience for the eventual winners - a group called Honey. Featuring Paul Cross on bass guitar, Alex Henderson on drums, Rita McCusker on vocals and ex-Golden Fleece members Pat Lavin and Pete Dyne, the band (which specialised in cover versions of New Seekers' numbers) was the only one from Corby to reach the finals. Having beaten thirty-six acts from all over the area, Honey were presented with a cheque for £100 and offered a season's holiday work in Italy. Vocalist Glen Stewart (the runner-up) won £30. Other finalists in the contest, which had been organised by Corby Town Supporters Club, were a group called Misty, a duo by the name of Friends and vocalists Agnes Gallagher and Martine Shelton. Hundreds of people attended the finals in order to watch the eight lucky acts and to dance to music provided by the Kathy's Flair band. Sitting on the panel alongside Ross Jones were Harold Lear (Chairman of Corby Council) Leonard Lucades (Managing Director of Spartan International) Richard Shaw (Manager of Woolston Dairies) and Ken Cox (a director of Dawn Promotions and one-time manager of St Cecilia).

Across the road from the Civic, Dougie King started up a new disco in the Strathclyde Hotel. In spite of his decision (on leaving Corby Bowl) to quit the music scene altogether, the lure of his beloved twin-turntables proved irresistible to Dougie - hence he was soon back in business. In typical Dougie style, the ebullient DJ announced that the new disco was to be restricted to those over the age of eighteen and would provide 'something that doesn't exist in Corby on a Saturday night.' Offering further detail, Dougie said: "Standards of dress will be observed - but that doesn't mean it'll be a suit and tie job! The Strath' disco won't be aimed at those who roll up in their Triumph Spitfires, but we are hoping to attract a slightly older crowd than the Bowl. There will be bouncers - but not big burly blokes with bow ties who throw their weight around". He concluded: "The potential is terrific". (Sadly, the new disco lasted barely two months - the hotel's management team put paid to it following the discovery of vandalism in the toilets!)

In the meantime, Corby Bowl opened the Exclusive Club. Managed by Bob Petch and with Tom Haworth as DJ, the venue was pitched in direct competition with the Strathclyde disco. The town's first nightclub, advertised entertainment to a clientele 'who enjoy good food, good music and good company in attractive surroundings'. What people didn't realise at the time was that the club, with a change of name, would eventually become one of the most popular (and infamous) institutions in the somewhat chequered history of 'Little Scotland'.

Tom Howarth: "The name Shafts came about because we thought the club needed something trendier. As the film *Shaft* was a massive cinema hit that year, the Exclusive Club became Shafts Exclusive Club. We resisted the urge to change the name completely because it would have involved a lot of paperwork and liaising with the licensing authorities. The club was open seven nights a week until 2a.m. and was a great success - partly due to the shift system operated by the steelworks. It meant that we always had plenty of people in the club. Our customers were mainly between the ages of eighteen and thirty. Many would be people with a disposable income who had rushed home from a backshift to get changed and go out. In 1979 the closure of the steelworks - and the redundancies - had a massive impact on the venue. That's when it was reduced to two or three nights a week."

Working as doormen at the club were John Brown and ex-boxer Sammy Rodgers. John: "Shafts had its fair share of trouble with drunks and louts - and that was only the women! I remember one night when we let a group of girls in and they started a big argument with us. They reckoned that we'd diddled them on the entrance fee and they were reluctant to cough up. Because they were shouting and becoming abusive, in the end I bawled at them 'Get out!' All of a sudden, one of the girls kicked me in a delicate place, so to speak, and I creased up in agony. Let's just say - for a minute or so I didn't know if I was going to end up being Horace or Doris!" Later on Sammy said to me, 'When the little ugly one said 'Leave it to me - I'll sort him out' I thought she meant that she'd got the extra money to get them in!'

Another time it was Sammy who was on the receiving end. At Shafts there was always a queue of revellers who drifted in from the pubs at closing time. They were looking for a late drink and, if they were lucky, a bit on the side! Anyway I remember that it was extremely boisterous that particular night. People were kicking the door to attract our attention; there were even some who were pleading to be let in. We always used to look through the little hatch in the door before admitting anyone, and I can recall Sammy opening the hatch in frustration that night and shouting, 'You lot can bugger off because you're all barred!' Then he slammed it shut again. Feeling rather pleased with himself, Sammy then stepped back and remarked 'That told them!' However, as was his wont, curiosity soon got the better of him. Just as he reached for the hatch - to take another peek outside - a big fat fist crashed straight through it and landed squarely on his (already broken) nose. Now it was Sammy's turn to be floored and wish that he was a thousand miles away. Remembering my 'points defeat' at the hands of a mere slip of a girl, of course I couldn't help but laugh!"

The Freewheelers Club in Dalkeith Place was Kettering's answer to Shafts. There were some old hands on the door at that place i.e. Brian Perrin, Terry Page and Arthur Horseley) (all of whom had worked at the Town Band Club during the 1950s.) Horseley, who was notorious throughout the district for his strong-arm tactics, behaved in much the same manner when off-duty. Johnny Steel from Corby says that he can remember being involved in an altercation with him outside Shafts. Here Johnny describes the incident. Johnny: "Trouble had been brewing between us for quite some time - mainly due to Horseley's aggressive behaviour in clubs in and around Corby. My brothers and I were fast losing patience with him, and by autumn 1973 things had finally reached boiling point. One night I was sitting at a table in Shafts, with my brother Tommy and some friends, and was just minding my own business. Suddenly, for some unknown reason, Horseley kicked my foot and then claimed that it had been me who had tripped him up. When I told him that he should watch where he was going, the big guy said that my feet were too big and that he'd see me outside. At that, I followed him out on to George Street - telling Bob Petch to shut the door behind us and to lock it. Once we were outside Horseley straightaway made a move to head-butt me, however, I got in first and decked him with a good right-hander! In fact I hit him so hard that he literally *flew* backwards, bounced off of the safety barrier and landed face down on the pavement. Consequently, he was taken to Kettering General Hospital to be treated for breaks to his nose, collarbone and arm."

Corbert Bond, who witnessed the confrontation, remarked at the time that he had never before seen anyone land a punch of such intensity. Corbert said: "While the big fella was lying flat out on the floor, the safety barrier that he'd struck was still vibrating - just like a giant tuning fork!"

Johnny: "The following night my elder brother told me of a telephone conversation that he'd had with Brian Perrin. Andy said that Brian had asked him if he'd fancy working a shift at the Freewheelers club in Kettering that night. When Andy asked him why, the response came 'because Horseley can't make it - he's in hospital. Your brother put him there!' Horseley left town shortly after that.

In spite of a national craze for going to discos and nightclubs, the humble game of darts was still very much on the agenda for Corby folk. In fact it could be said that the sport had never been so popular. On Monday and Thursday nights there was still a large turnout for town & district league matches, and (because teams often took a large following of supporters to away games) the landladies of the pubs involved had their work cut out to supply enough sandwiches and titbits. Journeying with their supporters from the Raven Hotel, the Diddymen from Corby continued not only to invade the local pubs, but also to forage further afield in pursuit of trophies - much to the annoyance of the 'away' opposition teams! Kitted out in their now famous uniform and waving the obligatory two-pint beer mugs, they harassed weary bar staff from far and wide with their orders for the mandatory "Two pints please innkeeper". In addition to providing neutral spectators with plenty of laughs, the attendant commotion (which always accompanied a visit by the Diddymen) would often undermine the host team before an arrow was even thrown!

Darts teams in the days before 'trophy-hunters' (i.e. players of more than average ability who - in their quest for darts superstardom - would attach themselves to whichever pub was currently doing well) were usually selected 'in house' from the best of a bank of players who on match days were willing to come in early to warm up, stretch their arms and 'get their eye in'. Only occasionally did a team include scratch players. This was a situation that clearly irked Corby's Tommy McAuley (who was a painter and decorator in BSC by day and Catholic Club 'News of the World' house champion by night.) McAuley was critical of the Corby Darts League because he felt that it was being dominated by players from Kettering. He said: "There are only three teams who ever get anywhere in the league - the Shire Horse, the Nags Head and the Phoenix, and they're mostly made up of Kettering players."

It wasn't all doom and gloom though - the Corby game had its fair share of characters for whom trophies were of lower priority than a fun night out at the pub. Jimmy 'Hamish' Cox (a carpenter by trade who was well known to those on the local darts circuit) had watched with growing disdain as the American game of pool had slowly infiltrated the British pub bar. What's more, Jimmy was

Clockwise: a) The Shire Horse darts team show off their haul for the season. L-R: Back Row - Dave Smith, James 'Hamish' Cox, Bobby McCallum, Archie 'Baldy' Eccles, Rob Wood. Front Row - Ian Foulton, the landlord of the Shire Horse, Johnny Morrison, Dave Lang and Davy McNeil. b) Winning pairs: Top to bottom - D. Hadden and J. Cox, B. McDowell and R. McGoldrick. J. Morrison and H. McKay. c) Press cutting: Brian McDowell. d) Sporting partners, Johnny Morrison and Rod Bailey. e) Johnny Morrison takes aim.

unable to hide his feelings of contempt for those players who arrived at the pub carrying their own personal pool cue in an expensive-looking case. He dismissed them as nothing more than posers. Customers at the Open Hearth were astounded, therefore, when Jimmy turned up one night (supposedly for an important darts match) and was carrying a rather spectacular wooden case. He made a big show of carefully placing the highly-polished, six foot long wooden construction on a table - aware that all eyes were on him, all minds wondering if he had transferred his allegiance to the new American intruder. Slowly, and with more than a touch of the theatrical, Jimmy opened the case. Lo and behold! There were his beloved darts - held in place by three small sets of brackets. Jimmy Cox had made his point!

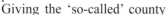

Billy Woods

Giving the 'so-called' county superstars a run for their money was a veteran player from the Nags Head - Billy Woods from Stephenson Way. "I've got ten good years left in darts!" boasted the eighty-one-year-old Yorkshireman. Prior to making a name for himself in the local leagues, Billy claimed to have been a poacher, wrestling champion, schoolboy rugby league prospect and illegal whippet chaser. Billy: "At a whippet meeting in Blackpool, one of my dogs won her heat to qualify for the final - the prize for which was a bountiful £1,000 purse. However, when the scrutineers discovered that I had placed bits of cork under her paws (in order to stabilise her on the corners) we were immediately disqualified by the stewards. It was a shame because she was a fast dog anyway. In fact she still holds the lap record at the Bradford track!"

Before the First World War Billy played rugby league at schoolboy level for Wakefield, winning two caps, and as a wrestler he was undefeated within a twenty mile radius of Pontefract. Unfortunately, the WW1 trenches and the campaigns at Ypres, Somme and Loos, left him with a shattered shoulder, torn side and several bayonet wounds - actively putting an end to his sports career. "So I took to gamekeeping and then poaching," Billy confessed. "In those days there were no fines. You went straight to prison if you were caught (and the police would be waiting for you when you came out!) It was for that reason that I came south to Gretton - and then carried on!" Also a good dominoes player, in his time Billy Woods, won titles in the Corby, Kettering, Welland Valley and Uppingham leagues. He said: "I could beat players half my age - but then they used bad language when I did!"

Johnny 'Redmondo' Redmond (a Diddymen supporter) was one of the more outrageous characters who frequented the Raven Hotel. When Johnny was around there was always a danger that something unexpected would happen. The problem was that he didn't care much for darts night etiquette and on more than one occasion upset and embarrassed unsuspecting visiting teams with his unseemly behaviour.

One night during a close contest between the Diddymen and a Kettering team, just as the match was reaching its climax, Johnny decided that he needed to pay an urgent visit to the gents - or so he claimed. To his dismay (if he is to be believed) Redmondo found that there wasn't any Izal toilet paper in his cubicle. Assuming it to be a simple oversight on behalf of the pub's cleaners, he folded his trousers, draped them neatly over his arm (waiter style) and casually strolled into the bar to ask the landlady if she would be kind enough to supply a roll! With the opposition looking on in astonishment, Johnny stood patiently at the bar in his underpants and jacket. Needless to say, the Raven won that night - leaving the visiting team looking rather puzzled. Many doubted whether the extraordinary scene, which had been played out before their very eyes, was indeed genuine or was just clever gamesmanship.

The game of darts was also gaining increased exposure at a national level, mainly through the medium of television. ATV was the first channel to feature the game - on a show called *Double Top*. Coming live from the studios in Birmingham, the programme was presented by Gary Newbon and former Wolves and England footballer Billy Wright (at that time Head of ATV Sport.) The inaugural show featured Hector McKay the Domino pub's star player and at the time, Corby's leading dartsman. (He was also county champion). On the show, Hector's challenge was to take on 'the best of the rest' of Britain in a studio pub which had been specially constructed for the series. An added attraction of the venue was that it would present Hector with a golden opportunity to meet and rub shoulders with some of the most famous characters ever to have appeared in the British soaps - namely Meg Richardson, Shughie McFee and Amy Turtle from *Crossroads*. Although Hector failed in his bid to become the national champion, he says that meeting Meg (Noele Gordon) and company, and getting 'wee' Shughie's autograph, more than made up for his lack of success on the oche.

Alas, the day was to end in disgrace when the Corby contingent let down themselves (and the town) by drinking to excess and causing too much background noise whilst on air. To the huge embarrassment of those watching locally, they were all asked to leave.

Hector's number one supporter, Dougie Bean, took umbrage at being asked to rush his pint and categorically refused to budge until he had finished it in his own good time. All in all, for Hector it was a memorable but ill-fated day. However, he wasn't the only one to suffer some bad luck - Denis Philkes, the London bus conductor and eventual winner of the competition, was knocked down by a bus on his return home to the capital!

The filming of the qualifying rounds for the *About Anglia Darts Trophy* was yet another occasion when visiting players from Corby outstayed their welcome. Although the town's finest were at Irthlingborough Working Mens Club to do 'battle' for a place in the Final (which was being held at the Anglia Television studios in Norwich) they appear to have taken the challenge a little too literally. What began as a pleasant evening soon turned ugly. The trouble began after a complaint from one of the Corby team that a member of the other side was persistently encroaching over the oche, in an attempt to steal a couple of inches and thus get nearer to the board. Things quickly turned nasty, and when the Corby players were set upon by their opponents, a full-scale riot ensued. Police were then called in to break up the fighting and the competition was subsequently abandoned.

At the extraordinary disciplinary meeting that took place in the wake of this debacle, all teams from Corby were barred from the County Super League. After an appeal was lodged they were reinstated - but only on condition that they wouldn't stay behind to socialise at away matches!

Twelve months after being called upon to hand out paper knickers in Corby Market Square, Dougie Martell (former roadie for St. Cecilia) was working at the Victoria Bars Club in Weymouth. His new employment was with Barn Promotions Management Company (owned by Chas Chandler ex-member of the Animals.) According to the *Weymouth News and Echo*, it was a very fortuitous move indeed. The newspaper reported that Dougie's 'lip - plus personality - has brought the offers rolling in. Doug, aged 22, the resident DJ at Victoria Bars, is seen as a hot property and is being considered for work by a number of radio and club show bosses.'

Entering a national DJ competition that was being sponsored by *DJ & Radio Monthly* magazine, the former failed Chi Rho freely admitted that he was 'never gonna be any good on guitar' and had at last found his niche. He went on to win the competition and walked away with tickets (presented by

DJ Ed Stewart of the BBC) for a mammoth sixteen-day whistle-stop working tour of New York, Nashville, Phoenix, the Grand Canyon, Las Vegas, Los Angeles and San Francisco.

Dougie: "After that the offers came flooding in. I did the *Radio One Roadshow* from Brands Hatch and had several offers from commercial radio. Most of the local clubs asked me to pop in and see them about arranging future dates. I was riding the crest of a wave. I seemed to be doing nothing but considering offers."

The month that Dougie spent stateside gave him invaluable experience, e.g. guesting on talk shows and working with the Woodstock rock and roll band Sha Na Na. He even did a spot of news reading. Well and truly bitten by the travel bug, for the next three years Dougie worked in the hotels, nightclubs and discotheques of Europe - playing music for all age groups. He eventually ended up in Denmark and decided to settle there after meeting his future wife Jonna.

Back at home two of his former sidekicks were now establishing themselves as songwriters. Dave Martin and Ian 'Robbie Stewart' Eccles were writing and recording their own material under the name of Wellington. Dave said in 2005: "We did really well together - Robbie was the lyricist and I

Although hoping for a taste of Noel Edmunds' champagne lifestyle, Dougie Martell has to settle for sharing a bottle of Piper Heidsieck with the famous DJ.

wrote the music. By sending demos to disc jockeys all over the country, we managed to get quite a lot of radio work. One interview that sticks in my mind was at Radio Leicester. Whilst we were on the air somebody phoned in from a corset factory and invited us down for a visit. Unfortunately we couldn't make it as we had to catch the train to London. It was a pity really, but that day we were working to such a tight schedule that our movements were quite restricted.

Mick Harper (who at the time was singing with Paper Lace) made a demo of one of our songs. It was called *The Wanderer*. Mick told us to take it to Campbell Connelly, the music publishers in Denmark Street, and to mention his name. When we entered the office we saw that a huge ornament was sitting on a table near the door. It was a gift from Lieutenant Pigeon - thanking the firm for its successful collaboration on their massive hit record *Mouldy Old Dough*. We knew then that we were in the presence of greatness! Later on we discovered that 'Dough' was recorded in some woman's house. If you listen carefully, you can hear a tray of tea cups tinkling as she enters the room!

Connelly's took our record without any trouble. In actual fact we went on to write loads more material for them - and still receive royalties to this day. Although it's not a mint, it's better than nothing! There was even a suggestion (although it didn't come to anything) that the Rubettes was going to record one of our songs - it was called *Smile*. Incredible as this may seem, the number eventually went on to become popular in Lebanon!"

Dave Martin eventually went back on the road with a band that had been cobbled together by Dave Dean and included John McConnell on drums and Andy Brown on bass. The Valentinos (as they called themselves) were managed by a guy named John Kenrick. John was able to secure regular bookings for them at venues such as the Stardust Social Club in Corby, and it was there that they took to the stage as the supporting act to 1960's icons Emile Ford, Kathy Kirby and Wee Willie Harris.

In February Ireland's Thin Lizzy (who had been recently hitting the charts with *Whisky In The Jar*) gave a rocking performance to a packed audience at the Central Hall in Kettering. There to greet the Irish rockers and take full advantage of the hall's renowned hospitality was an exuberant Corby-Irish contingent.

Fans of the silver screen were stunned when news leaked out concerning a possible closure of the Granada Cinema in Kettering.

Above: Representing his band Wellington, Ian Eccles is pictured striking a Napoleonic pose on the cover of their first record release, entitled 'Swoop Down On You'. Other members of the group included: John Grimley, Jack Murphy, Dave Martin and Ned McGuigan. Right: Their second release 'Catch Us If You Can' was taken up by an American recording company - fuelling the group's dreams of a transatlantic breakthrough. However, like its predecessor the number failed to swoop up the charts!

They were alarmed to hear that there were plans afoot to turn the stately old picture palace (and sometime pop venue) into a bingo hall. "This is the latest in a long line of Kettering cinema closures," complained Councillor John Bradley of Kettering

Town Council Health Committee, referring to the application for a bingo licence that they received from Granada Theatres, London Ltd. A spokesman for GTL said: "We have to protect the company's commercial interests and the first stage is to get a bingo licence." The general feeling at GTL was that while there was an increasing demand for bingo, cinema audiences appeared to be on the wane. Councillor Bradley was undeterred, saying "The cinema is a valuable asset to the town and one that Kettering can ill afford to lose. There is little enough live entertainment in the town as it is." This was a sentiment shared wholeheartedly by the majority of 18-30 year-olds living in Kettering.

There were some in the town who were willing to blame bingo for all of society's ills, and, according to one of the academics at Manchester University, they needed to look no further than eight miles up the road for confirmation of the harm that it could inflict on a community. Dr. Bill Beswick, Dean of the Faculty of Psychological Medicine at Manchester University, reported:

Dave 'Oscar' Martin. As well as performing with several local bands (including Oscar and Freedom), Dave was also a partner in the Eccles/Martin songwriting team. The Corby tunesmith passed away in 2008, following a long illness.

> 'Society is changing and Corby is a typical example of a new town in this day and age. Wives complain that husbands are spending their money on horses and rent is falling behind. I welcome moves by the government to make the family allowance paid directly to the wife. Better to make sure the money is not squandered on gambling by the husband.'

The report continued:

> 'The Corby Candle belches its flames of white hot fire, lighting the sky with eager industry - a silent symbol of Corby's booming prosperity as a key 'new town'. The flame that never dies at British Steel is a space age industrial Olympic torch, never to be doused and spells out fat pay packets for work hungry men. Men, rejected by their hometowns because of unemployment, arrive in ever increasing numbers into Corby. But in this new town with its dangled carrots of big wages, lesser working hours, easy facilities within the framework of a complex of concrete and steel, an insidious enemy is creeping up in carpet slippers - threatening to strangle a virtually classless society - boredom. Bored and with ready money jingling in their pockets, a social and immoral cancer is quickly sprouting in Corby as more and more men and women turn to a major outlet - gambling. Bingo, horses, one-armed-bandits and poker schools are a daily feature.'

Despite Ken Dodd's refusal to sponsor them (owing to his existing charitable commitments) the Diddymen darts team from Corby were nevertheless willing to pledge their support to his backing of a national campaign to 'Bring Back the Jam Butty'. The campaign (launched at Liverpool's Albert Dock by Ken and the genial characters whose moniker had been borrowed by the Corby darts team) was intended to revive interest in the traditional jam sandwich. The intention was to re-establish it as a staple of the nation's everyday diet, and to publicise the merits of the quick and tasty snack.

Dodd denied that his involvement had been prompted by the recent success of 'Doughnut Week', saying: "This latest activity from Purely Preserves - the UK Jam and Marmalade Awareness Initiative - has an overall objective to raise awareness of British jam and the many varieties on offer. I have been invited to front the campaign due to my long-term association with the Jam Butty Mines of Knotty Ash." He continued: "Jam Butties are the original fast food for kids. I grew up on them, and so did the Diddy Men. They're tartifilarious!"

Hard at it! Granite performing in Queen's Square, Corby. Amongst the musicians that day were L-R: Bob Grimley and Pete Bonas are on guitars, with Jake Pressley, Dick Kirk and Ron Kirk providing the brass-section.

One of the highlights of the 7th Corby Arts Festival was a 'Rock Night' that included performances from Granite, the Average White Band and Vinegar Joe (featuring Elkie Brooks and Robert Palmer.) Then in mid-week Brewers Droop and Bob Kerr's Whoopee Band appeared in the Willow Room. Together with Sam Spoons and Vernon Dudley Bohay-Nowell, Kerr was one of the original members of the jazz/comedy outfit Bonzo Dog Do Dah Band.

Introduced and presented by Trevor Wright, the evening was described in the *Evening Telegraph* as 'a feast of musical and audio mayhem from a collection of multi-talented and eccentric musicians'. Trevor recalled: "The band included a mad saxophone player named Evil John Gieves. What a nutter! He dressed up as a Canadian Mountie to go on stage, played the cello with a sword and sang *Indian Love Call*. He then changed into an Arab costume, placed a tray of sand on the stage and performed the *In A Persian Market* song and dance routine. The auditorium was in hysterics! The stage area was littered with props - dummy heads, tiger's heads and fancy dress. During the act an occasional firecracker would explode, making it sound as though the Civic was being blown up. Smoke then filled the room and people began to scream from the shock. Next minute they were falling about once more. It was crazy, total madness but the atmosphere was fantastic, absolutely brilliant! At the end I went on stage to thank the band for a great night of entertainment and to request a final encore - which of course the crowd loved!"

On the first Saturday of the festival the jazz-oriented band Granite provided some home-grown talent during a lunchtime session in the Queen's Square shopping precinct. Speaking prior to his death in August 2008, guitarist Bob Grimley said: "Granite's constantly changing line-up evolved around a small core of musicians - Jake Pressley, Ron Kirk and his brother Dick. My most vivid memories of that day revolve around us setting up our gear outside the John Menzies shop. It involved putting in place a bank of PA equipment - which meant that there would be miles of cable stretching everywhere. I remember that we had only just finished when the manager of the shop came out and told us to move it all. At that point there was already a crowd of more than four hundred people waiting for us to begin playing. I looked at them and then I said to the manager, 'Are you gonna tell them that we've got to move?' At that he went back inside - and it was just as well because the crowd was getting restless. Many of them were suffering from that days withering heat and were jumping into the ornamental pond to try and cool down. As you can imagine, they were in no mood for interruptions!"

Throughout 1973 the band were kept extremely busy and had the good fortune to be selected for a short tour with First Choice (a female soul trio from Philadelphia) who were touring on the back of their hit singles *Armed And Extremely Dangerous* and *Smarty Pants*. It was a punishing schedule and would have dented the enthusiasm of many a younger band. Bob recalled: "It was great fun, if not tiring! We impressed the girls right from the start, by learning all their material in just six hours of rehearsals. Although they were gracious enough to mention this in their subsequent *NME* interview, in all honesty - it wasn't that difficult. The tour kicked off on Saturday July 7th. We did an early evening performance at Whitchurch in Shropshire, followed by a late night spot at the Speakeasy Club in Crewe, then on the Sunday we played at both USAF Ruislip and at Mr. Dee's Club in

A member of Philadelphia's First Choice (centre left) enjoys a relaxing drink with Jake Pressley and Bob Grimley of Granite. The Corby jazz/fusion group supported the hit making band during a 1973 British tour which had been arranged to capitalise on the American combo's hit 'Smarty Pants'. Jake's wife Lou is on the right.

Peckham, South East London. The next couple of days took us to Stafford, Wolverhampton and Southend - from where we headed back to the capital for a date at the London Speakeasy Club. After a day off in mid-week (to recharge our batteries) we travelled down to Portsmouth for another two engagements, and then we set off again for Goole, Doncaster, Nottingham and Lincoln. All in all, it was a busy week!"

Big Band enthusiast Mervyn Sumpter was so impressed by Granite's 'ensemble' approach that he decided to form a band of his own along similar lines. He called them the New Sessionaires. For drummer Mervyn it was simply a way of being able to hear more of those great sounds played by the likes of Glenn Miller and Syd Lawrence. Explaining his 'easy on the ear' philosophy to the music critic of the local newspaper, he said: "I regard this kind of venture as a challenge and one that enables me to play music purely for my own pleasure. The band currently consists of ten members and we want to expand to about seventeen. We desperately need piano, bass and baritone sax players. This will ensure that we have a complete range of players - even if one or two have to drop out for various reasons."

Finding himself at a loose end following his spell as a roadie for St Cecilia, bass player Jim Smith joined Ricky and the Avengers (Ricky

Ricky Geoghegan (Man of a Thousand Pop Personas) is seen here with his latest line-up Ricky and the Avengers. Featuring Tommy Chapman on drums and Alan Palmer on bass guitar, the band is pictured warming up before a gig at the Corby Candle.

Geoghegan's latest project) who at various times featured Frank Porch, Ian Smith, Mark Plant and Tommy Chapman. Jim: "We played mainly in dance halls and as far afield as Huntingdon, St. Neots and beyond. Over the course of time we shared the bill with 1960's favourites the Searchers and Gerry and the Pacemakers." The band also played under the names of Ricky and the Boys, the Acoustics, and then Love Train. By that time the line-up included ex-Drumbeat Charlie Parr, Bob

Burlison from the Uglys, Malcolm Wright from Boot Z and folk-singer Dave Wolstenholme.

Following his tenure with Ricky and the Avengers, Jim Smith was invited to join Auction - one of the most popular bands on the circuit. Jim recalls: "Although Auction only lasted for three years, we were working constantly. We did a number of bookings down south and in the holiday camps, plus we also auditioned for the television talent shows *Opportunity Knocks* and *New Faces*. Much to our disappointment, however, we failed to make it onto either of the programmes because they wanted artists with original material. With a singer like Mick Harper - who could sing almost anything - we had never really considered trying to work out some material of our own. Auction was a great band, even though there were occasions when we had to play without lead guitarist, Reggie Knowles. I remember one weekend when we were playing in the Corby Candle pub, whilst Reg was banged up in the cop shop across the road (the reason being he hadn't made his child maintenance payments.) Billy Mathieson suggested that we should go over and ask the desk sergeant if we could borrow him for the night! Failing that, an alternative option was to enquire whether Reg's guitar lead could be extended - so that he could play from his cell!"

A perennial problem for rock and roll bands was transportation, and Auction found themselves to be no different in this respect. Jim: "We had been booked to play at RAF Mildenhall (the US air base in Suffolk) and, on the day of the gig, by sheer bad luck, our six wheel transit van wouldn't start. In desperation, we loaded the gear into the back, hooked it up to my Ford Cortina and then I towed it all the way down there and back. It was an extremely uncomfortable expedition - but turned out to be one marked with moments of sheer hilarity! In those days everyone in the group, except for Billy, wore a red suit on stage. Mathieson's suit, however, was bright yellow. One night, after performing in Harlow, we dropped Billy off at a nightclub and the rest of us went elsewhere in the town. After enjoying a few pints we set off home, minus Billy. Next day we found out that he'd had to make his way back to Corby by train - dressed like a canary! Although he called us a few choice names, eventually Billy saw the funny side of it!

In Corby's old village Jim Tibbs of the Nags Head was making steady progress. Tibbs: "We tried out lots of different ideas. Dougie King was with me at that time - working mostly as a DJ at the private parties that we were endeavouring to promote. Weddings and private dances were quiet lucrative at this time and always guaranteed a room-full.

Things didn't really click until I met Bip and we struck a deal to put on discos in the back room. Although they weren't exactly an overnight success, we stuck at it - in fact we worked together for over five years. Through thick and thin we got them in! With the Friday and Sunday night discos doing well, and then the weddings and private parties on Saturday, things were definitely looking up! I was of the opinion that Thursday could be a good night, however, it never worked until Trevor Wright (who eventually became landlord of the Everard Arms) put me on to a Coventry group called Patsy Powell and the Playboys. They were a country and western band whose music, unlike that played by some of the more traditional country outfits, was guaranteed to get everyone up on the dance floor. In fact they were such a huge success at the Nags that they ended up performing there every Thursday night for five years! Patsy herself was a great singer and the crowd loved her to bits. It therefore proved a great disappointment when, at the end of 1974, she decided to leave the band. Fortunately, that didn't stop the Playboys from packing them in.

Going back to 1973, the brewery had by then decided that we were doing well enough to justify revamping the pub, so they invested £40,000 to cover the cost of improvements. The two rooms at the back were knocked into one, a long bar was installed and then a new entrance built. At that time we were the only pub in the area to have a cloakroom. Mind you, that didn't prevent the coats from going astray - all it did was slow down the rate of attrition. At the end of most nights there was some irate customer or another who was missing a coat. Looking back, I don't know how those cloakroom girls put up with the abuse that was hurled at them.

Once the pub was ship-shape, it was time to turn our attention to the bouncers - Harry McCardie and Duncan Currie. I remember them looking very smart in their new blue blazers, grey slacks and bow ties, however, I'm sure they took some stick from the punters - though I don't think it was ever to their faces. Harry and Duncan were brilliant at the job and not to be messed with! Corby had quite a hard reputation but the boys were well up to the job! As we were now running quite a posh place, we also felt the need to impose dress standards on our customers and decided that men should be required to wear a tie (even if it meant Harry and Duncan renting them the very latest in trendy neckwear.)

We would open up the back room at 8 p.m., and amazingly, by 8.30 p.m. we'd have over two hundred people in there - at which point we'd shut the doors. Brilliant!

I had some excellent members of staff and many of them worked there for a long time. At the height of the business I employed more than thirty people to keep us up and running. Who would have wanted to be a cleaner at the Nags after five hundred carousing customers had passed through it?

After splitting with the Playboys, Irish-born Patsy Powell (far right) became a sought-after solo performer on the UK and Ireland club circuit. She retired from the music business in 1982.

Several of the Gallagher family worked for me. Paddy was a great barman, Pat worked as a barmaid and cook, Nuala was another of my barmaids and Manus worked as a doorman/barman. Then there was Celeste - the wife of Cyril Marsh. Cyril was responsible for booking some of the acts who appeared at the Nags. He always seemed to be on the phone but was very good at persuading acts to accept competitive rates. Cyril eventually left to run the Open Hearth after Bip took over from me at the Nags Head.

We were booking bands that played at the Marquee Club in London and on the student hall circuit. Some were good, some were very good and some were lousy. When you only paid twenty-five quid (for a four-piece band who'd come all the way from 'The Smoke') you never knew what to expect - you just hoped that they'd go down well.

On Sunday night we ran a disco. Bip Wetherell and his brother Stuart came up with the idea of a 'double DJ show' featuring two DJ s on stage at the same time. There'd be two sets of decks, alternate spins and plenty of banter in-between. It was a great format which the crowd loved.

Back then I was on good terms with the manager of Bailey's nightclub in Leicester. He and I came to an arrangement whereby I would use some of his weekend acts in a Monday night cabaret at the Nags. We ran it once a month at £5 per head. Amongst the acts that we put on were the Swinging Blue Jeans (from the Merseybeat era.) We put on Wee Willie Harris - who turned up carrying his own gear! He was a lot of fun. Then there was Screaming Lord Sutch, who had a great show but was a real nutter - nearly burning down the place when his swinging cauldron broke loose and set fire to some furniture! Solomon King was a bit big-headed - but that was par for the course - because he was a Yank! Nevertheless he put on a great show. In addition, a number of well-known comedians appeared. They included Jimmy Marshall and (my favourite) Dougie Brown from the TV series *The Comedians*. Then there was Jim Bowen and Mike Reid. The latter turned up in a Rolls Royce on his way to do the Palladium. Cyril had worked hard on that booking and I think Reid only came in order to stop Cyril from ringing him! He brought his family with him after I'd agreed that they could have free food and drink. George Roper, whose jokes were clean and inoffensive, was a big guy. He took one look at me and announced, 'I've met my long lost brother'. I think it was something to do with size!

A rare occurrence in 1970s' Corby - a taxi firm having to advertise for trade.

We put on several stag-nights (featuring a comedian and two strippers) that were very well received. In fact they were so successful that we tried a hen-night. What a mistake - the women were uncontrollable! After putting on about six shows, playing to a full house each night, the staff, the doormen and even Bip refused to do any more. I must say that I had to agree with them because, in spite of our first-rate doormen, the women went absolutely crazy. The barmaids were subjected to verbal insults and on one occasion Bip was pulled from behind his record decks and very nearly hauled from the stage. Give me stag-nights any time!

Being within easy walking distance of the steelworks, on a Friday we were the first port of call for scores of workers who had been on night shift - or were due to start a back-shift and had been down to the works early to collect their wages. I had to put on as many as five bar staff at lunch-time to cope with the demand. Card schools were the big thing in those days and no matter how many times I told the customers that it was illegal to play brag, poker or any other game where money was on the table, they just ignored me. Wives were known to come into the bar of a Friday lunch-time and demand the housekeeping money, fearing that there might not be any left when the husband got home! Then of course, closing times were a nightmare because the clientele just didn't want to leave.

There were a lot of cabbies (from Flanagan's, Donovan's and Knight's taxis) who came in every morning after the steelworks run. Taxi firms did quite well out of the trade from the Nags. Most of their drivers were on the dole and liked to play pool between fares. We had two of the first pool tables in Corby and I was amazed at just how much money they took weekly at 10p a game. We also had a video jukebox. It didn't really show videos but Super-8 films, and on the odd occasion the film would jam, causing the projection lamp to burn a hole in it. Next morning the engineer would come out and splice it together. The only problem was that when the record was next played and, let's just say for instance there was a topless girl dancing around in the kitchen, it would suddenly jump from there to the living room, to the garden, then back again to the bedroom or the kitchen. It was hilarious to watch. One night the police raided us and confiscated the jukebox alleging that it was obscene. Whatever the case might have been - none of us ever saw it again!"

Bip Wetherell: "On Mondays (our only night off during the week) Tibbs and I used to go over to Baileys to watch all the touring cabaret acts. We saw the Three Degrees, the Detroit Emeralds, Edwin Starr and many others. It was there that I watched Jim eat a dinner for four -

Frankie Avalon calls for a ladder so that he can view the video jukebox. Regulars of the Nags Head in Corby shared the same problem - that is until police impounded their machine!

all by himself! He was a great landlord as well as being a really nice guy to work with. Although we had the occasional tiff, it didn't prevent us from having a good working relationship.

On the eve of the publication of British Steel Corporation's annual report, the recently formed Corby Action Group warned that the future of Corby was at stake and that the town must unite in a fight to safeguard the jobs of its 6,500 steelworkers. The group claimed that Corby was now being looked upon as nothing more than a stop-gap steel production plant, whilst money was being invested elsewhere - in larger plants that would form the basis of a new steel industry. Spokesman George McCart said: "We will not be hit for five years. But there is no doubt that then we will be hit, and hit hard. The Government's White Paper on steel implies that there is a possibility of closing the Corby steel plant."

Fears grew after a meeting in Corby between union officials and Dr. Finniston, Acting Chairman of BSC. Dougie Reid (a turner in the tube works and union convener) told the Action Group: "The message came loud and clear that in five years the minerals department and iron and steel plant will be designated for closure," The following day Harry Armitage, the resident director of BSC in Corby, seemed more optimistic. In an attempt to reassure workers, he told reporters: "Corby's future is not in danger. As long as steel is produced here at a cheaper rate than the rest of the country, the town's 6,500 jobs are assured."

A few days after what, in hindsight, would appear to be an act of perfidy by Armitage, Sir Henry Chisholm, Chairman of Corby Development Corporation, addressed a well-attended public meeting at the Civic Centre. Speaking with a degree of confidence about the future of the town, he said: "The

Development Corporation's schemes to attract new industry into the town are meeting with a measure of success." On the question of the steelworks, however, although Sir Henry supported the views of the Action Group, he was less than emphatic when issuing his rallying call, conceding that people in Corby were 'right to be concerned about the future of the steelworks. We must all take steps to ensure that they remain intact, and in that way we will postpone the evil day - should it ever occur.'

Following the demise of Golden Fleece, on September 15, 1973 Pat Lavin (after a brief flirtation with a group called Honey) unveiled his new outfit Harry Garter and his Elastic Band. Included in the new group was Frank Mullen - one of Pat's work mates from BSC. Frank, who had lived in Corby as a youngster but had returned to Scotland during his teens, was already an accomplished guitarist when he met Pat, having played in and around the Clydeside area with several bands - including the Buddy Holly influenced rock 'n' roll group Airport. Joining Pat and Frank in their new venture were Dennis May on drums and Willie Thompson on bass guitar, and it was this line-up who made their debut at the wedding of Jimmy Heron (whose brother Johnny had played in Golden Fleece.)

Jimmy: "I had originally booked the Fleece to play at my reception in the Lodge Park Community Centre, but, as luck would have it, they folded just before the big day and I was left to ask Pat if he and his new band would take over. Although I knew all about Pat and Johnny's altercation at the RAF base, Pat and I bore no grudges over what had happened. As far as I was concerned, it was good of Pat to step in at short notice to fill the breach.

My stag night was equally memorable. A crowd of us went down to London and we ended up watching a band playing at a pub at Chiswick. Unfortunately for us, with the exception of one of their guitarists - who was quite obviously a 'pro' - they turned out to be pretty dire. On overhearing a chance remark of mine about how talented the lead player was, an American standing near us came over to enlighten me. He said that the guy, a fellow countryman of his, was actually just sitting in. He explained that his main reason for coming over here was to work with the singer Kiki Dee on a track that she was recording with Elton John's band. 'Only trouble is,' he said, 'we need a drummer'. At that, I pointed to my brother Johnny and said 'There's the best drummer around!' In response, the American chap handed over his business card and told Johnny to turn up for an audition at Elton's Mayfair studio. Johnny didn't take his offer seriously, and it was only when Elton's first No 1 (*Don't Go Breaking My Heart* - featuring Kiki Dee) came out the following year that he realised what an opportunity he'd missed!"

Pat Lavin: "The name Harry Garter and his Elastic Band was suggested to us by Willie Restorick - a work mate of mine. When we asked him why, Willie said: 'Well, I saw you playing at the Welfare Club last night, and if you lot think you're gonna make it as pop stars - you're stretching it a bit!' I just laughed at him, but then I thought to myself - hey, that's a great name for a band!" Overstretched or not, signing up with John Newman ensured that they were given plenty of work. Frank Mullen: "Newman, who was based in Leicester, used to say that although the bands from Corby were great - they were all alcoholics!"

On more than one occasion during their time together, the band ran into trouble over some of the more outrageous aspects of their act. Sometimes things would start out quite innocently, and then Pat's wicked sense of humour would go into overdrive - with the result that all hell would break loose. The following anecdote provides a perfect example of this. Pat: "It was at a time when it was fashionable to wear tight-fitting jeans with the zip showing, and I remember that on this particular night we were just about to go on stage at the Welfare Club when the little catch at the top of mine snapped. Without a second thought, Frank Mullen gave me the crucifix from around his neck and told me to hook it into my zip, to prevent it from coming undone. Unfortunately, as soon as we started playing, the crucifix dropped out and ended up dangling between my legs - much to the amusement of the audience (or should I say the majority of the audience.) The room was packed that night and so, just for a laugh, I asked if anybody would like to come up and kiss my cross! A woman sitting next to the stage was incandescent. 'That's blasphemous!' she yelled. The place then erupted as everyone else began cheering and laughing. After that the cross became an integral part of the act!"

Frank: "Pat was a smooth-looking character and a real poser, and because of that we'd be called all sorts of names - such as 'poofs' and 'queers'. We just played up to it though; we thought we'd give them something to talk about! When we introduced into our set the Carpenters song *Close To You*, it really brought out the worst in us. I'd get my guitar and rub it up against Pat's legs, thrusting it back and forth between them! It was all very crude and wildly over the top, but it was done in fun."

Be that as it may, the antics of the band were considered by some to stretch the bounds of common decency, and before long propelled them into the British tabloids. 'Pub Bans A Sizzling Pop Singer' screamed one newspaper headline.

Harry Garter and his Elastic Band. Despite the Cambridge gig being advertised as a free event, the band's ethos didn't stretch to 'playing for pints' à la Rod Stewart and the Faces. L-R: Alistair Brodie, Pat Lavin, Frank Mullen and Willie Thompson.

The accompanying article explained: 'A pop group has been banned from a Northamptonshire pub, the Phoenix in Corby, because the singer is too sexy. Harry Garter and his Elastic Band has been told that there will be no more sessions for them.' Landlord Tom Taylor explained: 'It was the way singer Pat Lavin wriggled his hips on stage that caused the trouble. During one number, *Do You Want To Touch Me*, Pat holds the microphone and thrusts his hips at it. Some customers complained. The group is very good musically but the singer puts it over a little too hot. We had to draw the line somewhere. Some of the singer's movements were too suggestive.'

Once he was back at work in the Engineering Shop, Pat had to put up with all the expected stick from his workmates. The ban and the subsequent press coverage in the *Sun* and the *Daily Mirror* brought him more grief than he ever could have imagined. It was the reaction from his boss, Dougie Milligan, which upset him the most. Pat: "Dougie was a bit on the dour side and we were all frightened of him. When you saw Dougie coming, you made sure that you were looking busy - so that he couldn't catch your eye. Well this one morning he came marching out of his office with steam coming out of his ears. 'You!' he bellowed at me, in that big Jock voice of his.

I looked at him and asked 'Me?'

'Yes' he said, 'You.' He went on: 'From now on keep your private life to yourself. That telephone hasn't stopped ringing all morning and I'm fed up of people asking for Pat Lavin. Get yourself up to the flyover at the work's gate - 'cause there's a posse of reporters and photographers waiting to see you.'

'No way,' I said, 'I'm in my overalls.' Nevertheless, Dougie ordered me up there to get rid of them. It was absolute bedlam!"

Reminiscing about some of the band's other experiences, Frank Mullen recalled a trip to Derek Tompkins' recording studio in Wellingborough. Frank: "I always used to argue with Pat about the backing vocals - which I felt were crap due to his singing too high. The problem was that I couldn't get my voice as high as his, especially when we were covering stuff like *Maggie May* and *My Girl* etc. I remember that over at the studios we spent about eight hours trying to perfect this one song - playing it time and time again. In the end my head was pounding (probably because we hadn't eaten all day) and so I told Pat that I couldn't carry on and that what we'd recorded would have to do. It was the only way I could get him to stop!"

Beck Sound Recording Studios were in Lister Street, Wellingborough. Housed in what was basically an old whitewashed warehouse; they were able to accommodate with ease around twenty musicians and provided for their use a Leevers-Rich eight-track recording machine. John Douglas and Vic White (the managing directors of the studios) were responsible for the administrative side of the business, and this left Derek Tompkins free to take care of the recording side of the operation. Tompkins was a gifted engineer whose professional confidence and skill allowed musicians to work to the best of their potential. In addition to Harry Garter and his Elastic Band, artists who passed through Beck Studios included the Barron Knights, Family, Gypsy and Black Widow.

After playing in the mid-1960s with the Midnighters and the Cascades, Alistair Brodie spent seven years living away from Corby. On his return, the opportunity to 'sit in' with the Roy Bishop Sound helped to rekindle his enthusiasm for playing again and led to him joining Harry Garter and his Elastic Band. Alistair: "Pat was outrageous and had a tendency to annoy most people - particularly those in the band! John Grimley played with us from time to time and, more often than not, ended up having a barney with him. The lasting memory that I have of my time with the band doesn't relate to that aspect though - its about the night when (because our manager, Basil Barnard couldn't make it) I was given the responsibility of driving his van and looking after the money. After the gig in the early hours of the morning I parked the bus and was walking along Norton Road, towards Willowbrook Road, when this shifty-looking couple - a guy and his girlfriend - approached me and demanded that I hand over the bag of money. Without thinking, I socked the pair of them in the mouth - then legged it!"

Two brothers who had undoubtedly paid their dues to the local pop industry were twins Mick and Tony Haselip from Weldon. Although in 1966 Tony replaced guitarist Graham Henderson in the Pacifics (the latter having left to join Rhubarb Tree), later he joined forces with his bass-playing brother Mick by becoming a member of Magnetic Storm. Following a subsequent brief spell with the Lykes of Witch, the Haselips then turned professional. Along with brothers Stuart and Jimmy Irving and Kettering drummer Steve Short, the siblings then embarked on a tour of United States Army bases in Germany, appearing under the name of Alias Jon Smith. Tony: "Before going to Germany with Alias Jon Smith, three of us (Mick, Stuart and I) had all completed apprenticeships with British Steel in Corby. As this was to be our first job as professional musicians you can imagine what a buzz it gave us to see that printed on our passports. We were so proud of ourselves! As it turns out, the trip proved to be a real eye-opener. Although it seems unbelievable now - on six nights a week we were expected to play five sets lasting forty-five minutes each! Yet we were always broke!

While we were in Germany the agreement was that we would be paid twenty-five per cent of our wages, plus expenses, and the balance was to be sent back to the UK for safe keeping. Our management had told us that it was the only way to avoid paying tax in both countries. As this seemed plausible at the time, we gave the matter no further thought.

After returning to the UK we had another 'adventure' trying to trace our money. We went down to Bournemouth to look for our agent - Harry 'Honest it's true' Goldblatt - but he had disappeared. So we never did get the dosh!

The Lantern public house in Burghley Drive, Corby. Situated on Corby's Exeter Estate (or 'the Ponderosa' as it was known locally) the Lantern was decorated in nautical style and was a purveyor of Flowers' beer. It also had a great jukebox and was an occasional venue for live music. Later renamed the Fox and Hounds, the pub was for many years an integral part of the estate's social life, however, over the years it became run-down and was eventually demolished.

Shortly after arriving in Germany, I remember that on one occasion we played a US base at Wildflecken on the border between East and West Germany. This was before the reunification of those two countries, and it was where the Americans had their crack ski troops positioned - just in case the Russians decided to attack across the mountains" Originally a training centre (between the years of 1937-39) for the Wehrmacht/German Army, by the time Alias John Smith arrived the base was being utilised as a military training camp for the use of all NATO partners. In 1958 Elvis Presley was stationed there whilst serving in the United States' military.

Tony continued: "It wasn't only the war that was cold - it was the middle of winter and the temperatures were down to -20°C! Although we got to the base easily enough, that evening the snow was relentless and around 8p.m. the guardroom informed us that the main autobahn was closed.

Fortunately for us, the officer in charge of entertainment kindly offered to put us up for the night in the sergeants' quarters - a decision that he was later to regret! Although this was only going to provide us with the most basic of amenities - i.e. a bunk and a sink - we had little choice but to gratefully accept his hospitality. That night the club was packed because there was nowhere else to go. There was a captive audience so to speak! After we had finished playing (at our normal time of around midnight) the CO suggested a game of poker. The deal was that we'd play a song if we lost, and he'd buy a round of drinks if he lost. Anyway the game went on until about 3.00 a.m. - at which point it came to a halt because Steve had fallen off of his drum stool!

It was then time to go and find out where our resting place for the night was to be. To our great relief, our genial host offered us a lift in his cars (a 4x4 pickup and gleaming Cadillac saloon that were parked outside the club, at the bottom of a small hill.)

A glimpse into John Grimley's scrapbook reveals a musical CV that few local performers could match. John travelled the motorways of Britain in order to play for some of the top stars of the period. Among them was the 1950s' rock 'n' roller Marty Wilde.

While we gently helped him to clear away the snow from, what we soon realised, were his 'pride and joy', the officer told us the story of how he'd managed to con the US Army into flying them both out from his hometown in Texas. We then all piled into the vehicles. The CO drove the pickup - with Stuart Irving and myself sitting with him up front, whilst his Sergeant drove the Cadillac - with Mick, Steve and Jimmy in the back (busily checking out the drinks cabinet!) By then the road was completely submerged in snow and was so slippery that even the 4x4 struggled to get up the hill. On the first attempt, just short of the crest it slithered to a halt. Its driver then decided that it would be wiser to reverse back down the hill. The sad part about it is that in doing so he lost control of the vehicle and, in one fell swoop, succeeded in writing off both it *and* the Cadillac!

When we were in Germany we were based at the Hotel De France in Wiesbaden, near Frankfurt. It was a good central location and enabled us on most nights to get 'home' to the hotel. However, the longer we stayed in Germany the more difficult it became to do this - the reason being that the old Ford transit van was struggling with the extra mileage and the extreme temperatures. It wasn't long before it took four of us to drive it! There'd be one person at the steering wheel and another with a piece of string connected to the carburettor - as the accelerator cable had snapped. A third person would be operating the windscreen wipers, because the motor had packed in, and the fourth would be demisting the windows - due to a heating malfunction! What kept us going was the thought that back home we had all that money waiting for us. We imagined ourselves buying some new gear with it, or perhaps taking a holiday. It was nice to dream."

On their return to the United Kingdom, the group (with John Grimley now in the line-up) successfully auditioned to tour with British rock 'n' roll stars Marty Wilde and Joe Brown. John recalls their first meeting with Wilde. He said: "We were in Derby to audition for a job over in Jersey, and, although we lost out on that one, Marty's manager happened to be there and invited us to try out for his client. Hal Carter, a well-known figure who counted the Kinks amongst his clientele, informed us that we'd need to travel up to Hull for this. When we got there and had set up our gear, Marty asked us to play a rock 'n' roll song, a ballad and then a pop song. Whilst this was going on, he set off around this big hall in his sheepskin coat, listening to us as he walked. When we'd finished playing Marty asked, 'Have you got any stage gear?' We showed him our suits and that sealed it. He said, 'I like your sound - you'll do for me.' Marty then wanted to know which one of us was Jon Smith. 'None of us' I replied. Then he asked me, 'Do you know what my real name is?' I said 'No'. Marty's response was: 'It's Reg Smith. You can call me Reg from now on!' (That was the start of a terrific few years for us and eventually led to me landing a three-year contract with Ace Kefford - the ex-Move bass player).

Our first rehearsal took place at the Corby Bowl. We had a run-through of some of Marty's hits: *Sea Of Love*, *Bad Boy*, *Teenager In Love* etc., with Stuart and me providing the backing vocals. I remember that it was on the day when the venue opened its doors for the very first time as the Exclusive Club. We were supposed to be playing there that night - together with a band called Boot Z - then suddenly we were told that we would be making our debut with Marty instead, at the Royal County Theatre Club in Bedford. Apparently we were to go on stage as a late replacement for the Peddlars, who had been forced to cancel because their drummer had fallen from his drum stool and fractured his arm".

Despite such short notice, the band's performance was the subject of an encouraging review that appeared in the *Bedford Chronicle*.

It stated:

> *'It was memory lane once again... when Marty Wilde came on stage and did his thing. His backing men are the Alias Jon Smith group and they presented a few numbers on their own before the top of the bill. This group was a little slow in starting but once they got into the swing of things they were really quite good and interesting to watch - particularly their lead singer, a very versatile, funny young man by the name of Stewart. It has been said about Marty, and quite truthfully too, that the basis of nearly all pop music is rock 'n' roll, and listening to the big voice of Marty you could see why. It was a pleasure to see a male entertainer who didn't have a tiny, wasp waist and dainty little black patent leather dancing shoes. He was a big man, full of masculine charm and he turned on more than one female in the audience. Marty and his group had a right old go at 'Blue Suede Shoes' - and many old hits made the rounds. Among them were 'Teenager In Love', 'Rubber Ball', 'Donna', and 'Singing The Blues' - all delivered with much wit and laughter all around. There was a great deal of variety and one of the best numbers was Joni Mitchell's 'Woodstock'. Very nicely done and the Jon Smith backing group really outdid themselves with it'.*

THE GRIMLEY FAMILY.
At the forefront of live music in Corby for over half a century.

John Grimley: "Next day we drove up to North Shields for a booking - this time without Marty. It was a sign of things to come. We'd play for Marty twice a night, for two weeks in a row, and then we'd spend the next two weeks gigging without him. It was a hectic schedule which saw us perform at venues like the She Club in Liverpool on one night, whilst the following night we might be playing at a working men's club in Bristol. We'd be in Barrow-In-Furness one week - and in Welwyn Garden City the next. It meant two years of living out of a suitcase. Some of the digs weren't particularly brilliant either! If you were booked into what they called 'theatre digs' then that was fine. You would be able to get a breakfast at lunchtime in any of them.

We played in South Wales a lot. In fact, it was in Swansea that Steve Short and I had a bit of an altercation. After we'd finished playing at this club one night, we decided to have a few drinks. I remember that Steve kept having a go at me about something or other, and eventually we ended up fighting. Although Marty tried to intervene - it was just as the bouncers turned up. Unimpressed by celebrity culture, they threw us all out. 'I've never been thrown out of a club in my life!' shouted Marty. To which I replied, 'You have now!'

Our usual routine began with Alias Jon Smith playing a couple of numbers and then Marty would casually stroll out onto the stage, walk up to the microphone and say 'Good evening'. At this point he would stretch out his arm behind him, without looking, and I would hand him his Gibson semi-acoustic. We'd then go straight into Elvis's *Burning Love*. It was corny - but good crack. One night I even passed him a cheap, plastic guitar from Woolworth's - but he took it all in good fun. It was lucky for me that he did. Marty was a big bloke and not one to be trifled with - as Ricky Valance (who had a one-hit wonder with *Tell Laura I Love Her*) discovered when he overstepped the mark. There was this one night when Ricky made a sarcastic remark about Wilde to the audience, and when he came off stage Marty was waiting for him. He grabbed Ricky and pinned him up against the dressing room wall, threatening to do him over!

Marty's wife Joyce, together with his kids Ricky and Kim, would often show up on tour - although this was long before Kim became a huge star.

Probably the highlight of my time with Marty was a rock 'n' roll tour that we did with Billy Fury, Billy J. Kramer and Heinz. I discovered that Fury and Kramer were nervous wrecks - they'd each down a bottle of whisky before going on stage!

I eventually stopped playing for Marty because I was fed up of being ripped off by his manager, Hal Carter. To begin with Hal paid us a weekly wage and we would normally have a Wednesday night off, however, after a while it became a regular occurrence for him to inform us on the Tuesday that we would be playing the next day. At this point we'd ask to see the contract, to which Hal always replied that it was in the post and that the extra nights work would be included in our pay packet. It soon became clear though that he was pocketing our share of the extra money - and that's why I jacked it in. I remember being surprised by Marty's reaction when I told him that I was leaving. He seemed genuinely upset and asked me why I was going. I told him straight, 'It's because Hal Carter is ripping us off' (meaning not only me but the Irving brothers as well.) He replied, 'I think he's ripping me off too'."

In 2004 Hal Carter died after a long illness. He was sixty-nine. His funeral was attended by many showbiz friends and associates - including Marty Wilde, Stuart Irving and Bip Wetherell. Bip: "I knew Hal very well. He was the Tornados' agent when I played with them in the nineties. He also managed the Swinging Blue Jeans. Hal would do all of his own promotions and he expected everything to run like clockwork. If it didn't - no matter who you were - he would chew your ear! Hal was Billy Fury's roadie when he first started out, and he always claimed the credit for the 'false getaway car' idea. He used to send out the limo with a member of the band in it, and then he and Billy would hide in the back of the van which was carrying the kit. Remember, all this was before the days of the Beatles!'

On October 3, 1973 a party of Manchester United supporters travelled from Corby to Old Trafford for the Denis Law testimonial match against Ajax of Amsterdam (skippered by Johan Cruyff.)

Amongst the group was David Black - for whom the night turned out to be especially memorable. David: "Through a combination of good luck and an uncharacteristic lapse in security, I was able to gate-crash the post-match reception for my all-time favourite footballer, Denis Law." The Manchester United supporter went on to explain: "After the final whistle my brother John ran on to the pitch and followed the departing teams down the tunnel. Concerned about his well being, I then made my way out of the stadium and around to the main entrance - where I was caught up in a mad crush of people who were seeking entry to (what I was informed) was a private event. With difficulty I managed to attract the attention of a uniformed concierge and went over to ask him if anyone by the name of Black had just been ejected. 'No' came the abrupt answer.

Puzzled as to where John could be, I turned to go - only to find that I was trapped on the inside of a security cordon that had been thrown hastily around the entrance. A few seconds later a Rolls Royce drew up at the door and a group of men and women wearing afghan coats and bedecked with beads alighted from it. (Although I've since forgotten their name, I recognised them at the time as being members of a well-known pop group). Anyway, as these celebs were making their way into the reception area, it suddenly dawned on me that I too might have a chance of gaining access to the event, and therefore, pretending to be one of their party, I joined the group as they breezed past the guard on the door. It was that easy. Looking back, I am ashamed to say that - in the excitement of the moment - all thoughts had gone regarding the whereabouts of my errant brother.

I followed the group upstairs and then I held back to assess the situation. From the landing I could see the director's lounge, in which there appeared to be some kind of reception taking place, however, I was unsure of my best course of action and so I nipped into a nearby toilet to gather my thoughts and decide what to do next. I checked my dress code in the mirror and what I saw (I was wearing a dark brown velvet jacket, turquoise blue shirt and faded blue jeans covered with numerous tartan patches) convinced me that the trampish figure looking back at me was as likely to be taken for a pop star as any of my erstwhile companions from the 'Roller'. That being the case, I decided to join the party. When I went in no one took the slightest bit of notice or indicated that anything was amiss. Then within seconds I spotted members of the Anderson and the King families (whom I knew from back home in Corby) and once I had spoken to them I felt more at ease.

At one point I even found myself being given a brief introduction to Denis Law and the rest of the players who were present. I wasn't aware of Johan Cruyff's presence in the room, but in any case, even if he'd been there, I wouldn't have been interested - to my mind Denis Law was a much better footballer.

After a while I went downstairs to the reception area, and it was whilst there that I could see my brother John, and our friend Johnny McShefferty, standing outside and gesticulating to me that they wanted to go home. I shouted to them 'Give me half another half hour and I'll be with you.' As I turned to go back upstairs to the bar, a sign above a nearby door caught my eye. It read 'Players Lounge'. Unable to resist the urge to explore, I walked along the corridor and through an open door into the bar. So much for the players lounge - in actual fact it was nothing more than a Nissan hut! The structure had a curved, corrugated roof that extended halfway down the walls, and was built both into and below the South Stand of Old Trafford - just to the left of the main entrance. As far as the décor was concerned, it had enjoyed a lick of very vivid (almost fluorescent) green paint and there were a few tables and chairs scattered around. That was as good as it got. Inside the room I could see Manchester United midfielder Paddy Crerand standing alone at the small crescent-shaped bar. I went over and offered to buy him a drink but he politely declined, so I ordered a pint for myself and attempted to engage him in conversation. A few minutes later George Best, John Fitzpatrick and David Sadler walked into the bar. George ordered a round and asked me what I was drinking. 'I'll have a pint please, George', I replied nonchalantly. So there was I, standing at the bar, chatting to the players and listening to them talking shop. When their glasses were empty I bought Best and 'Fitzy' a drink (Paddy and John Sadler said that they were only having the one) and shortly after that I paid a visit to the gents. On my return I bumped into George Best and Fitzpatrick just as they were about to leave. Best asked me if I would like to accompany them to a party. He said that Crerand and Sadler had decided not to go. I found myself declining George's offer. With hindsight, I now realise that I would have been able to dine out on that story for life, however, at the time I had other things in mind - like getting back up those stairs in order to try and engineer a one-to-one chat with the world's greatest living Scotsman! This I managed to do by weaving my way into a small circle of well-known football personalities who were standing chatting near the bar. The group included Denis Law, Tommy Docherty and Willie Ormond. Among the subjects being discussed were the 'famous five' who had played for Hibernian F.C. during the 1950s and, oddly enough, stock market fluctuations.

Above: George Best. This portrait perfectly captures the balletic skills of the most gifted footballer ever to have graced 'the beautiful game'. However, even Georgie couldn't hold the attention of one United fan from Corby who was anxious to get back to worshipping at the feet of King Denis!

Eventually I managed to engage Denis Law in conversation and we spoke for about ten minutes. Later on that night the lads who had been waiting downstairs for me would ask what Denis had said. To be honest with you, I couldn't remember a word of our conversation then - or to this day. After all, it's not every day that you find yourself in the presence of a King!

At the end of the night Sir Matt Busby came into the director's lounge and called 'Taxi for David Black.' I thought who's gonna believe this one? The great man himself was paging me for a cab! I casually raised my hand and responded 'Over here, Matt,' then made my way over to the exit, thanking him as I left. As I went out Sir Matt shook my hand and I can remember thinking what a gracious man he was.

Back in Corby, some weeks later I was in the Welfare Club and bumped into Jocky Anderson (Matt Busby's brother-in-law.) Jocky informed me that he had told Sir Matt all about my escapade and that his response had been: 'I'd like to meet that young man - as there are not many who manage to breach Old Trafford's security arrangements'. I did meet Matt Busby on two subsequent occasions but was careful not to remind him of the events of that evening. I often wonder what he would have said to me. Would he have reproached me, or would he have offered me a role in the United forward line - in recognition of my undoubted ability to unlock a defence?"

Alex Dawson of Corby Town Football Club was fined two weeks wages for refusing to travel to a Saturday away match at Merthyr Tydfil - his excuse being that he had just worked a nightshift. Unfortunately, the explanation offered by Dawson (a former 'Busby Babe' at Manchester United) didn't sway the club's management. A spokesperson for them said: "This shows that no player is bigger than the club." One can only conclude that the fools in charge of the club at that time had lost all sense of proportion, decency and common sense. Dawson (who at Manchester United set a footballing record that in fifty-two years has yet to be equalled) remains too much of a sporting gentleman to have ever revealed his true thoughts on playing for such a heartless and dictatorial shower. One suspects that in this case the player really was 'bigger than the club'.

Under Ron Atkinson's astute managership, in that same season Kettering Town Football Club secured their first Southern League Championship for nearly twenty years. Even back then the young manager (who would one day become a big name in British football) was bursting with confidence and charisma. It was as though he could already sense that he was on course to achieve greater things in the game, and his enthusiasm and ebullience inevitably wore off on his team, affecting the way in which they conducted themselves both on and off the pitch. The Kettering squad included many of Ron's old mates from Oxford United (i.e. Jim Hastie, Roy Clayton and Jim Harrington.) When added to journeymen like Mick Goodall, Roger Ashby and goalkeeper Dick Dighton, they provided the perfect title-winning combination and created a buzz about the Rockingham Road ground that had not been felt for many a year.

When looking back at those days, some thirty years later Corby lad, Dick Dighton, agreed that there had been a tremendous atmosphere at the club, and he acknowledged that it was mainly down to Atkinson. Dick recalled that Big Ron treated the team as if they were in the First Division of the Football League. He said: "Although Ron introduced pre-match luncheons, special diets and strict training routines, underlying all that he installed a steeliness to win - and to be the best. Furthermore, he encouraged us to do it in style. Atkinson expected victory, and when it arrived there'd be great celebration. On those occasions the champagne would flow (especially on away trips.) This was where Ron would be at his best - joining in with the players and the fans, sharing the banter and the singing."

Even so, playing for 'Bojangles' wasn't all a bed of roses. For a start, his players weren't exactly a set of robots and yes-men. You will find a few rebels in any group of fit and healthy young men - and even more so in a successful football team. That said, in order to achieve the right balance within a side, it is often necessary to include the odd player or two with a rebellious streak. Kettering's championship line-up also had a touch of devilment to it, as Dick Dighton remembers. Dick: "Over the Easter weekend we played two crucial matches down at Weymouth and Yeovil. Although we stayed overnight in a hotel, Ron placed us under a strict curfew on the night before the match with Weymouth. Having a night out at the seaside was too good an opportunity to miss though, and like naughty school kids we all disappeared down the fire escape and went out on the town. Big Eddie Dilsworth, the midfielder from Sierra Leone, got absolutely legless. Quite a few of the others didn't have a leg to stand on either!"

Of course, Big Ron knew exactly what had been going on behind his back, because next morning (presumably by way of punishment) he had the whole team sprinting up and down a deserted, windswept beach and running in the ice-cold surf. The shock treatment evidently revived them, as not only did Kettering Town manage a creditable 0-0 draw against Weymouth, they also shared the points with a strong Yeovil side on the following day. Some thought that the entire weekend only served to emphasise the tremendous team spirit that already existed within the club. Whatever the case, two away draws - at clubs that were in contention for the championship - were more than satisfactory.

A cynic might claim that even if the team had gone to bed early, they would still have been in with a fighting chance, however, there is a sneaking suspicion (amongst those who knew him well) that Big Ron might have had them running through the breakers anyway!

Another game which Dick remembers vividly is one that took place at Plough Lane in Wimbledon. That year the Dons were joint-favourites to win the league, and so their match with the Poppies was deemed a big one for both clubs. At half-time the scores were level at 0-0, then when Kettering Town ran out for the second half, Ron Atkinson held back Dighton and promised him that there'd be an extra fiver in his pay packet if he managed to keep a clean sheet. Atkinson then gave him a punch in the ribs for good luck. By sheer bad luck, just two minutes after the restart Wimbledon scored a goal - without Dighton having a single touch of the ball. As Dick says, all he could think of was 'there goes my fiver!'

Although the Poppies pulled back to make it 1-1, their goal was overshadowed by a second goal from the Dons which was enough to secure the points and put a dent in the championship aspirations of the visitors. "It was a great goal all the same." Dick later admitted. As for Big Ron? Ron decided to keep his wallet (if not his mouth) firmly shut. It would be the last time that he'd offer a financial incentive to his goalkeepers!

Later that season the Poppies were scheduled to play a match down at Dartford - one which was destined to be of special significance to Dick Dighton. Dick: "It was the first and only time in my career that I was sent off. The referee had awarded a dubious penalty to the Darts (at least that's the way I saw it) because he judged that I'd brought down one of their forwards just inside the box. Seething with anger, I protested that the player involved had taken a dive - but to no avail. An exchange then took place between the ref and myself which saw us trading insults - that is until I finally snapped and called him a prat. At this point he had no alternative but to dismiss me." Dick says he was replaced in goal by defender Mick Goodall, and that, much to his surprise, Mick managed to save the penalty. Dighton's abiding memory of the game was that whilst Goodall left the field to wide acclaim (his acrobatics having enabled Kettering to grab a point) the teams bona fide goalkeeper was reduced to sitting on the touchline and feeling sorry for himself!

As footballing history reveals, 'Mr. Bojangles', went on to achieve far more than he could ever have dreamed was possible back then. Not only did he win the F.A. Cup with Manchester United, but he also became manager of Spanish side Atletico Madrid. Following these two appointments, Atkinson remained a high profile - if somewhat controversial - figure in English football for many years to come.

In autumn 1973 British Steel Recreation Club in Corby installed in their newly-opened billiard room what were claimed to be the country's first automatic barmaids. The pair of coin-operated beer dispensers proved to be such a success that within a week another two were ordered. Mick Burns, a shift-worker in BSC's Bar Storage Dept., quipped: "They're not so bonnie as the real thing - but just as effective,"

Mr. John Broad, the chairman of the Occupation Road club, explained: "I first saw the dispenser at an exhibition in Blackpool and immediately realised its potential. These are probably the first ones in the country to be put into operation. Although they will never take the place of a barman or barmaid I can see a great future for them. Before the advent of 'our latest members of staff', if a man came into the club off shift-work at 10 p.m. and he wanted a quick pint, then he had to wait. Now he can get it straight away and be off home in time to watch *Match Of The Day*."

November saw the country struck once again by industrial unrest. The National Union of Miners (supported by the electricity workers) began an overtime ban that forced Peter Walker, the Secretary of Trade and Industry to declare a state of emergency. In light of this, a decision was taken to reduce petrol and fuel deliveries by 10 per cent, and motorists were asked to observe a voluntary 50 m.p.h. speed limit.

The situation was exacerbated when there was a cutback in crude oil production by Arab states. One week later a thousand miners were sent home without pay and production was halted due to a lack of weekend maintenance cover. In an effort to break the deadlock, Prime Minister Heath met miners' leaders at Downing Street - but to no avail. His next step was to order stringent measures to conserve electricity. From December 17, to December 30, industrial and commercial users were to be limited to a total of five days' power consumption. Then from December 31, they would be limited to three specified consecutive days each week, and would be prohibited from working longer hours on those days. Workers on a three-day week would be entitled to one day's unemployment benefit in the second week, followed by two days' benefit in subsequent weeks. Essential services such as restaurants, food shops and newspapers were to be exempt.

The year ended on a sour note after police officers with dogs were drafted in from other areas to break up a riot at the BSC Recreation Club in Corby. At a dance with four hundred young people in attendance, violence had erupted during a power failure - resulting in six people being taken to hospital by ambulance for treatment to cuts and bruises. Local firefighters were on standby and came to the rescue with emergency lighting after the club was plunged into darkness.

During an hour of terror the dance hall was turned into a battleground as youngsters smashed glasses and overturned tables and chairs. Young girls screamed as apprentice steelworkers fought on the floor in pitch darkness. Guitarist Derek Cowie (who at the time was performing on stage with his group Auction) recalls having to whack a couple of guys with his microphone stand when they tried to climb up onto the rostrum. Derek explained: "I was just protecting myself and worrying about them getting our gear and doing damage."

Following the night's events a senior police officer in the town had this to say: "It was an extremely grave situation. Every available policeman in Corby was called out and extra forces were brought in from outside the town. Arrests were made and a special court will be held today". PC John Plowright (one of the policemen who had been on the front line and therefore directly facing the violence) said:

"It was disgusting - I felt like the bull's eye on a dartboard as the missiles were thrown at us".

In her account of that night's events, nineteen-year-old Joan Ritchie said that the lights had failed in the middle of a dance and that for almost an hour she and her sister had been forced to take shelter beside a wall - because they were too frightened to move. The dance, which just a few minutes earlier had been the source of great fun, suddenly turned into a real nightmare. Joan described it as being like the mob riots shown on television, adding that a pint beer glass had missed her head by inches. It had been a terrifying experience!

Welfare Club assistant manager Buchin 'Barry' Littlejohn samples a pint of IPA bitter from the club's new push button beer vending machine which dispensed with the need to wait in line at the bar.

A spokesperson for Kettering General Hospital reported: "A special casualty room was set up for the people who were badly cut. We treated at least seven people for cuts to heads, hands and mouths - the usual result of a punch-up. None of the casualties were detained overnight." The club's manager, Ron Watson, told the *Northamptonshire Evening Telegraph*: 'It was the annual dance for young apprentices from the steelworks. At about 11.15 p.m., I had just closed the bars and some of the people were beginning to go home when the lights went out. The hall was pandemonium - all hell was let loose. Fighting broke out and glasses were thrown. It went on for about an hour with screaming and shouting. For a lot of the time we were in darkness and there was nothing we could do. In my 20 years at the club I have never seen anything like it.'

PC Joe Grun, who has now retired from the police force after thirty-three years of service, recalls the night well. Joe: "I was on traffic patrol duty when a call for assistance came through from Dave Panter - who was on Panda car duty. When I arrived at the Welfare it was in complete darkness, so Dave suggested that he go into the hall with his torch in order to see what was going on. I told him 'No way!' (It was absolute bedlam and I could just imagine what would have happened if they'd seen a copper in there with a torch!) I decided to radio for more help and a call for reinforcements went out to Kettering, Wellingborough and Northampton.

We convened at the Raven and waited for the Chief Inspector to decide upon what action we were going to take. When we went back round to the Welfare, we discovered that the fire brigade had turned up and installed some emergency lighting. We also found that there were still a few lads scuffling and causing agro, and so we arrested them for their troubles. It was just a typical night out in Corby!"

Joan Ritchie and boyfriend Stuart Wallace were just two of the innocent victims caught up in the violence that erupted during the BSC Apprentices' Dance at the Welfare Club.

The following day, while efforts were being made to clear up extensive damage to the club, Corby police appealed to other clubs and places of entertainment in the town to make alternative lighting arrangements. Their statement read: 'This was a very serious disturbance which caused terror to a lot of innocent victims. It was incredible that no one was seriously hurt in the full-scale fighting.' John Broad, the chairman of the Welfare revealed that although the club's battery-powered emergency lighting system had been tested only two weeks before the dance, on the night in question it had failed to switch on automatically when the lights went out. He also announced that he would be scrapping the dance for junior apprentices from then on, saying: "A minority element caused the disturbance and we are calling the dances off. The dance has been for people aged between 18 and 21. Most of them are well behaved but unfortunately the majority has been made to suffer." Two of those responsible for the trouble were charged with assault and with threatening and abusive behaviour towards PCs Plowright and Fawcett. They were both fined £40 for each assault and £29 for possessing an offensive weapon.

On Christmas Eve, lunch-time drinkers at the Corinthian in Queen's Square had to dash for the exits when the sprinkler system began to dowse them with water. Saxophone player Bob Crawford, who was in the pub at the time, recalls: "It was the Saturday before Christmas and the Corinthian was heaving with customers. I was there setting up with my newly-formed band (of Dave Johnson, Bob and John Grimley, Jack Murphy, Johnny Herron and Bob Clark) when I spotted Joe Doran holding up his lighter to a heat-sensitive cell in the ceiling. This of course set off the sprinkler system and flooded the bar." Whilst his soaking wet customers were beating a hasty retreat, landlord Jack Lewis called the police and the fire brigade. His distraught wife Josie said later: "Christmas was ruined for a lot of people because of one stupid person. I could have cried. I *did* cry. We had a band booked to play and they were ready to plug in - but we couldn't allow it because it would have been too dangerous. I hope that whoever did it had as happy a Christmas as I did!"

Normally fearless in a crisis, even PC Joe Grun was forced to exercise caution when faced with the riot at the BSC Apprentice Dance in December 1973. PC Grun has now retired from the force and spends his leisure time tending his allotment in Gretton.

When pensioner Donald Gooding began to feel a bit randy, the last thing he needed was cold water to cool him down. You see, Donald had a problem - he reckoned that it was the water that was turning him on in the first place! He explained: "At my age, an upsurge of virility can be extremely embarrassing." Eventually, the retired salesman (from Hatfield Peverell, near Chelmsford in Essex) became so frustrated about the matter that he complained to his local council. Mr. Gooding's gripe centred around his conviction that there were sex hormones in his water supply, and he blamed nearby Braintree Rural Council for the resultant unwanted side effects. Threatening to withhold his rates, sixty-nine-year-old Mr. Gooding said: "It's something in the water. Although it has made me feel twenty years younger, and sexier with it, I feel ill sometimes - and it has given my wife stomach ache."

The man with the 'sex urge on tap' believed that hormone weed-killer in the River Stour was responsible for his renewed vigour. Donald: "I was told by the Water Board that they were taking supplies from a river in the area - and I put two and two together. We all know what hormones can do to you. I have always congratulated myself on having good health. Lately, however, I have been wondering what has been happening to me. I hope my protest will succeed in getting something done about this serious problem."

A Health Department spokesman said that it was improbable that small quantities of hormone weed-killer in the water would cause increased virility, but conceded that it was not impossible.

Despite his campaign for redress, Mr. Gooding later admitted that both he and his wife Margaret, aged sixty-eight, were still drinking the rejuvenating water at a rate of several cupfuls per day!

On reading about Mr. Gooding's misfortune (or good luck, depending on your point of view!) Oona Campbell smirked:" I think I'll have a quite word wi' the barman in the Welfare Smoke Room - tae see if he'll put some of that water in my Shuggie's whisky. Mind you, Shuggie would need to quaff a lot more than a few cupfuls a day. Talk about raising the dead!"

The low point of the year for Mrs. Elizabeth Johnson of Polegate Court had been the lethargy surrounding the Queen Mother's trip to the town in April. Speaking outside Corby's Rangers club on New Years Eve, she complained: "Enthusiasm for the visit seemed to flag. Every shop that I went into expressed surprise that I wanted to buy a Union Jack. It was such a big occasion and yet no one seemed to want to make much of it." Elizabeth continued: "I was so disgusted that I even tried to make a flag myself!"

As things turned out, it appears that the Queen Mother was in fact delighted by the reception that she received in Corby. A letter sent by Sir Martin Gilliat (the Queen's secretary) to Mr. David Moon stated: 'I am commanded by the Queen Mother to thank you for the warmth and kindness that she received during her visit'.

Pictured circa 1973: The Corinthian public house in Queen's Square, Corby, - where Joe Doran (literally) put a dampener on the pub's Christmas festivities.

The Odeon Cinema on Rockingham Road (which later became the Rutland Cinema - and later still - the Rutland Theatre and Bingo Club) finally stopped showing late night films in 1973. One of the cinema's most keen patrons, Queenie Lattimore of Stephenson Way in Corby, was left to have the final word on the demise of the old picture house. She said mournfully: "No longer does Roy Rogers ride the range, Bugs Bunny battle for carrots, or the Monster from the Deep make faces at us from the screen." As for Ginger Graham - on hearing of the Odeon's closure, the Corby film buff and sometime philosopher was almost reduced to tears.

At the Empire Pool, Wembley, (in front of an audience of eleven-thousand people) Corby's Ray and Ann Brett were presented with the Country Music Duo of the Year Award. In addition, they collected a cheque and a new guitar.

1973 was also the year during which the people of Corby witnessed the disintegration of one of the quirkiest darts teams that Northamptonshire had ever known. On their way to winning the Kettering and District Licensed Victuallers Darts League Championship in both the 1969/70 and 1970/71 seasons, the Diddymen had marmalised their opponents, whilst brightening up an otherwise staid pub sport. As for the celebrated gravy wells of Knotty Ash - they very nearly drank them dry!

Top: A final hurrah for the team. In 1973 Diddymen supporters are pictured wearing for the last time their trademark hats with the slogans 'We are the Diddymen' and 'We'll marmalise you!' Back Row: Angie Robertson, Joe Gamble, Jimmy McCabe, Jackie Campbell, Peter Robertson, Davy Jones. Seated: Harry 'Cash' McShane, John Heaney and Andy McGowan. Bottom: A group of former Diddymen (complete with two-pint mug) reunite at the Raven Hotel on June 3, 2010. L-R: Alan Griffin, Johnny Morrison, Roger Johnson, David Black and Mick Matson.

When Will I See You Again?

It was a gloomy start to the New Year - the fuel crisis was now beginning to affect everyone. Four hundred thousand workers had been laid off on December 27, and, to add to this, restrictions had been imposed on the use of lighting in all commercial premises, shops, offices and streets. Furthermore, panic-buying was rife amidst fears that a potential rise in the price of petrol would lead to spiralling food bills. There came even more bad news when the price of a packet of twenty cigarettes went up by 1p, and the bread industry gave advanced notice that (due to the rising cost of wheat) the 16p loaf was just around the corner.

In Kettering and Wellingborough, a shortage of toilet rolls reached crisis-point - despite customers having been warned by shopkeepers that there would be a run on them. "The situation's getting desperate," complained one local retailer. Pat Board, a regular shopper and the product of an older generation, told an *Evening Telegraph* reporter: "I never thought I'd see a return to the days when I had to cut newspapers into quarters and hang them on a nail behind the toilet door!" She added, resignedly: "We'll just have to wait for the situation to bottom out."

Sugar was also in short supply following a blockade by workers at the Tate & Lyle refinery in London's East End. Housewives were quick to accuse the supermarkets of hoarding this vital commodity, in an attempt to cash in on the 5p increase, and there were calls for sugar to be rationed. There were also pleas for emergency provisions to be supplied from the vast Common Market stockpiles - so that old people's homes and drug manufacturers were not affected.

In the middle of all this consumer angst, it seemed that there were some scoundrels who were determined not to go short of anything. It was reported that thieves had broken into the Pluto pub in Gainsborough Road, Corby, and had raided the cellar, escaping with £1000 worth of spirits and cigarettes. Landlord Gordon MacDonald, who had been upstairs asleep during the raid, told police that he hadn't heard a sound. He said: "I can't understand it because we have two big dogs who normally bark their heads off at the slightest noise. The attending officer, Police Constable Grun, believed that he held the key to the mystery. On inspecting the scene of the crime, P.C. Grun had spotted what looked like dozens of empty crisp packets strewn around the cellar floor, together with two apparently well-nourished dogs fast asleep in the corner. It didn't require a Sherlock Holmes to deduce: "The thieves must have fed the dogs crisps to keep them quiet!"

It was just as well that there were some optimistic souls around who could see light at the end of the tunnel. According to Brigadier Hugh Hamilton, General Manager of the Corby Development Corporation, 1974 was going to be a boom year for the town. With the Urban District Council having become a District Council, and with a population of 53,741 people, Corby was now officially the second largest town in Northamptonshire. Brigadier Hamilton extolled: "The list of firms wishing to come to the town has never been so long - an indication that the prospects for Corby, once we are

The sign belonging to the Pluto pub in Gainsborough Road, Corby. Honouring Corby steelworks' contribution to Operation Pluto (Pipe Lines Under the Ocean), the lounge bar of this once popular pub was adorned with artefacts, photographs and technical drawings relating to the project. Work on the pipelines began on August 14, 1942, with successful trials taking place six weeks later. Their purpose was to transport fuel to allied forces in France, following the D-Day landings, on 6 June, 1944. Eight months later almost one million gallons a day were being pumped across the Channel to Normandy. Sadly the pub closed down in 2004 and was demolished in 2009. The pub sign itself is now lodged at the East Carlton Heritage Centre.

over the three-day working week, are as bright as ever." He also revealed that work was to begin on the building of three-hundred and thirty new houses, a Littlewoods store was to open in the town's shopping centre, plus a new block would be built to house the Post Office. In addition to all that there were at least eight new factories due for completion.

At the beginning of the year Corby's enduring links with Scotland had been reinforced when large numbers of the community celebrated Hogmanay in traditional fashion. As per usual, fights and brawls taking place during the early hours of January 1, had resulted in a hectic night for the town's ambulance men (those poor souls charged with the unenviable task of ferrying injured partygoers to the casualty department of Kettering General Hospital.) It came as something of a surprise, however, when a spokesman for the emergency services reflected: "Although the ambulance service had a very busy night, by and large it was one of the quietest New Year's Eve's that the town has enjoyed for many years." A senior police officer concurred: "It was a comparatively quiet night. I think the fog and bad weather did a lot to keep revellers indoors."

1974 also had its fair share of deaths and departures: In the wake of the Watergate scandal, The United States of America saw the back of disgraced president Richard Nixon. Lord Lucan disappeared into thin air following the mysterious murder of his daughter's nanny (and amidst rumours relating to his possible implication in the crime.) Fourteen-stone Mama Cass (formerly of pop group the Mamas and the Papas) died after choking on a ham sandwich whilst watching television in bed. John Stonehouse MP (the former Postmaster General) staged his very own re-enactment of television's *The Fall and Rise of Reginald Perrin* by faking his own death and scampering off to start a new life in the Antipodes. Alf Ramsey got the boot as manager of England's football team. Councillor Jimmy Kane went to ground - so to speak - after a disparaging article appeared in the *Lodge Park Citizen* (a monthly magazine representing the views of a local tenants association in Corby). In September Corby youth worker Nellie Connaughty retired again, ("This time it's for real" said Nellie). When all of that 'leave-taking' was added to striking miners, steelworkers, bakers and candlestick-makers, one might readily conclude that the Three Degrees' monumental hit record of that year (*When Will I See You Again?*) was indeed a perfect anthem for the time.

When will I see you again? might well have been a question posed by Jim Dale's former Rothwell chums - when news of his 'overnight success on Broadway' created a few newspaper headlines this side of the Atlantic. As part of the cast of Terence Rattigan's *French Without Tears*, the former stand-up comedian and pop singer (a graduate of Joan Strawson's Dancing School in Kettering) had been playing to packed houses at the Brooklyn Academy of Music. Only twelve months before that Dale had been starring in *Scapino*, in London's West End, and had been informing the newspapers that he had no ambitions of going to America. In the eyes of British television viewers and theatre audiences, the thirty-nine-year-old was regarded as a well-liked but only moderately successful entertainer, whereas in America he was described in the New York press as a 'young and supercharged Danny Kaye gone berserk.'

Jim Dale says that he was bitten by the showbiz bug at the age of nine - when he and his family travelled down to London to see Lupino Lane star in *Me And My Gal*. Jim: "I remember sitting there in the theatre and laughing at the little man - and when I looked around I could see that everyone else was also laughing. On the way home I told my mum and dad that I too wanted to be an entertainer." Taking him at his word, Jim's mother duly enrolled him at the local dancing school.

During the late 1950s (just at the time when the skiffle craze was taking off) Jim moved to London to further his ambitions, and it was there that he had a top ten hit with *Be My Girl*. Produced by George Martin (who later worked with the Beatles) the record set him firmly on the right path. Speaking in 2008 from his apartment on New York's 5th Avenue, Jim revealed that he'd had many reservations about the whole 'pop star' thing. He said: "The adulation made me feel uneasy. I was grateful, but I was also bewildered - even frightened - at the prospect of being elevated to the status of teenage idol. Admittedly, the audiences used to scream throughout my act, but then they did that for everybody. I didn't get any satisfaction from it at all, for the simple reason

Jim Dale, Northamptonshire's most successful entertainer.

that I'd always wanted to be a comedian. Comics seemed to last longer than pop singers." In 1958 Jim quit singing and returned to comedy - only to find that no one was interested. Jim: "My wife and baby daughter lived on beans-on-toast for over a year. I had been a big star and I didn't like it."

Dale's professional life changed for the better, however, when he joined the cast of the 'Carry On' films and went on to appear in fourteen of them - starring alongside the unforgettable Syd James, Charles Hawtrey and Hattie Jacques etc. As a sideline from his new film career, Jim began composing songs and had a massive hit with the Seekers' *Georgy Girl*. When he was given the chance to play Autolycus (in a production of Shakespeare's *The Winter's Tale* at the Edinburgh Festival) Jim found himself racked with nerves. He explained: "I had never read a word of Shakespeare or seen any of his plays. I always had to look up the words to see what they meant." A year later he played Bottom in *A Midsummer Night's Dream*, following which Lord Olivier invited him to become a member of the National Theatre - where he stayed for over four years. It was whilst commuting between London and his Kent cottage (which was near to Lord Olivier's country retreat) that Dale enjoyed a tremendous '£1,000 per week' stint as compere of the world-famous London Palladium. His greatest success to date came in 1980 when he was the winner of a coveted Tony Award (America's highest accolade for stars of the stage.) It was awarded for his performance in *Barnum* - the mega-successful Broadway musical which was based on the life of legendary circus showman P. T. Barnum. 'The boy from Rowell' had done good, and had undoubtedly come a long, long way since starting out all those years ago from the town's Gladstone Street School.

Something else that had come a long, long way was the pop music business. Indeed by 1974 the industry had changed out of all proportion and had reached a place which, frankly, wasn't to everyone's liking. 'It is to the degree to which tastes have become terminally bland' groaned the *Melody Maker*, adding that this was evident 'with the Swedish pop quartet Abba having the number one single and the Carpenters the number one album this year.' Bored with the amount of (what it considered to be) generally limp material on offer, the magazine decided to dedicate an article to the rise of heavy metal music. Featuring the burgeoning talents of bands like Grand Funk, Black Sabbath, Hawkwind and MC5, the publication defined the genre as being 'screaming guitars and basic riffs, lyrics that gloat over the macabre and the sick, mindless audiences and outrageous performers - that's heavy metal music.' Thus a brief insight was given into the alternative to what was fast becoming a rapidly declining and lack-lustre pop industry.

On the plus side that year was the release of Paul McCartney's best-selling album *Band On The Run*. Its cover design depicted some of the ex-Beatle's friends (including Michael Parkinson, Howie Casey and boxer John Conteh) being caught in the spotlight as they attempted a jailbreak.

By coincidence, train robber Ronnie Biggs was also still on the run (following his 1965 escape from Wandsworth Prison) and he too was waxing lyrical about a new record release - this time his own, entitled *Mailbag Blues*. The elusive fugitive was by this time holed up in Brazil, after escaping the clutches of the law in Australia, and was constantly taunting the British establishment with tales of his lavish lifestyle in Rio. Described as an avant-garde jazz composition, and recorded and released with the help of a group of young musicians from Brazil and also the U.S.A. Biggs caused outrage by claiming that the disc gave 'musical expression to the robbery.'

Another novelty record which was released in 1974 (and became famous for initiating a new craze) was *The Streak* by Ray Stevens. At high profile sporting events it soon became commonplace to see some bright spark or another 'streaking' across the football/rugby pitch etc., clad only in his (or her) birthday suit!

Corby lad Ginger McClelland bravely decided to 'give it a go' when he and fellow Rangers Football Club supporters went up to Goodison Park to watch their team play in a testimonial match for Everton and England right-back Tommy Wright. Much to the amusement of his drinking buddies from the Strathclyde Hotel, McClelland streaked across the turf and was promptly arrested by a pair of Liverpool 'scuffers' - who quickly bundled him out of the ground and into a cell. On the day after the match, readers of the *Scottish Daily Record* were treated to a photograph of Ginger (naked, except for his Tammy and tartan scarf) being apprehended by the two policemen. Unable to pay the magistrate's fine of a hundred pounds, two days later he was still in police custody - that is until a mysterious benefactor came to his rescue. It appears that a London lawyer had read about the case in his newspaper and was so appalled by the size of the fine that he felt moved to pay half of it. The Good Samaritan had this to say on the matter: "A man had recently streaked at Twickenham during an England v Australia rugby match and had gotten off with a lecture. One can only suppose that, because it had been a rugby match, the local bench thought it was a good jape."

Although Ginger readily accepted the lawyers kind offer of financial assistance, the 'Gers' supporter subsequently declined an invitation to visit the gentleman in question's flat - in case his new-found friend had expectations of being shown more than just gratitude!

THE WAY WE WERE: (as at March 31st 1974) The population of Corby stood at 53,741. British Steel Corporation employed 11,767 male and 1,172 female workers. Other firms in the town employed 6,761 male and 6,903 female workers. Corby Development Corporation and Corby Urban District Council between them rented out a total of 11,953 houses (with a further 209 dwellings under construction) whilst there were 2,864 privately-owned homes and 221 more under construction. 4,284 domestic garages were available for rent with 220 under construction. The Development Corporation's annual income from domestic housing rent was £1,520,367. On the health front Corby had 1 diagnostic centre and 1 maternity unit and 1 health centre. There were 14,360 pupils attending schools in the urban district and 124 full-time, 639 part-time (day) and 1,487 part-time (evening) students were enrolled at Corby Technical College. We were entertained in 1 Civic Centre and 36 halls. Our taxes paid for 1 Public Library and 1 Technical Library. Our souls were soothed by 18 churches and our thirsts quenched at 20 public houses and 2 hotels. We slept safely in our beds courtesy of 1 fire station, 1 police station and 1 magistrates' court. Finally we were laid to rest in either of two cemeteries or 1 parish church graveyard.

...AND WHERE WE WORKED

The background of Corby's mainly Scottish population was considered by some to be a contributing factor to the violent image that was associated with the town and which dated back to the 'pioneering' days of the 1930s. Probation Officer Don Martin offered his considered opinion on the subject, saying: "The problem is that the hard-drinking, hard-working Scots bring their way of life and traditions with them to Corby and sometimes have difficulty fitting into a new town environment. It may be that violence is more socially acceptable in the areas where these people originate from. One of the faults of a one-industry town is that it tends to become a working-class ghetto of sorts. Corby is an interesting town with plenty of character - though less violent now than when it was first developing."

While Don was airing his views, elsewhere in the town a man was found hurling a dustbin though his neighbour's living room window - bringing to a head a nine-year dispute over the size of an overgrown *Cupressocyparis leylandii* - 'more effective that a solicitors letter!' Not long after that Kevin Forde of Corby committed a crime of a lesser nature after spotting a tailor's dummy standing outside Hepworth's in Corporation Street. After first pretending to box with the mannequin, Forde then went on to steal the wig from its head. In court he pleaded not guilty to a charge of theft - claiming that he'd found the item lying on the pavement outside the men's clothing store. Constable Bob Dibble, the arresting officer, told the court: "He was arrested walking through the Market Square wearing the wig". Forde was found guilty and fined £15.

Rowdy behaviour was high on the agenda at the February meeting for residents of Corby Old Village (which was held in the Rowlett School hall.) As one would quite rightly expect, those who lived in the area were fiercely opposed to proposals for the opening of two further nightclubs in their neighbourhood. Addressing the meeting in his usual forthright manner, Councillor Tom Sykes argued: "With the White Hart, Nags Head, Cardigan Arms, White Horse and Old Legion all within yards of each other - there are more than enough licensed premises in the village already." He continued: "Most of their trade comes from other areas of the town and it is mainly those people who are causing the trouble - wandering around after the pubs shut and being drunk and rowdy. I have had to deal with many complaints from old age pensioners who have had their homes broken into by these people. The residents of the old village want to retain the friendly village atmosphere, and to that end I say - bring back the birch for these delinquents!" Unfortunately, it was a heartfelt plea which received little support from the floor. Councillor Peter Huckle responded: "You cannot solve the problem of violence by meeting it with more violence."

In a climate of local hostility towards the drinking establishments of the old village, the Nags Head's cause wasn't helped any by the emergency evacuation that had to be effected following an act of tomfoolery by one of the members of a visiting rock band. When firecrackers (a popular prop during live performances) had been set off that evening by the drummer, smoke had filled the room and sent choking customers rushing for the emergency exits. Struggling to breathe, and with the fire alarm bells ringing in their ears, anxious night-clubbers opened windows and took huge gulps of air whilst waiting to make their escape.

Strike-fever gripped the nation. To begin with Corby's dustmen went out on strike, and then the signalmen from the Southern Region Railway went down the same track. The crisis was undoubtedly linked to events of the previous autumn - when war in the Middle East had sent oil prices soaring. First of all, in November the miners had introduced an overtime ban, and then the electricity workers had promptly followed suit. As a consequence, when the railway workers walked out in January, Prime Minister Edward Heath was forced to declare a state of emergency (bringing into effect a three-day working week and petrol rationing - resulting in 885,000 people having to register for unemployment benefits). Although the Arab-Israeli War had indeed caused oil prices to spiral, many members of the Government claimed that the miners (who had gone down from first to eighteenth position in the industrial wages league) were exploiting the energy crisis for their own purposes. Be that as it may, what couldn't be disputed was the fact that in just one year the price of four-star petrol had leapt from 42p to an exorbitant 72p a gallon. Meanwhile, inflation had pushed up the cost of a

Mini to £1000. Throughout the UK relations between the industrial unions and the Government were becoming hostile, as, in an attempt to help the nation, the Tories tried to impose a pay freeze and other restraints. On February 9, the miners (who had voted to take industrial action if their pay demands were not met) walked out on strike.

In turn, Ted Heath called a snap General Election for February 28, and then promptly called on the miners to have a rethink and suspend their action until voting had taken place. In a broadcast to the nation, the Prime Minister (who firmly believed that the country would support his measures) asked: "Who's running Britain - the Government or the Miners?" Heath insisted that the miners had already been treated as a special case, adding that the 16.5 per cent pay rise on the table was far more than six million other trades unionists had settled for. His message to the electorate was clear: "Industrial strife has got to stop and only you can stop it. Use your ballot to show the miners how you feel!"

Open and closed for business at Corby

THE recently opened sub-branch at Corby Works has been welcomed by British Steel Corporation employees. In the picture on the left, Mrs M R Wilson (Cashier) serves her first customer at the sub-branch. But the opening ceremony was not all business, a fact proved by the picture on the right. At present the sub-branch staff consists of three cashiers and an enquiry clerk.

Opened as a concession to BSC's thousands of employees, this sub-branch of Lloyds Bank certainly did a roaring trade over the years. Bank worker Margaret Wilson was the duty cashier on the day of the launch. As reported in the bank's newsletter (see above) the event was celebrated in typical Corby style - sandwiches and beer!

The strike had the potential to harm the nation's industries with devastating effect - for instance, half of the workforce at BSC in Corby faced being laid off if it were to be extended. Unfortunately, NUM leader Joseph Gormley announced that he was unable to suspend the action. He deemed that it would be preferable for the election to take place in a calm climate rather than during a period of industrial unrest. Nevertheless, prominent left-winger Arthur Scargill was in favour of going ahead, saying: "A general election won't solve anything." In the end, the prime minister's pleas for wage restraint fell on deaf ears - the Conservatives were defeated and the country welcomed back Harold Wilson to Downing Street. Forty-eight hours later, and following a 35 per cent pay offer from the new Labour administration, the miners called off industrial action. (Which in four short weeks had seen coal production come to a complete standstill.) The pay settlement saw around 260,000 miners accepting increases ranging from between £6.71 to £16.31 a week - more than double those on offer from the previous government, and in March 1974 the UK finally returned to a five-day working week.

Back in Corby the election campaign had been dominated by concerns over the future of the steel works. Jim Haigh, the Liberal Party candidate, had boldly stated at the time that steelmaking in the town would be guaranteed for another hundred years if his party was to form a government. He said

"In the face of spiralling prices worldwide, full use should be made of Corby's raw materials. Since the White Paper was published in 1973, we have seen oil prices quadruple and have seen shortages of other raw materials forcing up prices. Corby is the only plant in Britain making steel from native iron ore. The setting up of Corby Steel Action Group to safeguard steel jobs was justified but it wouldn't be necessary if Liberals took power."

In the event, Sir Geoffrey DeFrietas retained his Labour seat and was likewise confident about the situation saying: "The rapidly rising cost of imported iron ore assures Corby's future as an integrated iron, steel and tube-making complex. The long-term prospects are good."

His comments were greeted with muted enthusiasm by those residents living within the 'pollution umbrella' of the steel works. Following the setting up of the residents' Watchdog Committee (the aim of which was to monitor the dirt and smell coming from the works) Ambrose Finan declared: "The last seven weeks have been the worst in the plant's history, and we are far from confident that BSC is doing as much as it could to control the pollution. The problem used to be red dust - now its black dust. One can taste the sulphur in one's mouth." Thomas Hector, a neighbour and fellow watchdog, was equally sceptical. Thomas said: "A veil of secrecy appears to have been drawn over this issue. I think it would a good idea if some of the steel company's top brass were forced to live down here for a month, and then they might realise just how bad it is."

In July 1974, BSC announced a record profit of £50 million for the proceeding year. However, in spite of this encouraging news, the company's chairman, Dr. Monty Finniston, poured water on the previously aired optimism of Sir Geoffrey DeFrietas by stating in his report that the future of Corby's steel-making remained in the balance. Although declaring that the tube-workers' jobs were secure, Finniston indicated that there would be a review of steel-making at the end of the year. 'Corby and Scunthorpe are the only plants to be using home ore. We shall have to consider whether we can go on processing domestic iron ore with low iron content beyond 1980. But against this consideration are the rocketing prices from abroad, where manganese ore has gone up 85 per cent in the last year. Nevertheless, beyond 1980 it will be anyone's guess on iron and steel-making, and I'm not prepared to make a guess.'

While the debate dragged on a crisis was developing at BSC - in the guise of a round-the-clock battle to restart iron-making. Two of the three blast furnaces that were still in operation had been shut down for emergency relining, and so when the third suffered a water leak, iron production had to be halted completely. As the furnaces had recently been plagued by a variety of problems, rumours began to spread that the crisis was merely a plot to phase out Corby's steel works - a fact which was strenuously denied by Bob Scholey (one of BSC's top men) who proclaimed that such speculation was a 'load of rubbish'. Scholey went on to deliver a blunt warning to the workers. He ordered: "Get your fingers out, get moving and get the furnaces going!" (A fourth furnace, which had just been rebuilt to the tune of £5million, was not due to come on stream until December).

As a diversion from the perpetual doom-mongering which surrounded the future of the steelworks, the arrival at Harringworth of a giant dragline caused quite a stir. *Sundew* as it was quirkily named (after the 1957 Grand National winner) had reached the village after completing a thirteen mile walk from Exton in Leicestershire, and was ready to dig even more holes in the countryside surrounding Corby. In a journey lasting nine weeks, the monster had traversed ten roads, a river, a main railway line, twenty-four hedges and fences, and had gobbled up over £2000 worth of electricity. It therefore came as no surprise to learn that compensation claims, to the value of £250,000, had been submitted by distinctly unamused landowners whose property had stood in the dragline's path.

There were plenty of other people who didn't see the funny side when on April Fool's Day 1974 the county boundaries were redrawn by the government. In the process counties with charters dating back to the Middle Ages disappeared overnight, alongside others which had been chronicled in the Doomsday Book. Only ten of the forty-five English counties survived unchanged, and there was just one out of thirteen Welsh counties. Cumberland, Huntingdonshire, Westmoreland and Rutland (England's smallest county) were all wiped off the map. Despite official claims that the changes would make local government more efficient, it has to be said that the affected counties didn't go down without a fight. Although Rutland had already succeeded in defeating two previous post-war attempts to remove its county status, this time its defences crumbled and outraged Rutlanders found themselves being unwillingly drafted into neighbouring Leicestershire. Appalled at the logic of Lord Redcliffe-Maud (the government official who had been responsible for the changes) Rutland vowed to obtain a reversal of the decision. It was a battle which the proud Raddlemen did eventually win - even though it took them until 1997 to do so.

Above: Sundew - pictured during its marathon walk to Corby. Despite its attempt at good manners, the giant dragline still managed to inflict a considerable amount of damage on the surrounding countryside.

Sundew was the name given to a large electrically-powered dragline excavator that was used in mining operations in Rutland and Northamptonshire. Built by Ransomes & Rapier (who christened it after the 1957 Grand National winner) the machine began work that same year at a Stewarts & Lloyds iron ore quarry in Rutland. Weighing in at 1,675 tons - and with a reach of 86 metres and a bucket capacity of 27 tons - at the time of its construction Sundew was the largest walking dragline in the world and was able to move a substantial amount of material in a relatively short period. Propulsion was via two large feet which 'walked' it backwards and forwards, whilst directional control was provided by a large circular turntable beneath the body of the machine. *Sundew* remained at Rutland until operations at the quarry ceased in 1974. The idea of dismantling such an enormous piece of equipment and then reconstructing it elsewhere (estimated to cost £250,000 and take two years to complete) was deemed a non-starter, and so, over a nine week period, in 1974 *Sundew* was walked thirteen miles from the village of Exton in Rutland to a site north of Corby. During the walk the dragline crossed three water mains, ten roads, a railway line, two gas mains and a river, before finally reaching its new home.

In March country and western fans enjoyed a rare treat when a touring show (bearing the name *The Nashville Cavalcade*) visited the Granada in Kettering. Featuring a line-up of famous artists such as Bobby Bare, Dottie West, Chet Atkins and Jim Ed Brown, the extravaganza was attended by a large crowd of enthusiasts from Corby, including John Black of Gilchrist Avenue. Not content with just watching the show that night, John also hoped to meet some of his favourite stars in person. John: "Atkins and Brown were well-known guitarists who'd played with Elvis, and so I decided to try and get their autographs. Without knowing where they were leading to, I walked up some stairs and opened a door. Behind it, to my great surprise, was Dottie West - standing in her bare feet as she waited to go on stage. Although Dottie appeared to be a little startled by my sudden appearance, she was kind enough to sign my programme anyway. After the show was over three of us even managed to get on to the tour bus - Chet Atkins had opened the vehicle's doors himself and welcomed us aboard. We were amazed - and that's putting it lightly! As we walked up the aisle and shook hands with everyone, I suddenly spotted Bobby Bare and his wife sitting towards the back of the bus. Although Bobby had a cowboy hat pulled down over his eyes (pretending to be asleep) I couldn't let the opportunity to pass to ask if it was himself or Mel Tillis who had written *Margie At The Lincoln Park Inn*. The country singer lifted up his hat and fixed me with a look of utter contempt (supposedly for betraying my ignorance of such matters) 'Tom T. Hall', he drawled, before pulling it down again. At this point I suddenly realised that the bus was moving and that we were all still on it, whilst the rest of our gang were outside banging on the windows and shouting to us to get off. Then suddenly the driver called out 'Next stop Liverpool!' Needless to say we were down those steps in a flash!"

Following *The Nashville Cavalcade*, the next act on at the Granada was Roy Wood and Wizzard of *See My Baby Jive* fame. It was March 22, and, unfortunately, a night when an unresponsive audience made it clear that they weren't in the mood to jive. A clearly disappointed Ian Easton said: "The show didn't really get going until the last three numbers. There had been no screams or scarf-waving and there had been very little bopping in the aisles. Even the bouncers looked bored! The Irish folk duo Tir Na Nog tried to liven things up a bit, but it was a case of being in the wrong place at the wrong time."

Sharon Coles from Kettering, another Wizzard fan, totally disagreed. She remonstrated: "Mr. Easton can't seriously be a Wizzard fan. I thought the show was brilliant and so did all of my friends. Regarding the bouncers being bored - isn't that good news? And the lack of screams underlined how enraptured the audience was by Roy Wood's music."

The future of the Granada cinema was sealed when (for the second time in twelve months) it was announced that plans to convert the theatre into a bingo hall were going ahead. A spokesman for the company reiterated their position by saying: "We cannot continue as a cinema. Falling audiences have made the screening of films an uneconomic proposition. During the year 1964-65 average attendance was 23,000 a month. Now it's down to 9,000 a month and still falling - this despite the popularity of a rash of Bruce Lee Kung Fu films." After that tirade no one was left in any doubt that the Granada was for the chop! The final curtain call for the Kettering cinema came on June 8, when the film *Zardoz* was shown - starring Sean Connery. Not exactly a distinguished swansong!

In spite of this, the venue continued to draw crowds with its live music shows. Country star Slim Whitman and Scotland's Bay City Rollers (who were enjoying chart success for the first time since 1971) were amongst the most popular acts to appear that year. However, according to the *Kettering Leader*, November's *The Morecambe and Wise Show* was the pick of the crop. 'Three and a half thousand fans packed the theatre out and for more than an hour the sparkling stand-up fun rocked along like a carefully runaway train. When the Johnny Wiltshire band launched into *Bring Me Sunshine* (the pair's signature tune) the first chuckle rippled through the stalls. The ripple surged into waves of laughter as Eric - peeking over his spectacles - said: "Thank you. You've been a great audience. You can all go home now."

By the time the show ended, Eric was still teasing the duo's adoring fans. "We'd love to carry on," he said, "but there's half a dozen people waiting outside for the second show"… and many exited the Granada in pains of laughter.'

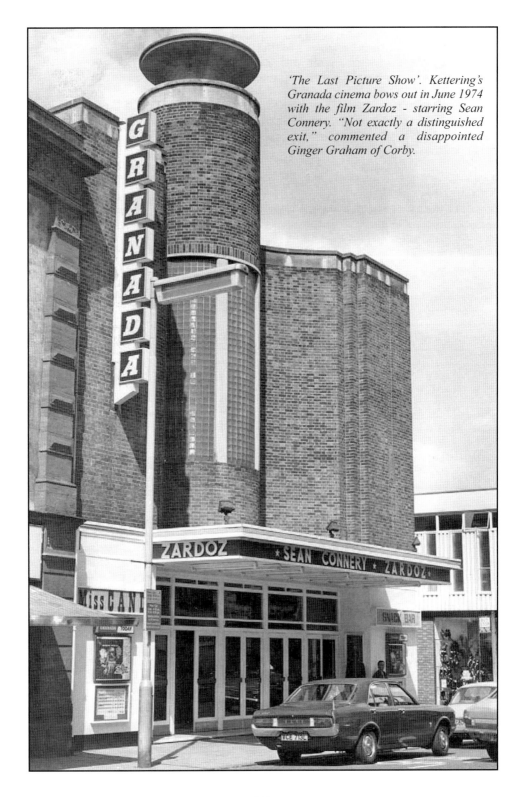

'The Last Picture Show'. Kettering's Granada cinema bows out in June 1974 with the film Zardoz - starring Sean Connery. "Not exactly a distinguished exit," commented a disappointed Ginger Graham of Corby.

That March the seven-piece Alex Welsh Band appeared at the Central Hall in Kettering and 'evoked memories of riverboat shuffles, Beaulieu Jazz Festivals and all the trappings of the jazz era.' One learned critic - who was more at ease with Welsh than Wizzard - gushed: "It is over twenty years since Alex burst onto the scene on BBC TV's *The Six-Five Special* and caused controversy among jazz fans with his non-purist style. Witnessing him play items tonight like *Doctor Jazz* and *Wild Man Blues*, plus a superb version of Lionel Hampton's *Vibes Boogie*, was a real treat."

That gig was undoubtedly the inspiration behind yet another attempt to establish a jazz club at the White Hart in Corby. Those behind the idea were a group of enthusiasts (including Dick Kirk, Billy McHarg, dance band drummer Bill Clark and ex-Marylander Jake Pressley) who proposed to bring back a real 'jazz groove' to the town. Bill, who was said to set the place alight when performing, confessed to doing just that when playing one night at a retirement dance in the Corby Supporters Club. He said: "I couldn't figure out where the smell of burning was coming from. It wasn't coming from the electric plugs, or from any of the wires on stage, and so I just carried on playing merrily away - that is until I became aware that I was surrounded by smoke. It finally dawned on me that a stray match had landed in my pocket and had set my jacket alight!"

Despite the sterling efforts of its founding members to popularise the venue, attendances at the White Hart Jazz Club were soon flagging to such an extent that a dejected Bill Clark lamented: "Because we're failing to get the message across, only handfuls turn up to support us." Seemingly non-plussed, landlord Stuart Charley refused to accept defeat, saying: "As soon as membership picks up we'll start booking top names."

On a local level, live jazz and folk music had been in the doldrums since the days of Studio 41 (back in the 1960s at the Nags Head.) The next attempt to launch a jazz/folk club in Corby came with the setting up of one at the town's Strathclyde Hotel. Bob McLean, his wife Lella, Sue Harris and husband Dick (otherwise known as the Furrow Folk) 'did a good night's work as the resident band, providing plenty of variety in their music, and they were accompanied admirably by Tony Callaghan and his squeezebox. However, the best was kept till last - when Jake Pressley, Leo Gale and Trevor Wright got together for some 'hilarious jazz'.

The Strathclyde went the same way as the White Hart - after some initial success support for the venture dwindled. Around that time the Thrapston Folk Club also closed due to lack of interest, and although the Corinthian and Rockingham Arms filled the gap for awhile with their Sunday lunch-time jazz sessions, the only bright light on the horizon was over at the Fir Tree in Wellingborough. It was there that regular shows were being presented with top name artists such as Humphrey Lyttleton and the equally superb Horace M. Smith Jubilee Serenaders.

Unsurprisingly, the fastest growing club in the area was the Solo club in Corby's Rutherglen Road. Held in the Co-operative Hall, it catered for widowed, single and divorced people of all ages, and managed to attracted over one hundred people in its first four months of existence with several additional members joining on a weekly basis thereafter. For those with not-so-lonely-hearts, a good old-fashioned night out was still to be had at the 'Works' in Kettering, where the Nashville Teens put in an appearance that year, or else at Shafts in Corby - which played host to Liverpool's Merseybeats. Over at the Civic Centre in Corby, a continuing lack of local support saw the future of live productions come under threat once more. The District Council's Leisure and Amenities Committee admitted that attendances had been very disappointing and that there was to be a review of the situation. Despite being mystified as to the type of live entertainment most desired by the people of Corby, Lance Garrett (who was new to the committee) remained undeterred in his quest to introduce to the public a range of activities that would embrace the whole spectrum of entertainment. For example, Garrett proposed screening special events (such as Test Matches and Cup Finals) and suggested that there might also be an audience for films based on the lives of famous composers. "Sounds like a winner to me!" grinned Manchester United supporter Brian King.

Once hailed - rather misguidedly - as Ireland's answer to the Beatles, the Bachelors' were the latest in a long line of artists whose shows at the Festival Hall in Corby were met with unanimous disapproval in the local press. In answer to those who had labeled the Irish trio's concert as 'shambolic' theatre manager Reg Campbell countered: "We welcome fair and justified criticism but I feel in this instance I must put the record straight. First of all, the Bachelors and supporting cast were due to arrive at 3p.m. They failed to do so - in fact the advance party didn't arrive until 5.30p.m. Our technical staff was on standby and was ready to accommodate their every requirement from 3p.m. onwards. When the group did eventually arrive (virtually in Indian file with the last one turning up just 5 minutes before the performance was due to start) it was much too late in the day to iron out the technical difficulties we encountered. The second fact is that the Bachelors' road manager was the compere - and one of the conditions of engagement was that he was in charge of the whole presentation of the show. Lastly, I take the point that we are lacking in certain articles of expensive equipment - it is unfortunate that in the Festival Hall we have no 'draw back curtains'. These, together with effective lighting, could make all the difference to a successful show."

Above left: The Co-op hall in Rutherglen Road, Corby. A popular venue for wedding receptions (and later the Corby Singles Club) it was eventually demolished to make way for an extension to the store itself and to enable the construction of adjoining retail units.
Above right: In October 1951 Jimmy Kane (future local Councillor, Leader of Northamptonshire County Council and Deputy Lord Lieutenant of Northamptonshire) is photographed setting off on honeymoon with new wife Cathy - following their reception at Corby's Co-op hall.

Still on the subject of music, Ray and Ann Brett, (who were pictured that night being introduced to the Bachelors) had recently been voted by *Daily Record* readers as the best duo in their field. At the time, Corby's king and queen of country and western music were busy recording their debut LP *Somebody Loves You*, and in spite of all the accolades coming their way, the married couple remained unfazed by all the attention.

Clive Wells from Peterborough, who was by night a country and western singer (and by day the driver of *Sundew* - one of the two giant draglines working the ore fields around Corby) might have done well to adopt the Brett's laid-back approach to life and music. Whilst driving one night to a booking at the Domino pub in Corby, Wells found himself being overtaken by a vehicle and forced off of the road and up on to a roundabout. When he realised that the other car contained a young couple whose minds weren't on the road because they were kissing and canoodling, an incensed Clive gave chase, stopped the car, hit the driver in the face and advised the pair to do their courting in a field. Although he later told Corby Magistrates' Court that the girl 'had her arms around the driver's neck', Clive was nevertheless fined £25.

The eighth Corby Arts Festival received the usual plaudits when a 'grand feast of music' from folk stars Julie Felix and Jake Thackeray kicked off the week (although things very nearly came off the rails when, due to illness, 10cc dropped out of the Saturday night rock show at the eleventh hour - forcing Trevor Wright to again prove his worth by securing short notice replacements in the form of the Sutherland Brothers and Quiver.

Speaking after the festival, John Sandy from British Steel's Transport Department articulated: "Trevor and his committee deserve full praise for organising such an exciting week. For me though, it was the local talent who stole the show - Granite were hard to beat."

The band's 'Back from the dead' one-off reunion gig in Queen's Square had kept everyone's mind off of the weather that day when rain threatened to spoil proceedings. In an hour long performance which began with Ashton, Gardner and Dyke's *Resurection Shuffle*, Granite also covered numbers by Blood, Sweat & Tears, Neil Young and Chicago - all of which went down extremely well with everyone.

Voicing the thoughts of the entire crowd, Danny Coyle (brother-in-law of Jake Pressley) said: "The festival has at last given young people in the town some music that didn't insult their appreciation of good rock." Danny was also thrilled with the performance given by the Red Hot Peppers (one of the main British pub rock groups of the early 1970s) and with Radio One DJ John Peel - who had filled the Wednesday 'Late Night Rock' spot.

One of Trevor Wright's biggest coups turned out to be his booking of blues singer Cousin Joe to play in the Willow Room - as the New Orleans veteran had only recently appeared on BBC's T*he Old Grey Whistle Test*. Joe shared the bill that night with trombonist Gene Connors, who (with a backing of local musicians including Jake Pressley, Bob Grimley, Dick Kirk etc) began his stint with *Hi Heel Sneakers* and *Goin' to Chicago*. Despite a lack of rehearsal time, the band coped admirably - with Dick Kirk playing some excellent saxophone solos. They were followed by a short interval and then Cousin Joe took to the stage and began tickling the ivories. His first words to the audience were: "I'm in love with my woman... and I'm in love with my wife!" Good old bluesy corn that had them eating out of the palm of in his hand. A glance at Trevor Wright told you that there was a 'cat' that'd definitely got the cream!

Although Granite may have lost touch with their home crowd, the group could be forgiven this because they had been out on the road for nigh on two years and had been working constantly. In fact they had already paid two visits to Germany during that same year (playing to audiences of several hundred people) and had been hailed as a great success at the International Festival in Velbert. Rob Purdie, later a partner of Franny Lagan and Aivors Zakss in their Sidewinder Promotions venture, had witnessed the event. Rob: "There were more than a thousand people packed into the festival tent - and they were going wild! It was the same again when Granite played at the Youth Centre in Velbert. All in all, they gave two tremendous performances."

Jake Pressley, Granite's trombone player and chief organiser, explained why they had put in so few appearances in Corby. Jake: "Although we have always been given a good reception in Corby, we are an eight-piece band and we may have become too expensive. Apart from playing the Nags Head once or twice, and at the Arts Festival, we haven't done much else locally." The band's line-up consisted of Jake and the two Kirk brothers, Peter Bonas on lead guitar, Phil Spinnelli on drums, Chris Newman on bass, Bob Grimley on guitar and Bip Wetherell on keyboards. Drummer Spike Gowen and ex-Invaders' guitarist Rodger Buckby 'depped' during the Germany weekends.

Following a shambolic (and very late) appearance at Corby's Festival Hall by Irish chanters the Bachelors, award-winning local singing duo Ann and Ray Brett appear to reassure the tardy trio that 'they' still believe.

Jake Pressley, who was born in Scotland, learned his trade with Ian Menzies of the Clyde Valley Stompers. He moved to England whilst still in his teens but later emigrated to South Africa - thus bringing his career with Granite to an end. When Jake first arrived in Northamptonshire he started playing with bands from the New Orleans Jazz Circle. After that he played in one of the big bands - led by trombonist and pianist John Betts, and later still with Professor Hugh McDonald's Cambridge-based MC2. Jake then went off to London in order to dabble in the capital's jazz scene, before coming back to join Granite. On emigrating to South Africa, soon after arriving in Johannesburg he formed the Jake Pressley Jump Band (which was based on the small group jazz favoured by the Ellington sidemen.) Whilst on a trip to the UK in 1983, Jake managed to persuade his former bandleaders to part with some of their charts, and when he arrived back in South Africa he founded the Fat Sound - a classic eighteen-piece unit which rapidly earned a reputation as one of the best-loved jazz orchestras in that country. The Fat Sound played at the immensely popular Radium Beer Hall, in Orange Grove, for more than fourteen years.

Members included a nuclear physicist, a research chemist, an engineer, an optometrist and Bruce Cassidy (formerly of Blood Sweat & Tears.) Jake Pressley is now retired but remains a close friend of Trevor Wright. He recently told Trevor that these days he 'just wants to help kids play jazz'.

With an estimated seven thousand discos and twenty-five thousand mobile discos operating in Britain, in 1974 the *Melody Maker* asked yet again 'Are discos killing live music?' With those who earned more than £20,000 a year being taxed at a rate of 75p in each pound, many of Britain's best-loved musicians were following the example set by the Rolling Stones two years previously and were fleeing into tax exile. The *Melody Maker* therefore concluded that the combination of high taxation and the vast number of discos was leading to an unprecedented crisis for the nation's live music industry.

No. 7001 on the list was the Touchdown Disco at Corby Rugby Club. It was fronted by DJ Alan Wetherell who (as a reminder that his brother Bip didn't hold the franchise on bullshine) placed the following advert in the *Evening Telegraph*. It stated: 'Every Thursday share the adventures of Super Soul Alan Wetherell. Yes! He's back with the Big Bad Boozy Bone Show. Plus guest DJ Irene - the one and only female Disc Jockey in town!'

Over the next three years Alan's disco became one of the hottest nightspots in town and was regularly jam-packed. On three nights of the week a stream of taxis would transport punters to this Rockingham Triangle outpost. What people seem to remember most about the Rugby Club disco was the amount of Tenants lager that was consumed. They say that at the end of the evening the whole dance floor would be ankle deep in cans depicting scantily-clad Glaswegian women.

Scotland's Tennants Lager was a staple tipple for the Touchdown Disco regulars at Corby Rugby Club. Unfortunately, it was a widely held view at the club that the contents never quite matched up to the 'lager lovelies' who adorned the cans, one of whom Billy Robertson always claimed was his cousin.

Gloom engulfed Corby Town F.C. when (following a Northamptonshire County Court ruling concerning their inability to pay an Inland Revenue bill of £4,016) the club faced a real possibility of being wound up. A reprieve was only granted when the Corby Town Supporters' Club said that they would pay half of the debt and that, furthermore, they would organise fund-raising events in order to raise the remaining £2000. Council Chairman Willie Mawdsley added weight to the campaign by launching the 'Save Corby Town Fund' - chipping in a £10 from his own pocket to get it off to a good start. David Lang the Supporters Club Secretary, also came up trumps by agreeing to face a knife thrower at the Rangers Club to raise cash. "It made a change having knives thrown at me rather than taking them out of my back!" he quipped. The club's chairman, Ernie Leaker, suggested that by donating just a penny from their wages every week, people would be giving the club a brand new start and securing a much brighter future for it. The Fund realised £400 in its first couple of weeks - but not everyone was taken with the cause. Councillor Tom Sykes had this to say regarding a recommendation by colleagues that the council should donate £500. Tom: "Ratepayers have enough of a burden on their hands without paying for Corby Town's tax debts! Semi-professional football is on the way out. If people wanted football in Corby they would have swelled the gates - and the fund - long before now." Another football-related issue that was bound to displease Tom was the violence which erupted that February on the football park in Burghley Drive. Trouble began during an NFA Cup Tie between Corby Exeter Association and Titchmarsh F.C. when home supporters attacked the visiting goalkeeper in his goalmouth. This provoked players from both sides to join in - resulting in an almighty brawl which brought the game to a swift conclusion. The police were subsequently called and one person was arrested. With several of their team injured, a spokesman for Titchmarsh said that they would never play in Corby again - as this was the second such incident in two months on that same ground.

The previous month Titchmarsh's Matt Lambourne had been shot in the back with an air gun. Disturbing as the incident was, Matt remained remarkably calm about it, saying: "I was accelerating down the wing when I heard a shot and immediately realised that I had been the target. I dropped to my knees and when I looked down I could see that my shirt had a hole in it. In spite of that, I think it was a prank really." Titchmarsh secretary Jeff Coleman was less reticent, He asserted: "The referee asked us to continue playing - but we told him that we couldn't under those circumstances. Furthermore, we said that we would be reporting the matter to the Northants Football Association." A representative from the Corby club was equally disgusted with events. He stated: "For a thing like this to happen in amateur football is absolutely sickening!"

Playing full back for Titchmarsh that day was builder Peter Dorrington (recognised throughout the local leagues as a raw boned, uncompromising, take-no-prisoners defender.) At odds with his tough approach to the game, off the pitch Peter was affectionately nicknamed 'Doris'. He explained: "How it came about was because two young kids in Corby heard one of my teammates calling me Dorrie - and they thought that he'd said Doris!"

Thirty-five years later, Peter Dorrington says that the weekend game of football always came as a welcome distraction from the toil of the building sites. (In addition, his sporting career also took in playing cricket for his village team and rugby for Rushden and Higham.) Pete says that he can still remember the events of the Burghley Drive fiasco as though it was yesterday.

Still looking remarkably fit and healthy for a man of sixty-two, he said laughingly: "I haven't a badge on me!" (a football reference to scars collected on the field of battle.) Pete acknowledged the competitive nature of teams from Corby, saying: "The Corby teams played the game hard and they appreciated a good contest. Even now, if I bump into any of our old adversaries in a pub or somewhere, there's usually a big smile and a crack about the old days."

Titchmarsh was a bit of an anomaly back then as only half a dozen girls were born after the war, during the 'baby boomer' years, as opposed to around sixty boys (something that no doubt caused a few problems in later years!) In Great Britain, during the 1950s and 60s all a boy wanted to do was kick a football in the winter and play cricket in the summer. The lads from Titchmarsh were no different in that respect - and many were extremely gifted. Pete: "I was probably one of the least talented of the bunch, I couldn't spray passes around or dribble past three or four players. My biggest asset, however, was being able to stop other people playing - and I loved it! I always thought the harder the game the better. Along with Tony Harrison, who had played football for Peterborough United in the early 1960s, I was one of those long throw specialists. Tony and I had watched Chelsea's Ian Hutchinson doing it on the telly and we decided to hold a competition amongst our players to see who could be the most effective. It turned out that I was able to throw the ball from the touchline right to the far post, as could Tony. We scored no end of goals from those throw-ins.

Titchmarsh were one of the top local teams and were fortunate enough to secure promotion in four consecutive seasons in the Kettering Amateur Leagues. We were afraid of nobody, however, when we played any of the Corby teams; we always knew that we were in for a tough battle. The Hazeltree had a good team in those days and had good support. I remember there was this one guy over there, a fat boy, who was always steaming and dishing out abuse to me. During one of our games I was challenging for the ball with a Hazeltree player, and this took us right next to the touchline where the lad was standing. Anyway, I got to the ball first and belted it right out of play - and straight into the fat boys' stomach. 'That'll teach you,' I muttered to myself, as the force of the ball sent him sprawling backwards. He then sort of bounced back up again and promptly spewed all over the grass. Everyone saw the funny side of the situation - mind you I'm not sure about him!

Exeter Association was a different kettle of fish altogether. Even their changing rooms were dire - there were no lights or windows, plus they reeked of urine and stale air. As I said before, we weren't scared of anyone, but when we played at Burghley Drive we always made sure that we went as a unit when leaving and returning to the dressing rooms. We were actually winning 3-1 in that game where the air rifle incident interrupted proceedings. At that moment I was just about to take a throw-in and I shouted to winger Matt Lambourne (whom we'd taken on loan from Thrapston) when he suddenly dropped to his knees in front of me.

Peter Callum (captain of Tichmarsh F.C.) and his son Derek hold up one of the torn football shirts from a tempestuous match against arch rivals Corby Exeter Association F.C.

Confused, I asked him what he was doing, and he groaned, 'I've just been shot!' As I looked at him, wondering what the hell he was on about, two more shots were fired - one going past my head and the other past my chest. Matt showed me the hole in his shirt and that was when we all ran off the pitch! The referee asked us where we were going, and our collective response was, 'the changing rooms!' It was assumed that the shots had been fired from the 'banana flats' in Counts Farm Road, using a high-powered air rifle." With the game abandoned, the police began searching for the culprits, and, later that afternoon, after establishing that the shots had in fact been fired from a nearby railway embankment, officers arrested two youths and confiscated an air rifle.

A month later the two teams met in another fixture on the Burghley Drive pitch, in a Junior Cup match. This too ended in a battle. Pete Dorrington: "We were 3-0 up and they were kicking lumps out of us, therefore we responded in kind. The game was ugly - with studs flying everywhere. It all erupted when Exeter, who had already had two men sent off, were shown a third red card. Spontaneously, supporters behind the goal began to attack our goalkeeper - lighting the touch-paper for a mass brawl between players and supporters of both sides. Then, to cap it all, someone drove a lorry onto the pitch! It was a tipper-truck belonging to Smith and Grace of Thrapston, and had obviously been commandeered from one of the many nearby building sites. Incredibly, its driver proceeded to career round the pitch with it, in a mad attempt to run down the Titchmarsh players. Tony Harrison and Mick Corby, who were chased up the Oakley Road by Exeter supporters, said later that they were forced to seek sanctuary at the police station on Elizabeth Street! It was crazy! Our centre half, Steve Dankowych, had his shirt ripped off his back before being thrown over a hedge into somebody's back garden!"

In the words of Pete Dorrington, following the debacle the Northants F.A. "behaved like a right shower. They expelled both clubs from the competition - despite the fact that it wasn't us who started it! They then re-instated Weldon Reserves (a team that we'd beaten 7-0 in the semi-finals) and it was they who played in the final against Nether Heywood and got hammered 11-0! We'd have won that cup no problem!"

In a gesture of goodwill (and to demonstrate that not all Corby clubs were tarred with the same brush) a few weeks later Corby Albion F.C., who shared the Burghley Drive pitch, donated a new set of football strips to Titchmarsh F.C. A spokesman said: "Not every club in Corby is like Exeter F.C.". The response of the Titchmarsh squad was equally magnanimous: "It was a smashing gesture and we invited members of their club to our annual presentation and dinner night."

Footnote: In an effort to give a balanced view of the aforementioned incidents, before going to print the authors of this book contacted several former members of Corby Exeter Association F.C. for their version of events. Some who had admitted taking part in the games in question have since denied having done so, whereas others declined point-blank to speak to us. From a Corby perspective, it appears that no one is prepared to shed any further light on the subject.

The ambitions of Southern League champions Kettering Town Football Club were underlined on Monday May 4, 1974 - when a new main stand was unveiled to coincide with a visit from First Division Arsenal. Mr. Len Shipman (President of the Football League) officiated at the opening ceremony and then went on to watch a very entertaining match in which the Gunners won 3-0.

It was common knowledge that Poppies manager Ron Atkinson felt that his destiny lay in managing one of the bigger league clubs, and speculation was rife that he wouldn't see out the season at Rockingham Road. It came as no surprise then that (following an away draw to Fourth Division Swansea City in the F.A. Cup First Round) the replay at Rockingham Road proved to be Big Ron's final game before taking over at Fourth Division Cambridge United. It was also the last time that his brother Graham would play for the club - the inside forward having suffered an horrific injury as a result of a tackle from young Robbie James. During the incident a loud crack was heard around the ground, and the deathly silence which followed gave some indication of the severity of the injury. Atkinson's leg had been broken in two places and his football career was effectively over. In spite of all this, it had been a superb performance from Kettering, and one which saw them sweep Swansea comfortably aside in a 3-1 victory.

The F.A. Cup went back to Merseyside in May, after Liverpool's 3-0 win over Newcastle United. There to watch the match that day, albeit through beer goggles, was Open Hearth barman (and fanatical 'Red') Clive Smith. Clive, who had only managed to get hold of a ticket on the Thursday before the game, said: "Rothwell Town footballer Alan Fox won it in a raffle and promised to sell it to me for its face value of £5. I travelled down to London by myself for the match, but later teamed up with a couple of guys from Corby - one of whom was Corby Town F.C. favourite Neil Burns. On the way to Wembley I got absolutely legless, and when we got to Tottenham Court Road a police patrol officer threatened to arrest me - for wearing a traffic cone on my head!

When I got there I attempted to smuggle into the match a Newcastle supporter who didn't have a ticket (I'd hidden him beneath my trench coat.) The poor guy was promptly bundled out through the turnstile by a steward, and to this day I still haven't quite figured out why I wasn't booted out too. Needless to say, I saw the first half of the game through a drunken haze, and it's only with the help of videos that some twenty years later I've been able to piece together what took place on the field that day."

Competing with the Poppies for the title of 'Best Local Team' was the darts team from the Shire Horse in Corby, who had been KLV Champions for two years running. With just one defeat that year, in both the Corby and Kettering leagues, many were asking the question: "What makes them so hard to beat?" Johnny Morrison, their captain, was quite clear about it. He said: "Consistency is the key - and team spirit. We've had virtually the same team for five years, and they are all hard to beat. It's a squad of thirteen players who have a wealth of experience between them. Ian Fulton, this year's house champion, is known as 'Mr. Shire', Archie Eccles is a county player and John Pengelly is our *News of the World* champion." Although Morrison modestly omitted to name himself, incredibly he and Brian McDowell had won the Midlands section of the National Pairs Championship for the last three years in a row. McDowell (who in partnership with Moira Henderson had also reached the semi-finals of the National Mixed Pairs Championship) was equally modest, merely stating the obvious - that he was playing better than he had ever done before.

The Open Hearth's darts team were not only rivals to the Shire Horse in the Corby League, but were also on a roll and challenging for honours on several other fronts. One cup which they were in contention for was the Northants Evening Telegraph Trophy, which found them pitted against the Red Cow from Market Harborough (finalists from the previous season.) Word had it that the opposition team was expected to coast through to the third round, however, Graham 'Champ' Reilly, Shay O'Connor, Big Tam Carlin and the rest of the Open Hearth squad let it be known that they themselves were in impressive form - as was their vociferous crowd of supporters! As the match got under way the Harborough side took a 2-0 lead, but their opponents rallied and evened the score with victories from Graham Reilly and Bunny Norman. The Cow then went into the lead again - only for the Hearth's Jim Reilly to level the contest. The match reached an exciting conclusion when Corby's Mick Rafferty wrapped things up in style with a well-deserved win - making the final score 12-9 to the Open Hearth. After milking the applause from their ecstatic supporters and a somewhat grudging Cow, the victors set their sights on the next hurdle - a trip to the Fox and Hounds in Kempston. Unfortunately, despite recording a resounding win over the Bedfordshire team, that was as good as it got - they were beaten in the final by a side from Corby - the Shire Horse!

In 1974 Manchester United's manager, Sir Matt Busby, was the guest of honour at the opening of Lodge Park Sports Centre. It was also the year in which two Corby youngsters were recognised as potential football stars of the future, when David Gill and his fifteen-year-old Lodge Park schoolmate Brynley Gunn were invited to sign apprentice professional forms for Nottingham Forest (no doubt hoping to follow in the footsteps of Irchester's Phil Neal - who played for Northampton Town before joining Liverpool for a club record fee of £60,000.) Whereas Gill failed to make it at the City Ground and returned to Corby to sign for the Steelmen, Gunn eventually went on to make headlines as part of the Forest team who in 1980 won the European Cup.

The 10th World Cup Tournament took place that summer in Germany, and all those in Corby with Scottish connections were 'over the moon' that their team would be competing for the first time since 1958 - an achievement made all the sweeter by the absence of the 'auld enemy' England. Thousands of fans made the trip over there to watch it, including four Corby lads who drove the whole of the way in their Morris Oxford estate car. James Quarrie, Derek McGivern, John Spence and Henry Trzaskalski had tickets to see six matches during their three week holiday (for which they'd shelled out £50 apiece all in.) Derek was particularly upbeat about Scotland's chances, despite the fact that they were in the same group as the reigning champions Brazil. He said: "If we can just get past Brazil,

I think we'll have a great chance of winning the final." His optimism was shared by some other fans from Rushden - who had travelled over to the Rhineland in a minibus and were carrying enough food to last them the three weeks. They had also brought with them their mascot, belonging to Dick Beattie, which was in the form of a huge cardboard cut-out kilted Highlander and was affectionately known as 'Big Dunc'. Sadly, Dick and co. were to return to the UK with a week's worth of food untouched - after Scotland were eliminated following the first stage. Leaving behind what had proved to be a spectacularly 'unlucky' mascot, the dejected lads set off from Frankfurt for home. At a later date Jim said: "The funny thing was - when we were on the way home, everywhere we stopped the Scottish fans would ask us where the big fella was. 'Where's Big Dunc? they'd say. In response, we told them that he had been too cream-crackered to make the journey home - so we'd left him there in exile!"

Defeating Zaire by a mere 2-0 had been Scotland's downfall, as both Yugoslavia and Brazil had given the African team a hammering. Consequently, the Scottish team went out on goal difference, thus being named as the only undefeated team to be eliminated from the tournament was of little or no consolation. Remarkably Brazil didn't make it through to the end of the competition either - the final was contested by host team West Germany and the brilliant Dutch side. The match referee was Wolverhampton butcher Jack Taylor, who, by coincidence, had officiated ten years previously in the momentous Occupation Road F.A. Cup tie between Corby Town and Bristol City.

Left: James 'Jammy' McKinnon - Mr. Reliable on the oche. Right: Hector McKay - Corby's top darts player of the 1970s. Hector also held the title of County Champion during that period.

Between the months of February and September 1974, Albert Greer and self-styled troubleshooter Ian Eccles were joint publishers of a highly successful, though short-lived, magazine on behalf of the Lodge Park Estate Tenants Association. Aptly named the *Lodge Park Citizen*, the publication (which was produced on an old Gestetner print machine) was a vehicle for highlighting, amongst other things, the concerns of the residents of that estate. If the editors intended to stir things up, they certainly achieved their goal - as the L.P.E.T.A. became embroiled in a number of battles with the local authority.

As members of the Rushden Tartan Army set out for the 1974 World Cup in Germany, the supporter on the far left broods over the distinct possibility that (in the immortal words of Scotland's Tommy Docherty) he and his fellow exiles might be 'home before the postcards!'

Aimed at satirising Corby District Council, Issue No.1 contained the first installment of a controversial series entitled *Dragfeet*. As anticipated, the article provoked howls of indignation from council officials, followed by threats of legal action. For this reason the series was dropped, although Eccles claimed at the time: "Nearly everybody has welcomed our magazine, except for a few jobsworths who have taken exception to what is a harmless piece of fun - namely *Dragfeet*. We printed 500 copies which were quickly snapped up by residents. The response has been fantastic. The March issue will be even better and will include recipes and record reviews, as well as news coverage of what's happening on the estate. As far as pressurising the Council is concerned, our main objective is to force them into providing a community centre for the area. There are a lot of senior citizens on this estate who have nowhere to go if they want a coffee and a chat."

In January Members of the L.P.E.T.A. complained bitterly about the cable TV system that was in operation on their estate - calling it a 'piped television scandal'. Following reports from residents that the system (set up by British Relay Wireless Ltd. in conjunction with Corby District Council) provided a meager service and a poor reception, the *Lodge Park Citizen* decided to conduct a survey on their behalf and found that up to 40 per cent of tenants were dissatisfied. "It's a scandal!" fumed committee-man Ian Eccles, who went on to explain: "Thanks to the Council, British Relay is operating a monopoly and residents have no choice - they have to use the system whether they want to or not!" He also pointed out that, in spite a council ban, many of the residents had erected their own television aerials in order to get a better reception.

In a report which accompanied the survey, Mr. Eccles was able to quote two specific cases. One concerned a pensioner who had said that she watched television purely for company. The unfortunate senior citizen complained that, with the exception of greyish strips on either side of the screen, her screen was completely blank. A second woman (who said that she had rented television sets from BRW since moving to Corby) informed the survey that her TV had black corners on the screen, and that she had been told by British Relay that there was nothing they could do because it was too old. The woman admitted that she had to use a screwdriver in order to receive a picture, however, it was with the full knowledge of the BRW 'who say they can do nothing'.

BRW's response to the allegations was to say that they were untrue and were ridiculous. John Barrowman from Arran Way said: "British Relay has ruined our viewing. A month hasn't passed without having to call them to come and fix the TV. The picture is rubbish and the colour is even worse. We've only had this trouble since we moved into this area. We are forbidden to have an aerial and British Relay even tells us which corner of the room to put our telly!"

John MacPherson said the picture that he received at his home in nearby Laxton Close was atrocious, whilst Margaret Wilson, a resident in Grafton Drive, thought that the council ban was absurd. Ian Black another resident from Arran Way described his problem: "The picture was fuzzy, the colour was mixed and there was a 'ghosting effect' on the screen."

Mr. F. L. Cook (the manager of BRW) responded by saying that the criticisms that had been levelled at the company were both unfounded and untrue. He stressed: "We wired the houses as we were told to by the council." In the end Corby Council and BRW relented and residents were allowed to install their own aerials. "It finally put a stop to the tyranny that was the Council/BRW monopoly", said Eccles.

Six of the tenants association's committee members resigned in April. At a meeting that was to descend into a shouting match, problems arose when two opposing factions clashed over Secretary Anne Bailey's refusal to sign (until other members were present) a blank cheque for materials required in the production of the magazine. This led to the chairman, Albert Greer, asking for her resignation, and when Anne refused - he tried to sack her.

At a subsequent meeting, on asking for a vote of confidence in the chair, Greer was defeated by 4 votes to 3. Refusing to accept the result, he later sent out voting forms to all association members - calling for a further vote of confidence. This time the result was 276 votes for Greer and 40 against. Alec Clacher, Chairman of the Social Amenities Committee, resigned along with five others. Alec said: "We believed that the association was set up to help senior citizens on the estate. We had no idea that we would come across a chairman with such a dogmatic approach. He has his good points but his attitude is all wrong." Clacher continued: "The committee is run very badly. Half the time we don't know what's going on. We were supposed to see everything that went into the magazine before it was published, but we never have. As far as I'm concerned, it's a load of rubbish! Arguments over the cheque, and the personality clash, brought into the open all the things that are wrong. It was agreed from the start that the magazine would be non-political and non-sectarian - but six members of the committee maintain that the magazine contained political bias. They are also concerned over 'council-baiting'. No one does more - or has done more - in the town than councillor Jimmy Kane, yet he was insulted in the latest issue and has not been seen since at our meetings."

At the end of the meeting Greer steadfastly refused to comment on the issues that had divided the committee. All he did was voice his appreciation of the tenants who had voted for him and thank the departing committee officers for all their good work.

Ian Eccles: "Albert Greer was an excellent guy with lots of history. His wife was, I believe, the daughter of the founder of the Boilermakers' Union. Originally from Glasgow, Albert was a tremendous character and a first-rate trade union rep. He once warned a packed meeting of workers from Sealed Beams Ltd. - which was held in the Odeon cinema - that the company would close down if they went on strike. I remember that Albert was shouted down and another shop steward convinced the workers to strike. The rest as we know is history...

As far as I'm concerned, the two biggest achievements of the Lodge Park Estate Tenants Association were (a) an end to the compulsory use of the British Relay TV system and (b) the winning of compensation, under the Land Compensation Act, for those senior citizens on the estate who were forced out of their prefab bungalows so that the land could be used for new housing.

Looking back, I suppose the *Lodge Park Citizen* was a bit of a satirical rag. As regards the issue which provoked the Council's lawyers to threaten legal action if certain offending items were not removed, their letter was actually delivered by hand - so I guess they weren't kidding!"

The short-lived but controversial 'Lodge Park Citizen' became involved in many issues that affected the lives of residents on that estate. Amongst those companies and organisations to incur the wrath of the newsletter's editors were British Relay and Corby District Council. Above: Tenants congregate outside the Civic Centre in order to lobby councillors over the local authority's failure to recognise tenant's rights under the Land Compensation Act.

Ian (together with the rest of his buddies in the songwriting outfit Wellington) released a second record called *Catch Us If You Can* for which there were hopes of stateside success after a top American record label executive took a copy back home with him. By that time Eccles, Dave Martin, Ned McGuigan, John Grimley and Jack Murphy had been writing songs and working as session men for over a year, and had already gained one credit to their name with *The Wanderer* - a number which had been recorded by 1960's chart-toppers the Hollies and was a possibility for inclusion on their forthcoming *Gypsy* album. In addition to that, one of the top bands in Lebanon had recorded four of their songs and Shakin' Stevens' management company was interested in some of their material. Ian said: "I mentioned about the latter during an interview with the *Evening Telegraph*, and when the music publishers found out - all hell broke loose! Apparently it wasn't the done thing to reveal the identities of interested parties until deals were done and dusted."

Ian continued: "Dougie King was our roadie. He and I were very close back then and ran regular discos at the White Hart and Shire Horse. I even went along with him to his Radio Forth audition in London. I recall us having to put on a disco in order to raise the money for the rail tickets! In preparation for his audition, Dave Martin and I recorded Dougie's demo tape in which he spoofed being on Radio Caroline - complete with all the jingles."

John Grimley was also being kept busy. During this period he was hard at work recording with Kettering singer/songwriter Robin Goodfellow and making appearances with a band who were appropriately named the Variations (they were an assortment of local talent who occasionally pitched together for jamming sessions.) Members included Alan Booth and Roy Walker, keyboard player Bip Wetherell, sax players Joe McElvenney and Tony Paul, guitarist Bob Grimley, vocalist Tim Richards and lastly Jimmy Gourlay - who had begun his musical career in the early 1960s with vocal ensemble the Jack Knives.

Goodfellow's latest offering was the self-penned number *You Know Me Now*. Released on Dawn Records, and with a studio backing of John Grimley and his sister Lilian, Jack Murphy, Johnny Heron and Dave King, the new single's review in the local press almost pleaded for success.

> *'C'mon, c'mon, give local talent a chance... and if Kettering's clever Mr. Goodfellow doesn't make it this time I'll eat my copy of this tasty platter. It goes like a train all the way down to the hole in the middle - which gives you the compulsion to put it straight back on.'*

The song had been recorded at Derek Tompkins' Beck studio during a session which saw John Grimley become the butt of a joke. John explained: "Derek had asked me to sing the vocals on a track which we were making a demo of and I had agreed to do so. The problem was, however, I was never really any good at singing on my own - I could harmonise, but even then wasn't comfortable. Apart from that, Derek had this really off-putting habit of whistling down the headphones. Anyway, as the recording session got under way, I looked up at the control room and could see Derek and Robin creasing up with laughter. My immediate thought was that I didn't think I'd done too badly, and so I was somewhat relieved to find out that it had been the look on my face when I heard the whistling coming through the 'phones that had started them off!"

Following a chance meeting with ex-Size Seven drummer Ian Murray (during a Sunday lunch-time jam session in the Corinthian) John decided that September to head off to London to look for more regular work. John: "Ian invited me to audition for his band, the Michigan Flyers, but although I was one of the two people short-listed, I failed to get the job. He then fixed me up with an audition for a band called Country Routes and this time I was successful, so I moved to London and rented a flat in Ealing for £12 a week. I also took my driving test down there because I needed my own transport for work. I used my first car, a Morris Mini which cost me £85, to cart around my amp and guitar. The spooky thing was - its registration number ended in AMP. Weird or what! Working with Country Routes gave me greater experience and enabled me to learn a new style of music. Nevertheless, playing pubs and clubs virtually every night of the week was very hectic. We played Acton, Willesden, Southall - and even Wormword Scrubs!"

In 2006 Ian Murray travelled from his home in Frankfurt, Germany to visit his brother David and to catch up with some old friends. Ian recalled: "I left the Size Seven in October 1969 in order to follow my best pal Ade Holland (former guitarist with the Midnighters) down to London, where he had acquired a flat in Acton. Ade and I had a shared ambition to become professional musicians and would hang out regularly at Ronnie Scott's Club and at the Bulls Head in Barnes, which was another great jazz venue. We also played at all of the renowned venues on the Fuller's circuit - playing mostly country music. Within a year I had established myself there and was working with a variety of bands. I found myself living by the telephone, waiting for it to ring in the morning and tell me where I would be playing in the evening. It was hand-to-mouth stuff but it didn't half improve your technique as you never knew whether you would be playing country, jazz, blues, rock or a mixture of them all. With short spells in a variety of bands, some studio work and various trips to the Continent, this went on for five years or so, and then in 1974 I helped form a band called the Michigan Flyers. We came very close to 'making it' but like so many other 1970's bands we were ultimately ripped off by our so-called agent. The band was in the process of splitting when I got a call from Johnny Goodison (a singer/songwriter for Brotherhood of Man and various other studio bands.) Johnny told me that he'd formed a band called Big John's Rock 'n' Roll Circus, whose album had done nothing in the UK but two of its tracks had reached the charts in South Africa. An agent there had called him and suggested that he bring out the band for a six month tour and for a host of good times, good food, good women and good money! Johnny said that he'd got everyone he needed bar a drummer and that my name had been put forward by a mutual friend. Following our telephone conversation, one of his representatives turned up at Dingwalls in Camden Lock to watch the 'Flyers' play. When we stopped to take a break, this 'suit' came flying down the aisle and shouted up to me "You've got the gig". As you can imagine - it didn't impress the others!

Among the other members of Goodison's band was John Tebb, the ex lead singer of the Casuals (famous for *Jesamine*), Mike Gregory from the Swinging Blue Jeans and well-known session saxophonist Howie Casey. Howie played with us for a year before leaving to join Paul McCartney and Wings on their world tour. At the end of two weeks of strenuous rehearsals, we were just about to book our air tickets when we received a call from one of Johnny's buddies in Johannesburg. He had rung to inform us that the agent was ripping us off and that there was a good chance that we wouldn't get paid for the tour. We were all of us hard-nosed professional musicians by that time and therefore we just shrugged our shoulders, looked at it philosophically and concurred that was that. For his part, Johnny was determined that the band would survive, and so he contacted the boss of the Bailey's organisation in order to try and find work for us. As a result, in July 1975 we opened at Bailey's in Leicester. The band then continued in various forms until breaking up in January of 1990. Having travelled the world as part of a working band for fifteen years, I decided that I didn't want to see the insides of a hotel ever again. In 1992, on the advice of some friends I moved to Frankfurt and got a 'real' job. I eventually married a lovely German girl and now travel throughout Europe on behalf of a Japanese electronics company. For a hobby I bash the skins in a band called the Old Spice Boys. Music's like golf - you just can't give it up! Ade Holland did it the other way round - first he married the lovely girl and then he got the 'real' job. Ade then went on to buy a house, have kids and pay off the mortgage. Then what did he go and do? He turned pro of course! He now lives in Reading where (in addition to teaching guitar in several schools in the area) he plays regularly with some of the best-known musicians in West London."

Holland swapped the 'security' of Corby's tube works to work as the manager of a London petrol station. He said: I moved down to London in 1967 and then Ian Murray joined me (taking up residence in the spare room of my flat.) As time went on we played together in quite a few different bands.

A pensive-looking Jack Murphy wonders if tonight he will once again have to defend his corner against the brothers Grim(ley). Fortunately, on this occasion he needn't have worried as both John and Bob were settling their artistic differences elsewhere.

When I was working at the petrol station, one day I served this bloke who was wearing beads, had an afro haircut, a flash car and the lot. I said to him 'You've got to be a muso - dressed like that!' He replied, 'I know you - on Sundays you play jazz guitar at the Angel. I go in there just to listen to you.' He introduced himself as Ray Dorset of Mungo Jerry who incidentally had a record at number two in the charts at the time.) I was flabbergasted that he recognised me!

Around that time I bought an original 1930's Selmer Maccaferri guitar from Selmer's in London. It was expensive but I had to have it as by then I was playing (or thought I was playing) in the style of Django Reinhardt. Unfortunately, it wasn't actually suitable for the kind of work that I was getting, for which I used my 1963 Gibson 330, and so I only really played it at home. My wife Tina later persuaded me to sell it, so that we could buy carpets for the flat. With hindsight that wasn't a great idea as the carpets are probably in the bin now - whereas the Mac would be worth in excess of £30,000!

It was also around about then that I had a call offering me six months' work with Liza Minnelli's band, followed by six months at a new complex on Hayling Island. Tina had not long given birth to Nathan, our second child, and although I was tempted and really wanted to go - I just couldn't leave the kids. Instead I continued to play up to five nights a week in a function band, whilst doing a bit of teaching as well. That lasted for about thirteen years and then, after a spell as a sales rep/sales manager, I bought a greetings card shop near Oxford. I was there for about twelve years and during that time formed a hot club band called Fat Chance. We did quite well playing locally and got to support people like Martin Taylor and Acker Bilk in some of the small theatres - occasionally topping the bill ourselves. From time to time we also did some local radio.

After that assortment of jobs I was offered six months' work in Cyprus. As Sarah and Nathan had both reached adulthood by then, I accepted the contract. There was only one stipulation - we had to have a girl singer. Having chosen one, the sad part about it was that two weeks before

Ian Murray - a former member of Big John's Rock 'n' Roll Circus. The band also included Howie Casey (pictured right) amongst other veterans of British rock music.

we were due to fly out, her mother died and she had to pull out. While we looked for another singer, the agent put another band in for the first three months and then we did the following three. We had a fantastic time out there.

On the day that I arrived home I took a call from him, saying, 'Don't sit down - I've got another job for you.' This time it was for four months in Bahrain. Alas the threat of divorce won the day and so I had to decline. I went on to make a living out of teaching guitar in private schools - and still do to this day - but will play jazz with anybody who rings me up!

During the 1970s I was working Saturday nights at a hotel in Maidenhead. At that time, Ian Murray was touring Europe but would stay at my place when he was in this country. I remember Ian coming with me to the hotel and getting to know the night porter - who decided to fill my Mini Cooper with the contents of the kitchen. In fact there was so much stuff in the car that I could hardly squeeze in my amp and guitar. Despite my protests that the police were out in force, Ian didn't seem to be bothered, and so with a heavy heart I started to drive back up the A4 towards Reading. At the first roundabout two police officers stepped out into the road and flagged me down. As they approached, Ian (who was sitting in the passenger seat) came out with this gem. 'Pretend you're asleep' he said. Not a good idea if you happened to be the over-the-limit driver of a car sporting bald tyres and an out-of-date tax disc! Getting back to the story, the senior officer took charge whilst his subordinate, armed with his notebook and torch, gave my car the once-over. The exchange between me and the sergeant went something like this:

'Where have you been?'

'Just to the Kingswood Hotel.'

'What's all this stuff in the car?'

'I work there.'

'What do you do?'

'I'm a guitar player.'

'Really! What sort of guitar do you play?'

'A Gibson.'

'A Gibson! Can I see it?'

Above left: Ade Holland playing his estranged Selmer
Maccafferri guitar. Right: Ade in 2006

At that I proceeded to drag the guitar out of the back of the car - spilling all kinds of stuff on the road in the process. The officer opened up its case and, to my amazement, stood on one leg playing G and D on my Gibbo!

By this time his partner had filled the page with enough evidence to send the two of us to the gallows! An appreciative police sergeant said: 'Great guitar! By the way, you'd better get your number plates sorted out - or you'll be had up for having the letters stuck on one side of the bonnet and the numbers on the other. Now, off you go!'

As we drove away, Ian (who had even managed to conceal the loot in the foot well by covering it with his flares) said admiringly: 'Holland, If you fell into a pile of manure you would end up smelling of roses!'

My most embarrassing gig was probably one which took place back in 1966, when I was still working in the tube works. An entertainments organiser from the Civic Centre told me that he'd heard that I had a band, and, so (for some reason known only to myself) I shot back 'Yeah, - it's a seven-piece'. The guy then asked if we'd be interested in taking a booking for that New Year's Eve.

'What's the fee?' I asked him.

'Food, drink and £200.'

When he said that, it took all my control to temper my excitement, and therefore, feigning disappointment, I asked again 'How much?'

He said: 'We could probably go to £250.'

Naturally, I told him that he'd got a deal.

Pictured: Fondly remembered local accordionist Benny McGeachy. Hailing from Shotts in Scotland, Benny was a former musician with 'Jimmy Shand and his Band' during the 1950s. He later went on to make a home for himself and his family in Corby - where he lived and worked until his untimely death in 1982 at just fifty-eight years of age.

'What's the name of the band?' he then asked.

I replied, right off the top of my head, 'It's the Ade Holland Seven of course!'

Looking forward to seeing my name emblazoned on the poster, I think I even started swanking around in a suit and tie for awhile (very self-importantly!) However, then came the real test - to get a band together!

I decided that my old pal Ian Murray would be on drums and that another acquaintance, Bob Crawford, could be my tenor player. I also knew of a great alto player, who was called Roger, and I persuaded him to join the gang as well. From those days when I frequented the Chequers pub in Wellingborough, I had gotten to know a good chord-playing guitarist named Dave Selby, and he was able to put me in touch with a pianist called Pete. Thus the band evolved until it reached the requisite size. It's hard to believe it now - but the first time that we actually met up was on the stage at the Civic!

When we were asked to start off with a waltz, I muttered to myself 'That's not a problem.' (I vaguely knew Dave Brubeck's *Raggy Waltz*, and when we played it - boy - was it raggy!) As the dancers came gliding past the stage, we began to hear comments like 'What on earth's that?' and 'Play some decent music.' Pete took umbrage at this, and so he plugged in a mic that connected to the house PA system and started a running commentary on the dancers. It was along the lines of: 'Here she comes again - in the same dress as last year!' and 'Look at this one - I can almost smell the mothballs!' When the first set came to an end, the organiser came up to me and said, 'Hey pal, although I don't normally drink - tonight I'm out of my head!'

I replied, 'That's great. If you can't get a little merry on a New Year's Eve in Corby - then there's got to be something wrong!'

'There is something wrong!' he ranted, 'I've just been banned from booking bands here ever again!' Then he passed out.

In the second half we were joined by an accordionist named Benny McGeachy, - a lovely guy whom they'd plundered from the Labour Club. He got straight to work and instructed us to 'Follow me boys. Let's have *Scotland The Brave* - in C.' It was fantastic. The crowd loved it. He continued, 'The next one's also in C. Come on now - Here we go, Here we go…' I suppose you could say that Benny really saved the day for us - or should I say night!"

Ade continued: "A couple of years later, a guy who worked with Ian Murray (in his office in the tube works) suddenly started talking about music. Aware that Ian was a drummer, he remarked, 'Do you know something - the worst band I ever saw was a couple of years ago at the Civic Centre. They were called the Ade Holland Seven - or something like that.' Ian just raised his eyebrows and said 'Never heard of them.'

Following a second General Election in October 1974, Harold Wilson retained power after calling for national unity 'to tackle the gravest economic crisis since the war'. Wilson had won by only the narrowest of margins (a majority of three) and just two weeks later, when his Westminster home was broken into and some of his personal papers were stolen, Britain's own 'Watergate' appeared to be unfolding. Many claimed that Wilson was becoming paranoid, because he suspected the involvement of MI5, whilst others thought that he was a double agent working for the KGB.

In the meantime Edward Heath pondered his future and vowed to carry on as leader of the Conservatives, despite calls for him to step aside. (Waiting in the wings was the woman who would later take over from him - The Right Honourable Margaret Thatcher, MP for Grantham in Lincolnshire. In time she would become better known as the Iron Lady.)

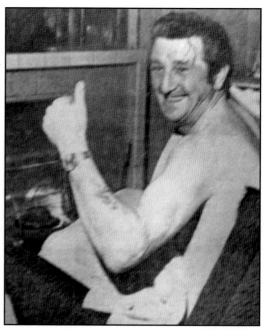

'It Had To Happen' reported the March 12, edition of the *Evening Telegraph*. The newspaper went on to tell the story of how steelworker Joe Smith (of Landseer Court in Corby) had streaked along Gainsborough Road in order to win a £3 bet with his mates from the Pluto. In spite of freezing conditions, Joe had stripped down to his socks and shoes and then hot-footed it home - to the astonishment and 'absolute disgust' of his horrified wife Jean. She said: "When I saw him dash past the window, with nothing on, I couldn't believe my eyes. I'm now too embarrassed to show my face to the neighbours."

Inspired by Ray Stevens' song 'The Streak', Joe Smith demonstrated what some would call bare-faced cheek(s) during his 300-yard dash from the Pluto pub to his home in Landseer Court.

Joe explained: "On Saturday night we were sitting in the pub, discussing streaking, and someone bet me that I wouldn't dare do it myself. On Sunday dinner-time I suddenly said to him, 'I'm all for brightening up people's lives and it will be the best laugh that Corby's had for a while'. Even so, I still needed a couple of bevvies to give me Dutch courage!"

The craze (sparked off by Ray Stevens' big hit) was becoming infectious, with two more reported cases in the Kettering area that same weekend. One concerned three men who were spotted dashing through the High Street and then huddling together in a shop doorway to try and keep their extremities warm. The other involved four lads who were seen running down Newlands Street - with their trousers held aloft in the air.

Regarding the 1970 death of the American saxophonist Albert Ayler, an article in *Rolling Stone* magazine appeared to contradict reports that he had jumped to his death from the Staten Island Ferry, instead suggesting that he had died at the hands of the New York mafia. According to John Swenson, who penned the article, Ayler was murdered for non-payment of a drug debt. The body of the celebrated musician was then tied to a jukebox and dumped in the East River.

Mr. John Sandy (acknowledged as Corby's pre-eminent authority on jazz) had this to say about the matter. John: "As far as I'm aware, there is no hard evidence to link Ayler with drugs of any description. More pertinently, I am certain that he wouldn't have been seen dead near anything as out-of-tune with his musical ethos as a jukebox!"

Fred Davies, the managing director of York Trailers Ltd., caused a storm in the vicinity when he sent a memo instructing fellow directors, to vet carefully all Scottish, Welsh and Irish nationals, who were seeking employment with the company. Davies had the audacity to opine 'they are either grossly evil or tremendously brilliant'. The memo, which was leaked to an outsider, brought the expected response. Margaret McCann, of Thames Walk in Corby, remonstrated: "Utter tripe! There are all levels of intelligence in all nationalities." Marion Murphy, who lived in Gretton but hailed originally from Londonderry, agreed that Fred was talking nonsense. She said: "Not all Paddys are thick - or brilliant."

Maggie Bell: 'Unique. Earthy. The greatest female blues singer ever to record this side of the Atlantic'.

That spring Maggie Bell (former vocalist with Stone the Crows) released her first solo album - *Queen Of The Night* - which was deemed 'well worth the wait' by the music critic from the *Northamptonshire Evening Telegraph*. Coincidentally, the Scottish rock singer had shared a childhood with Corby housewife Sylvia Johnson, although when the later left the Maryhill district of Glasgow in 1956, the two friends had lost touch with each other. Whereas Maggie went on to become Britain's top female blues/rock vocalist, achieving world-wide fame through her appearances with Stone the Crows, and later as a solo performer, Sylvia chose the path of domesticity.

Although her career reached extraordinary heights, Bell never forgot her 'wee pal' and also never gave up hope that they would one day be reunited. Happily that day came in October 2006 when the former Maryhillians met at Northampton's Royal & Derngate Theatre.

Above: The Johnson family on the eve of their departure for Australia. L-R: Gary, Roger, Darren and Sylvia. Right: Despite having to leave family and friends behind in Corby, a smiling Roger Johnson remains upbeat about his plans for a new life in Oz.

Seven years after moving to Corby nineteen-year-old Sylvia married the love of her life, local plasterer Roger Johnson, and went on to give birth to sons Gary and Darren. Despite beginning life in rented accommodation, the young couple achieved the first of their dreams by moving into a bungalow (on the Lawns estate) that Roger himself had built. Although the Johnson family eventually emigrated to Australia in 1975, Sylvia, an albino with 6 per cent vision, spent the next twenty years avoiding the Antipodean sun and yearning for a snow covered garden.

As more and more families in Britain faced up to the possibility of an uncertain future, a large number of them began to consider emigration as a solution to their problems. The *Daily Mail* reported that enquiries were markedly on the increase for the £10 assisted passage scheme (which had been in operation since 1947.)

One Corby travel agency even arranged for officials from Australia House, and New Zealand House to visit the town in order to help cope with the rush. Prospective emigrants were also given information on how to find a house and a job when they'd arrived down under. The travel agent explained: "Corby people are quick to move if they feel their jobs are put in jeopardy or their ability to earn a decent living is threatened. Most came to the town to work. If any doubts arise - they will just uplift their families and go. There has always been a constant stream of traffic between Corby and Australia, and it is steadily increasing."

Roger 'Jonah' Johnson explains how he and his family came to emigrate. Roger: "I was really fed up with life in Britain at that time. There were all the strikes, power cuts and price hikes to contend with, and then on top of those came the three-day working week. I thought that there had got to be a better way of living than the one we were experiencing over here, and when I spotted the article about emigration to Australia, I decided to look into the process."

After Roger had talked things over with his wife Sylvia, the couple then took the next step of travelling down to Australia House in London. Mr. Johnson says that when they were sitting on the train and were heading towards St Pancras station in London, they still harboured doubts about whether or not they would go (that is if the offer was still available.) Roger said: "What swung it for me was that when I told the embassy staff that I was a plasterer - they practically dragged me onto the plane!" He added: "My family and I were among the last people to get the £10 tickets."

On a bitingly cold afternoon in January 1975, Roger and Sylvia Johnson took their two young sons (Darren and Gary) on a visit to Corby's boating lake. Acutely aware that this was likely to be the last day that he would ever spend in his home town, the thirty-year-old plasterer had much to reflect upon as he accompanied his children on the ice-covered lake. Roger: "I remember thinking about the reality of growing up in a town that was in so many ways unique. To all intents and purposes Corby was almost a 'misplaced' settlement. For example, it had its own distinct heritage - which was mainly Scottish in origin but also included a liberal helping of Irish, Welsh and Eastern European culture (not to mention a smattering of English!)

I was preoccupied that day by thoughts of what the future held in store for me and my family. Not only that, there was the question of what would ultimately happen to Corby. I felt aggrieved over the fact that, due to circumstances beyond my control, I was literally being forced to leave behind the life that I'd known and had indeed treasured.

As I watched the boys enjoying the unexpected treat of skating on the frozen lake, my thoughts turned to John Plumb, one of my ancestors on my mother's side, who in 1782 married Rebecca Nailor at the St John the Baptist Church. A few years later the Plumbs left Corby to travel around the county in search of work, eventually putting down roots in Broughton, Earls Barton and Northampton. It was only when my parents - Cyril and Evelyn Johnson - returned to Corby in 1949 (on the back of the steelworks boom) that things came full circle. My father opened a shoe shop on the corner of High Street and Stocks Lane, where he practiced his trade as a shoemaker for the next twenty-five years. And so it came to pass that nearly two hundred years after John and Rebecca had married and moved away, I now found myself on the verge of taking a similar life-changing step and wondering if I or my family would ever return home. On the following day, January 9, 1975 we flew out from Heathrow. Two days later we arrived in Sydney - excited at the prospect of a better life. That isn't to say that Sylvia and I didn't expect Australia to be without its challenges."

For family and friends left behind in Corby, the future would also present huge challenges - as it would for 'Little Scotland' as a whole. There were to be dark days ahead - dark days indeed - for a town that had always been 'alive in the dead of night'.

Looking for something? How about a future? As he picks his way through the slag heaps, a lone steelworker ponders on the fate of the massive steelmaking complex in the background.